本书由重庆交通大学研究生教育创新基金支持出版
本书由重庆市研究生教育教学改革研究一般项目资助（yjg20163061）
普通高等学校规划教材

A Practical English Coursebook for Postgraduates
研究生实用英语教程

主　编　张周易　毛明勇
副主编　杨学云　郭敬谊

人民交通出版社股份有限公司
China Communications Press Co.,Ltd.

内 容 提 要

本书通过科技英语翻译篇、学术英语写作篇和实用英语写作篇三部分共29单元,介绍了常见的科技英语翻译技巧与翻译方法,力求强化学生翻译技能;讲解了英语学术论文从选题到撰写提纲、摘要、正文、参考文献的基本方法,为学生日后走上科研之路扫清障碍;罗列了撰写求学简历、工作经历证明,申请奖学金和学历、学位、奖励的方法,为今后有意赴国外深造的学子支招。

本书可作为非英语专业博士研究生、硕士研究生和英语专业本科生、研究生选修教材使用,也可供普通的英语爱好者使用。

图书在版编目(CIP)数据

研究生实用英语教程 / 张周易,毛明勇主编. —北京:人民交通出版社股份有限公司,2017.1
ISBN 978-7-114-13626-9

Ⅰ.①研… Ⅱ.①张… ②毛… Ⅲ.①英语—研究生—教材 Ⅳ.①H319.39

中国版本图书馆 CIP 数据核字(2016)第 319840 号

书　　　名:	研究生实用英语教程
著 作 者:	张周易　毛明勇
责任编辑:	刘永芬
出版发行:	人民交通出版社股份有限公司
地　　　址:	(100011)北京市朝阳区安定门外外馆斜街 3 号
网　　　址:	http://www.ccpress.com.cn
销售电话:	(010)59757973
总 经 销:	人民交通出版社股份有限公司发行部
经　　　销:	各地新华书店
印　　　刷:	北京盈盛恒通印刷有限公司
开　　　本:	787×1092　1/16
印　　　张:	23.75
字　　　数:	541 千
版　　　次:	2017 年 1 月　第 1 版
印　　　次:	2017 年 1 月　第 1 次印刷
书　　　号:	ISBN 978-7-114-13626-9
定　　　价:	55.00 元

(有印刷、装订质量问题的图书由本公司负责调换)

本书编委会

主　　编：张周易　毛明勇
副 主 编：杨学云　郭敬谊
参　　编：曹顺发　陈才忆　舒红凌　周洪洁　易　宇
　　　　　李　勇　张雪梅　廖彦婷　黄　鹂　易　毅

前　言

目前，市面上研究生英语方面的辅导书可谓多如牛毛，但大都集中在以通过某些所谓的"重要"等级考试为主的习题集上，很少有以培养学生应用能力为主的、让学生爱不释手的实用书籍。为此，我们特地组织了一批具有丰富教学经验、长期从事研究生英语教学工作的专家和教授共同编写了这本《研究生实用英语教程》。

本教材高举"实用"大旗，力求打造一本便捷的学习用书。学习的重要方式是读书，读书就要思考。"学而不思则罔，思而不学则殆"，由此可见学习与思考的重要性。全书共分为三大部分：

1. 第一部分为科技英语翻译篇，主要介绍常见的科技英语翻译的技巧与翻译方法，目的在于强化学生的翻译技能，为走上工作岗位奠定较强的翻译能力。

2. 第二部分为学术英语写作篇，英语作为一门外语，在英语和英语相关学术领域做研究和撰写论文是一个巨大的挑战。困难在于同学们缺乏足够的英语语言和研究工作所需的基本知识。本部分旨在介绍英语学术论文从选题到撰写提纲、摘要、正文、参考文献的基本方法，为日后走上科研之路铺平道路。

3. 第三部分为实用英语写作篇，重点在于为今后有意赴国外深造的学子如何撰写求学简历、工作经历证明，申请奖学金和学历、学位、奖励"支招"，为在国外学习、深造扫清障碍。

4. 每部分后附有参考答案，书中出现的所有练习的答案均能从中找到，使学习者做到既"知其然"又"知其所以然"。

本书在编写过程中参考了众多的英文著作、工具书和专业期刊论文，引用了不少其他作者的著作，还得到了外语界同行的热情关心和支持。由于编者水平有限，加之时间仓促，书中的疏误在所难免，恳请同行专家和广大读者批评指正。

编　者
2016 年 10 月

目　录

上篇　科技英语翻译篇

- Unit 1　科技英语特点 Characteristics of EST ······ 003
- Unit 2　词义的选择 Choice of Meanings ······ 049
- Unit 3　词义的引申 Extension of Meanings ······ 055
- Unit 4　词性的转换 Conversion of Parts of Speech ······ 062
- Unit 5　增词 Amplification ······ 075
- Unit 6　省略 Omission ······ 084
- Unit 7　反译 Negation ······ 093
- Unit 8　否定句的翻译 Translation of Negative Sentences ······ 097
- Unit 9　被动语态的翻译 Translation of Passive Voice ······ 106
- Unit 10　数字的翻译 Translation of Numbers ······ 116
- Unit 11　名词性从句的翻译 Translation of Nominal Clauses ······ 124
- Unit 12　定语从句的翻译 Translation of Attributive Clauses ······ 132
- Unit 13　状语从句的翻译 Translation of Adverbial Clauses ······ 146
- Unit 14　长句的翻译 Translation of Complicated Sentences ······ 156
- 参考译文 Reference Translation for Exercises ······ 168

中篇　学术英语写作篇

- Unit 1　论文简介 Introduction ······ 189
- Unit 2　论文选题 Negotiating a Topic ······ 193
- Unit 3　题目确定 Narrowing the Topic ······ 198
- Unit 4　文献笔记 Taking Notes ······ 210
- Unit 5　写作准备 Preparing to Write the Paper ······ 220
- Unit 6　摘要撰写 Writing an Abstract ······ 236
- Unit 7　论文写作 Writing the Paper ······ 241
- Unit 8　文献注释 Documentation ······ 253
- Unit 9　文献格式 Works Cited Format ······ 273

Unit 10　论文终稿 Final Presentation ·········· 310
参考答案 Answers to Exercises ·········· 323

下篇　实用英语写作篇

Unit 1　求学简历 CVs ·········· 335
Unit 2　申请过程中与大学的各种联络信件 Application Correspondence ·········· 346
Unit 3　申请奖学金 Scholarship ·········· 356
Unit 4　经济资助（助学金）及资助证明 Financial Aid & Certificates ·········· 359
Unit 5　学历、学位、奖励、工作经历证明 Relevant Certificates ·········· 365

参考文献 References ·········· 370

上 篇
科技英语翻译篇

Unit 1 科技英语特点
Characteristics of EST

任何作品均有特定的文体,原文的文体不同,翻译方法也随之而异。

科技英语是反映客观现实世界的工具,为了能准确地描述客观世界的实情,科技英语尽量在语言使用上规范地道,在语言形式上简明准确,在语义理解上直接明了,尽可能不出现语言变异现象。

科技文体崇尚严谨周密,概念准确,逻辑性强,行文简练,重点突出,句式严整,少有变化,常用前置性陈述,即在句中将主要信息尽量前置,通过主语传递主要信息。

试比较:

日常英语

People <u>get</u> natural rubber from rubber trees as a white, milky liquid, <u>which is called</u> latex. They <u>mix it with</u> acid, and dry it, <u>and then they send it</u> to countries all over the world. As the rubber industry <u>grew</u>, people <u>needed</u> more and more rubber. They <u>started</u> rubber plantations in countries with hot, <u>wet weather conditions</u>, but these still could not <u>give enough</u> raw rubber to <u>meet the needs</u> of growing industry.

科技英语

Natural rubber <u>is obtained</u> from rubber trees as a white, milky liquid <u>known as</u> latex. This is <u>treated with</u> acid and dried <u>before being dispatched</u> to countries all over the world. As the rubber industry <u>developed</u>, more and more rubber was <u>required</u>. Rubber plantations were <u>established</u> in countries with a hot, <u>humid climate</u>, but these still could not <u>supply sufficient</u> raw rubber <u>to satisfy the requirements</u> of developing industry.

日 常 英 语	科 技 英 语
1. 通俗化:常用词汇用得多	1. 专业化:专业术语用得多
2. 多义性:一词多义,使用范围广	2. 单义性:词义相对单一,因专业而不同
3. 人称化:人称丰富,形式多样	3. 物称化:多用物称,以示客观
4. 多时性:描述生活,时态多样	4. 现时性:叙述事实多用现在时
5. 主动性:句子倾向于主动态	5. 被动态:句子倾向于被动态
6. 简单性:单句、散句用得多	6. 复杂性:复杂句用得多,复合句用得多
7. 口语化:口语用得多,随意灵活	7. 书面化:长句用得多,书卷气浓

简而言之,科技文章的特点是:清晰、准确、精练、严密。科技文章的语言结构特色在翻译

过程中如何处理,是进行英汉科技翻译时需要探讨的问题,但在这之前我们首先应了解清楚科技英语的特点,现分述如下。

1. 大量使用名词化结构

《当代英语语法》(A Grammar of Contemporary)在论述科技英语时提出,大量使用名词化结构(Nominalization)是科技英语的特点之一。因为科技文体要求行文简洁、表达客观、内容确切、信息量大、强调存在的事实。

所谓名词化倾向,主要指广泛使用表示动作或状态的抽象名词或起名词功用的动名词。科技文章的语言特点之一是言简意明,简化语言结构的有效途径之一便是名词化。

科技英语中大量使用名词化结构可以缩短句子的长度,译成汉语时则不宜套用英语的这种模式,而是需要根据汉语的表达习惯灵活处理,有时也可将其拓展成汉语的句子。

➢ Archimeds first discovered the principle of displacement of water by solid bodies.
阿基米德最先发现固体排水的原理。

句中 of displacement of water by solid bodies 系名词化结构,一方面简化了同位语从句,另一方强调 displacement 这一事实。

➢ The rotation of the earth on its own axis causes the change from day to night.
地球绕轴自转,引起昼夜的变化。

名词化结构 the rotation of the earth on its own axis 使复合句简化成简单句,而且使表达的概念更加确切严密。例如:

➢ A distribution is described by its measures of central tendency and dispersion tendency.
对集中趋势和离散趋势的测量可以用来描述分布。

➢ By integrating measurement, documentation, and control systems, the use of the IC rollers allows for real-time monitoring and just-in-time corrections in the compaction process.
通过集成测量、文档编制和控制系统,智能压实压路机在压实过程中允许实时监控和即时修正。(IC = intelligent compaction,智能压实)

➢ During analysis of elevator drive system, it is concluded that torque, which is produced by an electric motor, is transmitted by a worm gear to the shaft.
在分析电梯驱动系统时,可以得出这样的结论:电动机产生的扭矩由蜗轮传递给轴。

➢ Reliability analysis in part design has been focused towards the electronic and digital disciplines since the emergence of reliability engineering in the late 1940's.
自从20世纪40年代后期可靠性工程出现以来,零件设计中的可靠性分析一直集中在电子和数字领域。

➢ The combination of these tire forces, which are essential for good curving performance of the monorail car, makes the dynamic motion of the monorail car complicated.
这些轮胎力的组合对于具有良好曲线通过性的单轨列车来说是必不可少的,这也使得单轨车的动力具有复杂性。

- The use of analysis/design software will complete the job and the selection of a bridge type for that situation will be automatic.

  采用分析/设计软件可以完成该任务且根据具体情况自动进行桥型选择。

- The increase in passenger traffic will result in greater tourism and economic activity on the Tibetan Plateau.

  旅客流量的增加给西藏高原的旅游业和当地经济带来了繁荣。

- Four wheel independently-actuated (4WIA) electric vehicle is a promising vehicle due to its potentials in emissions and fuel consumption reductions.

  四轮独立驱动电动车在降低排放和燃油消耗方面具有巨大的潜力,是一种很有发展前景的汽车。

- With the development of science and technology, the automatic transmission (AT) technology is broadly used on vehicles, especially on passenger vehicles for its advantages of convenience of manipulate, relieving drivers' tiredness, improving the comfort and safety when driving, and reducing the pollution of exhaust emission.

  随着科学技术的发展,自动变速器技术在汽车上得到广泛应用,特别是乘用车上。它具有操作方便等优点,可减缓驾驶员疲劳,提高驾驶的安全性和舒适性以及减少尾气排放污染的优势。

2. 广泛使用被动语态

在科技英语中被动语态使用频率较高,这是因为科技文章侧重叙事推理,强调客观准确,第一、二人称的过多使用会造成主观臆断的印象,因此应尽量使用第三人称叙述。另外,科技文章将主要信息前置,放在主语部分,这也是广泛使用被动态的主要原因。

试比较下面分别采用主动语态和被动语态表达的同义句子:

- We can store electrical energy in two metal plates separated by an insulating medium. We call such a device a capacitor, or a condenser, and its ability to store electrical energy capacitance. We measure capacitance in farads.

  我们可将电能储存在由一绝缘介质隔开的两块金属极板内。我们称这样的装置为电容器,称其储存电能的能力为电容。我们用法拉为单位来测量电容。

- Electrical energy can be stored in two metal plates separated by an insulating medium. Such a device is called a capacitor, or a condenser, and its ability to store electrical energy is termed capacitance. It is measured in farads.

  电能可储存在由一绝缘介质隔开的两块金属极板内。这样的装置称为电容器,其储存电能的能力为电容。电容的测量单位是法拉。

第二段话,虽然主语可以是人,如"we"等,但绝大多数情况都避免使用类似的人称主语,因为动作的发出者是不言而喻的,或是不受关注的对象,而动作本身是强调的对象,因此采用被动语态形式是最合适的。

这一段短文中各句的主语分别为：

Electrical energy; Such a device; Its ability to store electrical energy; It (Capacitance)

它们都包含了较多的信息，并且处于句首的位置，非常醒目。四个主语完全不同，避免了单调重复，使其前后连贯，自然流畅，足见被动结构可达到简洁客观的效果。

➢ The dynamic characteristics of the drive axle was analyzed through building the vehicle dynamics simulation model in virtual software.

在虚拟的软件中建立车辆动力仿真模型分析驱动桥的动态特性。

➢ Suspension, cable-stayed, and through-truss bridges are included in this category of main structure above the deck line.

悬索桥、斜拉桥和下承式桥梁都属于主结构在甲板线上方这一大类桥型。

➢ The arch form is intended to reduce bending moments in the superstructure.

(拱桥的)拱形是为了降低上部结构的弯矩。

➢ Alternatively, dynamic numerical models have been extensively used due to the recent advancement made in the computer technology.

另外，由于近来计算机技术的进步，动态数字模型已得到广泛使用。

➢ Road construction is often begun with the removal of vegetation and followed by the laying of pavement material.

通常，筑路的开始阶段是清除植被，然后铺设路面材料。

➢ Despite significant improvements in fuel and engine technology, the urban environments are mostly dominated by traffic emissions.

尽管燃料(的利用率)和发动机技术已经有了很大的改进，但城市环境污染问题主要还是受到机动车尾气排放的影响。

3. 常采用动词非谓语结构(非限定动词)

如前所述，科技文章要求行文简练、结构紧凑，而英语每个简单句(或复合句的分句)中只能有一个谓语动词，如果需要叙述几个动作，先选其中主要动作当谓语，而将其余动作用非谓语动词形式，才能符合英语语法要求。为此，往往使用**分词短语代替定语从句或状语从句**、使用**分词独立结构代替状语从句或并列分句**、使用**不定式短语代替各种从句**、使用**介词 + 动名词短语代替定语从句或状语从句**，这样可以缩短句子，又比较醒目。

汉语中则不存在这种结构，所以翻译时可酌情处理，或译成汉语动宾结构，或另起一句翻译。

试比较下列各组句子：

➢ A direct current is a current which flows always in the same direction.

A direct current is a current flowing always in the same direction.

直流电是一种总是沿同一方向流动的电流。

➢ Heat causes air currents to rise when it is radiating from the earth.

➢ Radiating from the earth, heat causes air currents to rise.
热量由地球辐射出来时,使得气流上升。
➢ A body can move uniformly and in a straight line if there is no cause to change that motion.
A body can move uniformly and in a straight line, there being no cause to change that motion.
如果没有改变物体运动的因素,那么物体将做匀速直线运动。
➢ Vibrating objects produce sound waves and each vibration produces one sound wave.
Vibrating objects produce sound waves, each vibration producing one sound wave.
振动着的物体产生声波,每一次振动产生一个声波。

1) 分词短语

➢ The transport of goods in and out of Tibet was mostly through the Qingzang Highway connecting the Tibet to the adjacent Qinghai province.
进出西藏的货物运输主要通过青藏铁路,该铁路将西藏与相邻的青海省相连。
➢ On the Internet itself there are lots of passionate non-commercial discussion groups on topics ranging from Hungarian politics to copyright law.
互联网上就有很多热闹的非商业讨论群,它们讨论的主题从匈牙利政治到版权法,应有尽有。
➢ Pushing their way through emerging cities like Barakar, India, automobiles carry unwanted cargo—CO_2 emissions.
汽车挤进像印度巴拉卡那样的新兴城市时,带来了不受欢迎的"货物"(污染物)——二氧化碳的排放。
➢ Comparing the actual performance with that anticipated in the design, we may do this by installing special instruments that measure movements, groundwater levels, and other important characteristics.
为了对比实际的(岩土)性能与设计预期的性能,我们可以安装特殊仪器来测量位移量、地下水位以及其他重要特征。
➢ Based on a first order method, the sensitivity of the failure probability with respect to the random input quantities is evaluated.
基于一阶矩法,对随机输入量的失效概率敏感性进行评价。
➢ The life safety requirements are more rigorous due to the greater number of people transported.
由于乘客通行量大,安全标准更严格。
➢ Compared with pure mechanism transmission, AT has the disadvantage of low transmission efficiency.
与纯机械变速器相比,自动变速器(AT = automatic transmission)具有传动效率低的缺点。
➢ The method of tunnel construction is determined based on such factors as the ground conditions, the ground water conditions, the length and diameter of the tunnel drive and the depth of the tunnel to be constructed.
隧道施工工艺的选择必须考虑诸多因素,包括地质条件、地下水状况、隧道开挖的长度和直径以及拟建隧道的埋深。

- Assuming optimal solutions are not unique, we consider two optimal trajectories shown in Fig. 4, both of which satisfy all necessary conditions and the boundary condition of PMP.
  假设最优解并不唯一,我们要考虑由图 4 所示的两条最优轨迹,它们都满足了 PMP 算法的全部必要条件和边界条件。
- For building frame with a regular outline, not involving unusual asymmetry of loading, the influence of sideway caused by vertical loads can be neglected.
  对于有规则轮廓、无异常不对称荷载的建筑结构而言,竖向荷载的附加影响可忽略不计。
- The basic mechanism causing earthquakes in the plate boundary regions appears to be that the continuing deformation of the crustal structure eventually leads to stresses which exceed the material strength.
  在板块边界区引起地震的基本机理似乎是地壳结构的持续变形最终导致应力超过材料强度。

2) 分词独立结构

- Both the first reason and the second considered, you will draw the conclusion that the differentials allow a perfect split of the motor and IC engine on each wheel.
  考虑到第一、二个原因,会得出这样的结论:分速器使得电动机和内燃机能对每个车轮的驱动做很好的切换。(differential,齿轮转动装置、分速器;IC = internal combustion,内燃机)
- Structural elements (parameters) connecting the disc and the ring represent the behavior of the sidewalls of the inflated tyre, those connecting the ring and the plate representing the effects of the local deformation of the belts near the contact area when a vertical load is applied.
  连接盘与环的结构单元(参数)体现了充气轮胎的侧面的性能,而连接环和面的单元,则表现了当施加垂向载荷时靠近接触域的帘线的局部变形效应。
- Almost all metals are good conductors, silver being the best of all.
  几乎所有的金属都是良导体,而银则是其中最好的。
- When people driving at night, pedestrians in images of a far infrared camera present very pronounced edges.
  夜间驾驶,行人在红外线相机中显现出的图像边界非常明显。
- Corruption prevailing in many developing countries, some observers are suspicious that the money will actually reach the people it is intended for.
  发展中国家贪污盛行,一些观察家怀疑这些钱能否到达应该得到它的那些人手里。
- An electron is about as large as nucleus, its diameter being about 10^{-12} cm.
  电子与原子核的大小大致相同,其直径大约为 10^{-12} 厘米。
- This current changing, the magnetic field will change as well.
  电流变化时,磁场也将发生变化。
- The sign of the integral depends on the direction of the path taken, a counter-clockwise direction being taken as positive.

积分的符号取决于所取路径的方向,我们把反时针方向取为正。

➢ There are several basic laws governing these interactions, <u>all of them discovered early in the nineteenth century</u>.

支配这些相互作用的基本定律都是在19世纪发现的。

3)不定式短语

➢ <u>To brainstorm</u> and develop approaches that simultaneously reached technical, cost and schedule to the minimum, design and construction personnel participated in constructability and risk reduction reviews.

为了提出和制定同时满足技术水平、成本及尽可能缩短工期的方法,设计和施工人员参与了可施工性和减少风险的评估。

➢ Kim et al. (1996) developed a logistic model and used it <u>to explain</u> the likelihood of motorists being at fault in collisions with cyclists.

Kim等人开发了一种逻辑斯蒂(回归)模型用来解释机动车驾驶人不小心与骑车人发生碰撞的概率。

➢ <u>To get</u> the optimal costate variable over the whole driving cycle, the variation of externals with multiple shooting methods is used in our study.

为了得到整个驱动循环中的最优共态变量,在研究中我们采用了"多重射击"方法的外界变量。

➢ As one of the bottleneck problems, the problem of reverse driving must to be solved <u>to improve</u> the whole performance of the machines, especially for those with high speed.

反向驱动作为瓶颈问题必须被攻克,从而提高机器的整个性能,尤其是高速运行的机械。

➢ The design build team was able to establish basic design parameters <u>to concurrently complete</u> the final design.

设计施工团队能设定基本设计参数以便同时完成最后的设计。

➢ The success of the management approach is mostly visibly demonstrated in the ability of the project <u>to retain</u> within budget.

项目管理方法的成功与否大部分明确地体现在预算内完成项目的能力。

➢ The regional flood protection system had been designed <u>to safely withstand</u> the storm surges and waves associated with a scenario roughly "typical" of a category 3 hurricane passing close to the New Orleans region.

设计出的地区防洪系统可安全地抵抗经过新奥尔良地区的3类台风带来的涌浪和波浪。

➢ Safe disposal of all human wastes is necessary <u>to protect</u> the health of the individual, the family, and the community, and also <u>to prevent</u> the occurrence of certain nuisance.

为了保护个人、家人和社区居民的健康,防止某些公害的产生,安全地处理所有垃圾是十分必要的。

➢ Two main strategies have been developed <u>to reconcile</u> these seemingly opposing interests: heat recovery and demand control ventilation.

为了协调热回收和通风控制需求这两个看似对立的方面,我们研发了两个重要策略。

➢ These systems use open spaces, called plenums between the concrete slab and raised access floor <u>to supply</u> conditioned air.

这些(通风)系统使用混凝土面和高架通道地板之间的开放空间(充气室)去提供调节的空气。

➢ This raised water level can cause damage by flooding and it allows waves <u>to attack</u> the coast and further inland.

水位升高能导致洪水灾害,使波浪袭击海岸及内陆地区。

4) 介词+动名词短语

➢ Likewise, disposal of solid waste <u>by incinerating</u> results in air pollution, which in turn is controlled <u>by scrubbing</u> with water, resulting in water pollution problem.

同样的,采取焚烧的方法处理固体垃圾导致空气污染,进而用水进行冲洗导致水污染问题。

➢ These criteria can best be met <u>by discharging</u> domestic sewage to an adequate public or community sewerage system.

生活污水排入公共的或者社区的污水处理系统能最好地满足这些标准。

➢ The goal is to improve vehicle dynamics, <u>by suppressing</u> resonances and <u>enlarging</u> the bandwidth for the yaw rate tracking dynamics so that the driver effort is reduced, and to improve stability.

通过抑制共振和扩大偏航率跟踪动态的带宽能达到改善车辆动力的目的,驾驶员省力,行驶稳定性也得到提高。

➢ In conclusion, the effect of change in radius of curvature on stress distribution is explained <u>by using</u> FEM and precautions which have to be taken to prevent a similar failure is clarified.

总之,我们利用有限元法(FEM = Finite Element Method)分析了曲率半径变化对应力分布的影响,也阐明了防止类似的失效再次发生所需采取的防范措施。

➢ Algorithm <u>for deriving</u> the equation of motion for the curving simulation was devised <u>by using</u> a multi-body dynamics method taking account of the forced input from the guideway to the truck though the tires.

采用了多体运动学方法设计了提取曲线仿真运动方程的算法,同时考虑了通过轮胎从导轨传入转向架的强制输入。

➢ At last, the ability of the controller to improve vehicle handling is evaluated <u>by using</u> a quite detailed (commercial) vehicle simulator.

最后,使用一个比较精细(商业)的汽车驾驶模拟器,评估了控制器提高车辆操纵性的能力。

➢ The lower-level controller allocates the required control efforts to the four in-wheel motors <u>for generating</u> the desired tire forces.

低层控制器将所需的控制力分配到四个轮毂电机来产生所需的驱动力。

➢ Because the infills in an infilled frame structure serve also as external walls or internal partitions, the system is economical way of stiffening and strengthening the structure.

由于填充框架结构中的填充物也可起到外墙或内墙作用,因此该系统是一种加固结构的节约方法。

➢ The horizontal stiffness of a rigid frame is governed mainly by the bending resistance of the girders, the columns, and their connections, and, in a tall frame, by the axial rigidity of the columns.

刚性框架结构的水平刚度主要受梁、柱及其连接件的抗弯能力控制,在高度较大的框架结构中,起主要作用的则是柱子的轴向刚性。

4. 后置定语

大量使用后置定语也是科技文章的特点之一。常见的结构大致有以下五种:**介词短语后置、形容词及形容词短语后置、副词后置、定语从句后置**。

1) 介词短语后置

➢ Nearly all vehicles have a chime or speaker in the dashboard instrument cluster for various alert functions.

几乎所有的车辆在仪表板上的仪表组配备了具有各种警示功能的报警器或扬声器。

➢ The vibratory roller for this investigation was an Ingersoll-Rand DD-138HEA double cylinder drum roller.

所调查的振动压路机为英格索兰公司制造的型号为 DD-138HEA 双缸轮压路机。

➢ The contact width of a cylindrical drum can be calculated from the geometry of the drum, the applied force, and the material properties according to Lundberg's theory.

根据伦德伯格的理论,一个柱形鼓的接触宽度可以由鼓的几何形状、对鼓施加的作用力以及鼓的材料特性计算出来。

➢ Simulations based on a high-fidelity, CarSim, full-vehicle model show the effectiveness of the control approach.

基于高保真 CarSim 的整车模型的仿真试验证明了该控制方法的有效性。

➢ Besides, a half vehicle model which is a linear approximation of the vehicle dynamics was used.

此外,该系统使用了一个车辆动力学线性近似的半车模型。

➢ The results therefore confirm that PCE of the studied street canyon is not improved and even become worse by using higher albedo materials for the exterior surface of buildings.

因此,结果证实了建筑物的外表面采用高反照率材料时,被调查的街道峡谷 PCE 没有得到改善,甚至变得更糟。

➢ Furthermore, the addition of electrical motors in the driveline provides regenerative braking and electric traction feasibilities.

此外,在驱动系统中增加电机来提供再生制动以及电动助力的可行性。

- The difference between logistic and linear regression is reflected both in the choice and assumption of parametric model.
  逻辑和线性回归的区别体现在参数模型选择和假设中。
- As stated in the introduction section, we aim to develop a method to build a costate approximation model which enables the use of the Pontryagin's Minimum Principle as an energy management strategy.
  正如引言部分所述,我们的目标是提出建立共态近似模型的方法,使作为能量管理策略的庞特里亚金极小值原理能够得到应用。

2) 形容词及形容词短语后置

- In this factory the only fuel available is coal.
  该厂唯一可用的燃料是煤。
- In radiation, thermal energy is transformed into radiant energy, similar in nature to light.
  热能在辐射时,转换成性质与光相似的辐射能。
- The speed necessary is 200km per hour.
  所需速度为每小时二百公里。
- All parties concerned (responsible) should attend the discussion.
  有关各方都应参加讨论。
- It is one of the stars visible to the naked eyes.
  它是肉眼可看见的恒星之一。
- Anyone drunk is not allowed to drive.
  任何醉酒的人都不许开车。
- A scientist is a good observer, accurate, patient and objective and applies persistent and logical thought to the observations he makes.
  一个科学家就是一个好的观察者,准确、耐心和客观,对观察结果做不断的逻辑思考。
- They produced gases almost as harmful as the gases from the factories.
  他们排出的废气几乎和工厂排出的废气一样有害。
- This is an article worthy of careful study.
  这是一篇很值得研究的文章。
- This is a question easily accessible to beginners.
  这是一个易于为初学者所理解的问题。

3) 副词后置

- Mountain ranges can block clouds, creating dry "shadows" downwind.
  山脉能阻止云,形成顺风面干燥的"雨影区"。
- In addition, all required FE calculations are performed automatically.
  此外,自动执行所有必需的有限元计算。
- The controlled power flow enables the car to take corners more directly and responsively.

控制功率流可使汽车在转弯时做出更直接的反应。

➢ A novel feature of the method is that the PSDs of various suspension responses can be obtained accurately and efficiently from the PSD of the road input.
这个(仿真)方法的创新点是,当输入路面功率谱密度时,该方法能准确而有效地得到各种悬架所响应的功率谱密度。(PSD = power spectral density 功率谱密度)

➢ If the instantaneous cost function is suitably defined, the result is close to the global optimum.
如果瞬时成本函数被适当地限定,其结果接近全局最优。

➢ Therefore, in what follows, we present a new rollover index which includes the lateral and roll dynamics simultaneously.
因此,接下来,我们提出一个同时包含外侧动力和辊动力的新的滚动指数。

➢ Shown in Figures 26-b and 26-c are the trajectories of the vehicle without and with the aid of the fuzzy active steering controller, respectively.
图 26-b 和 26-c 分别为车辆关闭和启用模糊主动转向控制器时的运行轨迹。

➢ The heat conduction problem is solved independently from the stress problem and phase state to obtain temperature history.
热传导的问题是通过独立求解应力问题和相状态,以获得温度历史。

➢ Desktop calibration of automatic transmission (AT) is a method which can reduce cost, enhance efficiency and shorten the development periods of a vehicle effectively.
自动变速器的桌面校准是一种能够减少花费、提高效率和有效缩短车辆研发周期的方法。

➢ Hence, the map of normalized s2 saliencies can be used directly as an edginess map.
因此,归一化后的 s2 显著性张量场可直接作为图像边界场来使用。

➢ The balanced suspension utilizes the "level" principle to distribute the axle load equally and to reduce the shock from the road irregularities.
平衡悬架采用"水平"的原则来使轴载分配均匀,并且减少路面不平度造成的振动。

➢ A method that is widely used is programming by demonstration, where the intermediate points to the goal position are recorded by sequentially moving the robot to each position using the teach pendant.
示范编程是一种广泛运用的方法,通过运用示教器顺序移动机器人到每个位置,并记录中间点到达目标点的路径。

4) 定语从句后置

➢ These fault lines divide the global crust into about 12 major tectonic plates, which are rigid, relatively cool, slabs about 100km thick.
这些断层线将全球地壳划分成十二大主要构造板块,这些构造板块是刚性的,温度较低,厚度约 100 公里。

➢ The pump compresses the diesel, which is then squirted into each cylinder in turn.
泵压缩柴油,然后依次喷射到每个气缸。

➢ In theory, traffic congestion is likely due to traffic volume that generates demand for a space greater than the availability and road capacity.

从理论上讲,交通堵塞有可能是由于交通量所需要的道路空间大于道路的可使用空间和承载力。

➤ The DAS, manufactured by IOTech, is equipped with an Ethernet port <u>which provides continuous data streaming to a laptop PC onboard the roller compactor, and has 16 programmable input voltage ranges</u>.

由 IOTech 公司制造的数据采集系统(DAS = Data Acquisition Station),配备有以太网端口,能为压路机上的笔记本电脑提供连续的数据流和 16 伏可编程输入电压。

➤ The point in the Earth's crustal system <u>where an earthquake is initiated</u> (the point of rupture) is called the hypocenter or focus of the earthquake.

地壳系统中,地震发生的位置称作地震中心或震中。

➤ The radial direction of the guide tires and the stabilizing tires, <u>which are contact with the side plane of the guideway</u>, are related to this displacement.

与导轨侧平面接触的导向轮和稳定轮的径向和(y 方向的)位移有关。

➤ In general, vehicle stability control systems <u>which prevent vehicles from spinning and drifting out</u>, have been already developed and commercialized.

总之,防止汽车侧滑和漂移的汽车稳定性控制系统已经开发并投入市场。

➤ The structural part is composed basically by three spokes <u>whose deformations (depending on the forces applied to the wheel) are sensed by means of strain gauges</u>.

结构部分是由三个通过张力测量仪感知变形量(根据施加在轮胎上的力)的辐条组成。

5. 普遍使用长句

科技英语一般指在自然科学和工程技术等方面的科学著作、论文、教科书、科技报告和学术讲演中所使用的英语,其表达客观准确、逻辑性强、结构严谨。有时一个英语句子里包含不少短语和从句,进行周密细致的限定和说明,所以句子往往偏长、结构复杂。

➤ But now that politicians and the green lobby are getting more worked up about emissions of global-warming gases, European car makers are terrified that regulations will be brought in to limit carbon dioxide emissions from cars, in the same way that toxic gases such as carbon monoxide or nitrogen oxides are subject to ever-falling statutory limits.

但由于政治家和环保团体正致力于全球温室气体减排,欧洲汽车制造商害怕新出台的法规将限制汽车二氧化碳排放量,同样,有毒气体如一氧化碳或氮氧化物也会受到要求排放量不断降低的法律限制。

➤ Such preview information can be obtained either from a look-ahead sensor which measures the road irregularity in front of the vehicle or by assuming that the road inputs at the rear wheels are the same as those at the front wheels except for time delays.

这种预知信息可以通过一个能感知车辆前方路面不平度的预处理传感器得到,也可以通过前后轮接受路面输入(除时间上延迟以外)是一致的假定获得。

6. 常见复合词与缩略词

大量使用复合词与缩略词是科技文章的特点之一，复合词从过去的双词组合发展到多词组合，缩略词趋向于任意构词。例如：

复合词
full-enclosed　　　全封闭的（双词合成形容词）
feed-back　　　反馈（双词合成名词）
work-harden　　　加工硬化（双词合成动词）
crisis-cross　　　交叉着（双词合成副词）
on-and-off-the-road　　　路面越野两用的（多词合成形容词）
anti-armoured-fighting-vehicle-missile　　　反装甲车导弹（多词合成名词）
radiophotography　　　无线电传真（无连字符复合词）
colorimeter　　　色度计（无连字符复合词）

缩略词
裁减式缩略词：
maths（mathematics）　　　数学
lab（laboratory）　　　实验室
ft（foot/feet）　　　英尺
cpd（compound）　　　化合物

用首字母组成的缩略词：
FM（frequency modulation）　　　调频
P.S.I.（pounds per square inch）　　　磅/英寸
SCR（silicon controlled rectifier）　　　可控硅整流器

混成法构成的缩略词：
TELESAT（telecommunications satellite）　　　通信卫星

1) 复合词

➤ The simplest frequency-domain analysis method used for bearing fault detection is Fast Fourier Transform (FFT).
FFT（快速傅里叶变换）是对轴承故障检测的最简单的频谱分析方法。

➤ By integrating measurement, documentation, and control systems, the use of the IC rollers allows for real-time monitoring and just-in-time corrections in the compaction process.
通过集成测量、文件编制和控制系统，智能压实压路机在压实过程中允许实时监控和即时修正。（IC = intelligent compaction，智能压实）

➤ In the events, a lot of victims died due to the time-consuming rescue, because the rescue for victims after the disasters is under extreme time pressure.
在那次事件中，很多受害者死于耗时过长的救援，（主要）是由于灾后对于受害者的救援面临着极大的时间压力。
- Virtual technology is widely utilized in various vehicle test-beds.
虚拟技术广泛应用于各种汽车试验平台。
- This week the EU approved a voluntary deal with car makers to reduce carbon-dioxide emissions by a quarter.
这周欧盟通过了一个自愿协议,让汽车制造商减少1/4的二氧化碳排放量。
- There are two types of vehicles used in the monorail system: straddle-type and hanging-type.
单轨系统中有两种类型的车辆:跨座式和悬挂式。
- The study of actions of high-speed moving loads on bridges and elevated tracks remains a topical problem for transport.
对桥梁和高架轨道上高速运动负荷特性的研究仍然是交通运输领域最受关注的问题。
- In case of high-rise buildings, forming intersections provides better ventilation at corners.
对于高层建筑,形成的交叉口会为角落提供更好的通风。
- The use of parallel-series structures of several cells of supercapacitors makes it possible to reach a voltage and a high current output.
超级电容电池以混(并/串)联形式组合在一起,可以实现电压和高电流的输出。
- While EGR can reduce the output of nitrogen-oxide, it can have unwelcome side-effect of increasing the level of particulates.
尾气再循环系统减少氮氧化物排放的同时,也带来了讨厌的副作用:增加了颗粒物的排放。(EGR = exhaust gas recirculation 尾气再循环)
- Behind this unlikely turn of events is a new generation of electronically controlled, high pressure fuel-injection systems combined with new "common-rail" technology.
令人意想不到的是新一代电子控制系统——高压燃油喷射系统结合共轨技术的产生。

2) 缩略词

- Field oriented control (FOC) is widely used in modern motor drives to achieve faster dynamic response and more efficient operation.
现代电机驱动广泛使用矢量控制(FOC)来实现更快的动态响应以及更高效的操作。
- In [10], two Rapidly Exploring Random Trees (RRTs) were rooted at the start and during the goal configurations.
在(文献)10中,两个快速探测随机模型(RRTs)被设置在开始和目标配置中。
- While EGR (exhaust gas recirculation) can reduce the output of nitrogen-oxide, it can have unwelcome side-effect of increasing the level of particulates.
尾气再循环系统(EGR)减少氮氧化物排放的同时,也带来了讨厌的副作用:增加了颗粒物的排放。
- After the Late Heavy Bombardment or Lunar Cataclysm period ended, mostly Near-Earth-Asteroids (NEAs) have peppered the terrestrial region.
在晚期宇宙大撞击或月球大灾难期结束后,大多数近地小行星已经布满陆地区域。

- The stochastic Finite-Element-Method (FEM) is a suitable tool to assess the reliability of life-time prediction models for complex components.

  随机有限元法(FEM)是一个评估复杂组件寿命预测模型可靠性的合适工具。

- According to the Federal Highway Administration (FHWA)'s terminology, Intelligent Compaction (IC) is defined as the compaction of road materials, such as soils, aggregate bases, or asphalt pavement materials, using modern vibratory rollers equipped with an integrated measurement system, Global Positioning System (GPS) based mapping, onboard computer reporting system, and (optionally) a feedback control.

  据美国联邦公路管理局(FHWA)的术语,智能压实(IC)定义为:利用配有集成测量系统、全球定位系统(GPS)测图、车载电脑报告系统和反馈控制系统(可选)的现代振动压路机,对路面材料,如土壤、混合地基或沥青路面材料进行压实。

- The knowledge of SR data is a prerequisite for the modeling and design of all photovoltaic (PV) systems.

  SR数据知识是建模和设计所有光伏(PV)系统的先决条件。

- However, gas turbines (GTs) are also used which make up around 28.7% of total installed capacity.

  然而,我们也使用占总装机容量的28.7%左右的燃气轮机(GTs)。

- In these conditions, the urban search and rescue (USAR) mobile robot can be dispatched to the collapse building to help the rescuers to complete the search and rescue task.

  在这些情况下,城市搜救(USAR)移动机器人能够被派遣到垮塌的建筑物中帮助救援人员完成搜救任务。

- Jerry Mahlman, director of NOAA's (National Oceanic and Atmospheric Administration) Geophysical Fluid Dynamics Laboratory at Princeton, however, has calculated that the surge use in coal and oil quickly increased the amount of sulfates aloft, prompting the cooling.

  但是,位于普林斯顿的美国国家海洋和大气局(NOAA)地球物理流体动力学实验室的主管Jerry Mahlman认为,大量使用煤炭和石油使空中的硫酸盐增加,促使空气变冷。

- A detailed standard CarSim small SUV (Sports Utility Vehicle) model is used in numerical simulations to analyze the responses of both the uncontrolled and the controlled vehicle.

  在数值模拟中,用精细的标准CarSim小型多功能车(SUV)模型来分析失控和受控车辆的反应。

- To examine stress distribution at the keyway and fracture surface, finite element method (FEM) was applied.

  有限元法(FEM)被用来检测键槽和断裂面的应力分布情况。

- The second comes about as a consequence of the growing use of the technologies of computer-aided design (CAD) and manufacturing (CAM) which employ databases with 3-D Cartesian positional reference systems.

  其次,使用具有3-D笛卡尔位置参考系统的数据库进行计算机辅助设计(CAD)和计算机辅助制造(CAM)的技术得到越来越多的运用。

> There has been increasing interest in short-distance transportation systems in city areas, such as the LRT (light-rail transit), subways and monorail.

在城市,短距离运输系统受到越来越多的关注,如轻轨、地铁和单轨。

> Then, a static output feedback based on optimal control LQR (Linear Quadratic Regulator) method is proposed to track a desired yaw rate reference.

然后,我们提出了基于最优控制线性二次型调节器(LQR)法的静态输出反馈来跟踪所需的偏航率参考值。

> This week the EU (European Union) approved a voluntary deal with car makers to reduce carbon-dioxide emissions by a quarter.

这周欧盟(EU)通过了一个自愿协议,让汽车制造商减少1/4的二氧化碳的排放量。

7. 时态的运用

1) 一般现在时

科技英语用一般现在时表达"无时间性(Timeless)"的概念,排除任何与时间关联的误解,可用于对科学定义、定理、方程(或公式)或图表等客观真理性的内容进行解说,还可对一些时常发生或不受时间性限制的自然现象、过程和常规等进行表述。

> The short answer is that diesel represents the industry's best hope of cutting carbon dioxide emissions.

(对这个问题的)简要回答是,柴油机代表了汽车行业对减少二氧化碳排放的巨大希望。

> The stochastic Finite-Element-Method (FEM) is a suitable tool to assess the reliability of lifetime prediction models for complex components.

随机有限元法(FEM)是一个用来评估复杂组件寿命预测模型可靠性的合适工具。

> That is because diesel engines are, typically, 30% more fuel-efficient than petrol engines.

这是因为柴油机的燃油利用率通常比汽油机高30%。

> It uses a moving coordinate system defined by the positions of the guide tires tracing along the guideway.

通过沿导轨方向运动的导向轮的位置来定义运动坐标系。

> From Fig. 1, it is clear that the management may induce a dynamic splitting of the driver torque between the front and rear drive.

从图1中可以很明显地看出,这个管理系统可能会导致前后驱动轮之间的驱动扭矩的动态分裂。

> The study of actions of high-speed moving loads on bridges and elevated tracks remains a topical problem for transport.

对桥梁和高架轨道上高速运动负荷的研究仍然是交通运输领域中最受关注的问题。

> Simulations based on a high-fidelity, CarSim, full-vehicle model show the effectiveness of the control approach.

基于高保真 CarSim 的整车模型仿真试验证明了该控制方法的有效性。

➢ The paper describes small scale wind tunnel experiments on the dispersion of contaminants discharged from the bottom of courtyards and other enclosed spaces.

这篇文章主要讲在中庭底部和其他一些封闭空间中做的污染物扩散小型风洞实验。

➢ Due to their many economic and ecological implications the possibility to predict tyre wear is of major importance to tyre manufacturers, fleet owners and governments.

考虑到经济和生态方面的影响,轮胎磨损的可预测性对轮胎制造商、车主和政府来说都显得非常重要。

➢ Among other benefits, EVs are more efficient and can reduce or eliminate the environmental noise and pollutants that are associated with conventional internal combustion engine (ICE) vehicles considerably.

除了这些优点,电动汽车(EV)效率更高,并且可以大幅度减少或消除传统内燃发动机(ICE)产生的环境噪声和污染物。

2)一般过去时

科技英语中在叙述过去进行的研究情况时,若不与现在情况发生联系,常用一般过去时。

➢ So, we used the PCA method to extract the typical features.

因此,我们采用 PCA 方法提取典型特征。

➢ Yet the Little Ice Age, an anomalous cold snap that peaked from 1570 to 1730 and forced European farmers to abandon their fields, was caused by a change of only half a degree celsius.

而在"小冰河时期",由于气温半摄氏度的改变而引起的异常寒流,却从 1570 年持续到 1730 年,迫使欧洲的农民放弃了他们的土地。

➢ Carbon dioxide concentration has been increasing about 0.3 percent higher than it was before the industrial revolution.

二氧化碳的浓度比工业革命之前增加了大约 0.3%。

➢ Problems became evident in the 1970's and 1980's as new political forms, economic relations, and restructured cities posed difficulties for the premises that underlie the tenants of modernist planning.

由于新的政治形势、经济关系以及城市的重建,(这一切)都对采用现代主义城市规划的住房造成困难,20 世纪 70 和 80 年代的这些问题变得突出。

➢ As no information with respect to the chemical composition of the shaft material was available, the first task in the failure analysis was the material identification.

由于没有轴材料化学成分信息,在失效分析中的首要任务就是材料鉴定。

➢ For example, the University of Iowa of the United States developed the world's most advanced National Advanced Driving Simulator (NADS) in 1999.

例如,美国爱荷华大学在 1999 年开发了世界上最先进的国家高级驾驶模拟器(NADS)。

➢ In the previous gear box, we used historical TTF data.

在前面的齿轮箱(例子)中,我们使用了历史 TTF 数据。
- The curving dynamics of a monorail car was simulated by using these dynamic models.
  单轨车的曲线动力是用这些动态模型进行仿真的。
- It was demonstrated that the output feedback based on optimal control LQR can improve the stability.
  结果表明,基于最优控制的线性二次型调节器(LQR = Linear Quadratic Regulator)的输出反馈可以提高稳定性。
- Sakai proposed a DYC system for a 4WIA electric vehicle, but only the vehicle lateral motion was controlled.
  Sakai 提出了四轮独立驱动(4WIA)电动汽车直接横摆角速度控制(DYC = direct yaw moment control)系统,但是该系统仅可以控制横向运动。

3)现在完成时

科技英语中在叙述过去进行的研究情况时,若与现在关系直接且影响较大则用现在完成时。现在完成时还用于表述已取得的成果或完成的工作,以及在加工过程中工序前后的顺序。

- Networking has made the advanced technology features for 2010—2011 model vehicles possible, including on board communications systems, control systems such as lane-departure warning systems, and (slippery) road-condition advisories.
  网络系统使 2010—2011 年款模型车辆具有先进的技术特点,包括车载通信系统,控制系统,如车道偏离警告系统,和(湿滑)路况通告。
- Recently, electric vehicles (EVs) have attracted a great deal of interest as an elegant solution to environmental and energy concerns.
  最近,电动汽车(EV)由于能够很好地解决环境和能源问题而备受人们的关注。
- Most current technological developments in electric vehicles have centered on improving energy efficiency.
  电动汽车领域最新的技术进步主要集中在能源效率的提高上。
- The different types of Stochastic Finite-Element-Methods (FEM) have been explained briefly.
  我们就不同类型的随机有限元方法做了简要的解释。
- Since the late 1700s, the burning of fossil fuels and other human activities have increased atmospheric CO_2 concentrations more than 30 percent.
  自 18 世纪末以来,化石燃料的燃烧和其他人类活动使得大气中的二氧化碳浓度增加了 30% 以上。
- Artificial intelligence techniques have been increasingly applied to bearing condition prediction, among which the most widely used models for prognostics are support vector machine.
  人工智能技术已越来越多地应用于轴承状态预测,其中最广泛使用的预测模型是支持向量机。
- Despite the space agency's resolve to think small, it has retained one big-ticket project from

the past: the $28 billion space station.

尽管航天局的决议是使花费尽可能少，但根据以往情况来看依旧是一个耗资巨大的工程：280亿美元的太空站。

➢ The recent terrorist attacks, also the large scale natural disasters, have brought huge property and life loss.

最近的恐怖袭击，加上大规模的自然灾害，已经造成了巨大的财产损失和人员伤亡。

➢ Methane, the principal ingredient of natural gas, has caused an estimated 15 percent of the warming in modern times.

在近代全球气温上升幅度中，约有15%是由天然气的主要成分——甲烷造成的。

➢ The United States, Europe, Japan, and Tsinghua University and Jilin University in China have carried out relevant researches, and made sample vehicles.

美国、欧洲、日本和中国的清华大学以及吉林大学进行了相关研究，并制作出了样车。

➢ There has been increasing interest in short-distance transportation systems in city areas, such as the LRT, subways and monorail.

在城市中，轻轨（LRT = light-rail transit）、地铁和单轨等短距离运输系统，已受到越来越多的关注。

➢ We have developed a curving simulation algorithm for a monorail car by using a moving coordinate system defined by guide tire positions.

我们已经利用导向轮位置定义的运动坐标系统研发了单轨车曲线通过性仿真算法。

➢ The present research work has been supported by International Campus on Safety and Intermodality in Transportation.

当前的研究工作获得了"国际校园安全"和"交通联运"的支持。

4) 一般将来时

在科技英语中，一般将来时可用于讨论计划中的项目研究。

➢ The results in terms of accuracy and dynamic performance will be discussed in the second part of the paper.

精度和动态性能方面的结果将在本文的第二部分讨论。

➢ Then, from 2007, environmentally friendly cars powered by fuel cells will begin to make an appearance.

2007年之后，由燃料电池驱动的环保型汽车即将面世。

➢ A tropical forest will soak up CO_2, but once cleared for cattle ranching, the same land becomes a source of methane.

热带森林会吸收二氧化碳，但是一旦砍掉森林改成牧场，这个地方就会变成甲烷的产生地。

➢ Soon it will be common to all manufacturers' models as an engine option.

很快，它将会成为所有制造商引擎模型的共同选择。

➢ In the cruise control mode, the virtual vehicle will run at the set speed until the driver has implemented any operation.

在巡航控制模式下,虚拟车辆将以设定好的速度运行,直到操作者执行其他操作。

➢ Beyond that the specific human effect on climate change <u>will remain</u> hauntingly indefinite until our knowledge increases and the models improve.

除非我们的知识得到丰富与模型水平得到提高,否则人类对气候变化的特定影响将还是个未知数。

➢ Recently, advancements in these technologies combined with emergent technologies, such as advanced sorbent injections, currently can attain the 2015 limits in many applications and <u>will continue</u> to gain ground on the incumbent SCR as the market opportunity expands.

最近,技术改进结合像洗烟塔这样的新技术能够在实际运用中达到2015年的排放标准,并且随着市场机会的增加,将继续取代现在的选择性催化还原技术(SCR = Selective Catalytic Reduction)。

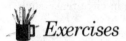

Exercises

1. Go through an English paper in your field recommended by your supervisor and review the characteristics of Science and Technology English.

2. Look through the following materials to get familiar with the special features of STE.

(1)大量使用名词化结构

➢ Unfortunately, it's those places that are now capturing the popular <u>imagination</u>, places that offer bomb-making <u>instructions</u>, pornography, advice on how to steal credit cards.

不幸的是,这正是让民众神往的地方,是能够提供制造炸弹的说明书、色情作品以及咨询如何窃取信用卡的地方。

➢ The <u>explanations</u> given above are valid if all uncertainties follow a Gaussian distribution and are statistically independent.

如果所有的不确定性服从高斯分布且在统计上是相互独立的,那么上面给出的解释是有效的。

➢ The <u>prediction</u> bearing <u>degradation</u> process is extremely important in industry.

在工业(生产)中,轴承损耗过程预测是极其重要的。

➢ Development of a systematic method for intelligent compaction data <u>analysis and management</u> is essential.

对智能压实数据分析与管理的系统方法的研发是非常重要的。

➢ A portable shape-shifting mobile system named as Amoeba Ⅱ(A-Ⅱ) is developed for the urban search and rescue <u>application</u>.

研发了一种被命名为A-Ⅱ的便携式变形移动系统来用于城市的搜救工作。

➢ Global climate depends on <u>combinations</u> of factors interacting in subtle and complex ways that we do not yet fully understand.

全球气候取决于以微妙复杂方式相互作用的因素组合影响,对此我们还未完全了解。

- The study of actions of high-speed moving loads on bridges and elevated tracks remains a topical problem for transport.
  对桥梁和高架轨道上高速运动的负荷的研究仍然是交通运输领域中最关注的问题。
- Due to the possible modeling error and parametric uncertainties, an adaptive control based higher-level controller is designed to yield the vehicle virtual control efforts.
  由于可能存在的建模误差和参数的不确定性,我们设计了一种基于高层控制器的自适应控制系统来对车辆进行虚拟控制。
- An analytic solution on how to distribute the higher-level control efforts is given, when the actuators constraints are not considered.
  在不考虑驱动器约束的情况下,本文提出了一种关于如何分配高层控制力的解析方法。
- This paper considers the stability control of a 4WIA electric vehicle.
  本文研究四轮独立驱动(4WIA)电动汽车的稳定性控制问题。
- Vehicle equations of motion in longitudinal, lateral, and yaw directions can be expressed as:
  车辆纵向动力方程、横向动力方程和角速度方程可以表示为:
- Many cities recently have provided urban design guidelines and suggested passive mitigation techniques to improve the pedestrian comfort and health.
  最近,许多城市都提供城市设计指南,建议采用被动缓冲技术以提高行人舒适和健康。
- Overall accuracy of measurement of trace gas concentration is about 10%.
  痕量气体浓度的测定整体精度约为10%。
- Increased traffic emissions and reduced natural ventilation cause build-up of high pollution levels in urban street canyons/intersections.
  汽车尾气排放量的增长和自然通风量的减少,造成城市街谷或十字路口的严重污染。
- In India, increased motorized transport in urban centers has led to problems of higher vehicular exhaust emissions, resulting in 64% of contribution in air pollution load.
  在印度,城镇中心日益增加的机动车辆导致了尾气排放量的增加,尾气排放量已经占到污染气体总量的64%。
- The objective of this study is to investigate an under floor air distribution (UFAD) system regarding thermal comfort, indoor air quality (IAQ), and energy consumption.
  该研究的目的是通过热舒适度、室内空气品质(IAQ)和能源消耗来调查地板送风系统(UFAD)。
- Examples are excessive speed during cornering, obstacle avoidance and severe lane change maneuvers, where rollover occurs as a result of the lateral wheel forces induced during these maneuvers.
  比如,弯道超速、避障和快速变道,都会因为轮轴横向力而发生翻转。
- This paper tackles the problem of driving stability for a hybrid vehicle.
  本文主要解决混合动力汽车的行驶稳定性问题。
- Simms and Wood performed multibody simulations of pedestrian impacts with a saloon car and an SUV.

Simms 和 Wood 用轿车和运动型多用途汽车(SUV = Sports Utility Vehicle)对行人碰撞进行了多体模拟。

➢ The use of linear regression models is inappropriate for making probabilistic statements about the occurrences of vehicle accidents on the road.
利用线性回归模型对道路车辆事故发生做概率性的陈述是不恰当的。

➢ The development of EV will provide needs and motivation to the development of relevant new and high technology industry.
电动汽车(EV)的发展为相关高新技术产业的发展提供了需求和动力。

➢ This paper presents a hybrid power source with the realization of batteries and supercapacitors.
这篇文献提出了一种由电池和超级电容组成的混合动力电源。

➢ Furthermore, with the considerations of all the physical constraints of the system, a formulation of nonlinear optimal control is presented.
此外,考虑到系统的所有的物理限制,我们提出非线性最优控制的公式。

➢ The uniqueness of the solution is possibly guaranteed in our problem when both the battery output voltage and the battery internal resistance are constants throughout the whole range of SOC.
在整个荷电状态(SOC = State of Charge)变化范围内电池输出电压和电池内阻保持一致,则能保证在这个问题中解的唯一性。

➢ The chassis is treated as a rigid body (six dofs) and each wheel has two degrees of freedom, the vertical travel and the rotation about its axis.
底盘被当作是刚体(六个自由度),而每个轮胎有两个自由度,垂直运行和绕轴旋转。

➢ The concepts and quantitative expressions of the steering road feel, steering sensibility, and steering operation stability are introduced.
本文介绍了转向路感、转向灵敏度、转向操纵稳定性的概念和定量表达式。

➢ An active steering system facilitates two major functions: realizing a variable steering ratio, and maintaining vehicle stability and maneuverability during emergency maneuvers or when driving conditions call for a change in steering response.
主动转向系统有助于实现两个主要功能:实现可变转向比,以及在紧急工况或转向驾驶条件需要改变时保持车辆稳定性和可操作性。

➢ Using the elite selection technique justifies a relatively high mutation rate, thereby facilitating the thorough exploration of the search space without losing the fittest members of each generation.
采用优胜劣汰技术证明了相对较高的突变率,从而有助于深入研究,并且不会失去每一代最合适的物种。

➢ The matching of the two-stage turbocharging system is mainly based on engine performance simulations.
二级涡轮增压系统的匹配主要基于发动机性能模拟仿真。

➢ Several factors may contribute to the formations of residual stress and deformation.
这几个因素可能会导致残余应力和变形(的地层)的形成。

- Despite such uncertainties, the computer programs used to model Earth's climate are improving rapidly.

  尽管有这些不确定性，用于模拟地球气候的计算机程序正迅速得以改进。

- As the key parameter for high-power battery management systems, the State-of-Charge (SOC) of a Li-ion battery directly indicates its residual capacity and thus reflects the remaining range of an electric vehicle.

  作为高功率电池管理系统的关键参数，锂电池的荷电状态（SOC）可直接表明电池剩余容量，并且可以反映出电动汽车可续航里程。

- Our prediction methodology evaluates the risk of a possible future accident based on the LTR and LSI.

  基于横向载荷转移率（LTR = Lateral-Load Transfer Ratio）和大规模集成电路（LSI = Large Scale Integrated circuit）技术的预测方法用来评估未来可能发生的事故的风险。

- However, detection of pedestrians from a moving vehicle is not trivial.

  然而，从行驶车辆中觉察到行人并不轻松。

- Methane, the principal ingredient of natural gas, has caused an estimated 15 percent of the warming in modern time.

  在现代全球气温上升幅度中，约有15%是由天然气的主要成分——甲烷造成的。

- Modern automobile electronic technology has shown an irreplaceable role in improving automobile power, safety, reliability, driving stability and comfort.

  现代汽车电子技术在提升汽车动力性、安全性、可靠性、行驶稳定性以及舒适性等方面已经展现出不可替代的作用。

- Therefore considerations of ride comfort and steering stability have led to much research into active and semi-active suspensions.

  出于对乘坐舒适性和操纵稳定性的考虑，人们积极开发主动和半主动悬架。

- The vehicle body vibration is transferred to the road surface through the suspension and tire as well.

  车身的振动通过悬架和轮胎传递到地面。

- So to address the question, we will assume that "alternative" refers to those fuels that are produced from a nonfossil source or to those fuels (fossil or otherwise) that would require substantial changes in automotive design or in the distribution and marketing strategies.

  所以为了解决这个问题，我们将考虑"替代燃料"。"替代燃料"是指非化石燃料，或是指由于汽车设计或分销以及营销战略而做出重大改进的燃料（化石或其他种类）。

- Along with fuel consumption, two other performance indicators of a hybrid vehicle are acceleration performance and exhaust emissions.

  除了油耗，混合动力汽车的其他两个性能指标就是加速性能和尾气排放。

- The combination of both model-based calibration and ANN-based error compensation methods can be an effective solution to enhancing robot position accuracy.

  采用基于模型校准和人工神经网络（ANN = artificial neural network）误差补偿方法，可以有效地提高机器人定位精度。

➤ The relentless accumulation of greenhouse gases has led the IPCC to project that in the next hundred years global average temperatures will rise by 1 to 3.5 celsius degrees.
由于温室气体的不断积累,政府气候变化专门委员会(IPCC)预测在未来的几百年全球的平均气温将上升1至3.5摄氏度。

➤ The impact of vibration generated by a bearing fault has relatively low energy and it is often accompanied by high energy noise and vibration generated by simultaneously-active equipment.
由轴承故障所引发的振动影响是相对较低的能量(振动),常常伴随同时运作设备所产生的高能量的噪声和振动。

➤ However, mechanical losses are incurred by the clutch and differential gears, during power transmission from the motor to the wheels.
然而,当能量从电动机传送到车轮时,机械损失会在离合器和差速器之间产生。

➤ In the recent years, there is an increasing need for flexible manufacturing systems, capable of adapting to different market demands and product-mix changes.
近年来,人们对柔性生产系统的需求日益增长,这种生产系统能适应不同的市场需求与产品组合变换。

➤ The surface properties of nitrided parts are closely related to the component phases of their compound layers and microstructure of their diffusion layers.
氮化工件的表面性能与其复合层的相组成和扩散层的微观结构密切相关。

➤ It was considered as the length of robot arm in the whole system.
它在整个系统里面被认为是机械手长度。

➤ This kind of design approach often results in the design conflicts, enables the designers have repeatedly modified the design of various subsystems, needs lots of tests to finish the development of vibration system, results in long product development cycle, and greatly increases the cost of the product design and testing.
这种设计方法往往导致设计间冲突,设计师需要反复修改各种子系统的设计,并且需要做大量的测试来完成振动系统的研制,从而延长了产品的开发周期,并极大地提高了产品的设计和测试成本。

➤ Simulation results suggest that "real-time" measuring of the actual forces at the tires can improve significantly the performance of the standard control systems.
仿真结果表明:在轮胎上"实时"测量实际作用力可以显著提高标准控制系统的性能。

➤ Computer simulation is an effective approach to analyze the dynamics of railway bridges under train motion along them.
计算机仿真是分析火车沿铁路桥梁运动的动力学问题的一种有效方法。

➤ As a result, in-vehicle networking has created a quiet evolution in automotive technology, resulting in the elimination of unwieldy wiring harnesses once used in control circuits.
因此,车载网络创造了汽车技术的悄然演变,从而消除曾用于控制电路笨重的布线。

➤ The modeling and prediction of the conducted EMI noises can serve as a fast design tool to optimize the EMC performance of high-density power supplies.

传导电磁干扰(EMI = Electro Magnetic Interference)噪声的模拟和预测可以作为快速设计工具来优化高密度电源的电磁兼容性(EMC = Electro Magnetic Compatibility)。

(2) 广泛使用被动句

➢ An overview of the instrumentation system is illustrated in Fig. 1.

设备系统简图如图 1 所示。

➢ Bearing is widely used in rotating machinery.

轴承被广泛应用于转动机械中。

➢ The basic and fundamental empirical model was proposed by Angstrom in 1924.

基础和基本经验模型是 Angstrom 在 1924 年提出的。

➢ It is designed with three degrees of freedom and two tracked drive systems.

它被设计成有三个自由度和两套跟踪驱动系统(模式)。

➢ More recent research is focused on the integration of such feedback systems into a centralized control system.

最近的研究集中在反馈系统和中央控制系统的结合。

➢ Elevator drive system is mounted at the bottom of the building.

电梯驱动系统安装在建筑物的底部。

➢ Virtual technology is widely utilized in various vehicle test-beds.

虚拟技术广泛应用于各种汽车试验平台。

➢ Reliability analysis in part design, indeed the very definition of reliability, has been focused towards the electronic and digital disciplines since the emergence of reliability engineering in the late 1940's.

自从 20 世纪 40 年代后期可靠性工程出现以来,在零件设计领域中,可靠性分析(真正对可靠性的定义)主要集中在电子和数字学科。

➢ All parts have a constant failure rate, and that part failure is modeled by the exponential mass density function.

所有的零件都有恒定的失效率,并且零件失效是以指数质量密度函数来模拟的。

➢ The front electric motor has a low power and it is mostly used for IC engine stop and start.

前面的电动机能耗低,主要用于内燃机(IC engine = internal-combustion engine)的停止和起动。

➢ Mechanical fixes of the investigated cameras were explicitly noted.

参与调查的相机的机械改进方式被明确指出。

➢ The analyses for moving load were developed in numerous papers [1-15].

运动载荷的分析在众多参考文献[1-15]中探讨过。

➢ Despite all these advantages exposed, some inherent issues of HEVs should be considered.

尽管混合动力汽车(HEV = Hybrid Electrical Vehicle)优势明显,但一些固有的问题还是应加以考虑。

➢ A vehicle stability control approach for four-wheel independently actuated (4WIA) electric ve-

➤ hicles is presented.
本文针对四轮独立驱动电动汽车提出了车辆稳定控制方法。

➤ An analytic solution on how to distribute the higher-level control efforts is given, when the actuators constraints are not considered.
本文提出了在不考虑驱动器约束的情况下分配高层控制力的解析解法。

➤ 4WIA electric vehicles employ four in-wheel (or hub) motors to actuate the four wheels, and the torque and driving/braking mode of each wheel can be controlled independently.
四轮独立驱动电动汽车采用四个轮毂电机来控制四个车轮,各个车轮的转矩和驱动/制动模式可以独立控制。

➤ A braking control method for electric vehicles was proposed in [10], and the studied vehicle was driven by independent front and rear motors, not by in-wheel motors.
文献10提出了一种电动汽车制动控制方法,其研究的车辆是由独立的前轮电机和后轮电机驱动,而不是轮毂电机。

➤ Control allocation algorithms are generally used to distribute the higher-level control signals to the lower-level actuators.
一般来讲,使用控制分配算法来把高层控制器信号分发给低层驱动器。

➤ The mechanical motion of a motor or a vehicle is much slower than a motor's electromagnetic dynamics, implying that the dynamic response of the motor driver and in-wheel motor can be ignored.
电机或者汽车的机械运动比电机的电磁运动慢很多,这意味着电动驱动器和轮毂电机的动态响应可以忽略不计。

➤ Dynamic programming (DP), Pontryagin's minimum principle (PMP), and equivalent consumption minimization strategy (ECMS) are described and analyzed, showing formally their substantial equivalence.
通过对动态规划、庞特里亚金最小值原理和等效燃油消耗最低策略的描述和分析,证实了它们的实质等同性。

➤ Numerous concepts for three-phase Power Factor Corrected (PFC) rectifier systems have been proposed and analyzed over the last decades.
在过去的几十年里,关于三相功率因素校正整流系统的很多概念已经被提出并加以分析。

➤ Moreover, UFAD systems offer improved ventilation effectiveness compared to overhead systems, as the supply air is delivered directly into the occupied zone, and contaminants naturally flow upwards into the return air system and out of the breathing area.
此外,和头顶送风系统相比,地板送风(UFAD = under-floor air distribution)系统能够改善送风效率。当供应的空气被直接输送到人员活动区域时,污染物自然朝上流向回风口,远离人员呼吸区。

➤ Rollovers are divided into two broad categories: tripped and un-tripped.
滚动分为两大类:倾翻和失倾。

➤ A rear electric motor has been added to the vehicle and the positive/negative torque generated

by this motor affects the driving conditions.
汽车增加了一个后置电机,该电机产生的正负转矩都对行驶状况产生影响。

> They showed that the negative binomial regression is a powerful predictive tool and one that should be increasingly applied in future accident frequency studies.
他们指出负二项回归是一个强大的预测工具,应该越来越多应用于未来的事故频率的研究当中。

> Because of its superiority in low cost and better driving performance, Hybrid EV is widely recognized.
由于具有低成本和较好驾驶性能的优势,混合动力电动汽车受到广泛的认可。

> Supercapacitors are used in series with a power battery to provide power requirement in transient state.
超级电容串联动力电池来提供瞬态动力需求。

> In the meantime, fuel saving technologies such as hybrid electric power-trains have both short-term and long-term values and are actively pursued by many car manufacturers.
同时,节省燃油的技术,比如混合动力传动系统,因具有短期和长期的价值而受到汽车制造商们热捧。

> Full-scale experimental tests were carried out with two Peugeot 406 cars on a road course in Italy.
用两辆标致 406 汽车在意大利公路上进行了全尺寸的实验测试。

> The developed model is evaluated by comparing its characteristics with the behavior of the FE tyre model.
通过和有限元(FE)轮胎模型的运行特点相比较,我们对改进的模型进行评估。

> The concepts and quantitative expressions of the steering road feel, steering sensibility, and steering operation stability are introduced.
本文对转向路感,转向灵敏度,转向操作稳定性的概念和定量表达式进行了介绍。

> The output of the fuzzy controller must be defuzzified and scaled before being used by the steering system.
模糊控制器的输出结果在被转向系统运用前必须去模糊化和规模化。

> The intercooler should be carefully designed and matched since the reduction of compression work of the HP compressor may not outstrip the power loss due to the corresponding pressure loss of the intercooler.
由于高压(HP = high pressure)压缩机的压缩功减少不能超过中冷器压力损失所造成的功率损失,所以中冷器须精心设计并与之匹配。

> In steels, martensite is formed from austenite containing carbon atoms and, in view of non-diffusion in its formation, it ideally inherits the carbon atoms of the parent austenite.
钢铁中的马氏体是从含有碳原子奥氏体形成的,鉴于其形成的无扩散性,它很好地继承了父奥氏体的碳原子。

> In active probing, special testing signals are injected into an unenergized phase.

在积极的探索中,特殊的测试信号可以送入一个未被激活的相电路中。

➤ To overcome the divergence of the current integral method, a closed-loop SOC estimation method based on the Kalman filter was proposed.
为了克服当前积分方法的误差,我们提出了一个基于卡尔曼滤波器的闭环电池荷电状态(SOC = state of charge)估计方法。

➤ Other techniques are based on extracting information from databases, which suggests that data from realistic, noncritical driving behavior could be used to parameterize ADAS.
另外一些基于从数据库中提取信息的技术表明,真实非关键驾驶行为的数据可以让自动驾驶辅助系统(ADAS = Advanced Driver Assistance Systems)数字化。

➤ Detection is achieved by searching for distributions of temperatures in the scene similar to that of the human body.
检测是通过在现场寻找与人身体相似的温度分布来实现的。

➤ The assumptions made in this research are that the vehicle can be driven at a speed of 20km/h on a horizontal plane and has a load of 70 kg.
本研究假设汽车负载70千克,在水平路面以每小时20公里的速度行驶。

➤ Through a systematic analysis, the result of developing tendency of all the electrical and electronic systems is developed.
通过系统分析,本文提出了(汽车)电气和电子系统的发展趋势研究结果。

➤ A series of failures are simulated and then compared with experimental tests on a demonstrator motor.
(对轮毂电机)一系列的故障进行了仿真,然后与电动机样机的实验测试进行对比。

➤ The primary fuels now used in auto-mobile, namely gasoline and diesel, are essentially derived from crude oil (petroleum).
现在用于汽车的主要的燃料——汽油和柴油都是从原油中提炼的。

➤ This is achieved by placing electric motors in the hub of the otherwise non-driven wheels.
这种(驱动)是通过将电机安装在非驱动轮轮毂实现的。

➤ In the above research, the least squares algorithm is used for parameter identification.
在上述研究中,最小二乘法被用于参数的识别。

➤ A target appearing in the sensor network can be sensed when sensor nodes detected strength beyond a predefined value.
当传感器节点检测出强度超出预定值,出现在传感器网络的目标就会被检测出来。

➤ These faults can be detected at early stages by employing suitable condition monitoring techniques.
在早期阶段采用合适的状态检测技术能够将这些故障检测出来。

➤ The first technique is to employ high-speed motors, so that motor volume and weight will be greatly reduced for same rated output power.
第一种技术是使用高速电机,在输出相同功率情况下,这种电机的体积和重量将大幅度减少。

➤ Moreover, additional batteries can be installed in the space that would otherwise be occupied by the mechanical gear.
此外,额外(备用)电池可以安装在原先机械齿轮的位置。

➤ The study was conducted using by x-ray diffraction (XRD) analysis and transmission electron microscopy (TEM).
借助 X 射线衍射分析和透射电子显微技术来进行研究分析。

➤ The motion trajectory of a robot arm is calculated using the geometric analysis.
机械手的运动轨迹是通过几何分析计算的。

➤ The railway bridge is considered as a flexible multibody system.
铁路桥被视为一种柔性多体系统。

➤ Linear flexible displacements of the body are described by component mode synthesis method.
用部件模态综合法来描述车体的线性弹性位移。

➤ Therefore, the MCU market is forecasted to increase from US＄3.9 billion to US＄5.5 billion, or by 41% during 2009 to 2014.
因此,预计(微程序控制器 MCU = Microprogrammed Control Unit)市场在 2009 年至 2014 年间,将从 39 亿美元增加到 55 亿美元,涨幅 41%。

➤ Because there is more air resistance, the diaphragm is heavier in a speaker with a 40mm diameter diaphragm and more power must be applied to drive it.
因为空气阻力增加,一个直径为 40mm 的振膜扬声器膜片更重,需要更多的能量进行驱动。

➤ A large indoor space that equipped by an UFAD system is used as the model space.
一个装备有地板送风(UFAD = under floor air distribution)系统的大型室内空间被用作模型空间。

➤ The joint compliance error is caused by the robot weight and the carried payload.
关节的柔性误差是由机器人的重量和附加的载荷引起的。

➤ Velocity profile measurements were made up in the centre of the basic courtyards by a pulsed wire anemometer.
通过脉冲式风速仪,我们在基础中庭中心测量风速剖面。

(3) 常采用非限定性动词

①分词短语

➤ The eccentric mass m_0e_0 has eight settings varying from approximately 1 kg·m to more than 2 kg·m, and must be changed manually.
偏心块的质量 m_0e_0 有八个设置值,这些值在大约 1kg·m 到大于 2kg·m 之间变化,并且必须手动进行设置。

➤ After 1970 the longer term effect of CO_2 and methane overwhelmed the short-lived aerosols, accounting for the temperature rise since then.
1970 年以后二氧化碳和甲烷的长期影响超过了短期的浮质影响,导致了从那时起气温的升高。

➤ A multi-criteria genetic algorithm is used to optimize the shapes and distributions of the fuzzy membership functions <u>associated with</u> the input and output variables in order to minimize the vehicle trajectory, yaw rate, and sideslip angle errors.
多标准遗传算法用来优化结合了输入和输出变量的模糊隶属函数的形状与分布,从而使车辆行驶轨迹、横摆角速度和侧滑角的误差最小化。

➤ The variable steering ratio is realized <u>using</u> a double planetary gear and an electric motor, <u>adding</u> additional steering angle to the driver's input at low speeds and counter-steering slightly at higher speeds.
利用双排行星齿轮和电机能实现可变转向比,即低速时增加额外的转向角输入,高速时略微输入反转向角。

➤ But the microbes that produce foodborne illness are bugs of a different order, capable of causing severe illness and even lasting damage—disorders <u>ranging from</u> temporary paralysis <u>to</u> kidney disease.
但产生食源性疾病的微生物是一种不同的细菌,能导致严重的疾病甚至持久的损害,比如暂时的麻痹和肾脏疾病。

➤ An increase in the resistances <u>caused</u> by the air filter before the LP compressor increases the compression work for achieving a certain total pressure ratio.
通过空气滤清器增加阻力,从而使低压(LP = low pressure)压气机增加压缩功实现了特定的总压比。

➤ Global climate depends on combinations of factors <u>interacting</u> in subtle and complex ways that we do not yet fully understand.
全球气候取决于以微妙复杂方式相互作用的因素影响,对此我们还未完全了解。

②不定式短语

➤ It is an important issue <u>to control</u> the robot arm using the inverse kinematics.
使用逆运动学原理来控制机械手是很重要的。

➤ The easiest way <u>to achieve</u> changes like this will be to switch to diesel.
实现这种改变的最简单的方式是转而使用柴油机。

➤ It makes sense for cyberspace participants themselves <u>to agree on</u> a scheme for questionable items, so that people or automatic filters can avoid them.
让网络空间的参与者赞同对付可疑问题的方案是很有意义的,可以使参与者或自动过滤器避开这些问题。

➤ <u>To meet</u> both pollution reduction requirements and plant performance goals, these markets are demanding a more cost-effective, in-process approach, which optimizes the combustion system to prevent emission generation.
为了满足工厂减排增效的目标,需要成本效益好的过程性方法来优化燃烧体系,防止污染排放的产生。

➤ If CO_2 emission increases are <u>to blame</u> for global warming, skeptics say, then temperatures should have risen appreciably during the postwar economic boom, when fossil fuels were burned in escalating quantity.

怀疑论者说,如果二氧化碳排放增加造成全球气温的升高,那么在战后经济兴旺时期大量的化石燃料使用,气温在那时就应该有明显的增加。

➢ To determine shaft material, the analysis of mechanical properties and microstructure was carried out.

要确定轴材料,必须对机械性能和微观结构进行分析。

➢ Energetic management choice may induce vehicle instability and it is not acceptable to use ESP to recover these situations.

能量管理的选择可能导致车辆不稳定性,且使用电子稳定程序(ESP = Electronic Stability Program)来恢复这些状况是不被接受的。

➢ Hybrid electric vehicles (HEVs) have the potential to reduce fuel consumption and emissions in comparison to conventional vehicles.

和传统汽车相比,混合动力汽车有减少油耗和排放的潜力。

➢ To promote the development of EV, developed countries are more willing to invest heavily in research and development.

为推动电动汽车的发展,发达国家更愿意投入大量资金进行研究和开发。

➢ Applying two-stage turbocharging system, a very high boost pressure as well as good efficiency can be obtained which provide the ability to achieve high brake mean effective pressure.

应用两级涡轮增压系统,可以得到非常高的升压以及良好的效率,从而实现高的制动平均有效压力。

➢ To obtain better results, more exact methods based on the extended Kalman filter (EKF) and the unscented Kalman filter (UKF) were proposed.

为了获得更好的结果,我们提出了基于扩展卡尔曼滤波(EKF)和无痕迹卡尔曼滤波(UKF)的更精确的算法。

➢ The aim of this system is to warn the vehicle's driver and reduce the reaction time in case an emergency break is necessary.

系统的目的是警示汽车驾驶者,在紧急制动时减少反应时间。

➢ This promises to make diesel as quiet and smooth as petrol, while offering much greater fuel economy.

这保证了柴油机跟汽油机一样,运行安静平稳且燃油经济性更好。

➢ To find the combination point of performance and fuel consumption, D-mode shift pattern is the optimized combination of perfect performance shift pattern and perfect economy shift pattern (as shown in Fig. 5).

为了寻求高性能和低油耗更好的结合,D-mode 换挡模式很好地把换挡模式的优越性能和经济性结合起来(如图5所示)。

➢ The CIEDE2000 formula [4], which estimates the perceptual color difference between two pixels p and q, ΔE_{pq}, has three parameters, k_L, k_C and k_H, to weigh the differences in luminance, chroma and hue respectively.

在文献[4]中的 CIEDE2000 准则是判别感知图像中任意两像素点 p 和 q 之间的差异 ΔE_{pq},(该准则)用 k_L、k_C、k_H 三参数来分别衡量的亮度、色度和色调差异。

➤ The balanced suspension structure is widely utilized <u>to achieve</u> axle load distribution.
平衡悬架结构被广泛用于实现轴载荷分布。

➤ However, it is difficult to use the existing methods <u>to resolve</u> reliability apportionment issues.
然而,用现有的方法解决可靠性分配问题很困难。

➤ All the incoming sunlight, with energy equivalent to about three 100-watt light bulbs per square yard, would strike Earth's surface, causing it <u>to emit</u> infrared waves like a giant radiator.
所有射进来的阳光能量相当于每平方码的面积上有 3 个 100 瓦的灯泡直射地球表面,使地球像一个巨大的散热器一样散发红外波。

➤ The approach based on the Unified Modeling Language needs <u>to implement</u> multidisciplinary collaborative modeling and simulation by providing a unified language.
基于统一建模语言的方法需要通过统一的语言来实现多学科协同建模与仿真。

➤ Three mechanical models of the smart wheel have been implemented <u>in order to</u> accurately predict the performances of the sensor.
为了更准确地预测传感器的性能,智能车轮上三个机械模型已安装完毕。

➤ <u>To show</u> the importance of bearing fault detection, induction motor's failure distribution is depicted in Figure.1.
为了显示轴承故障检测的重要性,感应电动机故障分布如图 1 所示。

➤ The main objective of this paper is <u>to propose</u> a simplified sensorless speed controller for the SRM drive system.
这篇文章的主要目的是提出针对开关磁阻电机(SRM = Switched Reluctance Motor)驱动系统的简化的无传感器的速度控制器。

➤ It is noteworthy that tire and suspension are two core transmission parts <u>to set up</u> the relationship between road and vehicle.
值得注意的是,轮胎和悬架是建立路面与汽车之间关系的两个核心传动装置。

➤ This paper proposed a new method <u>to achieve</u> bearing degradation prediction based on principal component analysis (PCA) and optimized LS-SVM method.
本文提出了基于主成分分析(PCA)和优化的最小二乘支持向量机(LS-SVM = least squares support vector machine)方法实现轴承损耗预测的新方法。

③介词+动名词短语

➤ The clever thing about common-rail technology, <u>by improving</u> combustion, dramatically reduces the level of both emission and noise.
共轨技术的优势在于通过改进燃烧状态大大降低排放量和噪声等级。

➤ The role of clouds is poorly understood, but they are known to both cool Earth <u>by reflecting</u> solar energy and warm Earth <u>by trapping</u> heat being radiated up from the surface.

人们对云的作用知之甚少,但大家都知道云能通过反射太阳能让地球降温,通过吸收从地表反射的热量让地球升温。

➢ The short answer is that diesel represents the industry's best hope of cutting carbon dioxide emissions.
简而言之,柴油机代表这个行业削减二氧化碳排放的最大希望。

➢ By putting every production process under one roof —from press machinery to welding, painting, assembly, and final quality checks—Toyota cut the overall investment required for the plant by 40%, to \$732 million.
将每个生产过程放在同一车间——从压机到焊接、喷漆、组装和最终质量检查,丰田工厂所需的总投入为7.32亿美元,减少了40%。

➢ Sustainable management is seen as a practical and economical way of protecting species from extinction.
可持续管理被看作是防止物种灭绝的实用及经济的方式。

➢ Quality of σ can be obtained by changing the constraints.
σ 的值可以通过改变约束条件得到。

➢ The proposed model has yielded a direct relationship between phase current and torque with considering the nonlinearity of the SRM drive.
考虑开关磁阻电动机(SRM = Switched Reluctance Motor)驱动器的非线性特征,拟建模型已经能在相电流和转矩之间产生直接的关系。

➢ There are different ways of changing energy from one form into another.
有多种不同的方法可将能量从一种形式转变成另一种形式。

➢ It would also reduce the times of validation work and shorten the development period by combining the theory and software simulation analysis to complete the desktop calibration work.
结合理论和软件模拟分析来完成桌面校准工作,能减少校验的次数,缩短研发周期。

➢ However, these models are the simplified models for heavy vehicles, without considering the property of balanced suspension.
然而这些模型都是重型车辆的简化模型,没有考虑到车辆的平衡悬架特性。

➢ Experienced robot programmers have to spend considerable time in order to optimize the robotic paths for each specific application by using conventional programming methods.
经验丰富的机器人编程员不得不花费大量的时间利用传统的编程方法来优化机器人每一个特定应用的路径。

➢ The approach based on the Unified Modeling Language needs to implement multidisciplinary collaborative modeling and simulation by providing a unified language.
基于统一建模语言的方法需要通过统一的语言来实现多学科协同建模与仿真。

➢ After this step, the joints geometry that allows the optimal stiffness values has been designed by applying topology optimization techniques.
这之后,拥有最佳刚度值的关节几何形状已经通过拓扑优化技术设计出来。

➤ It means that wheel to rail contact forces are obtained from simulation of a railway vehicle without taking into account vehicle-bridge interaction.
这意味着,车轮与钢轨的接触力是通过铁道车辆的仿真获得的,没有考虑的车—桥的相互作用。

➤ The sound from the front of the speaker is channeled out of the enclosure without losing energy to its surroundings.
声音从扬声器的前部传出,并没有能量损失。

➤ A virtual scene including roads and vehicles is developed by using the software.
使用软件来建立一个包括道路和车辆的虚拟场景。

➤ In the learning phase, a probabilistic roadmap is constructed by generating the robot's random free configurations and connecting them using a simple motion planner, also known as a local planner.
在学习阶段,概率路径图通过机器人自由随机布局生成,并用简单的运动规划器(也被称为本地规划器)来连接它们。

(4) 后置定语
①介词短语后置

➤ The left side velocity of the spring seat was greater than the right side in the vertical direction.
在垂直方向上,弹簧座的左侧速度大于右侧。

➤ It is beyond the scope of this paper to describe these ABS specific lifetime evaluation codes in more detail.
更加详细地描述这些 ABS 特定寿命评价准则,超出了本文的范围。

➤ China has become one of the world's largest importers of petroleum products, largely to fuel its burgeoning fleet of cars and trucks.
中国已经成为了世界上石油产品进口最多的国家之一,主要是为越来越多的汽车和卡车提供燃料。

➤ The merits of low cost and higher safety of the test-bed in the laboratory make it widely utilized.
低成本高安全的优点使实验平台被广泛利用。

➤ Figure 3 shows the model of the radial tire force.
图 3 显示了径向轮胎力的模型。

➤ The internal doors are simulated with additional cracks in the walls.
用更多的墙面裂纹来进行内门仿真实验。

➤ The 2½ hours' worth of inventory on hand is lower than at any other Toyota factory in the world.
2.5 个小时现场存货时间已低于全球其他丰田工厂。

➤ This paper presents a module for pedestrian detection from a moving vehicle in low-light conditions.
这篇文章提出了在低光照条件下,从行驶汽车中建立行人探测模型。

➤ Actually, the connection of the desktop calibration and vehicle calibration will reduce the work-

load, improve the efficiency, and shorten the period of calibration in some extent.
实际上,桌面校准和车辆校准的结合可以减轻工作量,提升效率,从某种程度来说减少了校准时间。

➤ This paper presents the analysis of parameter sensitivity of space manipulator with harmonic drive based on the revised response surface method.
这篇文章对基于改进响应面法的谐波传动空间机械臂的参数灵敏度进行了分析。

➤ The robot's final path is generated by connecting the recorded points via a robot controller, which tries to pass through all the points by taking into consideration the dynamic constraints of the robot.
机器人最终路径是通过连接由机器人控制器记录的各点生成的,这一方法试图通过考虑机器人动态约束来穿过所有的点。

➤ Linear flexible displacements of the body are described by component mode synthesis method.
用模态综合法来描述车体的线性弹性位移。

②形容词及形容词短语后置

➤ The Earth's climate system has demonstrably changed on both global and regional scales since the pre-industrial era, with some of these changes attributable to human activities.
自从前工业时代以来,地球的气候系统已经在全球和区域范围内发生明显改变,其中的一些变化是由人类活动引起的。

➤ While the Japanese powerhouse was figuring out how to build cars attractive to Europeans, it was also bearing down on costs to wield the efficiency needed to prevail in one of the world's lowest-margin auto markets.
日本政府在考虑如何制造对欧洲人有吸引力的汽车的同时,也在降低成本提高生产效率,希望在世界最低利润空间(竞争最激烈)的汽车市场之一占有优势。

➤ In the meantime, before hybrid and fuel-cell vehicles materialize, the conventional wisdom had been that ever-more refined petrol engines would dominate, better catalysts would clean up exhaust emission, more precise fuel injection would make engines leaner and more economical.
与此同时,在混合动力汽车和燃料电池汽车上市之前,人们普遍认为经改进的汽油发动机将占主导地位,更好的催化剂使排放更清洁,更精确的燃油喷射使发动机更省油。

③副词后置

➤ Despite such uncertainties, the computer programs used to model Earth's climate are improving rapidly.
尽管有许多不确定性,用来模拟地球气候的计算机程序正迅速得以改进。

➤ The controller must respond quickly and accurately to move the actuator through a specified distance to the desired position.
这个控制器必须反应迅速准确,才能使执行器移动特定距离到达目的位置。

➤ On the other hand, there is evidence that some kinds of events could change climate radically in the span of decades.
另一方面,有证据表明,在几十年间有些事件能大幅度地改变气候。

- If CO_2 emission increase is to blame for global warming, skeptics say, then temperatures should have risen appreciably during the postwar economic boom, when fossil fuels were burned in escalating quantity.
  怀疑论者说,如果二氧化碳排放增加造成全球气温的升高,那么在战后经济兴旺的时候大量使用化石燃料,气温就应该有明显的增加。
- Moreover, normalized CO concentration is decreased to below 1% and 5% within left and right sidewalks, respectively.
  此外,标准的一氧化碳浓度在左、右人行横道处分别降低至1%以下和5%以下。
- Exposure to emissions originating from building materials and their secondary effects can be reduced effectively with source control measures.
  利用源控制方法可以有效地减少暴露在建筑材料排放及其二次影响下的机会。
- In that time, climate had fluctuated drastically, from ice ages lasting tens of thousands of years to epochs of steamy heat.
  那个时候,气候急剧变化,从冰河时期持续几万年直到高温时代。
- Oceans store heat efficiently and transport it thousands of miles.
  海洋能高效地储存热量并把热量送到千里之外。
- Table 5 presents the results from fitting all the explanatory variables simultaneously.
  表5同时给出了适合所有的解释变量的结果。
- The voltage was then recorded continuously for 24 hours.
  24小时连续地记录电压读数。

④定语从句后置

- The trouble is that other methods of reducing nitrogen-oxide emissions depend on catalysts that react very badly to sulphur: it wears them out.
  问题是其他减少氮氧化物排放的方法都要依靠会和硫化物产生糟糕反应催化剂:这种现象会把催化剂消耗光。
- Clearly we should be happy with any method that simultaneously achieved the first three objectives.
  显然,我们应该对任何能同时实现前三个目标的方法感到高兴。
- Global climate depends on combinations of factors interacting in subtle and complex ways that we do not yet fully understand.
  全球气候取决于以微妙复杂方式相互作用的因素影响,对此我们还未完全了解。
- Planners should be aware of the forces and schools of thought that shape and change our cities.
  规划者们应该知道塑造和改变了我们的城市的有影响力的团体和学术流派。
- There is wide agreement that traffic should evolve into something that can be sustained in the future.
  人们广泛认为交通应该发展成未来可持续发展的事业。
- But the robot arm which is fixed on the platform, has limited work space.
  但是固定在平台上的机械手,其工作空间是非常有限的。

(5) 普遍使用长句

➤ The contribution of the paper is to give a simplified procedure to independently assign the steering dynamics eigenvalues and the wheel speed dynamics eigenvalues by an integrated action of the differentials of active front wheel steering and rear wheel steering.

本文主要是通过对前后主动转向轮差异的整合，提出一个独立分配转向动力特征值和车轮速度动力特征值的简化程序。

➤ Given this significant variation, the following discussion first seeks to provide a kinematic explanation and then to assesses the combined effects of vehicle speed and type, and pedestrian size, gait and speed on the frequency of occurrence of the different ground contact mechanisms.

鉴于这种重大的变化，下面的讨论首先旨在提供一个运动学的解释，然后评估车辆行驶速度和类型以及行人体态、步态和速度对不同地面接触机制发生的频率的综合影响。

➤ In short, this maneuver confirms that the cooperation between the fuzzy slip controller that was developed previously and the fuzzy active steering controller developed here has allowed the driver to accelerate the AUTO21EV on a μ-split road with the maximum possible traction forces on all four wheels, no spin-out effects on the wheels, and no side-pushing effect on the vehicle.

总之，该工况确认了先前开发的模糊滑移控制器和现在开发的模糊主动转向控制器之间的合作，从而允许该驱动程序让 AUTO21EV 的四轮以最大可能的牵引力在对开路面上加速，并且车轮不出现打滑，车辆没有侧滑。

➤ Dry storage of older fuel rods in specially designed metal casks or concrete modules is expected to grow over the next decade, with existing pool capacity being used for the 2000 metric tons of newly spent fuel generated each year by United States.

在接下来的十年里，用特制的金属桶或者混泥土模具干法贮存年代久远的燃料棒的方法将更加流行，而在美国每年新产生的 2000 吨乏燃料将贮存于现有的容量池里。

➤ It was used in different applications abroad based on AT technology and achieved a good performance of the vehicle compared with traditional AT technology which primary focuses on the drivability and fuel consumption.

在国外基于自动变速器技术有不同的应用，与主要集中于操纵稳定性和燃油经济性的传统自动变速器技术相比，这种方法让汽车有良好的性能表现。

➤ The superiority of the fuzzy PI controller compared to conventional controller is illustrated by simulations and experiments which confirm that the fuzzy PI controller effectively restrains the overshoot of position response.

通过仿真实验，我们发现，与传统 PI 控制器相比，模糊 PI 控制器的优势在于能有效控制位置响应的超调量。

(6) 常见复合词与缩略词

①复合词

➤ Almost every active steering system on the market today is based on the classical proportional-integral-derivative control system.

当今市场上,几乎每个主动转向系统是基于经典的 PID(比例—积分—微积分)的控制系统。

➢ A severe double-lane-change maneuver with obstacle avoidance was used to evaluate the effectiveness of each candidate controller.

严格的避障双移线工况被用来评估每个备选控制器的有效性。

➢ A hardware-in-the-loop driving simulator has been used to further evaluate the effectiveness of the proposed controller.

硬件在环(HIL)驾驶模拟器已被用于进一步评估所提出的控制器的有效性。

➢ Fig. 5 shows a general sensorless speed-controlled drive system.

图 5 展示了普通的无传感速度控制驱动系统。

➢ This research study focuses on the design and development of a small-scale in-wheel motor for electric vehicles.

这个研究主要是设计和开发一款小型的电动汽车轮毂电机。

➢ In turn, a ball vote can be seen as a ball-shaped tensor, $BT(p)$, with a strength controlled by the scalar factors $GS(p, q)$, $\eta_c(p)$ and $BV_c(p, q)$ each varying between zero and one.

反过来,球投票可以看成球形张量 $BT(p)$,其投票强度由三个范围在 0 和 1 之间的标量函数 $GS(p, q)$、$\eta_c(p)$ 和 $BV_c(p, q)$ 决定。

➢ The use of in-wheel motors, often referred to as hub motors, as a source of propulsion for pure electric or hybrid electric vehicles has recently received a lot of attention.

使用轮内电机(通常被称为轮毂电机)作为纯电动汽车或混合动力汽车的动力源,最近受到了广泛的关注。

➢ The traditional two-axle or quarter-vehicle model is still used to study heavy vehicle dynamic behaviors.

传统的二轴或四分之一车辆模型仍然在重型车辆的动态行为研究中使用。

➢ The high cost is often due to the relatively complex hardware, time-consuming calibration and special materials used in the manufacturing process.

成本高往往是由于在制造过程中使用了相对复杂的硬件、耗时的校准和特殊的材料。

➢ In the present study, a monorail way (a system of viaducts) and a monorail rolling stock (Figs. 1-3) are considered as two complementary two-dimensional rod systems with distributed parameters, including rigid elements with viscoelastic links (Figs. 4b-4d).

在目前研究中,单轨方式(高架桥的一个系统)和单轨车辆(图 1 ~ 图 3)被认为是两个互补的具有分布参数的二维杆件系统,包括具有黏弹性链路的刚性元件(图 4b ~ 图 4d)。

➢ The other is the PMP which uses a generalized Euler-Lagrange equation originated from the Calculus of Variation.

另一个是 PMP 算法,这个算法采用了从变分中得到的广义欧拉方程。

➢ As the key parameter for high-power battery management systems, the State-of-Charge (SOC) of a Li-ion battery directly indicates its residual capacity and thus reflects the remaining range of an electric vehicle.

作为高能量电池管理系统的关键参数,锂电池的荷电状态直接表明电池剩余电量,从而反映出电动汽车可续航里程。

②缩略词

➢ This paper presents the development of an energy management strategy of a Plug-in Hybrid Electric Vehicle (PHEV).

本文提出了插电式混合动力电动汽车的能量管理策略的改进方法。

➢ Such actuation flexibility together with the electric motors' fast and precise torque responses may enhance the existing vehicle control strategies, e.g. Traction Control System (TCS), Direct Yaw-moment Control (DYC), and other advanced vehicle motion/stability control systems.

驱动灵活性加上电机快速精确的转矩响应可以加强现有的车辆控制策略,例如牵引力控制系统、直接横摆角速度控制和其他先进的车辆动力性/稳定性控制系统。

➢ Global Positioning System (GPS) and Inertia Measurement Unit (IMU) have been proved to be an effective means of measuring vehicle states.

有证据表明全球定位系统(GPS)和惯性测量装置(IMU)可以有效评价汽车状态。

➢ Numerous concepts for three-phase Power Factor Corrected (PFC) rectifier systems have been proposed and analyzed over the last decades.

在过去的几十年里,很多三相功率因素校正整流系统的概念被提出并分析。

➢ An EMPD (effective moisture penetrating depth) deep model is used to simulate moisture buffering in the spaces.

有效湿量渗透深度模型被用于模拟空间湿度缓冲。

➢ An interrogation of the 9000 plus papers and reports in the AIVC (Air Infiltration and Ventilation Centre) database yielded only about a dozen references.

对 AIVC 数据库 9000 多份论文和报告进行搜索,只找到十几份参考资料。

➢ At a greater H/W (height/weight), the circulatory vortex is established inside the street canyon.

当高宽比更大时,街道峡谷就会形成循环涡旋。

➢ Computational fluid dynamics (CFD) methods are used to predict thermal comfort conditions of occupants, indoor air quality (IAQ), and energy consumption in this space.

计算流体动力学方法被用来预测居住条件的热舒适度、室内空气品质和空间能源消耗。

➢ EM (energy management) strategy is based on a highly simplified vehicle model.

能量管理策略是建立在高度简化的汽车模型基础上的。

➢ In contrast, the fuel consumption rate is not doubled in a pure engine driving mode because the high efficiencies region of brake specific fuel consumption (BSFC) is oriented to higher power region.

相反,燃油消耗率在纯发动机驾驶模式中不是翻了一倍,这是因为在制动燃油消耗率的高效区趋向于更高功率区。

- The vehicle model, in-wheel motor models, and advanced slip controllers have been implemented on a quad-core Peripheral Component Interconnect (PCI) Extensions from National Instruments, which uses the Laboratory Virtual Instrument Engineering Workbench (LabVIEW) real-time operating system to maintain precise timing during the simulation.
  将汽车模型、轮毂电机模型以及先进防滑控制器运用于美国国家仪器公司的四核外围设备互连(PCI)扩展,它采用了实验室虚拟仪器工程平台(LabVIEW)实时操作系统使其在仿真过程中保持精确定时。

- The ECM communicates with the PXI system over a Controller Area Network (CAN) bus, which is the standard in vehicular communication networks.
  ECM通过控制器局域网(CAN)总线与PXI系统进行通讯,这是车辆通信网络的标准。

- Downsizing the ICE by turbocharging technology is one of the most cost-effective technologies to improve the fuel efficiency and reduce CO_2 and NO_X emissions of internal combustion engines (ICE).
  通过涡轮增压技术缩小内燃机的尺寸是提高内燃机燃油效率、减少二氧化碳和氮氧化合物排放的成本效益最好的技术之一。

- To address these problems, this paper proposes an estimation method based on the Unscented Particle Filter (UPF) to estimate the SOC online.
  为了解决这些问题,本文提出了基于无痕迹的粒子滤波(UPF)在线估计SOC的估算方法。

- Advanced Driver Assistance Systems (ADAS) broaden the senses of a human driver with information that would not normally be available due to the position inside of the vehicle, as well as circumstances the driver fails to see.
  高级驾驶辅助系统用信息拓宽驾驶者的感知,而由于坐在车内无法感知周围的情况,一般情况下驾驶者是得不到这些信息的。

- A nonlinear tri-axle vehicle model with IBS (integral balanced suspension) is firstly proposed based on the detailed analysis of structural features of a heavy vehicle (DFL1250).
  基于重型车辆(DFL 1250)结构特性的详细分析,我们首次提出了包含整体平衡悬架的非线性三轴车辆模型。

- The study was conducted by x-ray diffraction (XRD) analysis and transmission electron microscopy (TEM).
  研究借助X射线衍射分析和透射电子显微技术展开。

- This paper presents a 6-DOF (6 Degrees Of Freedom) robot arm system and proposes a strategy for solving the inverse kinematics equations.
  本文介绍了一个6自由度机器臂系统,并提出了解决逆动力方程式的策略。

- This approach is mainly used in the military field, and has formed a relatively mature standard, such as distributed interactive simulation (DIS) systems based on the IEEE-1278 standard.
  这种方法主要用于军事领域,并形成了一个相对成熟的标准,如基于IEEE-1278标准的分布式交互仿真(DIS)系统。

- To improve its efficiency and competitiveness, modern trains are required to travel faster, with high levels of safety and comfort and with reduced Life Cycle Costs (LCC).
  为了提高其效率和竞争力,现代列车需要更快的速度、更高的安全性和舒适性,以及更低的寿命周期成本。
- It is estimated that today's well-equipped automobile uses more than 50 microcontroller units (MCUs).
  据估计,装备精良的汽车采用50多个微控制器。

(7) 时态的运用

① 一般现在时

- The purpose of this work is to investigate the influence of two-stage turbocharging system parameters on the engine performance and the optimization of these parameters.
  这项工作主要用来研究二级涡轮增压系统参数对发动机性能和优化参数的影响。
- DWI separators have similar composition, with a much higher population of fibers with diameters in the range of 0.2~0.4 microns.
  DWI隔膜有相似的特点:大部分纤维的直径处于0.2~0.4微米之间。
- It also needs to adjust the shift strategy to meet the demand of best vehicle performance and fuel consumption.
  这个(技术)也需要调整换挡策略来满足最佳车辆性能和最低油耗的要求。
- Space manipulator is an important tool for spacecraft to complete a variety of tasks in space.
  空间机械臂是航天器完成各种各样的空间任务的重要工具。
- Something in the American psyche loves new frontiers.
  美国人骨子里酷爱探索新领域。
- However, these error sources are specific to individual physical robots, so the method is not general.
  然而,这些误差源都是针对单个物理机器人,因此该方法不能通用。
- In the recent years, there is an increasing need for flexible manufacturing systems, capable of adapting to different market demands and product-mix changes.
  在最近几年,对于柔性制造系统的需求日益增长,该系统能够适应不同的市场需求和产品组合变换。
- Now, many experts believe, humans are imperiling their own ecological niche with the threat of global warming.
  现在,许多专家认为,全球气候变暖使人类的生态空间受到威胁。
- The new smart wheel described in the paper is relatively simple and it can be manufactured with conventional materials in order to make it less expensive.
  论文中所提到的新型智能车轮相对简单,并且为了让其更加便宜可以用传统的材料制造。
- It is an important issue to control the robot arm using the inverse kinematics.
  运用逆运动来控制机械臂是非常重要的。
- In this study, a metallurgical analysis based on phase transformation laws is performed to simu-

late the phase transformation during welding.
在这项研究中,用基于相变法的金项分析模拟焊接时的相变。

➢ Design of such an observer depends mainly on the nonlinear model of SRM.
设计这种观察器主要依靠非线性的开关磁阻电机(SRM = Switched Reluctance Motor)模型。

➢ Waves in water move like the waveform moves along a rope.
波在水中的移动像波形沿着绳子移动一样。

➢ Mathematics is the base of all other sciences, and arithmetic, the science of numbers, is the base of mathematics.
数学是所有其他科学的基础;而算术,即数的科学,则是数学的基础。

➢ The beauty of lasers is that they can do machining without ever physically touching the material.
激光的妙处就在于它能在不实际接触加工材料的条件下进行机械加工。

② 一般过去时

➢ The effects of the parameters investigated on contaminant concentrations were complex and quite variable, which allows for the possibility of designing courtyards to suit specific needs.
我们所研究的污染物浓度参数的影响是复杂多变的,这就为满足特定需求的中庭设计提供了可能。

➢ The structural model helps to clarify the role of driver behavior characteristics in the causal sequence leading to more severe injuries.
结构模型有助于澄清驾驶员行为特征在导致更多严重伤害的因果序列中的作用。

➢ In the fuel cell EV, the foreign business community set up transnational strategic alliances.
在燃料电池电动汽车(EV = Electric Vehicles)方面,外商建立跨国战略联盟。

➢ Based on these observations, in 2000 a three-year project named Tyre and Road Wear and Slip (TROWS) assessment was started.
根据观察结果,2000年开始了一项为期三年的名为TROWS的评估项目。

➢ The pore size and bubble point for DWI separators was slightly higher, but with the following advantages.
DWI分隔材料的空隙大小和泡点稍微有点偏高,但是它具有以下优势。

➢ We demonstrated our prediction method's validity using data acquired with the test vehicle of the French Institute of Science and Technology.
从法国科学与技术学院的测试车获取的数据证明了我们预测方法的有效性。

➢ The daring design was a hit.
这个大胆的设计是一个笑话。

➢ The most basic of parking auxiliary system form was single reverse radar, after that, video system was also used as parking assist device.
停车辅助系统的最基本形式是单一的倒车雷达,后来,倒车影像系统也被用作倒车辅助设备。

- Hence Hac applied a look-ahead preview control strategy to a quarter-car model to study its effects on ride comfort, road holding and power requirements.
  因此 Hac 把预见控制策略运用于四分之一汽车模型上,以研究这种控制策略对乘坐舒适性、路面承载能力和车辆动力要求的影响。
- Huang pointed out that it is unsafe to regard the two-axle or tri-axle loads as a group of loads acting on road once.
  黄(博士)曾经认为将两轴或三轴的负载视为一组载荷作用于道路是不安全的。
- Yu and Zhang proposed a flexible rotor beam element considering the flexibility of joint and link.
  考虑到节点和链路的灵活性,于和张提出了柔性转子梁单元(模型)。
- Malhotra discovered in previous research what this mechanism must have been.
  Malhotra 在以前的研究中发现了这种机制。
- The effectiveness of the identification algorithms was compared in the calibration study for SCARA robot by Omodei et al..
  Omodei 等人在 SCARA 机器人的校准研究中,对这些识别算法的有效性进行了比较。
- The probabilistic road-map path planning was introduced in [5] as a new method of computing collision-free paths for robots.
  在文献[5]中介绍了基于概率的路径图规划,这是用来计算机器人的无碰撞路径新方法。
- The APOLLO project's main objective was to develop and produce an "intelligent" tire in order to increase road traffic safety and improve the vehicle control systems.
  阿波罗项目的主要目标是开发和生产一个"智能"车轮,以增加道路交通安全和改善车辆控制系统。
- Flexibility of piers was not taken into account.
  桥墩柔性不予考虑。
- The first electronic computers used vacuum tubes and other components.
  第一批电子计算机使用真空管和其他元件。

③现在完成时

- Many studies have been carried out on the vehicle stability control.
  我们已经开展了许多对于车辆稳定性控制的研究。
- The application of three energy management strategies to a hybrid electric vehicle has been presented, showing how the optimal solution obtained with DP can also be computed by applying PMP.
  本文提出了三种能量管理策略在混合动力汽车中的运用,展示了使用动态规划(DP = dynamic planning)方法得到的最优解决方案也可以通过运用庞特里亚金最小值原理(PMP = Pontryagin minimum principle)计算获得。
- The effect of this assumption has been discussed by Steeman.
  Steeman 已经讨论了这种假设的影响。
- The description of the experimental procedures has been kept relatively brief here.

这个实验过程的描述已经相对简单化了。

➢ The presence of canyon vortex is first demonstrated by Albrecht and thereafter, and Georgii et al. have verified it.
Albrecht 是第一个证明了峡谷涡流存在的人,此后又有 Georgii 等人对峡谷涡流进行了验证。

➢ Sliding modes technique has shown to be an effective strategy to cope against uncertainties and perturbations.
滑模技术已被证明是一种应对不确定性和扰动性的有效策略。

➢ Human use of energy has evolved through the fire-wood era, coal era, and oil and gas era.
人类的能源利用经历了从薪柴时代、煤炭时代和油气时代的演变。

➢ Energy sustainability through development of clean and renewable energy sources have attracted a lot of discussion recently.
最近,针对研发清洁再生能源的能源可持续性发展已经引起了许多的讨论。

➢ Two separator companies have designed nonwoven separators specifically for double-layer electrolytic capacitor.
两家隔膜公司都设计了专门用于双层电解电容器的无纺布隔膜。

➢ In recent years, the SRM has received considerable attention in variable speed drive applications.
最近几年,开关磁阻电机(SRM)已经在变速传动应用中获得相当大的关注。

➢ It is possible that the warming observed during this century may have resulted from natural variations, even though the increase has been much more rapid than what the planet has witnessed over the past hundred centuries.
尽管地球温度的增长比过去几百个世纪都迅速得多,但本世纪观察到的变暖现象有可能是由于自然界的各种变化而引起的。

➢ Since 1990, the greatest warming has been observed between 40 degrees and 70 degrees north latitude—including Europe, Russia, and the northern half of the Untied States—where much of the world's industrial greenhouse gas emissions originate.
自 1990 年以来,人们在世界工业温室气体主要排放源——北纬 40 度到 70 度地区(包括欧洲、俄罗斯和美国的北半部),观察到了最明显的气温上升。

➢ Although many edge detectors have been proven effective, their performance decreases for noisy images.
尽管,许多边缘检测的方法已经被证实是有效的,但在噪声图像中效果不佳。

➢ The mechanics research of the interaction between vehicle and road is a way to solve the road damage problem and has recently received increasing attentions.
车辆与道路耦合的力学研究是解决路面损坏问题的方法,此法最近得到了越来越多的关注。

➢ The space manipulators have been widely used in satellites, space shuttles and many other spacecrafts.

空间机械臂已经被广泛应用于卫星、航天飞机和许多其他航天器。

➢ He has long suspected that two different projectile populations have been responsible for cratering inner solar system surfaces.
长时间以来,他怀疑是两个不同的流星族使内太阳系内(行星)表面出现了陨石坑。

➢ Many factories have addressed the modeling of the error sources of robots for calibration.
许多工厂已经解决了校准过程中机器人误差源建模的问题。

➢ The robot's final trajectory is highly dependent on the points recorded and the experience of the respective programmer, who has carried this out.
机器人最终轨迹很大程度上依赖记录点和参与记录这些点的每个程序员的经验。

➢ Much progress has been made in electrical engineering in less than a century.
不到一个世纪,电气工程就取得了很大的进步。

➢ The basic design of the steam engine has undergone no major change in over 200 years.
两百多年来,蒸汽机的基本结构没有发生任何重大变更。

④一般将来时

➢ No one knows for certain whether such things will happen.
没有人确切知道将来是否会发生这样的事情。

➢ The Palace Museum, also known as the Forbidden City, will limit the amount of visitors to 80,000 per day starting mid-June, the Beijing Times reported on May 15, 2015.
《北京时报》2015年5月15日报道,故宫(又名紫禁城)将于六月中旬起将每日游客数量限制在8万人。

➢ To meet the ever-increasing energy demand by one billion plus people in the course of building a moderately prosperous and modern society in an all-round way, China will build the world's largest energy supply and consumption system in the coming 10 to 20 years.
在全面建设小康社会的进程中,为满足十几亿人民日益增长的能源消费需求,中国将在今后一二十年内建成世界最大的能源消费和供应体系。

➢ For the real implementation, we are working on these "costate control" problems which will be presented in a future publication.
对于实时应用,我们正致力于解决这些"共态控制"问题,这将会在未来公开发表。

➢ If global warming retains unattended, Earth's ecosystems and the life that depends on them will be destroyed.
如果全球变暖再不引起重视,那么地球生态系统和以地球为生存环境的生命都将会被摧毁。

➢ The leaders will leave the copycat crowd behind, and will offer better products with tangible advantages.
领跑者将会远远甩开跟风者,以真正的优势提供更好的产品。

➢ Because of the low transmission efficiency, the fuel consumption of vehicle will increase.
由于传动效率低,车辆的油耗会增加。

➢ In the future, the meter will become information processing and display center.

在未来,仪表将会成为信息处理和显示中心。
- An artificial neural network (ANN) will be applied to compensate for these un-modeled errors.
人工神经网络算法将用于弥补这些未建模的误差。
- Flash capacities have recently risen to 3 MB and beyond, hence the next-generation engines will require far more.
闪存容量最近已经上升至或将超越 3 MB,因此,新一代的发动机将有更高的要求。
- These principles will be illustrated by the following transition.
这些原理将由下列演变过程来说明。

Unit 2 词义的选择
Choice of Meanings

英语的词汇翻译与语境是分不开的。英国著名语言学家、实践翻译理论家皮特·纽马克(Peter Newmark)认为:"Context is the overriding factor in all translation, and has primacy over any rule, theory or primary meaning."(语境在所有翻译中都是最重要的因素,它比任何规则、任何理论、任何基本词义都重要)。英国语言学家约翰·弗斯(John Firth)也强调说:"Each word used in a new context is a new word."(每个词用在新的语境中是一个新单词)。

例如:

	日常英语	科技英语
virus	病毒	电脑病毒
bus	公共汽车	总线路
memory	记忆	内存
menu	饭店菜单	电脑屏幕的项目菜单
plane	飞机	平面

同一词语在不同专业词义有变化,比如:

	专业	词义
transmission	电气工程	输送
	无线电	发射,播送
	机械学	传动
	物理学	透射
	医学	遗传
	土木工程	传递(荷载)
power	数学	幂,乘方
	光学	放大率,焦强
	机械学	(杠杆等)机械工具
	物理学	功率
	统计学	检验力
	电气工程	电力,动力
phase	土壤学	相(land phase,陆相; marine phase,海相)
	物理学	相

续上表

专业		词义
phase	电工学	相位
	数学	位相
	动物学	型
	天文学	周相
	军事学	战斗阶段
	土木工程	设计、施工阶段
resistance	力学	阻力
	电学	电阻
	机械学	耐受性,强度

英汉两种语言都有一词多类、一词多义的现象。一词多类就是指一个词往往属于几个词类,具有几个不同的意思。一词多义就是说同一个词在同一个词类中,又往往有几个不同的词义。

一词多类
根据词类选择词义。例如:

round

➤ An electron is an extremely small corpuscle with negative charge which rounds about the nucleus of an atom.
电子是绕着原子核转动带有负电荷的极其微小的粒子。(动词)

➤ The earth goes round the sun.
地球环绕太阳运行。(介词)

➤ Round surface reflector is a key unit for the solar energy device.
弯曲面反射器是太阳能装置的关键元件。(形容词)

➤ The tree measures forty inches round.
这棵树树围40英寸。(副词)

➤ This is the whole round of knowledge.
这就是全部的知识范围。(名词)

➤ Two rounds of waterstops are provided at immersion joint in immersed tube tunnel and one round is GINA gasket and the other is OMEGA.
在沉管隧道中,在沉管接头处安装两道止水带,一道是GINA止水带,另一道是OMEGA止水带。(名词)

base

➤ Plastics was at first based on coal and wood.
最初塑料是从煤和木材中提取的。(动词)

➤ As we all know, a base reacts with an acid to form a salt.
众所周知,碱与酸起反应变成盐。(名词)

- Iron and brass are base metals.

  铁和黄铜为非贵重金属。(形容词)
- The gravel bed is placed on ground base for immersed tunnel.

  在沉管隧道底部下方的地基铺设碎石垫层。(名词)

一词多义

根据上下文的语境来选择词义。例如：

power

- The electronic microscope possesses very high resolving power compared with the optical microscope.

  与光学显微镜相比，电子显微镜具有极高的分辨率。
- Power can be transmitted over a long distance.

  电力可以输送到很远的地方。
- The fourth power of three is eighty-one.

  3 的 4 次方是 81。
- The combining power of one element in the compound must equal the combining power of the other element.

  化合物中一种元素的化合价必须等于另一元素的化合价。
- Explosive technological development after 1940 gave the medical profession enormous power to fight disease and sickness.

  1940 年以来，随着技术的迅速发展，医学界大大提高了战胜疾病的能力。
- Semiconductor devices have no filament or heaters and therefore require no heating power or warmed-up time.

  半导体器件没有灯丝，因此不需要加热功率和加热时间。
- A car needs a lot of power to go fast.

  汽车高速行驶需要很大动力。
- Streams and waterfall are suitable for the development of hydroelectric power.

  溪流和瀑布适合用于开发水电能源。

1) 一词多类

since：*conj.* 既然；*prep.* 自……以后

- Since 85 percent of the large-greater than 300 megawatt facilities concentrated sources of NO_x already have been controlled through LNB and SCR solutions, the major utilities are shifting their focus to identifying the most economical solution for the mid-sized NO_x sources, which range from 100MW to 300MW.

  既然 85% 的超 300 兆瓦设备所产生的氮氧化物已通过 LNB 和 SCR 方法进行了控制，那么大型的公共事业公司将关注点转移到确认对 100 兆瓦到 300 兆瓦的中小型氮氧化合物源进行控制的最经济处理方法上。

➢ Since the late 1700s, the burning of fossil fuels and other human activities have increased atmospheric CO_2 concentrations more than 30 percent.

自 18 世纪末以来,化石燃料的燃烧和其他人类活动使得大气中的二氧化碳浓度增加超过 30%。

present: v. 提出,呈现; adj. 现在的;出席的

➢ This paper presents a module for pedestrian detection from a moving vehicle in low-light conditions.

这篇文章提出了在低光照条件下从行驶汽车中检测行人的模块。

➢ The present system has been implemented as part of the IVVI experimental vehicle.

当前的系统作为瞬时垂直速度指示器(IVVI = instant vertical velocity indicator)试验车的一部分已实现其功能。

2) 一词多义

diesel: n. 柴油;柴油机

➢ Strange as it may seem, diesel is staking a claim to be the environmentally friendly fuel of the future.

令人不可思议,现在柴油被视为一种未来的环保燃料。

➢ This promises to make diesel as quiet and smooth as petrol, while offering much greater fuel economy.

这(新一代控制方法)使得柴油机和汽油机一样运行安静而平稳,与此同时还能提供更高的燃油经济性。

as: conj. 因为;随着;虽然;依照;当…时
    prep. 如同;当作;以…的身份
    adv. 同样地;和…一样的

➢ But now that politicians and the green lobby are getting more worked up about emissions of global-warming gases, European car makers are terrified that regulations will be brought in to limit carbon dioxide emissions from cars, in the same way that toxic gases such as carbon monoxide or nitrogen oxides are subject to ever-falling statutory limits.

但因为政治家和环保团体正着手解决全球温室气体的减排,欧洲汽车制造商担心,新出台的法规将限制二氧化碳的排放量,就像一氧化碳和氮氧化物等有毒气体的排放量正在受日趋严格的法规限制一样。

➢ Strange as it may seem, diesel is staking a claim to be the environmentally friendly fuel of the future.

虽然好像很奇怪,但现在柴油被认为是未来环保型燃料。

➢ This promises to make diesel as quiet and smooth as petrol, while offering much greater fuel economy.

这就保证了柴油机能像汽油机一样安静平稳地运行,并且提供更好的燃油经济性。

➤ Recently, advancements in these technologies combined with emergent technologies, such as advanced sorbent injections, currently can attain the 2015 limits in many applications and will continue to gain ground on the incumbent SCR <u>as</u> the market opportunity expands.

近来,技术进步以及像洗烟塔这样的新兴技术,在实践运用过程中已经达到2015年的排放限制,并且<u>随着</u>市场占有率的增加,将继续替代现在的选择性催化还原技术。

➤ Buyers usually <u>see</u> this <u>as</u> a good competitive environment to receive better pricing.

买家们通常把这<u>看作</u>一种旨在获得更好的定价的良好竞争环境。

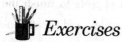

Exercises

1. Go through your professional papers and find the above linguistic phenomena.
2. Translate the following sentences.

(1) 一词多类

mean: *vt.* 意味; *adj.* 平均的; *n.* (*pl.*) 手段, 方式

1) Note that when the steering angle is zero, a = b = 0.5, which <u>means</u> that the driving force will be equally distributed to the left or right sides of the vehicle. (steering angle, 转向角)

2) Global positioning system (GPS) and inertia measurement unit (IMU) have been proved to be an effective <u>means</u> of measuring vehicle states. (GPS, 全球定位系统; IMU, 惯性测量装置)

3) For marine crossing bridges design and construction, the <u>mean</u> sea level under the bridge span shall be thoroughly considered.

study: *v.* 研究; 仔细观察; *n.* 研究

4) Many <u>studies</u> have been carried out on the vehicle stability control

5) A braking control method for electric vehicles was proposed in [10], the <u>studied</u> vehicle was driven by independent front and rear motors, not by in-wheel motors. (braking control method, 制动控制方法; in-wheel motors, 轮毂电机)

need: *v.* 一定; *n.* 需要

6) We have learned that a market crash <u>need</u> not lead to economic disaster.

7) The growing complexity in automotive electronics is amplifying the <u>need</u> for higher performance 32-b MCUs with more embedded nonvolatile memory. (higher performance, 高性能; embedded nonvolatile memory, 嵌入式非易失性存储器)

(2) 一词多义

mean: *n.* 均值; (*pl.*) 手段; 方式

8) The <u>mean</u> and variance of the transformed variable are accurate up to the second order of Taylor series expansion. (variance, 方差; transformed variable, 转换后的变量; the second order of Taylor series expansion, 泰勒级数展开式的二阶)

9) The tunnel is constructed by <u>means</u> of drill and blast construction method.

reverse: *adj.* 反面的; 倒车的; 颠倒的

10) The most basic of parking auxiliary system form is single reverse radar, after that, video system was also used as parking assist device.
11) Through the display screen, driver can see reverse images, map navigation, night vision displays and mobile TV etc.
12) A chart on the reverse of this letter highlights your savings.

development：*n.* 研发；发育；编制；设计

13) This kind of design approach often results in the design conflicts, enables the designers have repeatedly modified the design of various subsystems, needs lots of tests to finish the development of vibration system, results in long product development cycle, and greatly increases the cost of the product design and testing.
14) This is an ideal system for studying the development of the embryo.
15) This concept design is the development based on modern art of bridges.

efficiency：*n.* 效率；效能

16) There are many ways to increase agricultural efficiency in the poorer areas of the world.
17) Without efforts on focusing on your goals, you will lose your impact and your efficiency, and you will waste your resources by not realizing what is really important.

prepare：*v.* 准备；编制，写；预制

18) The artificial island shall be prepared for the installation of first tunnel element.
19) The employer is preparing tender documents.
20) All bridge girder segments shall get prepared in factory.

Unit 3　词义的引申
Extension of Meanings

在英译汉时,我们有时会遇到某些词,在词典上找不到表达恰当的词义,如果按照词典上的解释生搬硬套,逐字逐句直译,就会使人感到译文生硬晦涩,不能确切表达原文含义。如果出现这种情况,我们就要根据等效原则运用引申法,根据上下文的语境及逻辑关系,从该词语的基本意思出发,将词义进行引申,从而选择出恰当的汉语词汇来表达。

词语的意义要受具体语境的影响和制约,也就是说,只有在具体语言环境中,才有可能确定其真正的细致的含义。词典里提供的种种解释往往缺乏应有的细节,那是一种概括的孤立的说明。翻译时为了符合实际的人物和情节,必须对词典里的措辞进行一定程度的改动或引申,即依顺该词的基本意义,紧扣具体语篇的实在情况,选择较为合适的汉语词语予以表达(但汉源,1999)。由于词汇中包含着英汉两个不同民族的风土人情和生活习惯,仅仅依靠词典上的解释来选择词义是不够的,必须采取灵活的手法,从某一词的基本词义出发,根据上下文,引申词义,把该词所关联的深层意义表述出来(丁树德,2005)。

1. 专业化引申

英语科技文章所使用的词汇有些源自日常生活用语,但在科技语境中已经被赋予了不同于日常语境的专业化语义。因此,翻译时应基于其基本意义,根据涉及的专业引申出其专业化语义。

➢ Many manufacturers are also turbo-charging diesels to increase <u>air flow</u> and further improve <u>efficiency</u>.
很多汽车生产商还用涡轮增压柴油机来增加<u>进气量</u>,进一步提高柴油机的<u>热效率</u>。

➢ Six PWM <u>pulses</u> are then generated by this module and sent to the VSI to drive the SR-PM motor.
然后,六个脉宽调变(PWM = Pulse-Width Modulation)<u>脉冲信号</u>通过这个模块产生,送入电压源逆变器(VSI = Voltage Source Inverter)来驱动同步磁阻永磁(SR-PM = Synchronous Reluctance Permanent Magnetic)电机。

➢ But because the <u>pump</u> is driven by the engine, the injection pressure rises and falls along with the engine <u>speed</u>.
但因为<u>输油泵</u>由发动机驱动,所以喷油压力随着发动机的<u>转速</u>起伏。

➢ The Lupo is billed as the world's first three-liter car—the number referring not to the size of its engine, but to its <u>meagre thirst</u>.
Lupo 被宣传为世界上第一辆3公升车,这个数字并不是指它的发动机尺寸,而是指它的耗油量少。
- The univariate statistics, including the arithmetic mean or average, standard deviation (STD), histogram, 95% confidence level upper and lower limits, are calculated.
单变量统计量(算术平均,标准差,直方图,95%置信水平的上限和下限)被算出。
- A few simple experiments were conducted with the exemplar vehicle to establish parameters and verify some performance properties.
通过模型汽车做一些简单的实验来获取参数和验证某些性能属性。
- Virtual technology is widely utilized in various vehicle test-beds.
虚拟技术被广泛应用于各种汽车试验平台。
- Four coordinate systems, earth frame, body frame, tire frame and vehicle frame, were employed as shown in Figure 6.
如图6所示有四个坐标系统,分别为全局坐标系、车体坐标系、轮胎坐标系和车辆坐标系。
- That is because diesel engines are, typically, 30% more fuel-efficient than petrol engines.
这是因为柴油机通常会比汽油机节油30%。
- This should highlight the generally existing requirement of high switching frequency or high power density.
这应该强调突出普遍存在的高开关频率或者大功率密度要求。
- In the meantime, before hybrid and fuel-cell vehicles materialize, the conventional wisdom had been that ever-more refined petrol engines would dominate, better catalysts would clean up exhaust emission; more precise fuel injection would make engines leaner and more economical.
与此同时,在混合动力汽车和燃料电池汽车上市之前,人们普遍认为更加精炼汽油发动机仍占主导地位,更好的催化剂使排放更清洁,更精确的燃油喷射控制使发动机更省油。

2. 概括化和抽象化引申

英语科技文章中有些词语的字面意思比较具体或形象,但若直译成汉语,有时则显得牵强,不符合汉语的表达习惯,使人感到费解。在这种情况下,就应该用含义较为概括或抽象的词语对英文所表达的词义加以引申。英语中表示具体意义的词往往可用来表示事物的一种属性或一个概念,译时可将具体意义引申为某种属性或抽象概念。

- Much remains to be learned about Earth's carbon cycle and the role of the oceans as a "sink" for CO_2.
地球的碳循环以及海洋扮演的碳"汇"角色还有待研究。
- Thus it is important to evaluate the radial force of leading guide tire on the leading truck in order to design the light weight truck frame and the guideway.
因此,为了设计重量较轻的转向架与导轨,评价前转向架前导向轮的径向力非常重要。
- Alloy belongs to a half-way house between mixtures and compounds
合金是介于化合物和混合物之间的中间物质。

➢ No doubt, European car makers will give Toyota <u>a tough battle for every inch of ground</u>.

毫无疑问，欧洲的汽车制造商将与丰田<u>进行寸土必争的激烈市场竞争</u>。

➢ On a dollar-per-ton basis, the most economical solution for achieving <u>the umbrella requirements</u> for the foreseeable future involves integrated in-process technologies.

基于每吨一美元的理论，要实现<u>这一揽子要求</u>里关于可预见未来最经济的解决方案就是一体化进程技术。

➢ Typically, the <u>"me too" crowd</u> must offer unbelievable guarantees and warranties to differentiate their offerings from the other similar manufacturers.

通常情况下，<u>"山寨版"商家</u>必须提供非常难以置信的担保和保证来将他们的产品和其他类似的制造商的产品区分开来。

➢ This condition is not general in other optimal control problems but is fairly true for HEV with Li-Ion batteries which have <u>flat</u> voltage and resistance.

这个状况在其他最优控制问题中并不普遍，但对于安装了<u>稳定</u>电压和电阻的锂电池的混合动力汽车（HEV = Hybrid Electric Vehicle）来说却是普遍情况。

➢ Comparing Figure 10, which illustrates the control surface of the tuned fuzzy active steering controller, with Figure 4, it is clear that the scaling function has adjusted the membership functions of the output variable of the fuzzy controller such that the control surface extends to the <u>limits of the universe of discourse</u>.

图10举例明了调谐模糊主动转向控制器的控制面，比较图10与图4，可以很明显看出尺度函数已经适应了模糊控制器输出变量的隶属函数，从而使得控制面延伸到<u>最大论域</u>。

➢ Something in the American psyche loves new <u>frontiers</u>.

美国人骨子里酷爱探索新<u>领域</u>。

➢ <u>On the downside</u>, the performance of a computer vision application is very dependent on the illumination conditions.

<u>缺点在于</u>计算机视觉应用性能非常依赖光照条件。

➢ Steel and cast iron also differ in <u>carbon</u>.

钢和铸铁的<u>含碳量</u>也不相同。

3. 具体化和形象化引申

英语科技文章中有些字面语义颇为笼统或抽象的词语，若按照字面译出，要么不符合汉语表达习惯，要么就难以准确地传达原文所表达的意思。在这种情况下，就应该根据特定的语境，用比较具体或形象化的汉语词语对英文词语所表达的词义加以引申。将原文中词义比较宽泛、笼统的表抽象概念或一般行为的词引申为具体的意义或动作。词义的具体化和形象化引申的总趋势是缩小外延而丰富内涵，这样做可以避免照字面翻译造成的模糊性和词不达意，以确保译文准确到位，符合汉语的语义逻辑和表达习惯。

➢ The <u>clever thing</u> about common-rail technology is that, by improving combustion, it dramatical-

ly reduces the level of both emissions and noise.
共轨技术的优势在于,通过改善燃烧,显著地降低了尾气和噪声排放水平。
> In the United States one in four citizens suffers from a foodborne illness, and some 5,000 people die from something they ate each year.
在美国每年四个公民中就一个得食源性疾病,并且约5000人死于他们所吃的食物。
> The rest of energy warms earth and fuels its weather engine.
剩余的能量使地球变暖并且给天气引擎提供燃料。
> Pushing their way through emerging cities like Barakar, India, automobiles carry unwanted cargo—CO_2 emissions.
当汽车挤进如印度的巴拉卡一样的新兴城市,它同样带来了不受欢迎的污染物——二氧化碳排放。
> The voting process requires three measurements for every pair of pixels p and q:
投票过程中,每对像素 p 与 q 需要进行三次测量。
> Red neon numbers mounted high above the river of moving cars blink steadily, comparing the rate of completed autos with the company's goal.
安装在汽车生产流水线上的红色霓虹灯不停地闪烁,是为了将车辆生产速度与公司目标做比较。
> For the average consumer, voice-activated devices are a convenience; for the elderly and handicapped, they may become indispensable for a wide variety of chores in the home.
对一般使用者来说,声触发装置能提供方便;而对老年人和残疾者来说,它可能成为从事各种家庭杂务时不可或缺的帮手。
> A large segment of mankind turns to untrammelled nature as a last refuge from encroaching technology.
许多人都想回归自然,并把它看作躲避现代技术侵害的世外桃源。
> Her soft features effectively hid her strong mechanical foundation.
她柔媚的容貌巧妙地掩饰了她那强有力的机械躯体。
> Stability, sustainability, safety, aesthetics, durability are key drivers to the design.
稳定性、可持续发展性、安全性、美观性和耐久性都是该设计方案的关键因素。
> The choice of a suspension bridge is deliberate and the cost penalty is accepted because it creates a fixed link that is in perfect harmony from one end to the other.
悬索桥方案的选择是经过深思熟虑的,成本代价也是可接受的,因为这样的方案会创造出从一端到另一端都完美和谐的固定运输通道。

Exercises

1. **Find out the similar translation skills in your professional papers.**
2. **Go through the following sentences and focus on the translation skills concerned.**
   专业化引申
   > The Three Gorges power plant has put 21 power units into operation, and construction is under-

way on large hydro power plants in Longtan, Xiangjiaba and Xiluodu.
三峡电站已有21台<u>机组</u>投产,龙滩、向家坝、溪洛渡等一批大型水电站相继开工建设。

➤ As can be noticed, only the hub-belt lateral <u>stiffness</u>, the hub-belt longitudinal <u>stiffness</u> and hub-belt torsion <u>stiffness</u> seem to have a small influence on tyre wear.
可以注意到,只有轮毂帘线侧向<u>刚度</u>、纵向<u>刚度</u>和扭转<u>刚度</u>对轮胎磨损的影响小。

➤ Mountain ranges can block clouds creating dry "<u>shadows</u>" downwind.
山脉可以阻断云层,在顺风区形成干燥的<u>雨影区</u>。

➤ In active probing, special testing signals are injected into an unenergized <u>phase</u>.
在主动探索中,特殊的测试信号可以输入进一个未被激活的<u>相电路</u>中。

➤ <u>Spam</u> is an Internet slang for unsolicited email.
"<u>垃圾邮件</u>"是不请自来的电子邮件的互联网俚语。

➤ In this paper, we address this shortcoming and additionally derive a two-dimensional <u>discrete-time state-space equation</u> based on a combined model of the Li-ion battery.
在本文中,我们解决了这个缺点并且得到了一个基于锂电池组合模型的二维<u>离散时间状态空间方程</u>。

➤ On the <u>coupling</u> work condition of engine, the time of max average <u>power</u> and max efficiency of torque converter is the best work point.
在发动机的<u>耦合</u>工作条件下,变矩器的最大平均功率和最大效率的交点就是最佳工作点。

➤ Yet another <u>refinement</u>, exhaust-gas-recirculation (EGR), is being adopted as a way to cutting the amount of nitrogen oxide produced by diesel engines.
此外,另一项<u>改进技术</u>——废气再循环系统,被采用为削减柴油机氮氧化物排放量的方法。

➤ Since the motor is <u>housed</u> in the limited space within the wheel rim, it must have a high torque density and efficiency, and survive the rigours of being in-wheel in terms of <u>environment cycling</u>, ingress shock and vibration and <u>driver abuse</u>.
由于电机被<u>安装</u>在轮辋内有限空间里,所以电机必须具有较高的转矩密度和效率,并且适应<u>工况循环</u>、轮辋入口的冲击和振动以及<u>频繁驱动</u>等严酷的轮内工作环境。

➤ The balanced suspension utilizes the "level" principle to distribute the axle load equally and to reduce the shock from <u>the road irregularities</u>.
平衡悬架采用"水平"的原则来使轴载分配均匀,并减少<u>路面不平整</u>造成的振动。

➤ These approaches are based on an approximation of robot kinematic relationships, such as the relationship between the robot joint <u>readings</u> and its position errors or between the robot positions and its position errors.
这些方法是基于机器人运动学关系的近似法,如机器人关节的<u>读数</u>和位置误差之间的关系,或者机器人的位置和位置误差之间的关系。

➤ In [10], two Rapidly-exploring Random <u>Trees</u> (RRTs) <u>were rooted</u> at the start and during the goal configurations.
在文献10中提出,两个快速随机探测谱模型在开始和目标配置时<u>被安装上</u>。

> It is with some advantages services such as high efficiency, precisely repeated movements and good carrying capacity.
> 它(机械手)有一定的优势,如高效率、精确重复动作和良好的承载能力。
> The inter-face module analyzes data from both modules and then decides whether to fire the bag.
> 界面模块对两个模块数据进行分析,然后决定是否启动安全气囊。
> The mechanics research of the interaction between vehicle and road is a way to solve the road damage problem and has recently received increasing attentions.
> 车辆与道路耦合的力学研究是解决路面损坏问题的方法,该方法最近得到了越来越多的关注。
> Covering 70 percent of Earth's surface, oceans are the chief source of water vapor in the air.
> 海洋覆盖了地球表面的70%面积,是大气中水蒸气的主要来源。
> The air gap shall be kept between the two carriageways to allow for structure built in between.
> 两条行车道之间应保持间距,用来修建结构物。

3. **Translate the following sentences based on translation skills concerned.**

   概括化和抽象化引申

   1) There are three steps which must be taken before we graduate from the integrated circuit technology.
   2) The book is perhaps too high-powered for technician in general.
   3) The shortest distance between raw material and a finished part is precision casting. (precision casting,精密铸造)
   4) At the society much cross-fertilization of minds always takes place.
   5) The expense of such an instrument has discouraged its use.
   6) Industrialization and environmental degradation seem to go hand in hand.
   7) In the microbial transformation of contaminants, organisms can either "eat" the toxins or break them down in the process of consuming other substances.
   8) The research performed on smokers at rest indicates that smokers burn more calories than nonsmokers.

4. **Translate the following sentences according to the translation skills concerned.**

   具体化和形象化引申

   1) There are three things we have to know about every force in order to be able to understand the effect it produced.
   2) At high frequencies where the integration time is short, results will be displayed in rapid succession and possibly leave insufficient time for the user to record them. (integration time,积分时间)
   3) The purpose of a driller is to cut holes.
   4) The energy is so small that something must be done to prevent the complete loss of signal.
   5) The foresight and coverage shown by the inventor of the process are most commendable.

6) While the results may seem <u>discouraging</u> to smokers who'd like to quit without gaining weight.
7) In general, the design procedure is not <u>straightforward</u> and will require trial and error.
8) Steel and cast iron also differ in <u>carbon</u>.
9) <u>Plain</u> concrete is one type concrete without reinforcement.
10) Concrete <u>caring</u> requires highly of temperature and moisture control over fresh concrete.

Unit 4　词性的转换
Conversion of Parts of Speech

　　所谓词性转换,是指把英语原文中的某一词性转译成汉语的另一词性。同一意思在不同语言中可以用不同的词性来表达。

　　词性转换是英汉翻译常见、高效而且很重要的手段之一,运用得当,可使译文通顺流畅自然,否则译文可能生硬晦涩。英译汉过程中,过于追求原作与译文中的词性对等,可能会由于英汉差异引起的语言机械转换,使得译文貌合神离,翻译腔十足。因此,英译汉时我们需要按照汉语表达需要进行适当调整和转换,才能翻译出妥帖、顺畅的译文。尽管词性间的转换在英译汉中是没有限制的,译者可以根据不同语境自由地进行词性转换,但词性转换却有一定的原则,即忠于原意、可读性强、符合汉语的表达习惯。

1. 转换成汉语动词

1) 名词转动词

➢ It may take a decade or more of additional <u>research</u> to resolve those uncertainties.

这可能需要花费十年或更长时间<u>做</u>进一步<u>研究</u>来解决这些不确定性。

➢ Specific issues addressed in this paper include the <u>selection</u> and <u>placement</u> of accelerometers to capture the three-dimensional response of critical roller components, and the <u>measurement</u> of the rotating eccentric position within the drum.

本文中解决的具体问题包括:<u>选择</u>和<u>布置</u>加速计来捕获关键滚筒部件的三维响应以及<u>测量</u>振动轮内旋转位置的变化情况。

➢ Strange as it may seem, diesel is staking a <u>claim</u> to be the environmentally friendly fuel of the future.

令人不可思议,柴油<u>被认为</u>是未来环保型燃料。

➢ Therefore, there is an immediate <u>need</u> to develop a systematic IC data analysis and management method, in order to better take advantage of the IC technology and accelerate its implementation.

因此,为了更好地利用智能压实技术并加快实施,<u>需要</u>立即开发一个系统性 IC 数据分析和管理方法。

➢ This is an <u>application</u> of Newton's Third Law of force: equal and opposite forces.

这就<u>使用</u>了牛顿第三定律,作用力和反作用力。

- As curvature and the superelevation change during curving, the virtual body moves according to the <u>movement</u> of the tire frame as follows.

  如下所示，由于转弯处曲率和超高的变化，虚拟体的运动是随着轮胎坐标移动而<u>运动</u>的。

- The following sections will lay out the modernist approach to planning and problems associated with it, and <u>detail</u> the post-modernist approach and differences between it and the modernist approach.

  以下各部分罗列了现代主义规划的方法和与之相关的问题，并<u>详细介绍</u>后现代主义的手法，以及它和现代方法之间的差异。

- Higher air temperature means the increasing water <u>evaporation</u> and <u>melting</u> of sea and land ice.

  气温升高可能会<u>蒸发</u>更多的水，<u>融化</u>更多的海洋与陆地的冰。

- Further, it provides a separate <u>quantification</u> of vehicle-induced turbulence and turbulence produced by natural winds.

  此外，它（论文）对汽车引起的湍流和自然风引起的湍流分别作了<u>量化分析</u>。

- The voting process requires three <u>measurements</u> for every pair of pixels p and q.

  投票过程中，对每对像素 p 与 q <u>进行了三次测量</u>。

- Velocity profile <u>measurements</u> were made up though the centre of the basic courtyards using a pulsed wire anemometer.

  我们在基础中庭中心通过脉冲式风速仪<u>测量</u>风速剖面。

- Also there may be up to 1mm gap between still beam and liner plate to provide for adjustment for achieving correct weld size.

  底坎梁和衬板之间也要有1mm间隙，通过此间隙可以调节合适的焊缝尺寸。

2）形容词转动词

- Modern architects for their part, sought to design cities that would promote industrial efficiency in the face of massive housing shortages, standardized dwelling types <u>capable of</u> mass production.

  对于现代的建筑师来说，面对房屋大量短缺，他们寻求设计出能够提升行业效率的城市，以及能够批量生产的标准化住房类型。

- Managers <u>are able to</u> replace Excel and Access with no-risk, cost-effective, Internet-based tools that automate the review process of burdensome data analysis.

  经理们<u>能够</u>用无风险、成本效益好、基于互联网的工具来代替 Excel 和 Access，这个工具可以使烦琐的数据分析评审过程自动化。

- In order to make this maneuver <u>feasible</u> for a non-professional human driver, however, it was performed with an initial speed of 60 km/h.

  然而，为了使非专业驾驶员能够在该工况下<u>驾驶</u>，初始速度设置为60km/h。

- Hence, encoding these parameters results in shorter chromosomes and, consequently, <u>shorter</u> computation time.

  因此，编码这些参数导致染色体较短，从而<u>缩短</u>计算时间。

➤ Therefore, it is common practice to assume that deflections are negligible and parts are rigid when analyzing a machine's kinematic performance.
因此，通常的做法是在分析机器的运动性能时假定弯曲变形忽略不计，并且零件是刚性的。

➤ Grout equipment shall be capable of providing a continuous flow of 200 litre/min to the grout holes at pressures up to 1000kPa measured at the entry to the hole.
灌浆设备要能进行持续灌浆，速度为200L/min，井口压力达到1000kPa。

3) 副词转动词

➤ By selectively passing up to half the exhaust gas back through the engine, the amount of oxygen available for combustion can be reduced.
通过选择把一半的尾气重新送入发动机，可以减少参与燃烧的氧气。

➤ MLIB/MTRACE is the dSPACE library function, which aims at the seamless integration between MATLAB and dSPACE, and easily called by MATLAB.
MLIB / MTRACE 是维空间库函数，目的在于将MATLAB和数字空间无缝集成，并使MATLAB的调用变得容易。

➤ Two main strategies exist in contemporary building practice that allows to reconcile these opposing interests, namely the use of heat recovery units and the implementation of demand-controlled ventilation.
当代建筑实践的两个主要策略是调解这些对立的利益，换句话说，热回收部件的使用和需求控制通风的实现。

➤ If the symmetry S is not over a certain threshold, the ROI is deleted and will not be taken into account in the future.
如果对称的 S 不超过一定的阈值，ROI 就会被删除并在将来不予考虑。

➤ This will help to further the sciences.
这会有助于发展科学。

➤ Truth will out.
真相总有大白之日。

➤ The test was not over yet.
试验还没结束。

➤ Open the valve to let air in.
打开阀门，让空气进入。

➤ An exhibition of new products is on there.
那儿正在举办新产品展览会。

4) 介词转动词

➤ Those areas with an appropriate temperature, size, and position in the image are classified, by means of a correlation between them and some probabilistic models, which represents the average temperature of the different parts of the human body.

在图像中被分类的那些区域有合适温度、尺寸和位置,通过它们和一些概率模型之间的相关性来表示人体的不同部位的平均温度。

➤ A grass eating animal cannot exist without grass, a predator without prey, a plant without certain basic chemicals or certain kinds of soil.
食草动物没有草不能生存,食肉动物没有猎物无法生活,植物缺乏基本的化学物质或特定的土壤就无法生长。

➤ Numerical simulations play an important role in the design of advanced suspensions and in such simulations the road inputs can reasonably be treated as stochastic processes.
在先进悬架的设计方面,数值仿真技术起着非常重要的作用,运用这种仿真技术我们可以把路面输入视为一个随机过程。

➤ Life has prospered on this planet for nearly four billion years.
生命在地球上繁衍生息,已历时近40亿年。

➤ Its goal is to up its market share there to 8% by 2010.
它(丰田)的目标是在2010年提高市场份额8个百分点。

➤ It is our goal that the people in the underdeveloped areas will be finally off poverty.
我们的目标是使不发达地区的人民最终摆脱贫困。

➤ The robot's final path is generated by connecting the recorded points via a robot controller, which tries to pass through all the points by taking into consideration the dynamic constraints of the robot.
机器人最终路径通过运用机器人控制器连接记录点来生成,目标是尽可能在考虑动态约束的情况下通过所有的点。

➤ The contractor shall provide valves, by-passes, pressure hose, pipe and fittings as are necessary, in the opinion of the Engineer, to provide accurate grout pressure control regardless of how small the grout tank may be.
如果工程师认为有必要,即便灌浆桶很小,承包商也应提供阀门、迂回管、压力软管、刚性管和其他必要配件用于精确地控制灌浆压力。

2. 转换成汉语名词

1)动词转名词

➤ This technology forces the engine to operate at lower combustion temperatures, reducing the quantity of nitrogen-oxide produced.
这一技术迫使发动机的运转能在较低燃烧温度下进行,减少了氮氧化物的产生。

➤ Once-blah interiors sport higher-quality fabrics, dashboards, and knobs, while clean diesel engines are helping to power sales.
过去那种单调的内饰换成了质量上乘的织物、仪表盘和旋钮,而且配置污染小的柴油发动机,对汽车销量的增加有着很大的帮助。

- These test-beds generally need high investment, high cost and the tests on the actual roads are also highly dangerous.

  这些试验平台通常对投资、成本有着很高的需求,而实际道路上的测试也是非常危险的。

- Thus, in this study, we assume all of the required signals to be known.

  因此,在这篇文章中,我们做出了所有需求信号都已知的假设。

- This system will build on the knowledge and experience gained in developing the existing suite of software products.

  这个系统的基础是从开发现有的成套软件产品中所获取的知识和经验。

- All simulations were run over the heating season only.

  所有的仿真模拟的都只在供热季节运行。

- Gases differ from solids in that the former have greater compressibility than the latter.

  气体和固体的区别在于前者比后者有更大的可压缩性。

- The Earth's climate system has demonstrably changed on both global and regional scales since the pre-industrial era, with some of these changes attributable to human activities.

  自前工业化时代以来,随着人类活动对气候的改变产生影响,地球的气候系统在全球和地区范围内已经有了明显的改变。

- A higher SPL is needed to overcome interior noise, particularly at higher speeds.

  较高声压级(SPL = Sound Pressure Level)是克服内部噪声的需要,尤其在高速情况下。

- Drainage trenches shall be constructed as shown on the drawings or as directed by the engineer.

  排水渠的施工应按照图纸要求或是工程师的指导进行。

2) 形容词转名词

- That is because diesel engines are, typically, 30% more fuel-efficient than petrol engines.

  特别是因为柴油机的燃油利用率比汽油机高 30%。

- However, this is very often an inadmissible constraint to the probabilistic model.

  然而,这往往是概率模型所不允许的约束。

- Due to asymmetry in the machine and the potential nonuniform soil conditions, each roller drum and its surrounding frame assembly will potentially experience six degree-of-freedom motion (see Fig. 2).

  由于机器的不对称和潜在的地面条件不均匀,每个钢轮及其周围的车架部件都有可能经历 6 个自由度的运动(见图 2)。

- How credible are current projections?

  目前,预测的可靠性如何?

- A bridge engineer must have three points in mind while working on a bridge project: (1) creative and aesthetic; (2) analytical; (3) technical and practical.

  桥梁工程师在设计桥梁时必须牢记三点:(1)创新性和美观性;(2)可分析性;(3)较高的技术水平和实用性。

- Consumers are better educated about how to clean and cool meats and produce.
  消费者对如何清理和冷藏肉类和农产品接受了更好的培训。
- It is with some advantages services and such as high efficiency, precisely repeated movements and good carrying capacity.
  它(机械手)有一定的优势,如高效率、精确重复动作和良好的承载能力。

3)代词转名词

- A few of these may have run into one another, shattering each other into smaller bits.
  一些小行星可能会遇到其他小行星,彼此相撞变成更小的碎片。
- The development of intelligent vehicle requires that the structure of the vehicle itself and also its running process be intelligentized.
  智能汽车的发展要求汽车本身结构以及汽车运行的过程都智能化。
- This vehicle has a configuration similar to that of the commercially-available *Smart Fortwo*, but is equipped with four direct-drive in-wheel motors and an active steering system on the front axle.
  该车辆(模型)配置类似于市售 *Smart Fortwo* 的配置,但它装有四个直接驱动的轮毂电机和前轴主动转向系统。
- We need frequencies even higher than those we call very high frequency.
  我们所需要的频率,甚至比我们称作高频率的频率还要高。
- It is concluded by Altshuler, the founder of TRIZ, and other TRIZ experts.
  技术系统演化理论被 TRIZ 的创始人 Altshuler 和其他 TRIZ 的专家们总结出来。
- The second factor is introduced in order to prevent a pixel p previously classified as impulse noise from propagating its information.
  为防止像素点 p 在传递张量信息过程前被视为脉冲噪声,我们引入了第二个函数。
- If current rates continue, it will rise to at least twice pre-industrial levels by about 2060—and by the end of the century could be four times as high.
  如果按照目前的速度继续下去,大概到 2060 年,二氧化碳的含量至少将会上升到工业革命以前的两倍,到本世纪末将会是现在的四倍。

4)副词转名词

- The need to answer these questions becomes obvious if it is taken into account that the typical lifetime models are highly nonlinear and very sensitive with respect to some input quantities.
  如果考虑典型的生命周期模型是高度非线性的,并且对输入量非常敏感,那就必须回答这些问题。
- The system will warn (digital or voice hint) firstly if the spacing from the front car is too small to lead to rear-end collision.
  如果与前面车间距太小将导致追尾,系统将第一时间发出警告(数字或语音提示)。
- Much remains to be learned about Earth's carbon cycle and the role of the oceans as a "sink"

for CO_2.
关于地球二氧化碳循环和海洋碳"汇"作用的许多问题,还有待研究学习。

➢ In addition to supporting the vehicle weight, suspensions must also isolate the body from vibrations caused by road unevenness and keep its tyres firmly in contact with the road.
除了要承载车重之外,悬架还要把车身与路面不平所造成的振动隔离开来,同时也要保证轮胎与地面接触的牢靠性。

➢ Just as Microsoft Word can be used to automate spell check, EHS professionals now have tools at their disposal automatically to check air emissions data and information.
就像 Microsoft Word 可以做自动拼写检查,现在环卫局(EHS = Environmental Health Services)专家有很多手段实现检查空气排放数据和信息的自动化。

➢ In short, this maneuver confirms that the cooperation between the fuzzy slip controller that was developed previously and the fuzzy active steering controller developed here has allowed the driver to accelerate the AUTO21EV on a μ-split road with the maximum possible traction forces on all four wheels, no spin-out effects on the wheels, and no side-pushing effect on the vehicle.
总之,该工况确认了前面提出的模糊滑移控制器和现在提出的模糊主动转向控制器之间的合作,从而允许 AUTO21EV 的四轮以最大可能的牵引力在对开路面加速,并且车轮不出现打滑,车辆没有侧滑。

➢ Oxygen is one of the important elements in the physical world, very active chemically.
氧是物质世界的重要元素之一,其化学性质很活泼。

➢ Most people do not think that food poisoning can possibly occur in their home.
大多数人认为食物中毒发生在自己家的可能性不大。

➢ This artificial island is highly technical and beautifully designed.
该人工岛技术水平先进,设计精美。

3. 转换成汉语形容词

1)副词转形容词

➢ The trouble is that other methods of reducing nitrogen-oxide emissions depend on catalysts that react very badly to sulphur: it wears them out.
问题是其他减少氮氧化物排放的方法都要依靠一种会和硫化物发生糟糕反应的催化剂:这种现象会把催化剂消耗光。

➢ The most commonly known probabilistic method is the Monte Carlo Method.
最常见的熟知的概率方法是蒙特卡罗方法。

➢ Owing to the nonlinear nature of the coupled roller/soil system, the drum and frame acceleration response is not purely sinusoidal.
由于滚轴/地面耦合系统的非线性特性,钢轮和机架的加速度响应并不是纯粹的正弦曲线。

- Virtual technology is widely utilized in various vehicle test-beds.
  虚拟技术在各种汽车试验平台上得到了广泛的应用。
- Strange as it may seem, diesel is staking a claim to be the environmentally friendly fuel of the future.
  令人不可思议，现在柴油被视为未来的环保燃料。
- Despite such uncertainties, the computer programs used to model Earth's climate are improving rapidly.
  尽管存在不确定性因素，用来模拟地球气候的计算机程序依然得到了迅速的发展。
- Based on the pseudo-excitation method (PEM), a highly efficient and accurate probabilistic method is proposed in this paper.
  基于虚拟激励法，本文提出了一种高效而精确的概率统计方法。
- The supervisor must be suitably qualified candidate.
  监理候选人必须是合适的胜任的人选。
- Plant here is using the same advanced production processes that we use anywhere else in the world, and strives to meet the same requirements in terms of safety or environmental impact.
  这里的工厂所使用的生产工艺与我们在任何其他国家所使用的都同样先进，努力使这家工厂在安全和环保方面达到与其他各国相同的标准。

2）名词转形容词

- Behind this unlikely turn of events is a new generation of electronically controlled, high pressure fuel-injection systems combined with new "common-rail" technology.
  令人难以置信的是结合了共轨技术的高油压喷射系统的新一代电控技术的产生。
- Community standards should be enforced.
  公认的标准应该执行。
- With the controller enabled, however, the maneuver was found to require substantially less effort.
  然而，当控制器启用时，就会发现该操作非常轻便。
- Electronic computers and microprocessors ale of great importance to us.
  电子计算机和微处理器对我们来说都十分重要。
- The vehicle body vibration is transferred to the road surface through the suspension and tire as well.
  车身的振动通过悬架和轮胎传递到地面。
- This vehicle can travel up to 155 mi/h, so audibility of the alert functions at higher speeds is a necessity.
  该车车速可以达到155英里/小时，所以在更高速度下警报功能的可听性是必要的。
- They produce nitrogen oxides and particulates—tiny bits of hydrocarbon soot, the result of incomplete combustion.

这会产生氮氧化物和颗粒物——由不完全燃烧造成的细小碳氢烟尘颗粒。

4. 转换成汉语副词

1) 形容词转副词

➤ According to Steve Whelan of Ricardo, a consultancy that develops engines technology, this improves fuel efficiency, reduces the level of particle combustion produced, and makes the engine much quieter.
据 Ricardo 发动机技术研发咨询公司的 Steve Whelan 介绍，这项（技术）提高了燃油利用率，减少了燃烧产生的颗粒物，使发动机更安静地运转。

➤ Therefore, there is an immediate need to develop a systematic IC data analysis and management method, in order to better take advantage of the IC technology and accelerate its implementation.
因此，为了更好地利用智能压实技术并加快实施，需要立即开发一个系统性 IC 数据分析和管理方法。

➤ It is possible that the warming observed during this century may have resulted from natural variations, even though the increase has been much more than what the planet has witnessed over the past hundred centuries.
尽管地球温度的增长比过去几百个世纪都迅速得多，但本世纪观察到的变暖现象可能是由于自然界的各种变化而引起的。

➤ The engine has given a constantly good performance.
这台发动机一直运转良好。

➤ The common-rail system, in contrast, is more sophisticated, working with much higher pressure and more precise control of the fuel flow.
相反，共轨系统更复杂，使用更高的压力，能够更加精确地控制燃油流动。

➤ Only when we study their properties can we make better use of the materials.
我们只有研究这些材料的特性，才能更好地利用它们。

➤ Slight increase in the hydro carbon emission was observed.
我们可以观测到碳氢化合物的排放略微地增加了。

2) 其他词类转副词

➤ They reported they had succeeded in turning normal human cells into cancerous one.
报道说他们已成功地把正常人类细胞转化为癌细胞。

➤ In human society activity in production develops step by step from a lower to a higher level.
人类社会的生产活动，由低级向高级逐步发展。

➤ The added device will ensure accessibility for part loading and unloading.

增添这种装置将保证工件装卸方便。

➤ Rapid evaporation at the heating-surface tends to make the steam wet.

加热面上的迅速蒸发，往往使蒸汽的湿度加大。

➤ We shall develop the aircraft industry in a big way.

我们将大规模地发展航空工业。

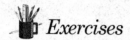

Exercises

Translate the following sentences into Chinese according to the skills concerned.

（1）名词转动词

1) However, detection of pedestrians from a moving vehicle is not trivial.
2) The voting process requires three measurements for every pair of pixels p and q.
3) In particular, they produce nitrogen oxides and particulates—tiny bits of hydrocarbon soot, the result of incomplete combustion.
4) Then, from about 2007, environmentally friendly cars powered by fuel cells will begin to make an appearance.
5) The reason is that natural processes are in balance, drawing about as much CO_2 from the air as they deposit.
6) As a result, in-vehicle networking has created a quiet evolution in automotive technology, resulting in the elimination of unwieldy wiring harnesses once used in control circuits. (in-vehicle networking, 车载网络; unwieldy wiring harnesses, 笨重的布线)
7) To make a decision on whether to activate the air bag, the system uses two key parameters: impact and loss of control.

（2）形容词转换成动词

8) Our river was dirty, our seas were polluted and our natural environment was destroyed.
9) The amount of work is dependent on the applied force and the distance the body is moved.
10) Kerosene is not so volatile as gasoline.
11) When is the next earthquake due?
12) They are sure that they'll be able to build the factory in a short period of time.
13) Humans are thought to be responsible for a large number of environmental problems, ranging from global warming to ozone depletion.
14) Living conditions is better a great deal.
15) The test piece shall be of length suitable for the apparatus being used.
16) Heat is a form of energy into which all other forms are convertible.

（3）副词转动词

17) The radio is on.
18) The electric current flows through the circuit with the switch on.
19) The two bodies are so far apart that the attractive force between them is negligible.

20) He took the machine apart yesterday.
21) The force due to the motion of molecules tends to keep them apart.
22) After careful investigation they found the design behind.
23) Motor vehicles, already the main source of city air pollution in rich countries, will increasingly pollute poor cities, too.
24) The experiment in chemistry was ten minutes behind.

(4) 介词转动词

25) The possibility of a real market-style evolution of governance is at hand.
26) This paper researches the yaw dynamics of a plug-in hybrid vehicle with powerful electric machine mounted on the rear shaft. (yaw dynamics, 横摆力; plug-in hybrid vehicle, 插入式混合动力汽车; rear shaft, 后轮轴)
27) Numerical simulations play an important role in the design of advanced suspensions and in such simulations the road inputs can reasonably be treated as stochastic processes. (simulation, 仿真; suspension, 悬架; stochastic processes, 随机过程)
28) With each change, sundry species have benefited and flourished.
29) With this in mind, a 2DOF vehicle model is used as a reference model to calculate the desired yaw rate of the vehicle, to which the controller attempts to match the nonlinear behavior of the vehicle. (desired yaw rate, 期望横摆角速度; 2DOF vehicle model, 二自由度车辆模型)

(5) 动词转名词

30) Mercury weighs about thirteen times as much as water.
31) The net and electronic commerce will foster a large number of free-lancers, and this will affect social structure in a big way.
32) PCs gave the world a whole new way to work, play and communicate.
33) He aims to become a computer expert.
34) In the life process, the animal works in the opposite way to the plant.
35) An electric current varies directly as the electromotive force and inversely as the resistance.

(6) 形容词转名词

36) Ice is not as dense as water and it therefore floats.
37) The different production cost is closely associated with the sources of power.
38) Glass is more soluble than quartz.
39) At constant temperature, the pressure of a gas is inversely proportional to its volume.
40) Both the compounds are acids, the former is strong and the latter weak.
41) The atmosphere is only about eleven kilometers thick.
42) The more carbon the steel contains, the harder and stronger it is.

(7) 代词转名词

43) Though we cannot see it, there is air all around us.
44) One would fall all the way down to the center of the earth without gravity.

45) The most common acceleration is that of free falling bodies.

46) Energy can neither be created, nor destroyed, although its form can be changed.

47) Radio waves are similar to light waves except that their wave-length is much greater.

48) We need frequencies even higher than those we call very high frequency.

49) According to a growing body of evidence, the chemicals that make up many plastics may migrate out of the material and into foods and fluids, ending up in your body.

(8) 副词转名词

50) Oxygen is one of the important elements in the physical world, it is very active chemically.

51) The quality of the operating system determines how useful the computer is.

52) India has the software skills and thousands of software developers who are English-speaking and technically proficient.

53) A look ahead gives petroleum an exciting role in the world of tomorrow.

54) The only naturally occurring substance used as fuel for nuclear power is U-235.

55) It was not until early 40's that chemists began to use the technique analytically.

(9) 副词转形容词

56) Mechanism 5a differs significantly from Mechanism 5b since whole-body rotation is in the opposite direction and head impact with ground occurs at much lower speeds (1.9 m/s on average). (whole-body rotation, 整个车体转动)

57) Another substantial advantage of an active steering system is its ability to electronically augment the driver's steering input to stabilize the vehicle. (active steering system, 主动转向系统)

58) What makes cyberspace so alluring is precisely the way in which it's different from shopping malls, television, highways and other terrestrial jurisdiction.

59) The wide application of electronic computers affects tremendously the development of science and technology.

60) The Earth's climate system has demonstrably changed on both global and regional scales since the pre-industrial era, with some of these changes attributable to human activities.

61) Strange as it may seem, diesel is staking a claim to be the environmentally fuel of the future.

(10) 名词转形容词

62) Electronic computers and microprocessors are of great importance to us.

63) The nuclear power system designed in China is of great precision.

64) In certain cases friction is an absolute necessity.

65) Patients may have to take them (drugs) for the rest of their lives, and the expense and complexity of the regimen keep them (drugs) out of reach for the 9 out of 10 patients who live in developing nations.

66) The doctors were operating on the patient, but the patient's nerve was continually on the stretch.

67) It is <u>no use</u> employing radar to detect objects in water.

(11) 形容词转副词

68) Some employers are <u>keen</u> to encourage employees to go green, and switch to small cars.

69) With <u>slight</u> repairs the old type of engine can be used.

70) The <u>wide</u> application of electronic machines in scientific work, in designing and in economic calculations will free man from the labor of complicated computations.

71) Very <u>significant</u> advances in lasers have been made in the past several years that open the door to more rapid progress in optical communications systems.

72) <u>Continual</u> smoking is harmful to health.

73) With <u>slight</u> modifications each type can be used for all three systems.

74) We have made a <u>careful</u> study of the properties of these chemical elements.

75) Below 4℃ water is <u>continuous</u> expansion instead of <u>continuous</u> contraction.

Unit 5　增　词
Amplification

作为翻译的一个普遍原则,译者不应该对原文的内容随意增减。不过,由于英汉两种语言文字之间所存在的巨大差异,在实际翻译过程中很难做到词句上完全对应,因此,为了准确地传达原文的信息,往往需要对译文作一些增减。

增词在科技英语翻译中是经常使用的翻译方法之一。所谓增译法,是指译者在英译汉时,在原文基础上添加原文中无其词却有其意的单词、词组、分句或完整句,从而使译文在修辞上,语法结构上,词义上或语气上与原文保持一致,达到译文与原文在内容,形式和思想方面对等的目的。

1. 增加表示名词复数概念的词语

➤ Quality can then be enhanced in both the direct and indirect respects referred to above.
产品质量将会在以上提及的各方面得到直接或间接的增强。

➤ There are a number of ways in which to classify bridges.
有许多划分各种桥型的方法。

➤ Signs that repair is needed are transverse joint faulting, corner breaks and lines at or near joints.
需要修补的各种现象包括横向接头损坏、角部断裂和接头处或附近出现的裂缝。

➤ Meanwhile, IC data produced by different roller vendors are presented in various data forms, which bring inconvenience and confusions to contractors when using multiple IC rollers.
与此同时,不同厂商制造的压路机所生成的智能压实数据呈现为多种不同的数据形式,所以使用不同IC的压路机会给承包商带来各种不便和困扰。

➤ The leaders will be the companies that invest for the future and try to add value beyond the status quo.
领军的那些企业将会是为未来投资,试图超越现状的那些公司。

➤ The following are typical design requirements for selection and design of the drive motor.
以下是驱动电机选型和设计的几项典型的设计要求。

2. 增加表示时态的词语

➤ All tunnels used for transport of people must have adequate fire escape safety provisions. The need has always been obvious in rapid transit tunnels, although in quite different degree.
所有的客运隧道必备完整的消防逃生安全设施。各种快速交通隧道都已经表现出(对安全设施)显而易见的需求,尽管程度上有所差异。
- Among the goals of intelligent soil compaction <u>are continuous monitoring</u> and identification of soil parameters and the feedback control of one or more of the following: vibration frequency, force amplitude, and forward velocity.
  智能土壤压实的目的是<u>连续监测</u>和识别土壤参数,并且反馈控制一个或多个以下参数:振动频率、振幅和碾压速度等。
- Battery electric vehicles <u>have been dismissed</u> as a colossal flop, so hybrid-electric vehicles, which use an internal-combustion engine for long journeys and an electric motor in town, will be a stop-gap to cut pollution and comply with law limiting vehicle emissions.
  电池电动车被认为是个巨大失败<u>已经被淘汰</u>。为了减少污染满足限制排放的法规要求,混合动力的电动车(长距离行驶时用内燃机驱动,城市中用电动机驱动)将成为权宜之计。
- Strange as it may seem, diesel <u>is staking a claim</u> to be the environmentally friendly fuel of the future.
  令人不可思议,<u>现在</u>柴油<u>被认为</u>是未来的环保燃料。
- Because creep behavior of the silty clay may affect excavation behavior, a series of triaxial compression and lateral extension creep test <u>had been conducted</u>.
  由于粉质黏土的徐变特性可能会影响开挖行为,<u>我们已经开展</u>了一系列的三轴压缩和侧向延伸徐变试验。
- If global warming continues to <u>raise</u> the Earth's atmospheric temperatures, the melting of the polar ice caps could be speeding.
  如果全球变暖继续下去,大气层的<u>温度</u><u>将会升高</u>,导致极地冰帽融化速度加快。
- Networking <u>has made</u> the advanced technology features for 2010—2011 model vehicles possible, including on board communications systems, control systems such as lane-departure warning systems, and (slippery) road-condition advisories.
  2010—2011年款的车辆网络系统已具备先进的技术特点,包括车载通信系统以及如车道偏离警告系统和(滑移率)路况报告的控制系统。
- Worldwide, researchers <u>are working</u> to develop more efficient drive systems for vehicles, in particular using electric motors.
  世界范围内,许多研究者<u>正致力于</u>开发出效率更高的车用驱动系统,特别是使用电机驱动的驱动系统。
- Most <u>current</u> technological developments in electric vehicles have centered on improving energy efficiency.
  <u>现在</u>电动汽车新技术的研究主要集中在提高能源效率上。

3. 增加表示句子主语的词语

- It is generally recognized that a suspension bridge is more seismic resistant than cable-stayed bridges.

大家普遍认为悬索桥比斜拉桥的抗震性能更好。

➤ Based on the modified Chinese criteria, the results of cyclic triaxial and simple shear tests, and the simplified liquefaction evaluation procedure, it was concluded that the weak layer would liquefy during the anti-earthquake design.

根据修改后的中国规范、周期三轴和简化的抗剪试验结果以及简化液化评价程序,我们得出了抗震设计时应考虑软弱层会发生液化的结论。

➤ Use the time domain analysis methods and frequency domain analysis methods to extract the statistical features.

本文应用时域分析方法和频域分析方法提取统计特征。

➤ The role of clouds is poorly understood, but they are known to both cool Earth by reflecting solar energy and warm Earth by trapping heat being radiated up from the surface.

虽然人们对云的作用知之甚少,但大家都知道云层通过反射太阳能给地球降温,通过吸收从地球表面辐射的热量增加地球温度。

➤ Extensive study of the so-called "Chinese criteria" was undertaken, and the criteria were applied in modified form to evaluate the liquefaction susceptibility of the weak clayey silt.

我们对所谓的"中国规范"做了广泛研究,并将这些修改后的规范用于评价软弱黏性粉土的液化趋势。

➤ The pre-stressed reinforced concrete piles were selected as the preferred method based on consideration of technical reliability, construction feasibility and environmental compliance.

我们考虑了技术可靠性、可施工性及环保性之后,选择了预应力钢筋混凝土桩这一最佳方法。

➤ Testing the geometric stability of several cameras in recent years has shown that the accomplished accuracies in object space are either limited.

近几年来,研究者们对多种相机的几何稳定性进行了测试,结果表明完成精度在对象空间是有限的。

➤ Earthquake-induced deformations of the strengthened dam were calculated using nonlinear finite element analyses.

我们采用非线形有限元分析法计算了加固大坝的地震变形。

➤ The piles were installed from floating plant with minimum disruption to project operations.

施工人员采用浮式设备沉桩,减少了对项目作业的中断。

➤ High-performance concrete has been primarily used in tunnels, bridges and tall buildings for its strength, durability and high modulus of elasticity. It has also been used in shotcrete repair, poles, parking garages, and agricultural applications.

高性能混凝土,因其强度高、耐久性好和弹性模量高,已经主要用于隧道、桥梁及高层建筑。高性能混凝土还已经用于喷射混凝土修补、支柱、停车场及农业设施。

➤ Based on quality engineering theory, the optimization algorithm is proposed by integrating the Monte Carlo descriptive sampling, non-dominated sorting genetic algorithm (NSGA-II) and 6-

sigma design method.

基于质量工程理论,本文提出整合了蒙特卡罗描述抽样、非支配排序遗传算法(NSGA-Ⅱ)和六西格玛设计方法的优化算法。

➤ Note that the amplitude and frequency associated with the first lane change is larger, since the first turn is slightly tighter than the second.

我们可以注意到:由于第一次转向比第二次略困难,所以与第一车道变换相关联的幅度和频率都较大。

4. 增加原文中省略的词语

➤ Meanwhile, much is known.

同时我们已经了解很多的相关知识。

➤ It is possible that the warming observed during this century may have resulted from natural variations, even though the increase has been much more than what the planet has witnessed over the past hundred centuries.

尽管这个世纪中地球温度的增长比过去几百个世纪都迅速得多,但本世纪观察到的变暖现象有可能是由于自然界的各种变化而引起的。

➤ To date, several billion dollars have been spent on site evaluation, studies of safety and environmental acceptability.

到目前为止,已经有数十亿美元投资在强辐射性废物处理站点的评估以及站点安全性和环境可接受性的研究。

➤ More than 50 different "designer" crops have passed through a federal review process, and about a hundred more are undergoing field trials.

超过五十种不同的"设计"农作物已经通过了联邦的审查程序,而且大约有一百种农作物正在试验田接受测试。

➤ If current rates continue, it will rise to at least twice pre-industrial levels by about 2060—and by the end of the century could be four times as high.

如果目前的速度继续下去,大概到2060年,二氧化碳的含量至少将会是工业革命以前的两倍,并且本世纪末二氧化碳的含量将会是现在的四倍。

➤ It is based on wireless PCM transmission (Pulse Code Modulation) technology, widely used in communications field.

商业性的遥测技术是基于无线 PCM 传输技术,现在广泛应用于通信领域。

➤ To better show the effectiveness of the proposed controller, the performance of an uncontrolled vehicle which runs on the same road was also compared.

为了更好展现本文提出的控制器的有效性,在同样行驶路面的条件下,将未受控制器控制的车辆行驶性能与受控制的车辆性能进行了对比。

5. 增加具体和明确化的词语

➤ The open web system permits the use of a greater overall length than for an equivalent solid web girder.
在相同部位,采用空心腹板系统的总长度可以比实心腹板梁总长度长。

➤ Current models do well in simulating seasonal variations and climate over thousands of years, leading most scientists to take their overall projections seriously.
现在这些模型在模拟数千年来的季节性变化和气候方面做得非常好,这一结果促使大多数科学家认真对待这些模型的整体预测。

➤ It is widely believed that the contact stress is a main reason for road damage, especially for cracking and rutting.
人们普遍认为,接触应力是导致路面损坏的主要原因,尤其是路面的裂缝和车辙。

➤ Frequently, this increase pushes the power above the level for which the speaker is rated, resulting in a significantly diminished sound quality.
通常,这种增加功率到扬声器额定的水平以上的方法,导致声音质量显著下降。

➤ But because the pump is driven by the engine, the injection pressure rises and falls along with the engine speed.
但由于输油泵由发动机驱动,所以喷油压力将会随着发动机的转速变换。

6. 增加起语气连贯作用的词语

➤ Modern architects for their part, sought to design cities that would promote industrial efficiency in the face of massive housing shortages, standardized dwelling types capable of mass production.
对于现代的建筑师来说,面对房屋大量短缺,他们寻求设计出能够提升行业效率的城市,以及能够批量生产的标准化住房类型。

➤ While these solutions effectively reduce NO$_x$ emissions, alternative technologies focused on pollution prevention are achieving the same results with added financial benefits and improved performance.
这些方案有效地减少氮氧化物的排放,而关注污染防治的替代技术也取得相同结果,从而使经济利益和性能都得到提高。

➤ The effect would be locally disastrous.
可想而知对当地会产生灾难性的影响。

➤ Consequently, simulation of this maneuver demands a driver model that can dynamically adjust the steering wheel according to the vehicle trajectory and yaw rate response at every time step of a simulation.
因此,模拟这种工况需要一个驾驶员模型,并且该模型可以根据每个时间步长的车辆轨迹和横摆角速度响应动态调整方向盘转角。
> Or they can wander freely if they prefer, making up their own itinerary.
或者他们可以随心所欲的自由漫步,以此来虚构他们的旅程。
> Bright white expanses of ice and snow reflect sunlight back into space, cooling the planet.
一望无际亮白色的冰雪把太阳光反射回太空,从而达到冷却地球效果。
> Using a transformer, power at low voltage can be transformed into power at high voltage.
如果使用变压器,低电压就能转换成高电压。
> Being stable in air at ordinary temperature, mercury combines with oxygen if heated.
常温下水银在空气中较稳定,但若受热便会同氧化合。
> Obviously, the study on the active safety of the running vehicle in the virtual environment is still insufficient, and it is worthy to develop indoor test-beds to research on intelligence vehicles.
显然,在虚拟环境中对运行车辆的主动安全性的研究仍然滞后,因此,开发室内试验平台来研究智能车辆是值得肯定的。
> But the technique of genetic engineering is new, and quite different from conventional breeding.
但是总的来说基因工程技术是新兴事物,而且完全不同于传统的饲养。

7. 增加概括性词语

> Ranching, rice farming and landfills have raised methane levels.
放牧、粮食耕种和垃圾填埋,这三种方式提升了甲烷含量。
> Half the Toyotas sold in Europe are built at factories in Britain, France, and Turkey.
在欧洲售出的丰田汽车,有一半都是由建立在英国、法国和土耳其三国的工厂生产的。
> The advantages of the recently developed composite materials are energy saving, performance efficient, corrosion resistant, long service time, and without environmental pollution.
最新开发的复合材料具有节能强、性能好、抗腐蚀、寿命长和无污染等五大优势。
> Now human beings have not yet progressed as to be able to make an element by combining protons, neutrons and electrons.
目前人类还没有发展到能把质子、中子、电子三者化合成一个元素的地步。
> The factors, voltage, current and resistance, are related to each other.
电压、电流和电阻这三个因素是相互关联的。
> The thesis reviewed the developments made in economy, traffic and environmental protection.
这篇论文评述了经济、交通以及环保三个方面的发展情况。
> Everything physical is measurable by weight, motion and resistance.
任何有形的物体都可以从重量、运动和阻力三个方面进行测量。
> The principal functions that may be performed by vacuum tubes are rectification, amplification,

oscillation, modulation and detection.

真空管的五大功能是:整流、放大、震荡、调制和检测。

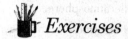 *Exercises*

Translate the following sentences according to the skills required.

(1) 增加表示名词复数概念的词语

1) After years as the poor, filthy relation to petrol engines, diesel has cleaned itself up.

2) The following sections will lay out the modernist approach to planning and problems associated with it, and detail the post-modernist approach and the differences between it and the modernist approach.

3) It is possible that the warming observed during this century may have resulted from natural variations, even though the increase has been much more than what the planet has witnessed over the past hundred centuries.

4) Planetary geologists have tried counting craters and their size distribution to get absolute ages for surfaces on the planets and moons.

5) In this sense, automobile companies such as Toyota, Honda, Chevrolet, Mazda and Ford, have invested a lot of efforts and money in developing hybrid cars.

6) Despite such uncertainties, the computer programs used to model Earth's climate are improving rapidly.

7) American, Japan and Europe are imposing ever-tighter rules to cut air pollution from cars.

8) Also, thanks to substantial improvements in electric motor and battery technologies, EVs now have driving performance metrics that are comparable to those of ICE vehicles. (ICE vehicles,内燃机车)

9) Toyota, a marginal player in Europe, is becoming a fearsome market force as it applies itself to winning a bigger share of the Old World's roadways.

(2) 增加表示时态的词语

10) Fuzzy logic controllers have emerged as the most effective controllers for motor drives. (fuzzy logic controller,模糊逻辑控制器)

11) Toyota is becoming a fearsome market force as it applies itself to winning a bigger share of the Old World's roadways.

12) Despite such uncertainties, the computer programs used to model Earth's climate are improving rapidly.

13) But there is little sure knowledge in this field.

14) Therefore, the dynamic models of the entire vehicle and the major assemblies are ignored, only the dynamic and kinematic analysis is considered.

15) In recent years HEVs are becoming very popular. (HEV,混合动力汽车)

16) The effect of this assumption has been discussed by Steeman.

17) America, Japan and Europe are imposing ever-tighter rules to cut air pollution from cars.

18) But now that politicians and the green lobby <u>are getting more worked up</u> about emissions of global-warming gases.
19) Human beings have little direct control over the volume of water in the atmosphere.
20) As a combination of electronic industry and car industry, automotive electronic technology <u>is developing</u> rapidly.
21) China <u>has become</u> one of the world's largest importers of petroleum products, largely to fuel its burgeoning fleet of cars and trucks.

(3) 增加表示句子主语的词语
22) Much remains to be learned about Earth's carbon cycle and the role of the oceans as a "sink" for CO_2.
23) The immediate benefits of IC technology have been proven by previous study, including at least the followings.
24) Eventually these vehicles, which will be able to run on hydrogen extracted from conventional hydrocarbon fuel, are expected to displace petrol and diesel vehicles.
25) There are several ways to address the problem of energy management control.
26) To better show the effectiveness of the proposed controller, the performance of an uncontrolled vehicle which runs on the same road was also compared.
27) There is wide agreement that traffic should evolve into something that can be sustained in the future.

(4) 增加原文中省略的词语
28) The changes in matter around us are of two types, physical and chemical.
29) Typically, the "me too" crowd must offer unbelievable guarantees and warranties to differentiate their offerings from the other similar manufacturers.
30) First, there are private email conversations, similar to the conversations you have over the telephone.
31) The trouble is that other methods of reducing nitrogen-oxide emissinos depend on catalysts that react very badly to sulphur: it wears them out.
32) For car makers, at least, being smaller certainly seems more beautiful.
33) To meet both pollution reduction requirements and plant performance goals, these markets are demanding a more cost-effective, in-process approach, which optimizes the combustion system to prevent emission generation.
34) It might help to leave behind metaphors of highways and frontiers and to think instead of real estate.

(5) 增加具体和明确化的词语
35) No doubt, European car makers will give <u>Toyota</u> a tough battle for every inch of ground.
36) The growing season in <u>the northern U.S.</u> has lengthened by about a week.
37) The Lupo is billed as the world's first three-liter car— the number referring not the size of its engine, but to its <u>meager thirst</u>.

38) Beyond that the specific human effect on climate change will remain hauntingly indefinite until our knowledge increases and the models improve.
39) This promises to make diesel as quiet and smooth as petrol, while offering much greater fuel economy.
40) Most of the warming has taken place at night—presumably because increased cloud cover shades the land by day and traps outgoing heat at night.

(6) 增加起语气连贯作用的词语

41) Diskettes that contain a computer virus will spread the virus to the computer. The virus will infect any other diskettes placed in that computer later. Experts say that you should keep your information diskettes write-protected if you can.
42) Hydrogen combines with oxygen, water being formed.
43) Since they burn less fuel, diesel engines produce less carbon dioxide.
44) What makes cyberspace so alluring is precisely the way in which it's different from shopping malls, television, highways and other terrestrial jurisdictions.
45) Were there no gravity, there would be no air around the earth.
46) Possessing high conductivity of heat and electricity, aluminum finds wide application in industry.
47) In addition to copper, there are many other metals which are good conductors.

(7) 增加概括性词语

48) The units of "ampere", "ohm", and "volt" are named respectively after three scientists.
49) The frequency, wave length and speed of sound are closely related.
50) PCs are either desktops or portables.
51) The article summed up the new achievements made in electronic computers, artificial satellites and rockets.
52) The chief effects of electric currents are the magnetic, heating and chemical effects.

Unit 6　省　略
Omission

　　词的省译或叫省略法,指的是原文中的有些词在翻译时不译出来。在科技英语翻译中,省略是一种比较常见的现象。科技文章具有高度的准确性、客观性、衔接性和逻辑性。省略是最常用的避免重复和冗长的翻译技巧。译文中虽无其词,但已有其意,或是属于不言而喻,译出来反倒累赘或是违背译文的语言习惯。通过保留一个单词,而删除其他相同表意的重复单词就可以使文章变得精炼。省略译法的目的就是为了使译文简明扼要、通顺。

1. 冠词的省略

- Wind wave action causes the most significant changes to a beach.
  风浪作用引起海滩发生巨大改变。
- A sequence of construction and the time to be allotted for each item is then indicated.
  工序和工件完成时间随后标明。
- The speedy execution of the project requires the ready supply of all materials, equipment and labor when needed.
  加快施工需要随时提供所需的材料、设备和劳动力。
- The design of the immersed tunnel includes the structural design of tunnel elements, joints, foundations and tunnel protections.
  沉管隧道的设计范围包括沉管、接头、基础和隧道保护层的结构设计。
- The aim of this system is to warn the vehicle's driver and reduce the reaction time in case an emergency brake is necessary.
  本系统的目的是在紧急制动情况下警告汽车驾驶者,减少驾驶者的反应时间。
- The amount of time allotted for the selection of methods of operation and equipment is readily available to the contractor.
  承包商随时有时间挑选设备和试验操作方法。
- The planning phase starts with a detailed study of construction plans and specifications.
  规划阶段从详细研究施工计划和规范开始。

2. 代词的省略

- The desert animals can hide themselves from the heat during the daytime.
  沙漠中兽类能躲避白天的炎热天气。

- Steel and iron products are often coated lest they should rust.
  钢铁制品常常涂上一层保护物,以免生锈。
- Once the HE sensor data has been resolved into a discrete square wave, it is possible to re-create the forcing function produced by the rotating eccentric mass.
  一旦 HE 传感器的数据被解析成一个离散的方波,就可以重新建立由旋转偏心质量块产生的强制函数。
- As a result, the yaw moments generated by the guide tire radial forces on the leading truck are larger than those on the trailing truck.
  结果表明,前转向架上导向轮胎的径向力形成的横摆力矩比后转向架上的大。
- The aim of this research study is to design and develop an in-wheel motor that reduces the power loss and power transmission in the vehicles.
  研究的目的是设计和开发一款轮毂电机,减少汽车的功率损耗和电力传输。
- If you know the frequency, you can find the wave length.
  如果知道频率,就能求出波长。
- Different metals differ in their conductivity.
  不同的金属具有不同的导电性能。
- A gas distributed itself uniformly through a container.
  气体均匀地分布在整个容器中。
- The volume of the sun is about 1,300,000 times that of the earth.
  太阳的体积约为地球的 130 万倍。

3. 连词的省略

- As the temperature increase, the volume of water becomes greater.
  温度增高,水的体积就增大。
- A lot of variables have a distinct influence on the performance of the system and consequently the performance of the system will be different for each set of parameters.
  大量的变量对系统的性能有明显的影响,因此不同的参数系统的性能将不同。
- The average speed of all molecules remains the same, as long as the temperature is constant.
  温度不变,所有分子的平均速度也就不变。
- In contrast, the hanging-type monorail car hangs on the guideway and runs under it.
  相比之下,悬挂式单轨车悬挂在轨道上运行。
- The inner and outer rings are graded and stored according to size.
  内外圈是根据尺寸分类存放的。

4. 动词的省略

- Thus the selection, design and detailing of the connections in a building frame has a very sig-

nificant influence on costs.
因此,建筑框架的类型挑选、设计以及连接细节对造价影响极大。

➤ The wire gets hot, for the current becomes too great.
电线发热,因为电流太大。

➤ Second, the monorail makes much less noise than a rail vehicle because its wheels consist of rubber tires.
第二点,由于单轨车辆采用橡胶轮胎,所以它比铁路车辆的噪声小。

➤ Friction always opposes the motion whatever its direction may be.
不管运动方向怎样,摩擦力总是同运动方向相反。

➤ The charged capacitor behaves as a secondary battery.
充了电的电容器就像一个蓄电池一样。

➤ The system makes use of a far infrared thermal camera to search for the heat that the pedestrians emit in certain condition.
该系统使用远红外线热成像仪来搜寻行人在一定条件下散发的热。

➤ And because so few cases of oral transmission have been documented, doctors conclude that the same antiviral compounds in saliva and stomach acids that protect us from a host of germ prove very effective against HIV in low concentrations.
由于鲜有口头传播病例的记录,医生的结论是在唾液和胃酸中有相同的可以保护我们免受宿主细菌侵害的抗病毒化合物,这种物质的低浓度溶液可以非常有效地防止 HIV。

5. 介词的省略

➤ The first electronic computer was produced in our country in 1958.
1958 年我国生产了第一台电子计算机。

➤ The critical temperature is different for different kinds of steel.
不同种类的钢,临界温度各不相同。

➤ The common feature of these projects is that they are developed by using real cars to do some safe driving researches on certain aspects of the real car.
这些项目的共同特征是都使用真正的汽车来做某些方面的研究,以保证驾驶安全。

➤ Engineering analyses can be carried out based on the information gained from the site exploration and characterization program.
现场勘探和特征程序的信息可用于工程分析。

➤ Slopes that are too deep to stand unsupported can be supported by a retaining wall.
可修建挡土墙来支撑不能自持的陡坡。

➤ So the final design drawings and specifications reflect the combined expertise of many individuals.
因此,最终设计图纸和规范体现了个人专业综合技能。

➤ Slopes may be formed naturally by erosion or built by excavation or filing.

侵蚀、开挖或填筑这三种方法均可成坡。
- However, in comparison with the base case with constant flow exhaust ventilation, the heat loss is slightly more sensitive to changes in the environmental parameters.
  然而，基本条件的通风与恒流排气通风相比，热损失对环境参数变化更加敏感。
- Sometimes the conditions encountered during construction are different, and this may dictate appropriate changes in the design.
  有时在施工过程中遇到不同地质条件，可能迫使设计方案做出适当改变。
- Furthermore, the braking torques on the front wheels are limited by the driver request at about 3.35 seconds, and on the rear wheels at about 3.42 seconds, which gradually bring the vehicle to a stop within 5 seconds.
  此外，驾驶员施加前轮制动转矩的时间约 3.35 秒，后轮约 3.42 秒，从而逐渐使车辆在 5 秒内停止。

6. 非人称代词"it"的省略

- It is common knowledge that the weight is a pull exerted on an object by the earth.
  众所周知，重量是地球作用在物体上的引力。
- It is a man's social being that determines his thinking.
  是人的社会存在决定人的思想。
- Obviously, the study on the active safety of the running vehicle in the virtual environment is still insufficient, and it is worthy of developing indoor test-beds to research on intelligence vehicles.
  显然，在虚拟环境中对运行车辆的主动安全性的研究仍然滞后，因此，开发室内试验平台来研究智能车辆是有意义的。
- From very beginning, the engineer must consider aesthetics in selection of spans, depth of girders, piers and the relationship of one to another and it is a responsibility that cannot be delegated.
  工程师从一开始就必须在挑选跨径、梁高、墩高的时候考虑美观以及各部分之间的比例，这份责任无法推卸。
- In fact, it is not inconceivable that automobiles would be fueled directly with hydrogen at pumping stations.
  事实上，在水泵站用氢直接给汽车加燃料并非是难以想象的。
- The equivalence with PMP and DP justifies its use as an optimal strategy and allows to tune it more effectively.
  与 PMP 和 DP 算法的等价证明了它（ECMS）是最优策略并且允许通过调整来使效率更高。
- As Contam is a ventilation model only, it cannot calculate transient room or duct temperatures.
  Contam 只是一个通风模型，不能计算空间或管道的瞬态温度。

➢ The Golden Gate Bridge was the longest suspension bridge span in the world when <u>it</u> was completed during the year 1937.
金门大桥于 1937 年建成时，是当世界上最长的悬索桥。

➢ <u>It</u> has been declared one of the modern wonders of the world by the American Society of Civil Engineers.
美国土木工程师协会宣称这座桥是现代的世界奇观之一。

➢ <u>It</u> is worth to mention that the conclusions of this study cannot be expanded to all street canyons.
值得一提的是本研究的结论不能适用所有街道峡谷。

7. "there be…" 结构的省略

➢ As such, drum vibration was monitored on the right side only where <u>there was</u> access to a non-rotating mount.
同样地，也只对(钢轮)右边进行滚筒振动监测，因为这里能够进行非旋转挂载。

➢ <u>There are</u> some most usually used time-frequency methods, such as: short-time Fourier transform (STFT), wavelet, empirical mode decomposition (EMD).
一些最常用的时频方法，如：短时傅里叶变换(STFT)、小波、经验模式分解(EMD)。

➢ Therefore, <u>there is</u> an immediate need to develop a systematic IC data analysis and management method in order to better take advantage of the IC technology and accelerate its implementation.
因此，为了更好地利用智能压实技术并加快实施，需要立即开发一个系统性 IC 数据分析和管理方法。

➢ <u>There are</u> a number of studies on flow field around an isolated building in neutrally stable boundary layers.
在中间稳定边界层做独立建筑周围流场的研究很多。

➢ Because <u>there is</u> more air resistance, the diaphragm is heavier in a speaker with a 40mm diameter diaphragm and more power must be applied to drive it.
因为空气阻力增加，一个直径为 40mm 的振膜扬声器膜片会更重，驱动它需要更多的能量供给。

➢ <u>There is</u> wide agreement that traffic should evolve into something that can be sustained in the future.
人们广泛认为交通应该发展成未来可持续的事业。

➢ But <u>there's</u> been too little data to prove it.
但是数据太少，很难证实是否就是如此。

➢ On the other hand, <u>there is</u> energy conversion from electric energy to mechanical energy or vice versa.
另一方面，能量转化可以从电能转化成机械能，反之亦然。

8. 同义词或近义词的省略

> Semi-conductor devices have no filament or heaters and therefore require no heating power or warmed up time.
> 半导体器件没有灯丝,因此不需要加热功率或加热时间。
> The signed insurance contract will be null and void if one party failed to obey the utmost honesty principle.
> 如果合同一方违背诚信原则,签订的保险合同将无效。
> Any default and breach of contract will be claimed.
> 只要违约就会遭到索赔。
> It is essential that the mechanic or technician understand well the characteristics of battery circuits and cells.
> 很好地了解电池和电路特性对技术人员来讲十分重要。
> Simple bar soup neutralizes HIV by breaking the chemical bonds of its lipids, or fats.
> 简单的棒汤通过破坏 HIV(病毒)脂质的化学键使其失效。
> The emerging of uncertainties of input quantities leads to two different problems or questions.
> 输入量不确定性的出现导致两个不同的问题。
> There has been extensive research and development into high quality vehicle suspensions, particularly since the 1950s.
> 尤其是 20 世纪 50 年代以后,人们对高质量汽车悬架做了广泛的研究。
> ICMV relates to the stiffness of the pavement system with an influence depth that may go into underlying layers and even soil foundation, while density is a measurement of single HMA layer.
> ICMV 与路面系统的刚度相关,它的影响深度甚至可能进入土壤基层,而密度仅仅是单个 HMA 层的一个测量单位。
> 4WIA electric vehicles employ four in-wheel (or hub) motors to actuate the four wheels, and the torque and driving/braking mode of each wheel can be controlled independently.
> 四轮独立驱动电动汽车采用四个轮毂电机来控制四个车轮,各个车轮的转矩和驱动/制动模式可以独立控制。

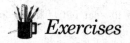
Exercises

Translate the following sentences according to the rules.

(1) 省略冠词

1) The rate of a chemical reaction is proportional to the concentration of the reacting substance.
2) The basic function of the triode is as an amplifier. (triode,三极管;amplifier,电流放大器)
3) It is a common tool used in geostatistics to describe spatial variation or uniformity. (geostatistics,统计学)

4) A virtual scene including roads and vehicles is developed by using the software.
5) Recent tests on the geometric stability of several digital cameras.
6) The results of the vehicle's calculated efficiency are depicted in Table 1.
7) The number and complexity of the connections have a decisive influence on the time for structural analysis and design.

(2) 代词的省略
8) The rest of the energy warms earth and fuels its weather engine.
9) Liquids are like solids in that they have definite volume.
10) When the signal we pick up has increased by 10 times as the gain may have been reduced by 8 times.
11) If we use electronic computers in hospitals, diagnosis will become quicker and more accurate.
12) Newton wasted much time on the theological studies toward the end of his life.
13) His left arm is paralyzed. He has no sensation in it.

(3) 连词的省略
14) The role of clouds is poorly understood, but they are known to both cool Earth by reflecting solar energy and warm Earth by trapping heat being radiated up from the surface.
15) Like charges repel each other while opposite charges attract.
16) In the abyssal zone, water temperatures are remarkably stable and remain virtually constant thought out the year.
17) The leaders will leave the copycat crowd behind, and will offer better products with tangible advantages。
18) If water is cold enough, it changes to ice.
19) Higher air temperatures can mean increased water evaporation and the melting of sea and land ice.
20) The microbes can also hide and multiply on sponges, cutting boards, dishtowels, sinks, knives, and countertops.
21) The salts of carbonic acid, or the carbonates, can be prepared by adding alkali to such aqueous solutions. (salts of carbonic acid,碳酸盐; alkali,碱; aqueous solutions,水溶液)
22) At the same time the Internet technology, optical fiber, Bluetooth technology and network technology will also be applied largely to cars, and further improving the car networking.

(4) 动词的省略
23) When heated, gases act in exactly the same way as liquid acts.
24) But in this age, it's hard to find a place where you can go and be yourself without worrying about the neighbors.
25) Positive force represents downward eccentric position and positive displacement is downward. (eccentric position,偏心块位置;positive displacement,正位移)
26) Just as Microsoft Word can be used to automate spell check, EHS professionals now have

tools at their disposal automatically to check air emissions data and information.

27) When the pressure gets low, the boiling-point becomes low.
28) From about 2007, environmentally friendly cars powered by fuel cells will begin to make an appearance.
29) The air we breathe keeps us alive in more ways than one.

(5) 介词的省略

30) Indeed, it might be good news for some farmers.
31) With each change, sundry species have benefited and flourished.
32) Their effects lift the death sentence of an HIV infection only for a time.
33) An overview of the instrumentation system is illustrated in Fig. 1.
34) In the future, nanotechnology will let us take off the boxing gloves.
35) This research study focuses on the design and development of a small-scale in-wheel motor for electric vehicles. (small-scale in-wheel motor, 小型电动汽车轮毂电机)
36) The war lasted four years before the North won in the end.
37) That means that diesel best fit in with the car makers' medium-term thinking about their industry.
38) Nearly all vehicles have a chime or speaker in the dashboard instrument cluster for various alert functions.
39) Three million people died of AIDS in 2000.
40) A comparison of the proposed detector with state-of-the-art methods is shown in Section 3.

(6) 非人称代词"it"的省略

41) It is possible that the warming observed during this century may have resulted from natural variations, even though the increase has been much more rapid than what the planet has been witnessed over the past hundred centuries.
42) It is common to analyze raw data as presented in Fig. 6.
43) It is not easy to determine which are governing and which are secondary or insignificant parameters.
44) The smaller the asteroid, the more it is influenced by Yarkovsky Effect.
45) Therefore, experts believe that it is vitally important to help people handle food properly.
46) It is necessary, then, to calibrate that sensibility.
47) It is widely believed that the contact stress is a main reason for road damage, especially for cracking and rutting. (contact stress, 接触应力; cracking and rutting, 裂缝和车辙)
48) It is estimated that today's well-equipped automobile uses more than 50 microcontroller units.
49) When solar energy penetrates the land surface, it is converted into heat, most of which radiates upward quickly.
50) It may take some convincing of the employees to accept this type responsibility and involvement but it will be worth the effort, I hope.

51) For vehicle suspension control problems, it is impossible to measure all state variables.

(7)"there be…"结构的省略

52) There is, however, a fly in the ointment。

53) Generally, there are two corresponding methods for developing vehicle test-beds.

54) There has been increasing interest in short-distance transportation systems in city areas, such as the LRT, subways and monorail.

55) On the other hand, there is evidence that some kinds of events could change climate radically in the span of decades.

56) There are two common approaches to solve deterministic optimal control problems.

57) There are other subtle examples of how individualist versus collectivist thinking plays out in national business cultures.

58) There has been extensive research and development into high quality vehicle suspensions, particularly since the 1950s.

(8)同义词或近义词的省略

59) China has become one of the world's largest importers of petroleum products, largely to fuel its burgeoning fleet of cars and trucks.

60) One is to fix or configure a real vehicle for actual road testing.

61) Heuristic methods do not involve explicit minimization or optimization; instead, the energy management is implemented with rules and regulations based on engineering intuition.

62) Typically, the "me too" crowd must offer unbelievable guarantees and warranties to differentiate their offerings from the other similar manufacturers.

63) I don't think of this as progress and I am not convinced the newly resurrected companies will last long enough to service the customers.

64) The government project is important and significant.

65) Technology is the application of scientific method and knowledge to industry to satisfy our material needs and wants.

Unit 7　反　　译
Negation

　　英汉翻译中有正译和反译两种技巧。所谓正译,是指把句子按照与英语相同的语序或表达方式译成汉语。而与之相对,反译是指把句子按照与英语相反的语序或表达方式译成汉语。正译与反译常常具有同义的效果,但有时候反译往往更符合汉语的思维方式和表达习惯,更为地道。

　　反译技巧常用在英汉否定表达中,英语在表达否定意义非常灵活复杂,在用词、语法和逻辑方面与汉语存在较大区别,英语否定句的范围和否定重点常要仔细区分。在英译汉时,往往需要将英语中正面表达的词或句子用汉语反面来表达,或英语从反面表达的词或句子用汉语正面来翻译。

1. 否定译成肯定

- A number which can be divided by 2 without remainder is an even number.
  能被2整除的数为偶数。
- There may be little or no oil left by the end of this century.
  到本世纪末,石油可能所剩无几或消耗殆尽。
- Those who do not remember the past are condemned to relive it.
  忘记过去的人,注定要重蹈覆辙。
- The fluid bearings never lose their accuracy.
  这些流体轴承的精度可永久保持。
- The advantages of nano-structured materials do not end here.
  纳米材料的优点还有很多。
- Until recently geneticists were not interested in particular genes.
  基因学家最近才开始关注特定的基因。
- No deposit will be refunded unless ticket produced.
  凭票退还押金。
- It was suggested that such devices should be designed and produced without delay.
  应该立即设计并生产这种设备。
- Ice is not as dense as water and it therefore floats.
  冰的密度比水小,所以能浮在水面上。
- These bacteria will not die until the temperature reaches 100℃.
  100℃的高温才能杀死这些细菌。

- Its importance can't be stressed too strongly.
  此事的重要性值得大力强调。
- Where no community sewer system exists, on-site disposal by an approved method is mandatory.
  如果社区缺乏污水处理系统，那么就强制采用已认可的现场处理方法。
- In summary, water resource management is the process of managing both the quantity and quality of the water used for human benefit without destroying its availability and purity.
  总之，水资源管理是对水的数量和质量的管理过程，使水为人类服务的同时保护水的可用性和纯净度。
- Existing utilities and buildings not only increase construction costs but also affect plants for the new construction of utilities.
  现有设施和建筑既增加了造价，也对建造新设施的厂房产生不利影响。

2. 肯定译成否定

- This is inefficient because the fuel is not always injected at the optimal pressure.
  由于燃料并非总在最佳压力下喷射，这种（工作方式的）效率不高。
- Compared with most other areas of civil engineering e.g. bridges, highways, water treatment facilities, coastal engineering design is less controlled by code requirements.
  与桥梁、公路、水处理设施等其他大多数土木工程领域相比较，规范对近岸工程设计的约束不严格。
- This is because of the less predictable nature of the marine environment and the relative lack of an extensive experience required to establish codes.
  这是因为海上环境的可预测性不高，并且缺乏建立相关规范的丰富经验。
- It is impractical to go about with a gas mask to treat impure air and with ear plugs to keep out the noise.
  戴着口罩应对污染空气，戴着耳塞防噪音是不切合实际的。
- Despite heavy rains in some regions, lack of rainfall in other regions brought a remarkable water shortage problem.
  尽管一些地区有强降雨，但在其他地区毫无降雨，造成了严重的缺水问题。
- Although the Chinese economy continues to grow at about 10% of gross domestic product (GDP), investments in urban construction are unable to meet demands in many cities.
  虽然中国经济以国内生产总值年均增长 10% 的增速持续发展，但是在许多城市，城市建设投资仍然不能满足需求。
- Figure 13 shows that the response amplitudes of front tire force with FRC tire model are slightly smaller than those with SPC model.
  图 13 显示，FRC 轮胎模型的前轮胎的响应幅值与 SPC 轮胎模型的响应幅值相差不大。
- Because the pump is not driven by the engine, the injection pressure can be optimised irrespec-

tive of the engine speed.

由于输油泵不再由发动机驱动，喷油压力可以达到最佳效果且不随发动机转速变化。

➤ There is little pre-existing natural immunity to H5N1 infection in the human population.

在人体内没有先天存在的天然的 H5N1 禽流感的抗体。

➤ The role of clouds is poorly understood but they are known to both cool Earth by reflecting solar energy and warm Earth by trapping heat being radiated up from the surface.

关于云的作用我们知道得不多，但是我们知道它能通过反射太阳能来冷却地球，并且通过吸收从地表辐射出来的热量来让地球升温。

➤ It will be good for the automotive industry here.

这对本地汽车工业没有坏处。

➤ There was a complete absence of information on the oil deposit in that area.

人们对该地区的石油储藏情况一无所知。

➤ The machine is far from being complicated.

这台机器一点也不复杂。

➤ The motor refused to start.

马达开不动（马达不能起动）。

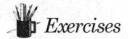

Exercises

Translate the following sentences based on the skills mentioned in this unit.

（1）否定译成肯定

1) An enhanced greenhouse effect may not necessarily be catastrophic.

2) Fi and Fb do not exist at the same time, and Fi doesn't exist on the horizontal road. (horizontal road, 水平坐标)

3) European auto makers such as Fiat, Adam Opel, and Ford, which can never seem to get out of the red, will feel the squeeze.

4) However, simply reducing ventilation rates has unwanted repercussions on the indoor air quality.

5) It is not easy to determine which are governing and which are secondary or insignificant parameters.

6) What is not in doubt, however, is the devastating effect humans are having on the animal and plant life of the planet.

7) No one knows for certain whether such things will happen.

8) However, the speed control of the SRM is not yet a perfected art. (SRM,开关磁阻电机)

9) What should not be overlooked are the vast changes taking place in automobile manufacturing.

10) The machine has two serious disadvantages.

11) There is no rule that has no exception.

(2) 肯定译成否定

12) The moon is a world that is <u>completely and utterly dead</u>, a <u>sterile</u> mountainous waste.
13) This drug is <u>contraindicated</u> in patients who are allergic to Penicillins.
14) Over 100 unites of this device have been ordered so far, and a complete listing <u>would require</u> too much space.
15) The mirror surface only needs cleaning <u>occasionally</u>.
16) There are many other energy sources <u>in store</u>.
17) In the high altitude snow and ice <u>remain</u> all year.
18) As rubber <u>prevents electricity from passing through</u> it, it is used as insulating material.
19) We have found your terms and conditions <u>agreeable</u>.
20) <u>More</u> instructions <u>should be contained</u> in this manual.
21) Sophisticated instruments <u>should be kept away from dust</u>.
22) An iron box <u>cuts off</u> the inside compass from the earth magnetic field.
23) It is <u>beyond our power</u> to sign this contract.
24) Their company is obviously <u>inferior to</u> their rival in product packaging and advertisement.

Unit 8　否定句的翻译
Translation of Negative Sentences

英汉两种语言在表达否定意义时,在语言习惯和表达方式上有很大差异。英语否定句种类繁多,形式灵活多变;汉语否定句相对固定、简单。本章将科技英语的全部否定、部分否定、双重否定、转移否定等英语中常见的表达否定的句式逐一列举出来,旨在帮助学习者弄清否定程度的差异,正确理解并能准确翻译英语否定句。

1. 全部否定

就现代英语中的完全否定而言,通常是由 no、not、none、no one、never、nobody、nothing、nowhere、neither...nor、not at all 等否定词构成,否定的是整体。

➢ Carbon dioxide does not burn, neither does it support burning.
二氧化碳既不自燃,也不助燃。

➢ Never is aluminium found free in nature.
铝在自然界从不以游离状态存在。

➢ Natural ventilation in urban streets canyons intersections is restricted because the bulk of flow does not enter inside and pollutants are trapped in the lower region.
自然通风在城市街道峡谷十字路口受到限制,因为大部分气流不能进入峡谷,污染物会聚集在下部区域。

➢ Since in a series of HEV there is no mechanical connection between the engine and the wheels, the engine speed can be set independently from the vehicle speed.
由于在一系列混合动力汽车中,发动机和车轮之间都没有机械连接,发动机速度可以独立于车辆速度之外进行设置。

➢ As a result, these models are not suited for detailed analysis of the distribution of contaminants in a single room.
因此,这些模型并不适用于详细分析污染物在一个房间的分布。

➢ Wheeled robot exhibits high velocity, but they can not climb over the obstacle higher than its radius of wheel.
轮式机器人速度快,但它们不能翻过障碍高于其车轮半径的地方。

➢ However, the active safety of the running vehicle is not taken into account at all.
然而,运行车辆的主动安全是不予考虑的。

➢ Due to the enormous heat capacity of the entire system, the temperature at the end of the shut-down is not equal to the ambient temperature.

由于整个系统的巨大热容量,在关闭时的温度不等于环境温度。

➢ Since the membership functions of the fuzzy controller must be tuned in a general sense and not based on the response of a specific driver or driver model, and also noting that the fuzzy controller is responsible only for the stability of the vehicle, the double-lane-change maneuver used in this work is performed as an open-loop driving test rather than a closed-loop test.

一般来讲,由于模糊控制器的隶属函数必须被调谐且不基于特定的驱动器或驱动模型的响应,并且模糊控制器只针对车辆的稳定性,所以本论文所用双移线工况是作为开环驾驶测试而不是闭环测试。

➢ Satellite surveying cannot take place indoors, nor can it take place underground.

卫星测量既不能在室内也不能在地下展开。

2. 部分否定

在英语中,当含有全体意义的代词或副词如 all、each、every(及其派生词)、both、always、often、entirely、wholly、some、many、every、everybody、everything 等用于否定式谓语的句子中的时候,构成部分否定句。

➢ Every electric motor here is not new.
这里的电机不全是新的。

➢ Both of the instruments are not digital ones.
这两种仪表不全是数字的。

➢ Every color is not reflected.
并非每种颜色都会反射回来。

➢ That goes for real life, too: genes are essential but not the whole story.
那也同样适用于真实生活:基因是必要的,但也不是全部。

➢ All the chemical energy of fuel is not converted into heat.
燃料化学能并未全部转化为热量。

➢ Not all bulk is spam.
并非所有的都是垃圾文件。

➢ Both the instruments are not precision ones.
这两台仪器并非都是精密仪器。

➢ Not everyone thinks the space station is a good idea.
并非每个人都觉得建立太空站是个好主意。

➢ Realistically speaking there are several fundamental questions we don't fully understand and have yet to answer: What causes the disease?
实际上,我们仍然有几个基本问题还没有完全理解,需要继续回答:什么导致了这种疾病?

➢ Notice that not all mechanical energy is kinetic energy.
要注意,并非所有的机械能都是动能。

3. 双重否定

双重否定即否定之否定,是两个否定词连用,否定统一单词,或一个否定词否定另一个否定词,其否定意义互相抵消而取得肯定意义,即我们常说的:"否定加否定等于肯定"。

- There is <u>no</u> modern communication mean that has <u>no</u> disadvantage.
  <u>没有</u>哪种现代通信手段<u>是没有</u>缺点的(现代通信手段都有缺点)。
- <u>Without</u> gravity there would be <u>no</u> sound of any kind.
  没有重力作用,就<u>不会</u>有任何声音(有重力作用才会有声音)。
- But the gains <u>won't</u> come <u>without</u> pain.
  但是<u>没有</u>牺牲就<u>没有</u>进步(但是有牺牲才会有进步)。
- What should <u>not</u> be <u>overlooked</u> are the vast changes taking place in automobile manufacturing.
  <u>不容忽视</u>的是在汽车制造业正在发生巨大的变化(我们应该看到汽车制造业正在发生巨大的变化)。
- A radar screen is <u>not unlike</u> a television screen.
  雷达荧光屏跟电视荧光屏<u>没什么不一样</u>(雷达荧光屏跟电视荧光屏一样)。
- <u>No</u> flow of water occurs <u>unless</u> there is a difference in pressure.
  <u>没有</u>压差,水就<u>不会</u>流动(有压差,水才会流动)。
- Though often beneficial, mindless use of antibiotics is <u>not without</u> hazard.
  使用抗生素虽然非常有好处,但如果盲目使用,就<u>难免没有</u>害处(使用抗生素虽然非常有好处,但如果盲目使用,也会有害)。
- Sodium is <u>never</u> found <u>uncombined</u> in nature.
  自然界中<u>从未发现不</u>处于化合状态的钠(自然界中的钠被发现都处于化合状态)。
- It is <u>not impossible</u> to control industrial waste waters to preserve the usefulness of the receiving water.
  <u>不是不可能</u>控制工业废水以保护进水的可用性(完全可以控制工业废水以保护进水的可用性)。
- There has <u>not</u> been a scientist of eminence <u>but</u> was a man of industry.
  <u>没有哪一个</u>有成就的科学家<u>不是</u>勤奋的(所有卓越的科学家都非常勤奋)。
- The profile will be perceived as a long, continuous line or ribbon of slender bridge spans <u>without</u> aesthetically <u>unpleasing</u> kinks.
  从纵截面看,桥梁的连续跨细长,看起来活像一条连续的线条或一条丝带,让绞结看上去<u>没有</u>感觉<u>不</u>美观(从纵截面看,桥梁的连续跨细长,看起来活像一条连续的线条或一条丝带,让绞结看上去非常漂亮)。
- <u>Without</u> this much of the opportunity for reducing risk, lowering cost, improving schedule and reducing delay and conflict brought about by the design, the build process <u>is lost</u>.
  <u>如果没有</u>如此多的机会可以降低风险、减少成本、加快工期、减少延误以及设计引起的冲突,施工过程就肯定<u>不会成功</u>(有如此多的机会降低风险、减少成本、加快工期、减少延误

以及设计引起的冲突,施工过程就肯定成功)。

4. 形式上的否定意义上的肯定

英语中有些句子形式上是否定的,但是内容含义上却是肯定的。常见的形式否定,意义肯定的固定句子结构有:

①cannot wait 后跟不定式,意为"急于做",表示强调的肯定。

②cannot/couldn't + too 意为"越……越……,非常,无论怎样……也不过分"。在此结构中,cannot 也可改用 can hardly、scarcely、never、impossible,too 也可改用 over、enough 等。

③not…until/ till…意为"直到……的时候才"。

④never (not)…but (that)…意为"每当……,总是……,没有哪次不是……"。

⑤not long before 意为"不久……就……"。

⑥no (none) other than 意为"仅仅,完全"。

⑦nothing like…意为"没有什么比得上…"。

⑧no/not/nothing + more + than 意为"不过"。

⑨no/not/nothing + less + than 意为"多达"。

⑩can not/ could not…more 意为"完全"。

➤ It was probably not until the 1880's that man, with the help of a more advanced steam locomotive, managed to reach a speed of one hundred mph.
直到 19 世纪 80 年代,人们才在更加先进的蒸汽火车头的帮助下,成功达到每小时 100 英里的时速。

➤ It was not until about 1600 BC when the chariot was invented that the maximum speed was raised to roughly twenty miles per hour.
直到公元前 17 世纪双轮马拉战车发明后,最快速度才被提高到每小时约 20 英里。

➤ The maximum power of this module is 300W and its efficiency is no less than 17%.
这个模块的最大功率是 300W,其效率高达 17%。

➤ Beyond that the specific human effect on climate change will remain hauntingly indefinite until our knowledge increases and the models improve.
除此之外,直到我们的知识增长和科研模型得到改进时,人类对气候变化的具体影响才能被确定。

➤ No doubt, European car makers will give Toyota a tough battle for every inch of ground.
欧洲的汽车生产商肯定会与丰田展开一场寸土必争的激烈市场竞争。

➤ An explosion is nothing more than a tremendously rapid burning.
爆炸只不过是非常急速的燃烧。

➤ It cannot be too much emphasized that agriculture is the foundation of the national economy.
农业是国民经济的基础,怎样强调也不会过分。

➤ That scientist has no small chance of success.

那位科学家很有可能会成功。
- Some oil wells produce nothing but salt water, while others always remain dry.

  有些油井只产盐水，而另一些油井却总是干的。

5. 含蓄否定

含蓄否定指英语中有些词或短语不与否定词连用，并且从句子的形式上也看不出任何否定的迹象，但其意义却是否定的。含蓄否定主要通过词汇、语法或修辞手段来表示。比如：lack, fail, deny, miss, neglect, avoid, decline, refuse, absence, failure, exclusion, deficiency, without, beyond, beside, against, above, beneath, above, hardly, seldom, few, little, instead of, but for, short of, free from, absent, blind, foreign to, last, too...to(for)..., rather than, more than, out of 等。

- Short of transformers, they make their own in their lab.

  没有变压器，他们在实验室自己制作。

- It is the last type of machine for such a job.

  这是最不适合这种作业的机器。

- The system of power supply in the city leaves much to be desired.

  该市的供电系统非常不完善。

- This lack of uniformity of the force of gravity results from a number of factors.

  引力的这种非均匀性是由许多因素引起的。

- The modern technique has made it possible to keep liquid hydrogen from being dangerously explosive.

  现代技术已能使液态氢不致发生危险的爆炸。

- It is a common expression to characterize something as "light as air", but air is hardly "light".

  通常人们总形容某个东西"轻如空气"，其实空气并不轻。

- And the assembly line—the organization of large numbers of men to carry out simple repetitive functions—is outdated.

  装配线——许多人在一起完成简单重复的工作，已不流行（过时）了。

- Geology is by no means without practical importance in relation to the needs and industries of mankind.

  地质学在涉及人类的需要和生产方面绝非毫无重要实际意义。

- The company declines, for competitive reasons, to identify the chemicals it uses to produce this polymer.

  出于竞争上的考虑，这家公司拒不披露生产这种聚合物所用的化学配方。

- Because the loads on the guide tires and the stabilizing tires are much smaller than those on the running tires, the contact force on the guide tire and the stabilizing tire can be neglected and only the contact force on the running tire should be considered.

  因为导向轮和稳定轮上的载荷比滚动轮要小很多，所以在导向轮胎和稳定轮胎上的接触力可以忽略不计,只考虑滚动轮上的接触力。

> If the wind speed out of the canyon is below some threshold value, the coupling between the upper and secondary flow is lost.

如果峡谷外的风速低于临界值,就不会有上层和二层的重合区域。

> As opposed to separate, vertical twin-shaft piers, the single-shaft piers provide less visual blocking and a lighter aesthetic weight when viewed at an oblique angle.

与分离式竖向双墩相反,从倾斜角度看起来,单墩墩身不会阻挡视线,看起来更为轻盈,因此更美观。

6. 转移否定

汉语句子中的否定重点一般是在否定词的后面,而英语却不然。英语句子中的否定词虽然往往位于谓语、主语、宾语等成分之前,但在意思上否定的却不一定甚至不是这些成分。因此在翻译时,需要把原文对于某一成分的否定转移到汉译中的另一成分的否定上去,这样才符合汉语的表达逻辑。否定的转移是指英语否定句在句中某一部分(常在谓语部分),但在语义上却是否定另一部分的现象。翻译这类句子时不要单纯依赖语法分析,而应从语义上分析,根据上下文理解句意。

> Nobody can set in motion without having a force act upon it.

如果不让力作用于物体上,就不能使物体运动。

> The motor did not stop because the electricity was off.

电机停止运转,并非因为电源切断了。

> No energy can be created, and none destroyed.

能量既不能创造,也不能毁灭。

> Most of all, a tunnel exists because there is demonstrated need: to move people or material where no other means is practical or adequate, or to accomplish the required movement more directly, more quickly, or less obtrusively.

首先,隧道之所以存在是因为对其需求是显而易见的:在其他任何方式都不实用、不充足或者不能直接、迅速或畅通无阻地完成运输任务的情况下,运送旅客或材料。

以动词think、suppose、believe、seem、expect、feel、anticipate等作谓语且后接不定式短语的否定句中,经常会出现否定转移现象。

> Liquids, except for liquid metal such as mercury, are not considered to be good conductors of heat.

除了液体金属如水银外,其他液体被认为是热的不良导体。

某些动词如believe、consider、regard、suppose、think、remember等否定式后带有从句或宾语补足语,否定往往转移至从句或宾语补足语。

> They do not consider that pure science is more important than applied science.

他们认为纯科学并不比应用科学更重要。

- Although the Japanese giant regularly ranks first in a variety of quality surveys across the Europe, consumers don't perceive Toyota as the quality leader.

  尽管日本品牌的车在欧洲的各项质量调查中经常拔得头筹,顾客仍认为丰田车的质量并不是最好的。

- Most people do not think that food poisoning can possibly occur in their home.

  大多数人认为食物中毒不可能发生在家里。

- I don't think of this as progress and I am not convinced the newly resurrected companies will last long enough to service the customers.

  我认为这不是进步,我相信刚刚复兴的公司不会长时间持续地服务客户。

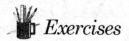

Exercises

Translate the following sentences according to rules picked up in this unit.

(1) 全部否定

1) No one knows for certain whether such things will happen.
2) This is no conversation about the lunch menu but a review of outbreaks nationwide of disease caused by food.
3) Complicating matter is the fact that there are no obvious solutions to the problem.
4) Solar energy is clean, quiet, abundant, and renewable energy source, which produces no pollution to the environment.
5) The virtual bodies were assumed to have no mass.
6) But cannot depict the actual cause for the instability.
7) People are taking serious notice, but no one has a good plan to combat it.
8) Despite decades of scientific research, no one yet knows how much damage human activity has brought to the environment.
9) Clearly, it makes no economic sense to delay harvest.
10) None of these transgenic animals have yet entered the market.
11) We haven't created a perfect society on earth, and we won't have one in cyberspace either.
12) They (infrared images) do not depend on the illumination of the scene.
13) Genetic modification is not novel.

(2) 部分否定

14) The fuel is not always injected at the optimal pressure.
15) It doesn't always get into our food, but when it does, it can cause encephalitis or meningitis in people with vulnerable immune systems and, in pregnant women, miscarriage or stillbirth.
16) Not all uncertainties really matter in the end.
17) There are a large number of variables of interest and it has not been possible to investigate all of them thoroughly here.

18) The environment is not fully controlled, so there is always an unknown probability of encountering an obstacle.
19) However, not all of the problems associated with the first generation systems have been overcome.
20) Opportunities come to all, but all are not ready for them when they do come.

(3) 双重否定

21) There is no rule that has no exception.
22) There is not any advantage without disadvantage.
23) Using this procedure the uncertainties having a lower impact on the failure probability are not ignored.
24) But the gain won't come without pain.
25) In fact, it is not inconceivable that automobiles would be fueled directly with hydrogen at pumping stations.
26) One body never exerts a force upon another without the second reacting against the first.
27) It is impossible for heat to be converted into a certain energy without something lost.
28) Bearings should not be unboxed or unwrapped until the moment for fitting has arrived.
29) Physiologic process cannot take place if there is not sufficient water.
30) A body at rest will never move unless it is acted on by an external force.

(4) 形式上的否定意义上的肯定

31) In a society that values individualism, workers will question the new method and probably not sign on until they figure out how it will directly impact them as individuals.
32) But we won't know for certain until the end of the year, when we have results from the first trail, begun in 1998—1999, in Europe and North America.
33) A person infected with HIV does not have AIDS immediately until the virus seriously damages his immune system, making it vulnerable to a range of infections, some of which can lead to death.
34) An enhanced greenhouse effect may not necessarily be catastrophic.
35) There is nothing like mineral water to quench one's thirst.
36) Pesticides can cause a lot of harm, so you can never be too careful when using pesticides.
37) These scientists could not believe the Curies more.
38) No less than 25 percent of the crops are polluted.
39) The importance of proper lubrication cannot be overemphasized.

(5) 含蓄否定

40) There is, however, a fly in the ointment.
41) Sustainable management is seen as a practical and economical way of protecting species from extinction.
42) But protease inhibitor, often combined with other HIV drugs such as AZT, is far from prevention or cure.

43) Since most legitimate businesses recognize the public's strong anti-spam sentiment, they <u>avoid</u> using it.

44) The role of clouds is <u>poorly understood</u>, but they are known to both cool Earth by reflecting solar energy and warm Earth by trapping heat being radiated up from the surface.

45) Spam is <u>rarely</u> sent directly by an advertiser.

46) Women in the developing world have <u>little</u> leverage to negotiate safe sex with their partners and are often abused for trying.

47) We find that they frequently fall into avoidable error because of a <u>failure</u> to reason correctly.

(6) 转移否定

48) After an insulator has been electrified, the electricity <u>does not</u> move through the insulator as it would through a conductor.

49) These free electrons usually <u>do not</u> move in a regular way.

50) Contrary to what is often thought, the earth <u>does not</u> move round in the empty space.

51) It is imperative to emphasize that <u>no</u> patient with a marked stridor should be submitted to general anaethesia. (marked stridor,明显喘鸣; general anaethesia,全身麻醉)

52) In general, <u>no</u> new substance forms in a physical change.

53) The engine did <u>not</u> stop because the fuel was finished.

54) The planets do <u>not</u> go around the sun at a uniform speed.

55) We <u>don't</u> consider melting to be chemical changes.

56) The doctors <u>do not</u> expect that the patient with breast cancer will recover.

Unit 9　被动语态的翻译
Translation of Passive Voice

被动语态在科技英语中使用非常广泛,其原因有二:一是被动语态比主动语态主观色彩更少,更能客观地反映事实,这正是科技产品所需要的;二是被动语态比主动语态更能说明需要论证的对象,因为在被动句中,所需论证、说明的对象充当句子的主语,其位置鲜明、突出,更能引起读者的注意。但由于被动语态在英语与汉语中的表达方式上的差异,如科技英语中用被动语态表达的概念在汉语中却常用主动语态来表示,这就给被动语态句子的翻译带来了较大的困难。因此,在翻译科技英语的被动语态句子时必须掌握一定的方法和技巧,才能译出忠于原文的地道的译文。对于英语原文的被动结构,我们一般采用下列的方法:

1. 译成汉语主动句

1) 原文中的主语在译文中仍做主语

在采用此方法时,我们往往在译文中使用了"加以""经过""用……来"等词来体现原文中的被动含义。

➤ In other words, mineral substances which are found on earth must be extracted by digging, boring holes, artificial explosions, or similar operations which make them available to us.
换言之,矿物就是存在于地球上,但须经过挖掘、钻孔、人工爆破或类似作业才能获得的物质。

➤ Nuclear power's danger to health, safety, and even life itself can be summed up in one word: radiation.
核能对健康、安全、甚至对生命本身构成的危险可以用一个词——辐射来概括。

➤ Two different lifetime limiting effects have been addressed, namely creep rupture and low cycle fatigue.
两种不同的限制寿命的影响已经解决,即蠕变断裂和低周期疲劳。

➤ This equation can be solved to obtain the controller parameters K_p and T_e.
这个等式可以用来获得该控制器的两个参数 K_p 和 T_e。

➤ A clear advantage of unidirectional converters regarding complexity compared with bidirectional converters is only given for three level converters.
跟双向变换器的复杂性程度相比,单向变换器一个显著的优点就是拥有三相层变换器。

➤ Natural ventilation in urban streets canyons intersections is restricted because the bulk of flow does not enter inside and pollutants are trapped in the lower region.

在城市街道峡谷十字路口自然通风受到限制是因为大部分气流无法进入峡谷,污染物会聚集在下部区域。

➢ The swirl diffuser was simulated as a rectangular shape divided into nine small cells.
涡流扩散器被模拟为九个矩形的小隔舱。

➢ The rule base of the fuzzy controller is developed from expert knowledge, and a multi-criteria genetic algorithm is used to optimize the parameters of the fuzzy active steering controller.
模糊控制器的规则库是通过专业知识开发的,并且多标准遗传算法被用来优化模糊主动转向控制器的参数。

➢ In addition, an elite selection rate of 2% was employed to ensure that the fittest chromosomes were retained unaltered from one generation to the next.
此外,2%的优选率确保染色体优胜劣汰。

➢ These criteria can be best met by the discharge of domestic sewage to an adequate public or community sewerage system.
将生活污水倒入公共或社区排水系统,从而完全满足规范要求。

➢ The storage reservoir may be elevated, or it may be at ground level. The stored water is used to meet high demand during the day.
可升高水库蓄水的水位,或保持与地面齐平。蓄水可用于满足白天较大的用水量需求。

2) 原文中的主语在译文中作宾语,并增译主语

增译的主语一般是"大家、我们、人们、他们、有人"等。另外下列结构也是通过这一手段翻译:

It is asserted that...   有人主张……

It is believed that...   有人认为……

It is generally considered that...   大家(一般人)认为

It is well known that...   大家知道(众所周知)……

It will be said...   有人会说……

It was told that...   有人曾经说……

It is considered that...   我们认为……

It is defined as ...   把……定义/解释为……

It is reported that ...   报道说……

➢ A variety of parameters within these shapes were investigated, including the depth of the walls around the courtyard, the presence of openings in the walls, the effects of wind direction, the presence of surface clutter and stratification of the air in the courtyard.
我们研究了多种形状内的参数,包括中庭壁面高度、墙壁上存在开口的情况、风向的影响、壁面存在的扰动以及多层空气分布。

➢ A nonlinear tri-axle vehicle model with IBS (integral balanced suspension) is firstly proposed based on the detailed analysis of structural features of a heavy vehicle (DFL1250).

基于重型车辆(DFL1250)结构特性的详细分析,<u>我们首先提出了包含整体平衡悬架的非线性三轴车辆模型</u>。

➢ <u>The semivariogram model was studied</u> to evaluate the compaction uniformity, and <u>the compaction curve was developed</u> to identify the optimum number of roller passes.

<u>我们研究出半变异函数</u>用以评估压实均匀性,并且<u>开发出压实曲线</u>来确定辊道的最佳数目。

➢ Generally, however, <u>it is considered</u> that solid waste is a problem to be solved as cheaply as possible rather than a resource to be recovered.

但是,<u>我们一般认为</u>固体垃圾是一个问题,这一问题应尽可能采用经济的方法来解决,而不是将固体垃圾作为资源回收。

➢ Silver <u>is known to</u> be better than copper in conductivity.

<u>大家知道</u>银的导电性比铜好。

➢ <u>It could be argued</u> that the radio performs this service as well, but on television everything is much more living, much more real.

<u>可能有人会指出</u>,无线电广播同样也能做到这一点,但还是电视屏幕上的节目要生动、真实得多。

➢ Television, <u>it is often said</u>, keeps one informed about current events, allows one to follow the latest developments in science and politics, and offers an endless series of programs which are both instructive and entertaining.

<u>人们常说</u>,电视使人了解时事,熟悉政治和科学领域的最新发展变化,并能源源不断地为观众提供各种既有教育意义又有趣的节目。

➢ <u>It is generally accepted</u> that the experiences of the child in his first years largely determine his character and later personality.

<u>人们普遍认为</u>,孩子们的早年经历在很大程度上决定了他们的性格及其未来的人格。

➢ <u>It is concerned about</u> reclaiming the city, re-establishing personal and collective roots and in general, the re-enchantment of the city through the re-enchantment of identity and community.

<u>人们关心的是</u>改造城市,重建个人和集体的根,通俗地说,就是通过重塑个人和集体魅力来重塑城市的魅力。

➢ <u>It is well known that</u> especially the location of the cooling channels has a significant influence on the mechanical integrity of the blades.

<u>众所周知</u>,尤其是冷却通道的位置对叶片的机械完整性有重要影响。

➢ And <u>it is imagined</u> that the operations of the common mind can be by no means compared with these processes, and that they have to be acquired by a sort of special training.

<u>许多人认为</u>,普通人的思维活动根本无法与(科学家的)思维过程相比,而且认为科学家的思维过程必须经过某种专门的训练才能掌握。

3）原文中的主语在译文中做宾语，而原文中的行为主体、用作状语的介词短语或其他词语则相应地译成主语

- A right kind of fuel is needed for an atomic reactor.
  原子反应堆需要一种合适的燃料。
- By the end of the war, 800 people had been saved by the organization, but at a cost of 200 Belgian and French lives.
  战争结束时，这个组织以二百多个比利时人和法国人的生命为代价，拯救了800人。
- Separation is a critical design consideration—as a speaker diaphragm vibrates, sound waves are produced by the front and back of the diaphragm.
  分离是关键的设计考虑，当扬声器膜片振动时，膜片前部和后部都能产生声波。
- The body frame was located on each rigid body and moves along the guideway.
  在每个刚体上建立物体坐标系，并沿着导轨运动。
- Drum and frame vibration was monitored in three dimensions using accelerometers.
  加速度计监测钢轮和机架三个方向的振动。
- Local wind flows inside the street canyons are greatly affected by the mechanical turbulence induced by moving vehicles.
  行驶汽车产生的机械湍流会对街道峡谷内的气流产生巨大影响。

4）原文中的主语在译文中做宾语，译成无主句

另外，下列结构也可以通过这一手段翻译：

It is hoped that...　　　希望……
It is reported that...　　据报道……
It is supposed that...　　据推测……
It may be said without fear of exaggeration that...　　可以毫不夸张地说……
It must be admitted that...　　必须承认……
It must be pointed out that...　　必须指出……
It will be seen from this that...　　由此可见……

- It should be mentioned that the average static pressure in the exhaust air vent is supposed to be equal to the atmospheric pressure.
  值得一提的是，排风口的平均静压力应等于大气压力。
- Great efforts should be made to inform young people especially the dreadful consequences of taking up the habit.
  应该尽最大努力告诫年轻人吸烟的危害，特别是吸上烟瘾后的可怕后果。
- By this procedure, different honeys have been found to vary widely in the sensitivity of their inhibition to heat.

通过这种方法发现不同种类的蜂蜜的抑热敏感程度也极为不同。

➤ Many strange new means of transport have been developed in our century, the strangest of them being perhaps the hovercraft.
在本世纪研制了许多新奇的交通工具,其中最奇特的也许就是气垫船了。

➤ In order to obtain the desired research goals, a tire model which predicts tire saturation and accounts for varying normal loadings and camber changes is needed.
为了得到预期的研究目的,需要一个预测轮胎的饱和度并解释各种正常加载和曲线变化的轮胎模型。

➤ The car body and the two trucks (leading truck and trailing truck) were assumed to be rigid bodies with lateral, roll, and yaw degrees of freedom.
假设车体和两个转向架(前、后转向架)是具有侧向、旋转、侧偏自由度的刚体。

➤ At the first stage, when solving the problem about a beam under the action of the simplest moving load such as a moving weight, two fundamental methods can be used.
在第一阶段,解决在诸如运动重力的最简单动载荷作用下梁的运动特性的问题,可以使用两种基本方法。

➤ It can be seen from Figure 13 that the normalized 4WS input curve is very similar to the 2WS curve.
从图 13 可以看出规范化的四轮转向系统的输入曲线和两轮转向系统输入曲线非常相似。

➤ In [1] it is shown that the required increase in pipe size in order to obtain proper separation of air from water.
在[1]中可以看到,需要增加管道口径以便能够更好地从水中分离出气体。

➤ It is reported that no maintenance was applied on the shaft during operation life.
据称,在驱动轴工作年限内不需要进行维修。

➤ It can be seen that LGC generates fewer edges than the others but misses some important edges and their strength is reduced for the noisy images.
由此可见,较其他方法而言,LGC 法可产生更少的边缘,但丢失许多重要边界,其强度在噪声图像中减弱。

➤ It was found that for this machine the predicted cogging torque is exceptionally low (0.025% of rated torque), as illustrated in Figure 5.
研究发现,本机的预期齿槽转矩非常低(为额定转矩的 0.025%),如图 5 所示。

➤ It is widely believed that the contact stress is a main reason for road damage, especially for cracking and rutting.
普遍认为,接触应力是导致路面损坏的主要原因,尤其是路面的裂缝和车辙。

➤ However, it has to be pointed out that further research into cost management and profit analysis is needed to make the retailer and supplier continuable system more perfect.
但是,需要指出的是,有必要对成本管理和赢利分析展开更深入的研究,使零售商及供应商的可持续系统更完善。

5) 把主语并入谓语合译

英语中有些成语动词含有名词(如 make use of、pay attention to 等)变成被动语态时可将该名词作主语,这是一种特殊的被动语态。汉译时,可以将主谓合译,译成汉语无主句的谓语。

➢ Attention must be paid to environmental protection in developing economy.
发展经济必须注意环境保护。
➢ Care should be taken not to damage the instruments.
注意不要损坏仪器。
➢ Care must be taken to reduce the coal to fine powers.
必须注意,把煤碎成细粉末。
➢ Account should be taken of the low melting point of this substance.
应该考虑到这种物质的熔点低。
➢ Stress must be laid on the development of the electronics industry.
必须强调电子工业的发展。

2. 译成汉语被动句

英语中的许多被动句可以翻译成汉语的被动句。常用"被""给""遭""挨""为……所""使""由……""受到"等表示。

➢ Early fires on the earth were certainly caused by nature, not by man.
地球上早期的火,肯定是由大自然而不是人类引燃的。
➢ Columns are defined as members that carry loads chiefly in compression.
柱被定义为主要承载压力的构件。
➢ These signals are produced by colliding stars or nuclear reactions in outer space.
这些讯号是由外层空间的星球碰撞或者核反应所造成的。
➢ Natural light or "white" light is actually made up of many colors.
自然光或者"白光"实际上是由许多颜色组成的。
➢ The behavior of a fluid flowing through a pipe is affected by a number of factors, including the viscosity of the fluid and the speed at which it is pumped.
流体在管道中流动的情况,受到诸如流体黏度、泵送速度等各种因素的影响。
➢ Therefore, a fuzzy adaptive PI controller was designed for the position control.
因此,模糊自适应 PI 控制器被用作位置控制。
➢ It has been applied to the probabilistic assessment of a gas turbine disk.
这种方法已经被应用于燃气轮机涡轮盘的概率评估。
➢ The acceleration of gravity is subtracted from the vertical acceleration data.
重力加速度被从垂直加速度中减去。
➢ The vehicle frame, used to calculate the relative displacement and the relative velocity, was as-

sumed to be located on the car body frame.
计算相对位移和相对速度的车辆坐标系被假设为固定在车体坐标系上。
- A novel feature of the method is that the PSDs of various suspension responses can be obtained accurately and efficiently from the PSD of the road input.
这个(仿真)方法的新的特点是,当输入一个路面功率谱密度激励时,各种悬架所响应的功率谱密度就被准确而高效地获得了。(PSD = Power Spectral Density,功率谱密度)。
- Correspondingly, the lower or upper output capacitor is charged, and thus the two output voltages—UPM and UMN—can be balanced.
相应地,下位或者上位段输出电容被充电,所以才能平衡 UPM 和 UMN 这两项输出电压。
- Vehicle dynamics is influenced by several uncertain conditions (weather, road, state, etc.) and perturbations (aerodynamic drag forces, undesirable yaw moments, etc).
车辆动力学受到几个不确定条件(天气、道路、状态等)以及扰动因素(空气动力阻力、不利的横摆力矩等)的影响。
- A severe double-lane-change maneuver with obstacle avoidance was used to evaluate the effectiveness of each candidate controller.
严格的避障双移线工况被用来评估每个备选(主动转向)控制器的有效性。
- The largest storm surge, however, was produced by waters from Lake Borgne which has been raised by the onshore storm surge from the Gulf.
海湾近岸的风暴涌浪使伯根湖的水位升高,湖水进而产生了最大的风暴涌浪。
- The levees in this area were simply overwhelmed and were massively eroded.
该地区的防洪堤被淹没,因而受到极大侵蚀。
- Large developed areas within all of the main polders were flooded, and they remained inundated for considerable periods of time before levee breaches could be repaired and the waters pumped out.
在所有主要围垦区中的大片填筑遭洪水淹没,这些地区在很长一段时间一直浸泡在水中,直到大坝缺口被修补以及水被抽干。

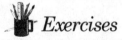
Exercises

1. Search the sentences with passive voice in your professional papers and translate them with skills in this unit.

2. Translate the following sentences based on the skills concerned.

(1)译成主动句:
原文中的主语在译文中仍做主语
1) By selectively passing up to half the exhaust gas back through the engine, the amount of oxygen available for combustion can be reduced.
2) This is inefficient, because the fuel is not always injected at the optimal pressure.
3) The existing prediction methods can be roughly classified into experience-based methods, model-based (or physics-based modals) and data-driven methods.

4) But because the pump is driven by the engine, the injection pressure rises and falls along with the engine speed.
5) Virtual technology is widely utilized in various vehicle test-beds.
6) Third, the monorail system can be built in crowded city areas because its cars can follow sharp curves and high gradients.
7) Ventilation is ambiguously related to the energy saving rationale originating from the mitigation of global warming.
8) In active probing, special testing signals are injected into an unenergized phase. (unenergized phase, 未被激活的相电路)
9) Detection is achieved by searching for distributions of temperatures in the scene similar to that of the human body.
10) When a vehicle is travelling on the road surface, the random vibration excited by the uneven road profile is transferred to the vehicle body through tire and suspension system. (suspension system, 悬架系统)

原文中的主语在译文中作宾语,并增译主语

11) To explore the moon's surface, rockets were launched again and again.
12) If one of more electrons be moved, the atom is said to be positively charged.
13) Yet another refinement, exhaust-gas-recirculation (EGR), is being adopted as a way to cutting the amount of nitrogen oxide produced by diesel engines.
14) The measurement techniques are explained in detail, and experimental data is presented to demonstrate the nature of the responses observed during field testing.
15) Control signals are read out by invoking library function MLIB/MTRACE of dSPACE. (library function, 库函数)
16) The car body and the two trucks (leading truck and trailing truck) were assumed to be rigid bodies with lateral, roll, and yaw degrees of freedom.
(truck, 转向架;rigid body, 刚体;lateral, roll, and yaw degrees of freedom, 侧向、旋转、侧偏自由度)
17) At the first stage, when solving the problem about a beam under the action of the simplest moving load such as a moving weight, two fundamental method scan be used.
18) The focus is shifted towards "green" or sustainable buildings, seeking concepts that allow to maintain or even further increase the comfort level that we are accustomed to, while significantly reducing the associated energy use in every aspect of human life.
19) The concepts and quantitative expressions of the steering sensibility, and steering operation stability are introduced.
20) Community standards should be enforced, but those standards should be set by cyberspace communities themselves, not by the courts or by politicians in Washington.
21) It is found that only the second method, that is the "engine" functions reading DS1103 board interface data through MLIB/MTRACE, is successful.

22) However, it has been known that conventional PI controllers generally do not work well for nonlinear systems.

原文中的主语在译文中做宾语,而原文中的行为主体、用作状语的介词短语或其他词语则相应地译成主语

23) But because the pump is driven by the engine, the injection pressure rises and falls along with the engine speed.

24) The methods of signal processing are introduced in Section 2.

25) In the present paper, the above problem is solved by using the method for the moving load analysis and a step procedure of integration with respect to time. (moving load analysis,动载荷分析)

26) However, little information is available in literature on the performance that can be achieved with different approaches to demand controlled exhaust ventilation.

27) Community standards should be enforced, but those standards should be set by cyberspace communities themselves, not by the courts or by politicians in Washington.

28) Foodborne disease is caused by consuming contaminated foods or beverages.

原文中的主语在译文中做宾语,译成无主句

29) A virtual scene including roads and vehicles is developed by using the software.

30) A vehicle stability control approach for four-wheel independently actuated (4WIA) electric vehicles is presented.

31) An advanced genetic-fuzzy active steering controller is developed based on this vehicle platform.

32) Vehicle safety must be considered in the event of catastrophic failure of one motor drive; this is of most concern when travelling at high speed.

33) The use of the term 'spam' (a trade-marked Hormel meat product) is derived from a Monty Python sketch.

34) It is required to evaluate the performance of the CFD model based on obtained sizes for the study domain and mesh.

35) It may be noted that active anti-roll-bar system is a common and desirable controller for heavy vehicles.

36) It may be used as an integrated starter/generator and also can be used to improve the internal combustion (IC) engine fuel consumption.

37) At high magnification, it can be seen that the competitor's materials are constituted primarily of fibers that range in diameter from 1-4 microns, with many fibers in the range of 1-2 microns, and very few fibers less than 1 micron in diameter.

38) In this study, it is assumed that the thermal properties of S15C steel are the same as those of S45C steel.

把主语并入谓语合译

39) Attention has been paid to this phenomenon.

40) Attempts were made to develop a new technique for breeding rice variety.

41) Allowance must, no doubt, be made for the astonishing rapidity of communication in these days.

(2) 译成被动句

42) They may have been a source of part of the atmosphere of the terrestrial planets, and they are believed to have been the planetesimal-like building blocks for some of the outer planets and their satellites.

43) Over the years, tools and technology themselves as a source of fundamental innovation have largely been ignored by historians and philosophers of science.

44) Whether the Government should increase the financing of pure science at the expense of technology or vice versa often depends on the issue of which is seen as the driving force.

45) The supply of oil can be shut off unexpectedly at any time, and in any case, the oil wells will all run dry in thirty years or so at the present rate of use.

46) Finally, the conclusions are given in Section 5.

47) Humans are thought to be responsible for a large number of environmental problems, ranging from global warming to ozone depletion.

48) Their approach will be modified and adjusted to be applicable to Kuwait taking into consideration the country's geographical parameters and climate conditions.

49) In these conditions, the urban search and rescue (USAR) mobile robot can be dispatched to the collapse building to help the rescuers to complete the search and rescue task.

50) Elevator drive system is mounted at the bottom of the building.

51) Virtual technology is widely utilized in various vehicle test-beds.

52) Several cameras were evaluated covering a wide range of brands and sensor formats.

53) The entire process is called the greenhouse effect.

54) The rest is trapped in the lower air layers, which contain a number of gases—water vapor, CO_2, methane, and others—that absorb the outgoing infrared radiation.

55) Two approaches are suggested to assign the bottom boundary condition for the soil.

56) In this section, the implementation of the building geometry in the model will be discussed first, followed by an overview of the use performance assessment parameters.

57) In the ECMS, the equivalent fuel consumption parameters between fuel usage and electricity usage are defined with two constants which are switched by the battery state.

58) In active probing, special testing signals are injected into an unenergized phase.

59) It also can be fully used on different kinds of AT platform in the developing process of various vehicles.

60) The balanced suspension structure is widely utilized to achieve axle load distribution.

Unit 10　数字的翻译
Translation of Numbers

科技中的很多重要信息是通过各种数量形式表达的。数字和量词的使用在科技英语中是一个重要的构成部分。在当今信息时代里,获取信息不仅要快,而且要准确。如果不能正确地理解原文的意思,翻译的数据不准确,就会带来不可估量的损失。因此,准确地掌握好各种数量表达的含义是一件十分重要的事情。本章将帮助大家厘清中英文在数字表达上的差异,梳理科技英语中数量用法的常用表达。

1. 倍数增减的译法

1) 倍数增加的译法

英语凡是表示倍数的增加,都包括底数在内,表示的都是增加后的结果。而汉语在表示倍数增加时却要区别是否包括底数在内的问题,如果不包括底数,一般说"增加了多少倍";如果包括底数,一般说"增加到多少倍"或"是……的多少倍"。因此,对英语中表示倍数增加的各种方式,翻译时都可以用以下两种说法表示:

- "增加了 N–1 倍"(表示净增,不包括底数)。
- "增加到 N 倍"或"是原来的 N 倍"(包括底数)。

英语中表示倍数增加的句型大概有以下两种:

- Be N times as + 形容词 / 副词 + as…
- Be N times + 比较级 + than…

这两个句型所表示的意义一样,可一概译为"增加了 N–1 倍"或"是……的 N 倍"。(此处的 be 动词也可换成动词。)例如:

➢ This machine is five times heavier than that one.
这台机器比那台机器重 4 倍。

➢ This railway is three times as long as that one.
这条铁路的长度是那条铁路的 3 倍。

➢ This substance reacts three times as fast as the other one.
这个物质的反应速度是另一物质的 3 倍。

➢ High concentration of CO_2 can have the fertilizing effect on plants, which is why some commercial greenhouses use the artificial indoor atmosphere containing CO_2 at about three times as high as that of the outside.

高浓度的 CO_2 对植物具有施肥的效果,这就是为什么一些商业温室使用人工室内空气,让二氧化碳含量是室外大约 3 倍左右。

➤ This book is three times as long as (three times longer than/three times the length of) that one.

本书的篇幅是那本的 3 倍(长 2 倍)。

用 double 和 twice 表示倍数。应译为"增加 1 倍"或"是……的 2 倍"。例如:

➤ The melting point of titanium is almost twice as high as that of platinum.

钛的熔点差不多比铂的熔点的高 1 倍。

➤ Within the next forty years, the world population may double.

在今后的 40 年内,世界人口可能增加 1 倍。

➤ If current rates continue, it will rise to at least twice pre-industrial levels by about 2060——and by the end of the century could be four times as high.

如果保持目前的速度的话,大约在 2060 年(二氧化碳)将至少增加到工业化前的 2 倍,到本世纪末将会增加到 4 倍。

用 treble 或 triple 表示倍数。应译为"增加 2 倍"或"增加到 3 倍"。例如:

➤ If you treble the distance between an object and the earth, the gravitational attraction gets nine times weaker.

如果把一个物体与地球的距离增加 2 倍,地心引力就会减弱到 1/9。

➤ The number of farm in the United States tripled between 1860 and 1910.

1860—1910 年,美国农场的数目增加 2 倍。

2)主语+谓语+倍数+比较级

这种形式特别易使初学者感到困难。其实只要牢记"N times"表示倍数,无论何种句型都包括基数 100% 在内,表示的是增加了后的结果即可。因此在理解时决不可以改变如 N times more than = N times + as + 原形 + as 的统一性(例如:N times easier = N times as easy),译为"是……的 N 倍",或"增加(N-1)倍"。

➤ The velocity of sound in water is 4900ft per second, or four times more than its velocity in air.

水中声速为每秒 4900 英尺,比空气中的声速快 3 倍多。

➤ Water conducts heat about 20 times better than air does.

水的传热能力较空气强约 19 倍。

➤ The energy of steering portability is 0.000041J after optimization, and it is 1.58 times bigger than that before optimization.

优化后的转向能量大约是 0.000041 焦耳,是优化前的 1.58 倍。

➤ The grain output is three times higher this year than that of last year.

今年粮食产量是去年的 3 倍。

表示增加意义也可使用行为谓语动词。主要的句型有:

①表示增加意义的动词 increase 等 + N times/ to N times/by N times + 对比对象；
②非增加意义的动词 + 倍数 + 表示增加意义的名词；
③increase 等表示增加意义的动词 + by a factor of N。
以上三种，都表示增加后的结果，译为"增长到 N 倍"或"增加了（N - 1)倍"。

> The production of integrated circuits has been increased to three times as compared with last year.
> 集成电路的产量比去年增加了 2 倍。

> Instead of simply transmitting the forces you exert, it amplifies them by a factor of ten.
> 它不是简单地传递施加的力量，而是把力放大到 10 倍。

> The drain voltage has been increased by a factor of seven.
> 漏电压增加了 6 倍（即增加到原来的 7 倍）。

> The presence of the iron in the coil has increased the magnetic induction to 5500 times what it would be if the coil were in vacuum.
> 线圈中铁芯使磁感应增强到线圈处于真空之中时的 5500 倍。

> A temperature rise of 100℃ increases the conductivity of a semiconductor by 50 times.
> 温度升高 100℃，半导体的导电率增加到 50 倍。

> Multiband transmission permits a reduction in error probability in exchange for at least a twofold increase in bandwidth and carrier power.
> 多频带传输能降低误差概率，但使带宽和载波功率至少增加了 1 倍。

> In case of electronic scanning the bandwidth is broader by a factor of two.
> 电子扫描时，带宽增加了 1 倍。

> The speed exceeds the average speed by a factor of 3.5.
> 该速度超过平均速度的 2 倍半。

系动词 + 倍数 + up on /over/compared with +……，表示超过（N - 1)倍。

> This year our industrial output is four times up on that of 1990.
> 今年我们的工业产量比 1990 年提高了 3 倍。

so much（或 many，fast 等形容词或副词）+ again as + 对比对象，主语 + 谓语 + again as much as + 对比对象，表示"前者是后者的两倍"，或"多一倍"。例如：

> Wheel A turns as fast again as Wheel B.
> A 轮转动比 B 轮快 1 倍。

be half as much（等）again as ;be half again as much as 这两个形式，表示"比……多半倍"。例如：

> Wheel A turns half again as fast as wheel B.
> A 轮转动比 B 轮快半倍（或 1 倍半于 B 轮）。

increase by N orders of magnitude，是一种涉及数量级（order of magnitude）的表达，意为"增加 N 个数量级，加上 N 个零，增加 N 位数"。increase by two orders of magnitude，意指"增加两

个数量级"。此外,若增加的倍数数目很大,如"increase by factors of hundred million"时,因 1 倍比较起来可以省略,当然译成"增长千百万倍"即可,"减一"之说显然已无必要。原文倍数为一个非常大的不定数词时都可以这样处理。例如:

> The thermal conductivity of metals is as much as several hundred times that of glass.

金属的导热率比玻璃高数百倍。

3)倍数减少的译法

从表面上看,英语中倍数减少的译法可以参照倍数增加的译法,但问题并不这么简单。英语中可以用倍数来表示减少的程度,但汉语中一般不使用"减少多少倍"的说法。按照汉语的习惯,减少一倍就等于零,减少一倍以上就是负数,因此,汉语大多用分数来表示减少的具体程度。例如,黄油价格由原来十二元降到四元,不能说降价三倍,正确的说法应是减少了三分之二。英语中凡是表示倍数减少的句型,翻译时都要换成分数,可以有以下两种译法:

- "减少了(N-1)/N"。
- "减少到1/N"或"是(原来)的1/N"。

英语中表示倍数减少的句型可以归纳为以下两种:

- decrease + by + N times;
- decrease + N times。

这两个句型表示的意义一样,均应译为"减少了(N-1)/N"或"减少到1/N"。例如:

> Since the introduction of new technique the switching time of the transistor has been shortened three times.

采用这项新工艺后,晶体管的开关时间缩短了 2/3。

> When the signal has increased by 10 times the gain may have been reduced by 8 times.

如果信号增大 9 倍,增益就可能减少到 1/8。

N times + 弱比较级 + (than);
N times + as + 表示差、少意义的形容词原级 + as。

这两个句型的意义一样,可译为"比……(弱)(N-1)/N"或"是……1/N"。例如:

> The moon is eighty times lighter than the earth.

月球的重量只有地球的 1/80。

> The new motor is five times as light as the old one.

新电机比旧电机轻 4/5。

> The power output of the machine is twice less than its input.

该机器的输出功率比输入功率小 1/2。

2. 数字、百分数等增减的译法

1)表示增减的动词 + to + 百分数;百分数 + (of) + 名词(或代词)

这两句型表示增减后的结果,包括底数在内。翻译时可以直接译出,或按倍数译法处理。

例如:

- Using the new process, the loss of metal can be reduced to 20 percent.
  如果采用这种新工艺,可使金属损耗下降到20%。
- In 1993, industrial output in the USA fell to 65 percent of the output in 1929.
  1993年,美国的工业产值降至1929年的65%。
- Its goal is to up its market share there to 8% by 2010.
  它的目标是在2010年将欧洲的市场份额增至8%。
- The total exhaust flow rate is reduced to 10% of the design flow rate.
  总排气流量减少到设计流量的10%。
- Moreover, the optimum return air vent position in this UFAD system can result 10.5 percent reduction in the amount of energy consumption compared to the mixing ventilation system.
  再者,和混合通风系统相比,使用地板送风系统(UFAD = under-floor air distribution)中的最佳回风位置可以减少10.5%的总能源消耗。

2) as + 形容词 + as + 数字,这一句型一般可译为"……达(数字)"

例如:

- When the sun goes down, the temperature on the moon may be as low as 160℃ below zero.
  太阳落下之后,月球上的温度可低达零下160摄氏度。
- Generated by bacteria in rice fields, decomposing garbage, cattle ranching, and fossil fuel production, methane persists in the atmosphere for nearly a decade and is now about 2.5 times as prevalent as it was in the 18th century.
  稻田里的细菌、腐烂的垃圾、牲畜放牧和化石燃料的生产所产生的甲烷气体在大气中会存在近10年,并且现在大气中甲烷的含量是18世纪的2.5倍。

在其他句型中,数字、百分数和分数,无论增减,一般均表示净增减部分,可以照译。

- The boiler cuts its coal intake by 22 percent when scales were removed.
  水垢清除后,锅炉的耗煤量减少了22%。
- The United States Census Bureau notes that the population of the world still is expected to increase by more than 25% in the next 13 years.
  美国人口普查局指出,在今后13年中,世界人口预计将增加超过25%。
- Carbon dioxide concentration has been increasing about 0.3 percent higher than it was before the industrial revolution.
  与工业革命前相比,如今二氧化碳的浓度增长了0.3%。
- When EGR rate is 0.4, the required total pressure ratio is nearly 50% more than that without EGR.
  当废气循环(EGR = Exhaust Gas Recirculation)率为0.4时,应达到的总压比没有废气再循环时多了近50%。
- Images developed with the Leaf (manufacturer of the digital back) software yielded approxi-

mately 18% better accuracy than images developed with Adobe Photoshop Camera Raw software

相比 Adobe Photoshop 相机原始软件处理的图像,经 Leaf 软件处理的图像准确性提高了大约 18%。

➢ European revenues rose 35.3% in 2003, to $19.5 billion.

2003 年,欧洲的收入上涨 35.3%,达到 195 亿美元。

➢ This week the EU approved a voluntary deal with car makers to reduce carbon-dioxide emissions by a quarter.

本周,欧盟(EU = European Union)批准了与汽车制造商的一份自愿协议,目的是把二氧化碳的排放量减少 1/4。

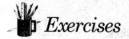
Exercises

1. Single out the sentences containing figures in your professional papers and translate them into Chinese.

2. Translate the following sentences based on the skills in this unit.

1) C is twice less than B.

2) Single mode operation could be achieved by reducing the length of the laser tube by a factor of ten.

3) The hydrogen atom is nearly 16 times as light as oxygen atom.

4) If you treble the distance, the gravitational attraction gets nine times weaker.

5) Every square mile on the sunny side of Mercury's surface receives seven times as much heat as a square mile on the earth.

6) The average energy consumed per head of population in the United Sates is over 100 times that of the world's poorest countries.

7) Radio waves travel almost a million times faster than sound.

8) The laboratory under construction will be as large again as this one.

9) The production of our factory this year is as much again as last year.

10) The two countries are scheduled to sign a long term agreement Tuesday, which is expected to double the trade between them.

11) When the voltage is stepped up by 10 times, the strength of the current is stepped down by 10 times, so that the power remains the same.

12) The water level in winter falls by a factor of three as against the average level.

3. Go through the following sentences and focus on the expressions of increase and decrease.

1) The relentless accumulation of greenhouse gases has led the IPCC to project that in the next hundred years global average temperatures will rise by 1 to 3.5 degrees C.

不断增加的温室气体让政府间气候变化专门委员会(IPCC)预测在接下来的一百年内,全球平均气温将上升 1~3.5 摄氏度。

2) Sales in Europe rose 20.6% in the first four months of the year, following a 10.4% leap in

2003, to 835 000 cars.

在2003年销售量猛增10.4%之后,丰田今年前四个月在欧洲的销售量增长了20.6%,卖出了835 000辆车。

3) European revenues rose 35.3% in 2003, to $19.5 billion.

欧洲的收入在2003年增长了35.3%,达到195亿美元。

4) In 2005, Toyota's local production will rise to 60%, nearly matching the level of local production in the United States.

2005年,丰田在当地的生产值将提升到60%,几乎达到在美国当地的生产水平。

5) Its height can increase from a meter or less to over 20 meters.

其高度可以从1米甚至更低增加到超过20米。

6) The growing season in the northern U.S. has lengthened by about a week.

美国北部的生长季节延长了大约1个星期。

7) Goldin pared the agency's workforce by 4,000 jobs and sliced its budget by $30 billion over an eight-year period.

戈丁预计在8年内把机构的职位削减4000个,并将预算减少300亿美元。

8) By putting every production process under one roof—from press machinery to welding, painting, assembly, and final quality checks—Toyota cut the overall investment required for the plant by 40%, to $732 million.

通过将每个生产过程安排在同一车间:从压机到焊接、油漆、装配到最后的质量检查,丰田公司所需的生产总投资减少了40%,降至7.32亿美元。

9) The company announced this year that it plans to trim head count by 4 800 through early retirement and voluntary departures.

公司今年宣布,计划通过提前退休和自愿离职将员工数量减少4 800人。

10) This implied that the ringflash in the Oldenburg test increased the maximum absolute LME of the Alpa camera by approximately 60 mm or, in other words, the ringflash degraded the accomplished accuracy by approximately 50%.

在奥尔登堡对阿帕尔相机的环形闪光灯的测试表明,它的长度测量误差(LME = length measurement error)的最大绝对值增加了近60mm,换句话说,环形闪光灯的精度降低了近50%。

11) For example, the root mean square of the rear dynamic tyre deflection response was reduced by 34%, i.e. from 9.096mm to 6.031mm.

例如,后驱动轮挠度响应的均方根减少了34%,即从9.096mm减少到6.031mm。

12) The results show that with the fuzzy adaptive PI control, the position response overshoot is greatly reduced from 23% to 1%.

结果显示,采用模糊自适应的PI控制,位置响应超调量从23%大幅下降到1%。

13) In the Northern Hemisphere, snow cover has decreased about 10 percent in the past 21 years, but no significant melting of the Antarctic ice sheet has been detected.

在北半球,积雪已经在过去的21年里减少了大约10%,但没有检测到南极冰块有明显的融化。

14) The European utilities recently implemented the Large Combustion Plant Directive, requiring the reduction of NO_X from coal-fired electric generating units to 500 milligrams per cubic meter (mg/m^3) by 2008 and to 200 mg/m^3 by 2015.

欧洲通用事业公司最近实施大型电站能源消费法令,要求减少燃煤发电机组的氮氧化合物的排放量,从2008年的500 mg/m^3减少到2015年的200 mg/m^3。

15) Moreover, normalized CO concentration is decreased to below 1% and 5% within left and right sidewalks, respectively.

此外,标准一氧化碳浓度在左、右人行横道处分别降低至1%以下和5%以下。

16) Any program should have realistic goals that lead to a slow, steady weight loss of no more 0.5 to 1 pounds a week.

任何计划都应该有每周减少0.5～1磅的缓慢、稳定而切实的减重目标。

17) It's worth pointing out that the word "nanotechnology", has become very popular and is used to describe many types of research where the characteristic dimensions are less than about 1,000 nanometers.

这里值得指出的是,"纳米技术"一词已变得非常流行,用来描述多种特征尺寸小于1000纳米的研究类型。

Unit 11　名词性从句的翻译
Translation of Nominal Clauses

英语的名词性从句就是起名词最主要的一些功能的从句,包括主语从句、宾语从句、表语从句和同位语从句等。翻译的时候,大多数可以按照原文的句子顺序翻译成相应的汉语译文。但是,有时候可以采用其他翻译方法来灵活处理。

1. 主语从句

以 what、whatever、who、whoever、whether、when、where、how、why 等词引导的主语从句,在翻译的时候,一般可以按照英语原文顺序来翻译。

- What makes this possible is a new kind of turbo-charged direction (TDI) diesel engine.
  让这成为可能的是一种涡轮增压式直喷柴油机的出现。
- What's likely to happen in cyberspace is the formation of new communities, free of the constraints that cause conflicts on earth.
  在信息空间极有可能形成新的团体,免受现实生活中导致冲突的条件约束。
- How to determine the area of IC data coverage used to correlate with the in situ tests would depend on the "influence area" of the specific type in situ tests and the desired number of roller passes.
  如何确定关联原位测试的智能压实数据覆盖面积,取决于原位测试中具体类型的"影响区域"和所需的滚筒数量。
- What should not be overlooked are the vast changes taking place in automobile manufacturing.
  不可忽视的是汽车制造业正在发生巨大的改变。
- What we call a machine is really a kind of tool that can do work for man.
  我们所称的机器实际上是能为人类工作的一种工具。
- How the brain manages to think is a conundrum with a millennial time scale.
  大脑如何思考是个千年不解之谜。
- When it was first invented is not known.
  它最初的发明时间到现在还不清楚。
- Where the water has gone can easily be answered.
  水到哪里去了,这很容易回答。
- Who will do the experiment first has not been decided.
  谁先做这个实验,尚未决定。

➢ Whatever concrete crack does occur will be of smaller width.

无论发生什么样的混凝土裂缝,裂缝宽度都会比较小。

用 it 作形式主语的主语从句,翻译时可以把主语从句放到汉语句子最前面。为了强调起见,it 一般可以译出来;如果不需要强调,it 也可以不译出来。有时候,如果主语从句仍然按照英语原句的顺序翻译的话,it 一般不需要译出来。在汉语译文的开始,一般可以用"……的是,……"这样的结构。

➢ It is possible that the warming observed during this century may have resulted from natural variations, even though the increase has been much more rapid than what the planet has witnessed over the past hundred centuries.

尽管地球的气温的增长比过去几百个世纪要迅速得多,但本世纪观察到的气候变暖很有可能是属于自然变化。

➢ It is unknown what factors affect the geometric stability the most, which would aid in identification of the weakest link or the place where stabilization measures should be most effective.

目前还不清楚是什么因素对几何稳定性有极大的影响,但了解清楚这一问题将有助于识别最薄弱的环节或需要稳定措施的地方。

➢ It is natural that the controller based on PMP needs a larger costate if the vehicle is able to recuperate more electric energy, or if current is higher than the desired level.

如果汽车有能力回充更多的电能或者电流高于所需水平,基于 PMP 的控制器自然需要一个较大的协态变量。

➢ It is evident that the equation has two roots.

显然该方程有两个根。

➢ It is still a mystery how that phenomenon was discovered.

那个现象是如何被发现的仍然是个谜。

➢ It is known that molecules are made up of atoms.

大家知道分子是由原子构成的。

➢ It has not been discussed how the method is used here.

(我们)尚未讨论在此如何使用该方法。

➢ It does not matter in which order two numbers are added.

两个数相加的顺序是无关紧要的。

➢ At first glance it does not appear that this integral fits any of the forms presented up to this point.

乍看起来,似乎这个积分并不符合目前为止所讲的任何形式。

➢ Concrete shrinks as it dries out. So it is advisable to minimize such shrinkage we should use concrete with the smallest possible amount of water and cement compatible with other requirements, such as strength and workability.

混凝土变干就收缩,因此,为了尽量减少混凝土收缩量,建议将混凝土的水灰比减到最小,同时满足如强度和合易性等其他要求。

➢ It was empirically determined that the effective damage done to the road is roughly proportional to the 4th power of axle weight.
根据经验可确定,对道路造成破坏与轴重的四次方约成正比。

➢ It is recommended that this testing can be done at night as during cooler temperatures, joints open, aggregate interlock diminishes and load deflections are at their highest.
建议在夜间温度较低的时段开展测验,此时接缝张开,集料咬接消失,荷载挠度最大。

2. 表语从句

英语中的表语从句放在系动词后面,充当表语成分,一般可以按照英语原文顺序直接翻译。

➢ Sending a signal from one place to another is what is called transmission.
把信号从一地发送到另一地,就是人们所说的传输。

➢ Weather is what happens outside your home this morning.
天气就是清晨屋外的风云变化。

➢ The drawback of the method is that the number of FE analysis still can be quite large.
该方法的缺点是,有限元分析的数量仍然相当大。

➢ The short answer is that diesel represents the industry's best hope of cutting carbon dioxide emissions.
简而言之,柴油机代表了汽车行业减少二氧化碳排放的最大希望。

➢ The common feature of these projects is that they are developed by using real cars to do some safe driving researches on certain aspects of the real car.
这些项目的共同特征是使用实车来做相关方面的安全驾驶研究。

➢ Another advantage of LDS is that these sequences are entirely repeatable, giving the same sequence every time.
低差异序列(LDS = low-discrepancy sequences)的另一个优点是这些序列是完全重复的,每次都给出相同的顺序。

➢ Vehicle calibration of AT is that vehicle shift gears is checked according to the performance and fuel consumption of desktop calibration.
自动变速器(AT = automatic transimission)的车辆校准就是根据桌面校准的性能和油耗来检查车辆变速齿轮。

➢ The basic criterion for design is that the settlements should be relatively small.
设计的基本标准是沉降量应该相对较小。

3. 宾语从句

用 that、what、how、when、which、why、whether、if 等引起的宾语从句，翻译成汉语的时候，一般不需要改变它在原句中的顺序。但"it"做了形式宾语或加了条件句，就要改变句子结构。

➢ At the same time, we know that the meteorites could not have delivered all of the water, because then the earth's atmosphere would contain nearly 10 times as much xenon (an inert gas) as it actually does.
同时，我们知道，因为那时地球大气包含的氙气（惰性气体）是现在的 10 倍，陨星不可能提供所有的水。

➢ No one knows for certain whether such things will happen.
没有人能够确认这些事情是否会发生。

➢ You've probably noticed that much of the spam you receive involves deceptive practices.
你可能已经注意到，你收到的大部分垃圾邮件涉及欺诈行为。

➢ Research suggests that currently circulating strains of H5N1 viruses are becoming more capable of causing disease.
研究表明，目前流行的 H5N1 病毒株更容易让人生病。

➢ The development of intelligent vehicle requires that the structure of the vehicle itself and also its running process be intelligentized.
智能车辆的发展要求车辆本身的结构以及汽车运行的过程都要智能化。

➢ Calibration results showed that digital cameras can be applied for an accurate photogrammetric survey.
标定结果表明，数码相机可以用于高精度的摄影测量。

➢ That means that diesel best fits in with the car makers' medium-term thinking about their industry.
这意味着柴油机与汽车制造商们对本行业的中期设想相吻合。

➢ The simulation results show that the optimized system based on quality engineering theory can improve the steering road feel, guarantee steering stability and steering portability and thus provide a theoretical basis for the design and optimization of the novel electric power steering system.
仿真结果表明，基于质量工程理论体系的优化方法可以提高转向路感，保证转向的稳定性和转向轻便性，从而为设计和优化新的电动助力转向系统提供理论依据。

➢ The preliminary results indicate that the proposed genetic-fuzzy active steering controller has the ability to improve the performance of the vehicle handling and stability considerably.
初步结果表明，所提出的遗传—模糊主动转向控制器能够大幅地提高车辆的操纵性和稳定性。
- The fuzzification block means that real world variables are translated in terms of fuzzy sets.
模糊模块意味着现实世界的变量能够以模糊集的方式转换。
- Some could argue that the overall economic decline is due to the events of September 11, but I think it had more to do with their lack of continued innovation and new product development.
一些人认为是因为"9·11事件"引起整体经济下行,但是我认为更多的是因为缺乏持续创新和新产品开发。
- Everyone realizes to what extent the world is dependent on petroleum.
大家都知道(当今)世界对石油的依赖到了何种程度。
- That means that people can choose where to go and what to see.
那意味着人们可以选择网站和浏览的内容。
- But the coming craze for diesel means that, sooner or later, they may have to dig into their pockets and comply.
但是,即将到来的柴油机热潮意味着汽车厂商迟早要自掏腰包以顺应(市场)。
- We are aware that environmental protection is an important challenge that we must meet as corporate citizen.
我们意识到环境保护是作为企业法人必须面对的重要挑战。
- These results seem to indicate that lane detection in the frequency domain has some inherent advantages over detection in the spatial domain, and so it has much promise in terms of being used to design a real-time lane detection and tracking system.
实验结果表明,基于频域的边缘检测算法较基于空间域的检测算法有其固有的优势,在实时车道线检测以及伺服跟随系统的设计中有更广阔的前景。
- Nutritional experiments have made it evident that vitamins are indispensable for one's health and growth.
营养实验已经证明,维生素在人们健康和成长中是不可缺少的。
- Since all of the loads on one-way slab must be transmitted in the short direction to the supporting beams, it follows that all of the reinforcement on the slab should be placed at right angles to these beams.
由于所有作用在单向板的荷载必须沿短方向传递到支撑梁上,因此,板上的所有配筋应该与这些梁成直角布置。
- Two-way slabs bend into a dished surface rather than a cylindrical one when loaded. This means that at any point the slab is curved in both principal directions.
双向板在受力时,弯曲成盘子表面形状而不是圆柱形,这意味着受力板在两个主要方向的任意点均发生弯曲。
- The report estimates that urban drivers pay an average of $746/year on vehicle repairs.
报告估计,城市司机每年平均花费746美元用于汽车维修。
- It has to be pointed out that opposed to boost-type PFC rectifiers, the main current is not direct-

ly impressed by the control, but is formed only by PWM without feed-back from a controlled DC current.

必须指出,与增压 PFC(Power Factor Correction,功率因素校正)整流器相反,主电流不是直接受控制器的影响,而是通过没有反馈的受控直流电流的 PWM(Pulse-Width Modulation,脉宽调频)获得。

4. 同位语从句

同位语从句主要是用来对名词作进一步的解释,说明名词的具体内容。能接同位语从句的名词主要有:belief(相信),fact(事实),hope(希望),idea(想法,观点),doubt(怀疑),news(新闻,消息),rumor(传闻),conclusion(结论),evidence(证据),suggestion(建议),problem(问题),order(命令),answer(回答),decision(决定),discovery(发现),explanation(解释),thought(思想)等。翻译同位语从句有以下几种方法:

①一般来说,同位语从句可以直接翻译在主句后面。

②有时候在翻译同位语从句时,可以将其放在所修饰的名词前面,相当于前置的修饰语,但不一定使用定语的标志词"的"。这种情况下,同位语从句一般比较简单。

③增加"即"(或者"以为")这样的词来连接,或用冒号、破折号直接分开主句和同位语从句。

> Despite the fact that there have long been law prohibiting junk faxes and unsolicited commercial calls to cell phones, there is currently no federal anti-spam act.
> 尽管禁止垃圾传真和手机上来路不明的商业电话的法律颁布已久,但现在联邦政府还没有反对垃圾邮件的行动。

> This trend results from the fact that at 40 km/h Mechanism 4 occurs frequently with the lowest values of the ratio BLEH/PED.
> 在每小时 40 公里的速度时,BLEH/PED 的最低比值常会伴随机制 4 产生,这就是该趋势产生的原因。

> Good citizens jump to a conclusion that better regulate it.
> 好公民们突然有了结论:更好地规范它。

> Evidence that main belt asteroids pummeled the early inner solar system confirms a previously published cosmochemical analysis by UA planetary scientist David.
> 主要小行星带撞击早期内太阳系这一证据证实了先前公开发表的 UA 行星科学家戴维德做的宇宙化学分析。

> There is wide agreement that traffic should evolve into something that can be sustained in the future.
> 交通应该发展成未来可持续发展的事业是人们广泛的共识。

> There is general acknowledgment that characteristics of an individual are a result of an interaction of genetics and environment.

众所周知，某一个体的特性是遗传和环境相互作用的结果。

➤ The century ahead will see the first laboratory proof that self-replicating systems can form from ordinary chemicals.
下个世纪将看到第一个实验室证据：自复制系统可以由普通化学物质形成。

➤ The idea that continents broke and drifted apart is known as the hypothesis.
认为大陆曾经断裂并漂离的设想叫作大陆漂移假说。

➤ The fill is made by the "compacted layer method" that a layer of fill is spread the compacted to specifications and this process is repeated until the desired grade is reached.
填筑采用"分层夯实法"，即铺设一层填料之后，立即夯实至规范要求的夯实度，重复此过程一直达到要求的坡度。

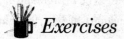 Exercises

1. Search Nominal Clauses in your professional papers and manage to figure out their Chinese expressions.

2. Translate the following sentences.

(1) 主语从句

1) It is known to all why metals have been widely used in industry.
2) These substances expand when heated and contract when cooled is a common physical phenomenon.
3) What the TV camera does is to break the picture up into a number of lines consisting of very small points of light.
4) Whether a body is in a state of motion or rest is always relative.
5) How hot the sun really is can hardly be described in word.

(2) 表语从句

6) This is what the second law of motion means.
7) Another property of acid is that they have ability to combine with compounds known as bases.
8) It is because a conductor carrying a current is surrounded by a magnetic field.
9) Galileo's greatest glory was that in 1609 he was the first person to turn the newly invented telescope on the heavens to prove that the planets revolve around the Sun rather than around the Earth.
10) The truth is that men are developed from anthropoid apes.

(3) 宾语从句

11) One may say that the energy of a body is the capacity of that body for doing work.
12) You should determine which of the following functions is analytic.
13) The conductance of a circuit is a measure of how easily current can flow through it.
14) Electrons always move toward where the potential is higher.

15) We must know at what distance the detected object is.

16) We must understand what is meant by the slope of a function.

(4) 同位语从句

17) The general statement can be made that wherever there is motion there is friction.

18) There can be no doubt that genetic engineering is a wonderful new tool.

19) The fact that copper and aluminum are widely used for electronic wire is well known.

20) Doctors are of the opinion that most people cannot live beyond 100 years.

21) However, the writing of chemical symbols in the form of an equation does not give any assurance that the reaction shown will actually occur.

Unit 12 定语从句的翻译
Translation of Attributive Clauses

在各种从句中，定语从句大概算是最难掌握的了，这种从句在形式和意义上的变化比较多，因此学生们在学习时常觉得很难理解，不好翻译，尤其是在科技英语中。定语从句一般由关系代词 that, which, who, as, whom 等和关系副词 when, where, why 等引导。定语从句有限制性和非限制性定语从句两种，两者的区别在于限制意义的强弱，且定语从句绝大部分因较长而放在所修饰的中心词之后。而汉语不用长定语，且所有的定语都要前置，也不涉及限制意义的强弱。故将定语从句翻译成汉语时，不宜一概将其翻译成汉语的修饰语，要对句子的结构、意义进行具体分析，适当调整、转换，才能使译出的句子通顺、流畅，符合汉语的表达习惯。根据具体情况，定语从句可译为先行词的前置定语，并列分句或状语从句，也可采用融和法。

1. 采用前置法

当英语定语从句比较简短，可将其译成带"的"的定语，放在被修饰词之前，从而将英语的复合句译成汉语的简单句。

➢ The pumps which are used on board ship can be divided into two main groups.
在船上使用的泵可分为两类。

➢ Ricardo engineers have developed additional technology that complements common-rail technology by optimizing the way air swirls as it enters the combustion chamber through two separate inlet valves.
里卡多公司的工程师们已经开发出了通过优化空气气旋经两个独立进气阀门再进入燃烧室的方式来完善共轨技术这项新的工艺。

➢ Four different demand control strategies were implemented on the basic exhaust ventilation system that is described in Section 2.1.
在 2.1 节描述的基础排气通风系统的基础上实现了四种不同的需求控制策略。

➢ Thus, there is a net force that has a component parallel to the orbital motion of the asteroid.
因而产生了与小行星轨道运行平行的净力。

➢ Desktop calibration of automatic transmission (AT) is a method which can reduce cost, enhance efficiency and shorten the development periods of a vehicle effectively.
自动变速器的桌面校准是一种能够减少花费、提高效率并有效缩短车辆研发周期的方法。

➢ There are a number of ways in which bridges are classified.
有很多桥梁进行分类的方法。

➢ The erector typically prepares an erection plan which specifies the erection practices and safety

measures which will be employed for the approval of the general contractor.
安装人员通常拟定一个安装计划,该计划规定了安装作业以及<u>经总承包商批准拟采用的安全措施</u>。

➢ Companies that will lead the marketplace in 2004 and beyond will be the ones <u>that continue to innovate and invest in research and development</u>.
要想在 2004 年及以后引领市场的公司必须是<u>在研发上持续创新和投入的</u>公司。

➢ Large diesel engines, <u>which have cylinders nearly 3 feet. in diameter</u>, turn at the relatively slow speed of about 108 rpm.
<u>气缸直径近三英尺的</u>大型柴油机,以每分钟 108 转的相对低速运转。

2. 译成并列句

　　定语从句比较长,意义上独立性较强,译为汉语定语时显得啰唆,或定语从句并不长,但译成汉语定义后不合逻辑或不符合汉语表达习惯,可把定语从句拆译成汉语并列的独立句,这时可重复先行词或用"这""那""其"作为独立句的主语。

➢ Centrifugal pumps consist of an impeller, <u>which rotates at high speed</u>, inside a casing.
离心泵有泵叶轮,<u>叶轮以高速度在泵壳内转动</u>。

➢ The yaw moments generated by the guide tire radial forces are the moment <u>that resist the moment generated by the air-spring forces and the side forces</u>.
通过导向轮胎径向力可形成横摆力矩,<u>这种横摆力矩可以平衡由空气弹簧力和侧向力形成的力矩</u>。

➢ Recent tests on the geometric stability of several digital cameras <u>that were not designed for photogrammetric applications</u> have shown that the accomplished accuracies in object space are either limited or that the accuracy potential is not exploited to the fullest extent.
最近对几种数码相机进行几何稳定性测试,<u>这些相机都是非专业摄影测量数码相机</u>,结果显示该类相机在物体空间所能达到的精度是有限的,或者说精度还没有发掘到最大程度。

➢ Figure 1 illustrates the AUTO21EV, which is a two-passenger, all-wheel-drive urban electric vehicle <u>that has been developed and modeled</u> in this work using the ADAMS/View and MapleSim software packages.
图 1 是两座、轮毂电机直接驱动的四驱城市电动汽车(AUTO21EV)模型,<u>该模型是</u>基于 ADAMS/View 和 MapleSim 软件包<u>开发与建模的</u>。

➢ The use of small but powerful direct-drive in-wheel motors allows for the implementation of the most advanced all-wheel-drive system <u>in which the optimal traction force can be generated on all tires by controlling the tire slips at all times</u>.
使用体积小但输出强劲的直驱轮毂电机有利于最先进的四轮驱动系统的实现,<u>该系统通过随时控制轮胎滑动,可以产生最佳的牵引力</u>。

➢ The superiority of the fuzzy PI controller compared to conventional controller is illustrated by simulations and experiments <u>which confirm that the fuzzy PI controller effectively restrains over-</u>

shoot of the position response.
经过仿真和实验,模糊 PI 控制器比传统 PI 控制器性能更为优越,<u>可以更好地限制位置反馈的超调量</u>。

➤ ICMV relates to the stiffness of the pavement system with an influence depth <u>that may go into underlying layers and even soil foundation</u>, while density is a measurement of single HMA layer.
ICMV 与路面系统的刚度相关,它的影响深度<u>甚至可能入进土壤基层</u>,而密度仅仅是 HMA 层的一个度量指标。

➤ However, additional CM filter stages have to be implemented on the mains side for the filtering of the noise currents <u>that result from the parasitic capacitances of the power semiconductors to the heat sink</u>.
然而,额外的 CM 滤波器台不得不执行对主载荷边噪声电流的过滤通过,<u>而噪声电流来自于功率半导体中的寄生电容的热沉降效应</u>。

➤ A retaining structure is a permanent or temporary structure <u>which is used for providing lateral support to the soil mass or other materials</u>.
挡土结构是一个永久或临时的结构,<u>用于侧向支撑土体或其他材料</u>。

➤ Other major greenhouse gases include nitrous oxide—produced by both agriculture and industry—and various solvents and refrigerants like chlorofluorocarbons, or CFCs, <u>which are now banned by international treaty</u> because of their damaging effect on Earth's protective ozone layer.
其他主要的温室气体包括农业和工业产生的氧化亚氮以及各种溶剂和含氯氟烃的制冷剂。为了让保护地球的臭氧层免受伤害,<u>国际条约现已禁止氯氟烃</u>(CFC = chlorofluorocarbon)的使用。

➤ Despite heavy rains in some regions, lack of rainfall in other regions brought a remarkable water shortage problem, <u>which is still problematic for many inland cities and one of their most serious problems</u>.
尽管某些地区大雨倾盆,降水缺乏却给另一些地区带来严重的水短缺问题,<u>这是许多内陆城市面临的最严重的问题之一</u>。

➤ Radioactive wastes are a product of the military and civilian uses of nuclear energy, <u>which emerged in the United States in 1945 and grew rapidly through the early 1980s</u>.
放射性废料是军用和民用核能的产物,<u>它于 1945 年出现在美国并且在 20 世纪 80 年代初快速增多</u>。

3. 译成状语从句

1) 译成时间状语从句

➤ Electrical energy <u>that is supplied to the motor</u> may be converted into mechanical energy of motion.
<u>把电能供给电机时</u>,它就能变成运动的机械能。

> This records both positive and negative velocities and also produces a reliable measurement of longitudinal turbulence intensity through the recirculating flow in the courtyard where reversed flow occurs.
> 这种(测量)记录了正反两种速度,同时,当中庭产生逆流时,通过中庭的回流也可以为纵向扰流强度提供可靠的测量数据。

> An electrical current begins to flow through coil, which is connected across a charged condenser.
> 当线圈同充电的电容器相连接时,电流就开始流经线圈。

> Very loud sounds produced by huge planes, which fly low over the land, can cause damage to house.
> 巨型飞机低空飞行时产生的巨大轰鸣,足以摧毁房屋。

2)译成原因状语从句

> Iron is not so strong as steel that is an alloy of iron with some other elements.
> 铁的强度不如钢高,因为钢是铁与其他元素形成的合金。

> Liquids, which contain no free electrons, are poor conductors of heat.
> 由于不含有自由电子,液体是热的不良导体。

> For an uncertainty analysis the experimental design plan should be centered around the expectation point, which is usually the starting point of the search for the most probable failure point.
> 不确定性分析的实验设计方案应该围绕期望点,因为研究的起点通常是最有可能出现故障的地方。

> Einstein, who worked out the photoelectric effect, won the Nobel Prize in 1921.
> 爱因斯坦因为提出了著名的光电效应理论获得了1921年诺贝尔奖。

> Evaporation of this incoming flow leaves the belt with a higher salt content than the rest of the North Atlantic, which is fed by substantial freshwater runoff from continental watersheds.
> 这股洋流的蒸发导致留下一片比北大西洋其他地方含盐量高的区域,而北大西洋其他地方含盐量略低是因为大量的来自大陆的径流注入。

> Thus, the leaf springs would present features of energy loss and nonlinear hysteresis features, which also have an important influence on vehicle ride comfort and road friendliness.
> 由于钢板弹簧对车辆驾驶的舒适性和道路的友好性有重要影响,因此它必须具有能量损失和非线性滞回特性。

> Instead of global village, which is a nice dream but impossible to manage, we'll have invented another world of self-contained communities that cater to their own members' inclinations without interfering with anyone else's.
> 因为地球村是一个美好但不能实现的梦想,我们将来要创造另一个能够在不影响他人的情况下满足自己需求世界。

3)译成条件状语从句

> An electrical current begins to flow through a coil, which is connected with a charged condenser.

如果线圈同充电的电容器相连接，电流就开始流过线圈。
- The melting point of steel, the carbon content of which is higher, is lower.
  如果钢的含碳量较高，其熔点就较低。
- The performance of the fuzzy active steering controller becomes clearer when looking at Figure 15, which compares the vehicle yaw rate and sideslip angle for both cases.
  如果比较以上两种状况下的车辆横摆角速度和质心侧偏角，图 15 更能清晰地表现出模糊主动转向控制器的性能。
- The systematic framework and the detailed modeling process for balanced suspension were proposed by Яценко, in which the rotational inertia of the balanced rod was not taken into account.
  在不考虑平衡棒转动惯量的条件下，Яценко 提出了平衡悬架的系统构架，详述了平衡悬架的建模过程。
- Food, which is kept too long, decays, because it is attacked by yeasts, moulds and bacteria.
  食物如果放置时间太久，就会腐烂，因为食物会受到酵母菌、霉菌以及细菌的侵蚀。
- Water, which is impure, causes serious illness.
  水如果不清洁，就会引起重病。
- For any machine, whose input force and output force are known, its mechanical advantage can be calculated.
  任何机器若知其输入力和输出力，就可求出机械效益。

4）译成目的状语从句

- The bulb is sometimes filled with an inert gas which permits operation at a higher temperature.
  有时往灯泡内充入惰性气体，是为了能在更高的温度下工作。
- There is a minimum size for the reactor at which the chain reaction will just work.
  要使链式反应刚好会维持下去，反应堆要有最小尺寸的限制。
- This balance of reinforcement and decay allows the selection of the shortest paths, which are traversed quickly and reinforced more often.
  这种强化和衰减的平衡允许对最短路径进行选择，使其能快速移动和经常强化。
- To meet both pollution reduction requirements and plant performance goals, these markets are demanding a more cost-effective, in-process approach, which optimizes the combustion system to prevent emission problems.
  为了达到减排增效的目的，市场要求本轻利厚的过程性方法，以便能优化燃烧系统防止（污染）排放问题。
- Although water vapor is the most potent greenhouse gas, evaporation also leads to cloud formation, which can have a cooling effect.
  虽然水蒸气是最强的温室气体，蒸发也导致云的形成，达到冷却效果。
- Second, there are information and entertainment services, where people can download anything from legal texts and lists of "new great restaurants" to game software or dirty pictures.

第二，(网络上)有大量的信息和娱乐服务，以便于人们可以网站上下载任何想要的资源：从法律文本到"新的高级餐馆"的名单以及游戏软件和黄色照片等，应有尽有。

➢ It's easy enough for software manufacturers to build an automatic filter that would prevent you or your child from ever seeing the undesired item on a menu.
软件制造商可以轻松地设计出自动过滤器（来屏蔽这些内容），以防你或你的孩子看到不希望看到的内容。

5）译成结果状语从句

➢ Copper, which is used to widely for carrying electricity, offers very little resistance.
铜的电阻很小，因此被广泛地用来输电。

➢ Matter has certain features or properties that enable to recognize different matters easily.
物质具有一定的特征或特性，所以（我们）能够容易识别各种物质。

➢ Meanwhile, IC data produced by different roller vendors are presented in various data forms, which bring inconvenience and confusions to contractors when using multiple IC rollers.
与此同时，不同厂商压路机的智能压实数据（IC）数据展现为各种各样的数据形式，所以在多台压路机共同使用时会给承包商带来各种不便和困扰。

➢ The model also provides a realistic calculation of the self-aligning torque at each front tire, which complements the steering system model previously discussed.
这个模型也提供了每个前轮的自回正力矩的实用算法，从而完善了之前讨论的转向系统模型。

➢ The two position sensors output two types of voltages, with the value of one voltage being twice as high as that of the other, which can reflect the output of pedal stroke.
两个位置传感器输出两种形式的电压，其中一种电压的值是另一种的两倍，从而可以反映出踏板行程的输出。

➢ These tire forces difference between the leading truck and the trailing truck is caused by the combination of guide tire radial forces and side force, which affects good curving performance.
前转向架和后转向架上的轮胎力差是由于导向轮径向力和侧向力组合产生的，从而影响了良好曲线通过性能。

➢ The existing technology today is to operate automobiles on CNG and LPG, which would meet the second objective.
目前的技术采用压缩天然气（CNG = Compressed Natural Gas）和液化石油气（LPG = Liquefied Petroleum Gas）给汽车提供能源，能够满足第二个目的。

➢ She took Chinese medicine which relieved her symptom.
她服了中药，缓解了症状。

➢ IC is also promising to reduce life cycle cost, which is the concern of construction industry.
智能压实有望降低使用周期成本，因此备受建设行业关注。

➢ Global warming has raised the issue of city flooding, which is becoming a big problem for most Chinese cities due to inadequate storm drainage utilities.

全球变暖已经造成城市洪灾,由于大多数中国城市的暴雨排水设施不足,因而成为棘手的问题。

6) 译成让步状语从句

➤ A gas occupies all of any container in which it is placed.
气体不管装在什么容器里,都会把容器充满。

➤ Friction, which is often considered as an obstacle, is of much help to the vehicles moving forward.
摩擦虽然被看作是一种障碍,但对车辆前行却很有帮助。

➤ Glass, which breaks at a blow, is capable of withstanding great pressure.
玻璃尽管一击就碎,仍然能承受很大压力。

➤ Photographs are taken of stars, the light of which is too faint to be seen by eyes at all.
虽然许多星体的光线非常微弱,眼睛根本看不见,但它们的照片还是被拍下来了。

➤ Scientists say that standard filters, which reduce the amount of tar inhaled by smokers, do not make the smoke less toxic to the cells.
科学家认为,普通过滤嘴虽然可以减少吸烟者吸入的焦油量,但不能减少烟雾对细胞的毒害。

➤ Penicillin drugs, which cured nearly all bacterial urinary-tract infections several decades ago, are now much less effective against them.
青霉素虽然几十年前曾治愈了几乎所有的细菌性尿道感染,但现在它的效果已经大大不如以前了。

➤ Potential energy that is not so obvious as kinetic energy exists in many things.
势能虽不像动能那样明显,但它却存在于许多物体之中。

➤ Atoms, which are very small, can be broken up into still smaller particles-electrons, protons and neutrons.
原子虽然很小,但还能分解为更小的粒子,如电子、质子和中子。

4. 采用融合法

主句为 there + 主语 + 定语从句的句型中,主要谓语的意义不在 there be 上,而在从句的谓语部分,翻译时可以把主语译成"有 + 名词",把从句译成谓语,从而融合为一个简单句。

➤ There are many properties that can be measured.
有许多特性可被测量出来。

➤ There are also chemicals called antibodies that the body manufactures specially and circulates in the bloodstream to give further protection.
还有一些被称为抗体的化学物质,是由人体特别制造的,并在血液中循环,增进对人体的保护作用。

有些带定语从句的英语复合句,当主句包含系表结构时,译成汉语可将英语主句压缩成汉语词组做主语,而把定语从句译成谓语,从而融成一个简单句。

➤ Strength, hardness and plasticity of metals are the properties that make them so useful for industry.
金属的强度、硬度和可塑性使其在工业上得到广泛的应用。

➤ Is it the blue print of a new-type lathe which you are checking?
你在检查一种新型车床的蓝图吗?

在带有定语从句的主从复合句中,从句与其所修饰的词的关系密且不可分割时,运用汉语的连动式或兼语式,把二者融合成一个整体,往往能简洁有力地表达原文的内在含义。

➤ The turbines drive the dynamos which generate the electricity.
涡轮机推动发电机发电。(兼语式)

➤ Once the crystal is oriented, it is placed on a diamond saw which slices the crystal into wafer.
晶体一旦定向完毕,就把它放在金刚石上锯成薄片。(连动式)

➤ The oil tanker carries crude oil to a refinery, there the oil is possessed.
油轮将原油运到炼油厂加工。(连动式)

➤ The molecules give up some of their energy of motion to push the position that does the work.
这些分子释放出一部分动能推动活塞做功。(兼语式)

5. 特殊定语从句的译法

1) as 引导的定语从句

as 单独引导定语从句时,修饰整个主句或主句中的一部分,可以放在句首、句中或句末。当 as 在从句中作主语时,从句的谓语通常是被动语态或系表结构;当 as 在从句中作宾语时,从句的谓语常用"情态动词+动词原形"构成。常见的结构如下:

as is known to all　　众所周知
as has been said above　　如上所述
as was expected　　正如预料的那样
as has been pointed out　　正如指出的那样
as suggested by　　正如……所建议的
as we all can see (know, hear)　　正如大家看到的(知道的、听到的)那样

➤ As seen from the earth, these planets appear to move in circles round the sun.
正如从地球上看到的那样,这些行星看来是围绕太阳作圆周运动。

➤ As is very natural, man can live without air.
没有空气人就不能生存,这是很自然的。

➤ The patient did not have a heart attack as the doctor had feared.
患者并没有像医生所担心的那样复发心脏病。

- Power is equal to work divided by the time, <u>as has been said before</u>.

  功率等于功除以时间,<u>这在前面已讲到</u>。

- <u>As is announced in the papers</u>, our country has launched another man-made satellite.

  <u>报上宣布</u>,我国又发射了一颗人造地球卫星。

2)由"but"引导的定语从句

一般和"no"连用,译成"没有……不"。

- There is no rule <u>but has exception</u>.

  凡规则都有例外。

- There has not been a scientist of eminence <u>but was a man of industry</u>.

  没有哪一个有成就的科学家不是勤奋的。

- With the introduction of the electronic computer, there is no complicated problem <u>but can be solved</u>.

  使用电子计算机,任何复杂的问题都能解决。

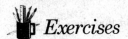 *Exercises*

1. Pick up the sentences with attributive clauses from professional papers in your field and translate them by the rules in this unit.

2. Translate following sentences according to the rules learned from this unit.

采用前置法,将下列各定语从句译成"的"字结构的定语:

1) The people who use biometric locks no longer have to worry about forgetting their keys.

2) Glass bottles and jars that hold food and drink allow us to see the contents.

3) The chemical processes by which iron oxide is stripped of their oxygen constituents are complex.

4) The day is rapidly coming when robots will be equipped with a multitude of sensors such as vision, touch, force and proximity.

5) There are many methods by which gastric resection may be accomplished.

采用分译法,将下列定语从句译成并列分句:

6) A computer is a device that takes in a series of electrical impulses representing information.

7) Computers, which make it possible to free man from the labor of complex measurements and computations, have found wide application in engineering.

8) The waves, which are commonly called radio waves, travel with the velocity of light.

9) Galileo was a famous Italian scientist by whom the Copernican theory was further proved correct.

10) To find the pressure we divide the force by the area on which it presses, which gives us the force per unit area.

将下列定语从句译成相应的状语从句：

11) We cannot live on the moon, where there is no air and water.

12) A transformer cannot operate on direct current, which would burn out the winding in it.

13) Reaction is often reduced by the formation of a thin oxide film which limits access of oxygen, water, vapor and other gases.

14) There was something original, independent, and heroic about the plan that pleased all of them.

15) Matter has certain features or properties that enable us to recognize it easily.

16) The generator is producing electricity, which is used for lighting.

17) We have to oil the moving parts of the machine, the friction of which may be greatly reduced.

18) Pieces of iron which are left in the rain become rusty.

19) The factory, which is small, produces a large quantity of machine every day.

20) A polished surface reflects more heat than a dull surface, which absorbs more heat than a polished surface.

21) Trains, which disappeared from Britain many years ago, are still used in several European cities.

22) The fact that the new alliance was locally generated and sustained should be a strong inducement of the US whose interests already dicate such support.

试译下列各特殊定语从句：

23) Spiders are not insects, as many people think, nor even related to them.

24) As is known to all, a body at rest will not move unless it is acted upon by a force.

25) Levers and pulleys, as shown in the experiment, change motion from one direction to another.

26) The book was written in 1940. It was the best reference book there was then on inorganic chemistry.

27) There is no material but will deform more or less under the action of forces.

3. Go through the following sentences and pay attention to the translation skills of attributive clauses.

➤ According to Steve Whelan of Ricardo, a consultancy that develops engines technology, this improves fuel efficiency, reduces the level of partial combustion produced, and makes the engine much quieter.

据 Ricardo <u>发动机技术研发</u>咨询公司的 Steve Whelan 介绍,这项(技术)提高了燃油利用率,减少了燃烧产生的颗粒物,使发动机更安静地运转。

➤ The 2004 Indian Ocean tsunami was an undersea earthquake that occurred at 00:58:53 UTC (07:58:53 local time) on December 26, 2004.

2004 年 12 月 26 日,发生在国际协调时间(UTC = Universal Time Coordinated) 00:58:53

(当地时间 07:58:53) 的印度洋海底地震引起了海啸。

➤ Clearly we should be happy with any method that simultaneously achieved the first three objectives.
显然,我们应该对任何能同时实现前三个目标的方法感到高兴。

➤ Global climate depends on combinations of factors interacting in subtle and complex ways that we do not yet fully understand.
全球气候取决于许多我们无法完全理解的微妙和复杂方式的相互作用。

➤ But in this age, it's hard to find a place where you can go and be yourself without worrying about the neighbors.
但是在如今这个年代,找到一个可以随心所欲而不必担心打扰左邻右舍的地方是非常难的。

➤ A lathe is a machine tool by which we can cut metal from the surface of a round workpiece.
车床就是我们用来切削圆形工件表面金属的机床。

➤ But we produce other greenhouse gases that intensify the effect.
但我们制造了其他温室气体,这加剧了(温室效应的)影响。

➤ Emissions of greenhouse gases and aerosols due to human activities continue to alter the atmosphere in ways that are predicated to affect the climate.
由于人类活动排放的温室气体和悬浮颗粒不断改变着大气(成分),这必将会影响气候状况。

➤ Someone who posted pornographic material under the title "Kid-Fun" could be sued for mislabeling.
那些将色情材料放在"童趣"网站上的人可能会因为乱贴标签而遭到起诉。

➤ The earthquake, at a magnitude of 9.0, generated a tsunami that was among the deadliest disasters in modern history.
震级为9级的这次地震,引发了海啸,它是近代历史上最惨重的灾难之一。

➤ An advertiser enters into an agreement with a spammer who generates email advertisements to a group of unsuspecting recipients.
广告商和发送邮件广告给许多毫无戒心的接收者的垃圾邮件发送者达成协议。

➤ In the United States one in four citizens suffers from a foodborne illness, and some 5,000 people die from something they ate each year.
在美国,每年每四个公民中就有一个遭受食源性疾病,大约5000人死于他们所吃的食物。

➤ They can put a rat gene into lettuce to make a plant that produces vitamin C or splice genes from moth into apple plants, offering protection from fire blight, a bacterial disease that damages apples and pears.
他们把老鼠的基因注入生菜,使其产出维生素C,或者把飞蛾的基因和苹果的基因拼接,使其不受火疫病(一种损害苹果和梨的细菌性疾病)的侵害。

➤ The early modernist planners held utopian attitudes and a belief in the future in which social

problems could be tamed and humanity liberated from the constraints of scarcity and greed.
早期的现代派设计者对于未来持有理想化的态度和信仰,认为一切社会问题能够得到解决,并且人性能够摆脱不足和贪婪的束缚。

➤ The same technology, which has already appeared in a BMW, is also hitting the road in a Mercedes, an Alfa Romeo, and in cars from Volkswagen, Rover, Peugeot and Citroë.
这种已经运用在宝马汽车上的技术也运用在了奔驰、阿尔法·罗密欧的一款车型以及大众、漫游者、标致和雪铁龙的多款车型上。

➤ The rest is trapped in the lower air layers, which contain a number of gases-water vapor, CO_2, methane, and others—that absorb the outgoing infrared radiation.
其余部分集中在含有许多气体(水蒸气、二氧化碳、甲烷及其他气体)的较低的大气层中,这部分较低的大气层吸收红外线辐射。

➤ Also the first measurement of each test uses all three FIDs for the same sampling point, which must agree.
每次试验的第一次测量用三个火焰离子检测器(FID = Flame Ionization Detector)测量同一个选样点,并且它们的数值必须相同。

➤ High concentrations of CO_2 can have a fertilizing effect on plants, which is why some commercial greenhouses use an artificial indoor atmosphere containing CO_2 at about three times the level outside.
高浓度的二氧化碳对植物有施肥效果,这就是为什么一些商业温室使用比外面二氧化碳浓度高大约三倍的人工温室。

➤ The physical model described here is created on the basis of the TreadSim model, which is developed around a simplified physical structure of a real tyre.
这里描述的物理模型是基于 TreadSim 模型建立的,这是根据简化的真实轮胎模型的物理结构研发的。

➤ Meanwhile, IC data produced by different roller vendors are presented in various data forms, which bring inconvenience and confusions to contractors when using multiple IC rollers.
与此同时,不同压路机生产商给出的智能压实数据(IC)呈现为各式各样的数据形式,这会带来使用多台智能压实压路机时的诸多不便和困扰。

➤ Eventually these vehicles, which will be able to run on hydrogen extracted from conventional hydrocarbon fuel, are expected to displace petrol and diesel vehicles.
以传统碳氢化合物燃料中提取的氢作为动力源的汽车,最终有望取代传统的汽油车和柴油车。

➤ The main purpose of this section is to identify the possibility of air drafts due to the UFAD system usage, which can cause local thermal discomfort for the occupants.
本章的目的在于确认使用地板送风系统(UFAD system)产生气流的可能性,这可能导致居住者的局部热不舒适性。

➤ The active front steering (AFS) consists of a double rows planetary mechanism and displace-

ment motor, which can realize variable transmission ratio control and steering intervention control.
前主动轮转向由一个双排行星齿轮机和变速马达组成,这可以实现变传动比控制和转向干预控制。

➤ For instance, BMW's active steering system is only able to apply up to 3 degrees of steering angle on the front wheels, which is equivalent to a driver steering wheel input of about 55 degrees.
例如,宝马主动转向系统仅适用于向前轮增加不超过 3 度的转向角,这相当于大约 55 度的方向盘转角输入。

➤ Lots of repetitive work had been done on calibration work of the vehicle, which would prolong the period and increase the cost of the development of the vehicle.
在机动车的校准工作上做了很多的重复性工作,这延长了研发周期,增加了研发费用。

➤ The tire property of filtering out the high-frequency excitation component is called enveloping characteristics, which was initially proposed by Lippmann.
轮胎能够过滤高频激励信号的特性称为包络特性,这最初是由李普曼提出的。

➤ The fundamental design conflict faced by conventional steering systems involves choosing a suitable geometric steering ratio, which affects not only the steering effort in the maneuvering range, but also the vehicle dynamics at higher speeds.
传统转向系统面临的基本设计冲突涉及选择合适的几何转向比,这不仅影响转向力度的操纵范围,而且影响在更高速度时车辆的动力。

➤ Program development can be greatly speeded by a dump analysis program, which makes the state of a program more visible to the programmer.
采用一种转储分析程序能够大大加速程序开发,这种转储分析程序可以使程序员更清楚地看见程序的状态。

➤ Using a new technique, Gary Blasdel and Guy Salama of the University of Pittsburgh in the US have produced pictures of the visual cortex of macaque monkeys that demonstrate the two systems in action.
美国匹兹堡大学的 Gary Blasdel 和 Guy Salama 使用一种新技术摄制了猕猴视觉皮层的照片,(照片)展现了这两种机制的运作情形。

➤ The sun is a mass of condensed gases or liquids, the temperature of which is about 10,000℃ on the surface.
太阳是由凝聚气体或液体凝聚成的团块,其表面温度约为摄氏 10000 度。

➤ He can use medications to combat infectious that have got into the patient's system and are causing trouble.
他使用药物治疗对付已进入病人器官系统并造成疾病的感染。

➤ Lab-technicians perform tests on the samples that may indicate the nature of the complaint. So the doctor can perceive just by scrutinizing the results of the tests.

化验员对这些标本所做的化验可以表明病痛的性质。因此，医生只要查看化验结果就明白了。

➤ Other diseases for which the cure has not yet been discovered may benefit somewhat from research that aims at diminishing the severity of the disease.

对于另一些疾病，虽然目前尚未找到治疗方案，但旨在减轻其严重性的研究可能多少会对它们有所帮助。

➤ The widespread use of antibiotics has resulted in the natural evolution of strains of disease germs which are resistant to such medications.

抗生素广泛的使用已经导致了对这种药物有抵抗力的致病菌株发生自然演变。

➤ Some bacteria release poisonous chemicals that harm the body.

有些细菌可释放出对人体有害的有毒化学物质。

Unit 13　状语从句的翻译
Translation of Adverbial Clauses

状语从句是指用来修饰主句或主句的谓语的英语句子。状语从句一般可分为九大类，分别表示时间、地点、原因、目的、结果、条件、让步、比较和方式。状语从句种类较多，在不同场合需要使用不同的连接词与主句连接，与汉语表述习惯存在较大差异。在科技论文中，状语从句随处可见，通常结构复杂，多重嵌套，有些从句中还包含其他类型的小从句等句式结构，给翻译者带来了极大的困难。因此，真实、简洁、通顺地翻译状语从句，需要翻译者的技巧和经验。

在翻译状语从句时，应注意以下几点：首先，应注意各类状语从句在英汉两种语言中的位置差异，在译文中适当调整语序，相应地译成符合译文表达习惯的状语从句；其次，应注意连接词，分清主句和从句之间的逻辑关系；第三，应尽量避免机械地照搬连接词的汉语对应词或译义，在准确理解主句和从句间的逻辑关系后，进行相应的句型转换，如可将英语的时间状语从句译为汉语的并列句或条件句，地点状语从句译为汉语的条件句等。

1. 时间状语从句

1）译成时间状语从句放句首

➢ After the Late Heavy Bombardment or Lunar Cataclysm period ended, mostly near-Earth asteroids (NEAs) have peppered the terrestrial region.
在后期宇宙大撞击或者说月球灾难时期结束后，大多数近地小行星已经布满类地行星区。

➢ We should take it as our obligation to maintain and nurture the ecology of this planet and pledge ourselves to the prudent, sustainable use of natural environment while we are striving to fulfill our historic missions of contributing to enhanced prosperity for all.
当我们努力去实现促进（经济）繁荣的历史使命的时候，应该把维护地球生态和保证谨慎而可持续地使用自然环境资源当作自己的义务。

➢ When solar energy penetrates the land surface, it is converted into heat, most of which radiates upward quickly.
当太阳能照射陆地表面时，它就转化为热能，其中大部分迅速向上辐射。

➢ Because the straddle-type monorail car is more stable than the hanging-type monorail car when subjected to external forces, such as wind, Hitachi has been developing the straddle-type.
当受到风等外力作用时，跨座式单轨列车比悬挂式列车运行更平稳，所以日立公司已经在研发跨座式单轨车。

➢ The upwind side of the canyon is called leeward and downwind, and it is windward <u>when the wind flow is perpendicular to the street canyon</u>.

峡谷的逆风侧称为背风面或者顺风面,<u>当气流与街道峡谷垂直时</u>,就成为迎风面。

➢ It is essential to guarantee the steering stability <u>while developing the novel EPS and the vehicle system</u>.

<u>在研发新型的电动助力转向系统(EPS = Electric Power Steering)和车辆系统的时候</u>,保证转向的稳定性是重要的。

➢ Therefore, it is advantageous to use steering intervention rather than braking intervention to generate a corrective yaw moment when controlling a vehicle on slippery surfaces, <u>where the limits of adhesion can be easily reached</u>.

因此,<u>在很容易达到附着极限的湿滑路面上行驶时</u>,使用转向干预而不是制动干预产生校正横摆力矩控制湿滑路面的车辆是很有利的。

➢ These thin elements may buckle locally at a stress level lower than the yield point of steel <u>when they are subjected to compression in flexural bending and axial compression</u>.

<u>当这些细薄构件在塑性弯曲和轴向压力作用下受挤压时</u>,在应力水平远远小于钢材屈服点的情况下,(细薄构件)局部就发生竖向弯曲。

2) 译成并列句

➢ While EGR can reduce the output of nitrogen-oxide, it can have unwelcome side-effect of increasing the level of particulates.

尾气再循环系统(EGR = Emission Gas Recirculation)减少氮氧化物排放,同时它也带来了令人讨厌的副作用:增加了颗粒物的排放。

➢ When a vehicle is travelling on the road surface, the random vibration excited by the uneven road profile is transferred to the vehicle body through tire and suspension system.

车辆行驶在路面上,不平整的路面所产生的随机振动通过轮胎和悬架系统传递到车身。

➢ The earth turns round its axis <u>as it travels around the sun</u>.

地球<u>一面绕太阳运行</u>,一面绕地轴自转。

➢ <u>While a rocket is fired</u>, a hot gas is formed inside it.

<u>火箭点燃时</u>,内部就形成一股炽热的气体。

3) 译成条件状语从句

➢ When the molecules of a solid move fast enough, the solid melts and becomes a liquid.

如果固体内的分子运动得足够快,固体就融化为液体。

➢ When information exists in digital form or is transferred into digital form it is digitized.

如果信息以数字形式存在,或被转化成数字形式,便是被数字化了。

➢ The oil companies are, unsurprisingly, reluctant to spend billion rebuilding refineries to do

this, especially when low oil prices are hitting them hard.
特别是在低油价的重创下,很多燃油公司不愿意把数十亿的资金投入新炼油厂的建设中,这并不奇怪。

➢ When warm water collects in one place, evaporation and cloud buildup may increase.
如果温暖的海水集中在一个地区,(海水的)蒸发与云层的形成可能会增加。

➢ When the angle sensor of steering wheel turns at a certain angle, the processor can determine the present absolute angle of the steering wheel through the pulse sequence.
当方向盘角度传感器达到一定的角度时,处理器就可以通过脉冲序列确定目前的方向盘的绝对角度。

➢ When the shear capacity of the beam is exceeded, the "shear failure" occurs by excessive shear of the gross area of the webs.
一旦超过了梁的抗剪能力,腹板总面积剪力过大从而导致"剪切破坏"。

2. 地点状语从句

1)译成地点状语从句放句首

➢ Furthermore, higher temperature might be most welcome where they most likely occur.
另外,最有可能出现(升温现象)的地方恰好就是较高温度最受欢迎的地方。

➢ Heat is always being transferred in one way or another, where there is any difference in temperature.
凡有温差的地方,热都会以这样或那样的方式传输。

➢ Where there is little rain, the reservoir would provide us with water.
雨水少的地方,水库就会给我们供水。

➢ Where high moments have to be resisted, high strength or friction-grip bolts or a full-strength welded splice may be required.
在必须抵抗高力矩的部位,可要求使用高强或摩擦握紧螺栓或等强度焊接进行加固。

2)译成条件或结果状语从句

➢ The belt cools and becomes denser as it approaches Greenland, where it sinks.
洋流带接近格陵兰岛时温度下降,密度上升,因此下沉。

➢ Where water resources are plentiful, hydroelectric power stations are being built in large numbers.
只要是水源充足的地方,就可以修建大批的电站。

➢ It is hopeful that solar energy will find wide application wherever it becomes available.
人们希望太阳能得到广泛的利用,任何地方都可以使用。

➢ Wherever conductors are needed, insulators will be indispensable.
凡需要导体的地方,就缺不了绝缘体。

3. 原因状语从句

1)译成表"因"的分句

> Some sulfur dioxide is liberated when coal, heavy oil and gas burn, <u>because they all contain sulfur compounds</u>.
> <u>因为煤、重油和煤气都含有硫化物</u>,所以它们燃烧时会放出一些氧化硫。
> To launch a space vehicle into orbit, a very big push is needed <u>because the friction of air and the force of gravity are working against it</u>.
> 要把宇宙飞船送入轨道,需要施加很大推力,<u>因为空气的摩擦力和地球引力对它起阻碍作用</u>。
> Engineers today plan swiftly and effectively <u>because they know how to measure and calculate</u>.
> 现在,工程师搞设计速度快、效率高,<u>因为他们知道如何测量和计算</u>。
> <u>Because column has axial compression as well as moment to bear</u>, it is given precedence in multi-storey construction.
> <u>因为柱能承载轴向压力以及力矩</u>,所以成为多层建筑结构的首选。

2)译成因果偏正复句的主句(从句译成主句)

> <u>Because energy can be changed from one form into another</u>, electricity can be changed into heat energy, mechanical energy, light energy, etc.
> <u>能量从一种形式转换成另一种形式</u>,所以电可以转变为热能、机械能、光能等。
> <u>As the mass of a body is constant</u>, the effect of the increase in applied force is to increase the velocity.
> <u>物质的质量不变</u>,所以增大作用力便会增加速度。
> <u>As the temperature is very high</u>, some method of cooling must be adopted.
> <u>温度非常高</u>,所以必须采取某种冷却方法。

4. 结果状语从句

1)顺译

> The industry's top companies will also have a strong international presence <u>so that they can continue to serve their customers</u> as they expand their manufacturing capacity overseas.
> 该行业的翘楚也会在未来有强大的国际影响,当他们在海外扩展制造能力时,<u>能继续为客户服务</u>。
> D-mode is applied most in common drive, <u>so it needs to highlight best fuel consumption</u>.
> 驱动器模式是最常见的驱动方式,<u>所以它需要强调最佳的燃油消耗</u>。

- Electronic monitors would watch over the public areas <u>so that there would be little crime</u>.
  电子监视器将对公共场所进行监视，<u>因此将少有犯罪行为</u>。
- Electricity is playing such an important part in the national economy <u>that industry cannot develop rapidly without it</u>.
  电在国民经济中扮演重要的角色，<u>少了它工业就不能迅速发展</u>。

2）省略连词

- Electronic computers work so fast <u>that they can solve a very difficult problem in a few seconds</u>.
  电子计算机演算神速，<u>一个难题几秒钟内就能解决</u>。
- Some elements exist in such small quantities <u>that it is difficult to get them</u>.
  有些元素非常稀少，<u>很难得到</u>。
- These piston rings are so worn <u>that they must be renewed</u>.
  这些活塞环磨损得相当严重，<u>必须更新</u>。
- The temperature in the sun is so high <u>that nothing can exist in solid state</u>.
  太阳内部的温度非常高，<u>任何物体都不能以固态形式存在</u>。

5. 目的状语从句

1）目的前置分句

- The blocks were close fitting when stacked together, <u>so that there was no significant leakage between them</u>.
  <u>为了使块与块之间没有明显的缝隙</u>，他们叠合在一起的时候必须极其吻合。
- All the parts for this kind of machine must be made of especially strong materials <u>in order that they will not break while in use</u>.
  <u>为了在使用时不致断裂</u>，这种机器的所有部件都应该用特别坚固的材料制成。
- An additional force is needed <u>in order that the motion of a body can be changed</u>.
  <u>为了改变物体的运动</u>，必须施加外力。
- A rocket must gain a speed of about five miles per second <u>that it may put a satellite in orbit</u>.
  <u>为了把卫星送入轨道</u>，必须使火箭达到每秒约五英里的速度。

2）目的后置分句

- Scientists are also using biotechnology to insert genes into cows and sheep <u>so that the animals will produce pharmaceuticals in their milk</u>.
  科学家们正在使用生物技术把相关的基因植入牛羊体内，<u>使牛羊的奶水中产生药物</u>。
- A mechanical interface is prepared on the spaceship <u>so that it can be used as a lifesaving boat for space station</u>, and at the same time the orbital module can also serve as a target spacecraft for future rendezvous and dockings.

在宇宙飞船上准备一个机械接口,可以用作空间站的救生船,同时轨道舱也可以作为一个未来交会对接的目标航天器。

6. 条件状语从句

1)译成"条件"或"假设"的分句

- They said if we had any problem, it would stop the lines.
  他们(工程师)说,一旦出现问题,就会使生产线停产。
- The need to answer these questions becomes obvious if it is taken into account that the typical lifetime models are highly nonlinear and very sensitive with respect to some input quantities.
  如果考虑典型的生命周期模型是高度非线性的,并且对于一些输入量非常敏感,那么回答这些问题的必要性变得明显了(那么就很有必要回答这些问题了)。
- If global warming retains unattended, Earth's ecosystems and the life that depends on them will be destroyed.
  如果继续漠视全球变暖现象,地球的生态系统和依赖它们的生命将会遭到毁灭。
- And even if all greenhouse gas emissions stopped tomorrow, the planet almost certainly would continue warm for several decades because of the gases' long atmospheric lifetime.
  即使明天就停止所有温室气体的排放,可以肯定地球会在未来几十年里持续变暖,因为温室气体的大气寿命很长。
- The system will warn (digital or voice hint) firstly if the spacing from the front car is too small to lead to rear-end collision.
  如果与前面车的间距太短将导致追尾,系统将在第一时间发出警告(数字或语音提示)。
- Simple P-type current controllers can be used if feed-forward of the mains voltages is applied.
  在提供前馈主电压的条件下,才能使用简单的P型电流控制器。
- A tropical forest will soak up CO_2, but once cleared for cattle ranching, the same land becomes a source of methane
  热带雨林吸收二氧化碳,但如果把它们砍光用来放牧,同样的土地则会变成沼气产生之地。
- If you require a computer to make a calculation or to solve a problem, you have to feed it with the necessary information.
  如果计算机要做计算或解决问题,就得输入必要的信息。
- A body at rest can't move unless a force is exercised on it.
  除非施加外力,否则静止的物体不可能运动。
- The average speed of all molecules remains the same so long as the temperature is constant.
  只要温度不变,所有分子的平均速度就不变。
- If there were no air, there would be no life on the earth.
  如果没有空气,地球上就不会有生命了。

- If the weld is made from one side, the throat thickness may be reduced.
  如果从一侧焊接,可降低焊喉厚度。
- If pinned connection is assumed, they should have sufficient flexibility to accommodate rotations without causing significant bending moments that may lead to premature failure of the connection or connected members.
  如果采用了铰接接头,这些接头应有足够的柔性以承受转动而不产生较大弯矩,否则,这些弯矩可能导致接头和连接构件发生过早失效。
- Where bolts are subjected to shear, and are not preloaded, some degree of slip is to be expected.
  如果螺杆受剪力,又没有经过预加载,就会产生一定程度的滑移。
- If an accurate basic control is established first, large errors can be prevented and minor ones controlled and localized, so that the small details of the survey fall automatically into place.
  如果首先建立准确的基础控制网,不仅可以防止产生重大误差,还可将小误差控制在局部范围,从而使测量的细节井然有序。
- Indeed, it is advisable that welded connections should generally be designed as full strength, since undersized welds may fail in brittle fracture if exposed to greater than expected moment resulting from differential settlement.
  的确,建议焊接接头通常设计为满强度接头,因为在不均匀沉降产生的异常大的力矩作用下,尺寸过小的焊缝会脆性失效。

2) 译成补充说明情况的分句

- Iron or steel parts will rust, if they are unprotected.
  铁件或钢件是会生锈的,如果不加保护的话。
- Anybody above the earth will fall unless it is supported by an upward force equal to its weight.
  地球上的任何物体都会落下来,除非它受到一个大小与重量相等的力的支持。

7. 让步状语从句

1) 前置或后置

- The subject of surveying is not difficult although a sound knowledge of certain branches of mathematics is necessary at advanced level.
  虽然在高级阶段必须有扎实的数学领域知识,但是勘察学科难度不算大。
- The researchers added that while sulforaphane was the most potent enzyme activator yet discovered, they still have much to learn about the chemical.
  研究人员补充说,虽然萝卜硫素是目前发现最有效的酶激活剂,但他们仍需要更多了解这种化学物质。
- Although the rise time of the fuzzy adaptive PI controller is slightly longer, the performance improvement is considerable.

尽管模糊自适应 PI 控制器的上升时间长一点，但其性能提升还是十分可观的。

➢ While these solutions effectively reduce NO$_x$ emission, alternative technologies focused on pollution prevention are achieving the same results with added financial benefits and improved performance.

尽管这些解决方案有效地降低氮氧化合物（NO$_x$）的排放，但替代技术在污染防治中取得了相同的结果，增加了经济利益并且提高了（防治）性能。

➢ Although dSPACE CAN module has been nested in the Simulink blocks, another CAN card is needed to serve as the medium between the computer host board and DS1103 board.

尽管数字空间的（dSPACE）的 CAN 模块镶嵌在 Simulink 模块上，但还需要另一个 CAN 卡来作为电脑主板和 DS1103 板之间的媒介。

➢ At this point, the optimal control problem is completely defined, although it is not particularized explicitly for any specific architecture.

在这点上，虽然并未明确具体的任何特定的体系结构，但是最优控制问题已经被完全界定了。

➢ Although water vapor is the most potent greenhouse gas, evaporation also leads to cloud formation, which can have a cooling effect.

尽管水蒸气是最容易引起的温室效应的气体，但这种蒸发过程也可以导致云层的形成，从而达到降温的效果。

➢ In addition, one of the main problems with simulation models is the uncertainty on input data, despite the fact that the sensitivity of the results to variation in the input data may be very high.

此外，尽管结果输入数据变化结果的灵敏性可能很高，仿真模型的一个主要问题仍是输入数据的不确定性。

➢ Features apparent in the flow around a single, isolated building are also present for a group of buildings, although their relative and absolute significance is generally affected by interactions within the group.

单个独立建筑周围的气流所存在的特征，也出现在建筑群周围的气流中，尽管它们的相对或绝对的意义通常会受到组团内相互作用的影响。

➢ Although the fuzzy active steering controller was not able to exactly match the actual vehicle yaw rate with the desired one at this speed, it was confirmed that the controller is capable of this performance at lower speeds.

在此车速下，虽然模糊主动转向控制器不能控制实际车辆横摆角速度达到预期值，但有一点是确认的，那就是在车速较低时，控制器能使横摆角速度达到预期值。

2）译成表示"无条件"的条件分句

➢ The best way to improve urban air may be to curb the use of cars, even though modern cars are far cleaner than earlier ones.

尽管现代汽车比以前的汽车污染要小得多，但改善城市空气质量最好的办法可能还是控制汽车的使用。

Exercises

1. Translate the sentences with adverbial clauses picked up in your professional papers.

2. Practice the rules harvested from this unit in the translation of following sentences.

(1) 时间状语从句

1) Meroney et al. report that the pollutant concentrations are almost independent of the wind speeds when the aspect ratio equals 1.

2) There are also questions about whether sustainable management is practical when it comes to protecting areas of great biodiversity such as the world's tropical forests.

3) When the waves of tsunami approach land, their appearance and behavior become dependent on several local factors.

4) When warm water collects in one place, evaporation and cloud buildup may increase.

5) As the electron beam scans the image, variations of light intensity of the image are converted into variation in electric energy.

6) People tend to store energy in good years to see them through lean ones. But when bad times never come, they will hardly get rid of it.

(2) 原因状语从句

7) The higher income tax is impractical in that it may discourage people from trying to earn more.

8) Because the body's defense system is damaged, the patient has little ability to fight off many other diseases.

9) The Sahara has retreated by 40 kilometers in the past four years because the rains have been good.

10) As the moon's gravity is only about 1/6 the gravity of the earth, a 200-pound man weighs only 33 pounds on the moon.

(3) 条件状语从句

11) If the wind speed out of the canyon is below some threshold value, the coupling between the upper and secondary flow is lost.

12) If the statistics holds true, most Americans suffer in this way from time to time.

13) The border's definition is higher if the difference between the pedestrians and the backgrounds temperature is significant.

14) And the Newmark-β method has an advantage of unconditionally stable integration if the suitable parameters are chosen. (stable integration,稳定积分)

15) Unless you know the length of one side of a square or a cube, you can not find out the square's area or the cube's volume.

(4) 让步状语从句

16) Although the pedestrian movement would be assumed to be linear, the movement of the camera, attached to an accelerating vehicle, is not.

17) Though we get only a relatively small part of the total power radiated from the sun, what we get is much more than enough for our needs.
18) Energy can neither be created nor destroyed although its form can be changed.
19) Though radar uses radio waves, it is somewhat different from radio and television.
20) Different as the forms of matter are, they are nothing but matter in motion.
21) While tallness is evidently a hereditary characteristic, any individual's actual height depends on the interaction between their genes and the environment.
22) Complicated as the problem is, it can be solved in only two hours with an electronic computer.
23) All living things, whether they are animals or plants, are made up of cells.

(5) 目的状语从句

24) A rocket must attain a speed of about five miles per second so that it may put a satellite in orbit.
25) Iron products are often coated lest they should rust.
26) Cables are usually laid underground that their life may be prolonged.
27) The temperature is raised so that water may be turned into steam.

(6) 地点状语从句

28) Generally, air will be heavily polluted where there are factories.
29) Where water resources are plentiful, hydro-electric power stations are being built in large numbers.
30) Both plants and animals could not exist where there were no sunlight, water and air.
31) Therefore, it is advantageous to use steering intervention rather than braking intervention to generate a corrective yaw moment when controlling a vehicle on slippery surfaces, where the limits of adhesion can be easily reached. （steering intervention,转向干预;braking intervention,制动干预;corrective yaw moment,校正横摆力矩;limits of adhesion,附着极限）

Unit 14 长句的翻译
Translation of Complicated Sentences

为了说理严谨、逻辑紧密、描述准确,科技英语中大量使用长句。一句话有时需要一系列的从句和短语来加以周密细致的限定和说明,从而使得句子比较长,结构比较复杂,所以我们需要掌握一定的长句翻译技巧,才能准确翻译。科技英语长句翻译中应注意以下问题:

①在借助语法进行句子结构分析时,要理清句子之间的逻辑关系、先后顺序和前提条件等。除此之外,还要根据专业知识来弄清各层意思之间的相互关系,以确定原文的真正含义。

②在弄清句子结构的基础上,接着就要确定关联词(连词、关系代词和关系副词)的基本词义。有时一个关联词有好几个词义,一定要根据上、下文和专业知识来准确地界定关联词的词义,这是长句翻译准确的关键。

③如果对翻译的内容不熟悉,一定要翻阅有关方面的资料或书籍,做到对这方面的专业知识有个大概的了解。切忌不懂专业知识,只靠查字典生硬翻译。有时,我们发现有些句子翻译出来后,语法上没错误,可译文却语义不通,这就是忽视专业知识理解造成的。

④翻译方法并不是固定的,翻译中不可拘泥不变,应采用合适的翻译手段。任何一个长句,只要弄清语法关系的眉目,看透技术上的来龙去脉,就可以适当变动原文结构,灵活处理。有效的翻译应以译文信息准确和完整,通顺和易懂为首要目标。

⑤在汉语表达上应力求文字严谨,避免层次不清,表达混乱,语言文字拖泥带水。同时,也一定要避免歪曲原文的精神实质。

科技英语长句的翻译方法概括说来有四种:顺序法、逆序法、分译法和变序法。

1. 顺流而下——顺序法

如果英文原文的表达顺序与汉语的表达顺序一致,可按照原文的顺序由前向后逐次译出。

➤ To protect against harvesters of email addresses, some websites use software that "poisons" the harvester—for example, generating bogus email addresses of directing the harvester to a nonexistent site.

为了防范电子邮件地址收割机,一些网站使用可以让收割机中毒的软件,例如,(软件)生成假的邮件地址将收割机引向不存在的地址。

➤ Therefore, for better power and less fuel consumption, output characteristic of coupling work condition must meet the demand of reaching max average output power within the work range of high efficiency area for coupling work condition or whole work range.

因此,为了更佳的动力和更少的燃油消耗,耦合工况下的输出特性必须满足在耦合工况或者整个工作区间的高效工作范围达到最大平均输出功率的要求。

- This simulation shows that the radial tire forces of the guide tires on the leading truck are larger than those on the trailing truck because the directions of the yaw moment generated by the air-spring forces on the leading truck are different from those on the trailing truck, while the directions of the yaw moment generated by side forces are identical.

  仿真表明位于前转向架上的导向轮胎径向力比后转向架上的导向轮胎径向力大,这是因为前转向架上的空气弹簧力产生的横摆力矩的方向与后转向架上不同,而与侧向力产生的横摆力矩方向是一致的。

- Such actuation flexibility together with the electric motors' fast and precise torque responses may enhance the existing vehicle control strategies, e. g. traction control system (TCS), direct yaw-moment control (DYC), and other advance vehicle motion/stability control systems.

  这种驱动灵活性,加上电机对转矩的快速精确响应,可能增强现有的车辆控制策略,例如,牵引力控制系统(TCS)、直接横摆角速度控制(DYC)和其他先进的车辆动力性/稳定性控制系统。

- The review provides a comprehensive literature on wind tunnel simulation studies in urban street canyons/intersections including the effects of building configurations, canyon geometries, traffic induced turbulence and variable approaching wind directions on flow fields.

  评论提供了一篇关于城市街道峡谷/十字路口风洞模拟研究的综合性文献,内容包括构建配置、峡谷构造、车辆引起的湍流以及可变侵入风向对流场的影响。

- In short, this maneuver confirms that the cooperation between the fuzzy slip controller that was developed previously and the fuzzy active steering controller developed here has allowed the driver to accelerate the AUTO21EV on a μ-split road with the maximum possible traction forces on all four wheels, no spin-out effects on the wheels, and no side-pushing effect on the vehicle.

  总之,该工况确认了先前开发的模糊滑移控制器和现在开发的模糊主动转向控制器之间的协作,从而允许 AUTO21EV 的四轮以最大可能的牵引力在对开路面上加速,并且车轮不出现打滑,车辆没有侧滑。

- Recent tests on the geometric stability of several digital cameras that were not designed for photogrammetric applications have shown that the accomplished accuracies in object space are either limited or that the accuracy potential is not exploited to the fullest extent.

  最近对非专业摄影测量的几款数码相机几何稳定性的测试显示,目前该类型的数码相机在物体空间所能达到的精度是有限的,或者说该精度还没有发掘到最大程度。

- Before any optical 3-D measurement system will be adopted by industry it must demonstrate not only that it is capable of producing the accuracies required, but also that the measurement process offers the potential of improving productivity.

  任何光学三维测量系统要想得到行业认可,必须能达到所要求的精确度,同时其测量程序必须有提高的潜力。

- Only by studying such cases of human intelligence with all the details and by comparing the results of exact investigation with the solutions of AI (Artificial Intelligence) usually given in the elementary books on computer science can a computer engineer acquire a thorough understanding of theory and method in AI, develop intelligent computer programs that work in a human-like way, and apply them to solving more complex and difficult problems that present computer can't.

只有通过详细研究人类智能案例,并把实际研究结果与基础计算机科学书上的人工智能结论相比较,计算机工程师才能彻底地了解人工智能的理论和方法,开发出具有人类智能的计算机程序,并将其用于解决目前计算机不能解决的更复杂和更困难的问题。

➤ Large-scale plans, development, and redevelopment activities can hardly be construed as being conducive to promoting the interests and wellbeing of those with less power as they are not in a position to participate in the planning process and gain the benefits of the outcomes of modernist planning.

大规模的规划、开发和再开发活动很少被认为有助于弱势群体的利益和福祉,因为他们不参与规划过程,也无法获得现代规划的结果所带来的好处。

➤ Due to the possible modeling inaccuracies and vehicle parametric uncertainties, an adaptive controller is designed as the higher-level controler to give the required forces to the left and right sides of the vehicle.

由于可能出现的模型误差和车辆参数不确定性,(我们)设计了一个自适应控制器,将其作为高层控制器来分配车辆左右侧所需的力。

➤ When it's unclear from the context whether we're using the specific definition of "nanotechnology" or the broader and more inclusive definition (often used in the literature), we'll use the terms "molecular nanotechnology" or "molecular manufacturing".

当从上下文也无法明确使用的是纳米技术的特定含义还是广泛含义,或者是更具包容性的定义(经常在文献中使用)时,我们将使用"分子纳米技术"和"分子制造"的术语。

➤ In contrast to the Kalman filter, the particle filter is a completely nonlinear state estimator based on the probability and can be a good candidate for SOC (State of Charge) estimation for a Li-ion battery.

与卡尔曼滤波算法相比,粒子滤波算法是一种完全基于概率的非线性状态估量算法,并且能够很好地估算锂电池的荷电状态(SOC)。

➤ The contribution of this paper is to find solutions to the rationing of energy use with the aim to preserve Kuwait's oil wealth and to prioritize future needs during the gradual shift towards the use of alternative and renewable energy in power generation, with emphasis on solar energy and PV (photovoltaic) generation.

本文的作用是找到能源使用配给的解决方案,目的是为了保护科威特的石油财富,在逐步转向使用可替代和可再生能源发电的同时优先考虑未来需求,强调太阳能和光伏发电。

➤ Just before the accident, two persons were leaving the elevator and because of sudden fracture of the shaft, connection between pulley and electric engine was broken, which lead the break system of the engine to fail.

就在事故发生前,两个人正准备离开电梯,由于突发轴断裂,滑轮和电动机之间的连接断开,从而导致引擎刹车系统的失灵。
- The development of intelligent vehicle requires that the structure of the vehicle itself and also its running process be intelligentized so as to improve the intelligent interaction with other vehicles and the surrounding facilities in road traffic, and to ensure the active safety of the running vehicle.

  智能车辆的发展要求车辆本身的结构以及其运行的过程都要智能化,以提高在运行中与其他车辆和周围设施之间的智能交互,并确保运行车辆的运行安全。

- Each failure mechanism acting on a mechanical part induces one or more part failure modes, and each part failure mode has one or more failure effects on the part and the upper design configurations in which the part is integrated.

  每个作用在机械零件上的失效机制会引起一个或多个零件的故障模式,并且每个零件失效模式都会对零件和与之整合的上层设计配置起到一个或多个失效作用。

- Examples are excessive speed during cornering, obstacle avoidance and severe lane change maneuvers, where rollover occurs as a result of the lateral wheel forces induced during these maneuvers.

  许多例子证明了在转弯、避障和突然变道时,车速太快会导致由外侧轮力量诱发的车辆翻转。

- Accident severity is of special concern to researchers in traffic safety since this research is aimed not only at prevention of accidents but also at reduction of their severity.

  事故严重性引起了交通安全研究人员的特别关注,因为本研究的目的是不仅要预防事故,也要减少事故的严重性。

- On the other hand, given the uniqueness of the solution, the control trajectory obtained by the algorithm is optimal for the arrived final, though it is not a desired final value, because the uniqueness means that there is not an alternative costate that satisfies the boundary conditions for the arrived final.

  另一方面,当给定唯一解时,即使这不是理想的末状态,在达到末状态时由算法得到的控制轨迹是最优的,因为唯一性意味着将不会再有另一个可以满足边界条件的协态变量。

- The aim of this work is to provide a simulation tool that takes into account both tyre structure and tyre tread design thus allowing to predict tyre wear for a given manoeuvre as the function of road and vehicle characteristics.

  这项工作的目的是提供一个仿真工具,它能考虑轮胎结构和轮胎面设计两个方面,作为一个道路和车辆特征函数的指定策略,能够预测轮胎的磨损。

- In order to meet the demand of engine power improving and high exhaust gas recirculation (EGR) rate for emission control, two-stage turbocharging technology is applied as one of the key technologies in the advanced internal combustion engines.

  为了满足通过提高发动机性能和废气再循环率来控制排放的需求,二级涡轮增压作为一项关键技术运用于先进的内燃机上。

- Steel is usually made where the iron ore is smelted, so that the modern steelworks forms a complete unity, taking in raw materials and producing all types of cast iron and steel, both for sending to other works for further treatment, and as finished products such as joists.

炼铁的地方通常也能炼钢,因此现代炼钢厂是一个配套的整体,从运进原料到生产各种类型的铸铁与钢材,再送往其他工厂进一步加工处理,制成成品如托梁。

➢ Since 1900, the greatest warming has been observed between 40 degrees and 70 degrees north latitude-including Europe, Russia, and the northern half of the U.S.—where much of the world's industrial greenhouse gas emissions originate.

自 1900 年以来,最大的升温集中在北纬 40 度到 70 度之间的区域——包括欧洲、俄罗斯和美国北半部,这些都是全球工业温室气体主要排放地区。

➢ The author also describes the prospect of energy technology development and stresses the implementation of energy strategy by further improving energy policy and related mechanisms, strengthening macro-management and the essential role of the market in resource allocation so as to ensure the economic and social development of China through reliable energy supply.

作者也描述了能源技术的发展前景,强调通过进一步改善能源政策和相关机制,加强宏观管理,更好地发挥市场配置资源的基础性作用来实施好能源发展战略,为中国的经济和社会发展提供有力的能源保障。

2. 逆流而上——逆序法

有些英语长句的表达顺序与汉语不同,甚至相反,如主句后有状语从句、后置的定语从句等。汉译时须从英语原文的后面译起,自后向前,逆着原文顺序翻译。

➢ On the other hand, the detained decomposition gas might become the cause of reducing the purity of the metal oxide coating adhered to the ribbon glass in the case the aforementioned decomposition gas is not thoroughly removed from the spraying locale.

另一方面,如果上面提到的分解气体在喷射处没有被彻底地清除掉的话,那么,留下来的分解气体就会使黏附在玻璃带表面上的金属氧化膜的纯度降低。

➢ However, the objects that have been battering our inner solar system after the so-called Late Heavy Bombardment ended are a distinctly different population, UA (University of Arizona) Professor Emeritus Robert Strom and his colleagues report in the article, "The Origin of Planetary Impactors in the inner Solar System".

然而,亚利桑那大学教授斯特罗姆和他的同事在文章《内太阳系行星撞击起源》中指出,在所谓的晚期宇宙流星大撞击结束后,撞击太阳系内的物体是完全不同的星族。

➢ The computer models used to project greenhouse effects far into the future are still being improved to accommodate a rapidly growing font of knowledge.

随着知识的快速积累,用于预测未来温室效应的计算机模型正在被改善。

➢ We should take it as our obligation to maintain and nurture the ecology of this planet and pledge ourselves to the prudent, sustainable use of the Earth's resources and the protection of natural environment while we are striving to fulfill our historic mission of contributing to enhanced prosperity for all.

当我们把促进社会繁荣当作历史任务来完成时,应该将维持和呵护地球生态系统及谨慎可持续地利用自然资源保护自然环境当作我们的义务。

➤ It is possible that the warming observed during this century may have resulted from natural variations, even though the increase has been much more rapid than what the planet has witnessed over the past hundred centuries.

尽管本世纪内地球温度的增长比过去几百个世纪都迅速得多,但本世纪观察到的变暖现象有可能是由于自然界的各种变化而引起的。

➤ This is why the hot water system in a furnace will operate without the use of a water pump, if the pipes are arranged so that the hottest water rises while the coldest water runs down again to the furnace.

如果把管道设计成热水上升而冷水下流返回锅炉,那么,锅炉中的热水系统不用水泵就能循环。

➤ Iron rusts at its exposure to the open air on account of the corrosion made by the destructive chemical attack of a metal coming into contact with such media as air, water and moisture.

金属在接触空气、水和湿气等介质时,会受到破坏性的化学侵蚀,因此,铁暴露在露天环境时要生锈。

3. 化整为零——分译法

原句包含多层意思,而汉语习惯一个小句表达一层意思。为了使行文简洁,将整个长句译成几个独立的句子,顺序基本不变,保持前后的连贯。

➤ A gas may be defined as a substance, which remains homogeneous, and of which the volume increase without limit, when the pressure on it is continuously reduced, the temperature being maintained constant.

气体是一种处于均质状态的物质,当温度保持不变,对气体施加的压力不断降低时,其体积可以无限增大。

➤ This link implies that strategies based on equivalent consumption minimization can be regarded as an implementation of the optimal solution to the energy management problem and therefore can be used with more confidence; furthermore, the coherent description of the optimal control problem and the ties between the three strategies allow for a more effective tuning of the ECMS.

此链接意味着基于等效消耗最小化的策略可视为能量管理问题的最佳解决方案的实现,因此可以更有信心使用。此外,最优控制问题的相关描述和三种策略之间的关系允许对ECM进行更有效的调节。

➤ More particularly, this invention relates to a method and apparatus for forming a film of metal oxides continuously on the surface of ribbon glass by spring thereon a solution of metal compounds at a point in the neighborhood of the inlet to a lehr or the inside thereof when the ribbon glass is being conveyed to the lehr after it has been formed from molten glass.

更具体地说,本发明涉及在玻璃带表面连续地喷涂一层金属氧化膜的方法和装置。当玻璃由液态成型为玻璃带后,在其被送往退火窑时,从退火窑入口附近或入口里将金属化合物溶液喷到玻璃表面上。

➢ With the development of science and technology, the automatic transmission (AT) technology is broadly used on vehicle, especially on passenger vehicle for its advantages of convenience of manipulation, relieving fatigue when driving, improving the comfort and safety, and reducing the pollution of exhaust emission.

随着科学技术的发展,自动变速器技术广泛应用于车辆上,特别是乘用车上。它具有操作方便,减缓驾驶疲劳,提高安全性和舒适性,并且能减少尾气排放污染等优点。

➢ Its simple construction is due to the absence of the magnets, rotor conductors, brushes, and high system efficiency over wide speed ranges make the SRM (Switched Reluctance Motor) drive an interesting alternative to compete with permanent magnet brushless DC (Direct Current) motor and induction motor drives.

它(开关磁阻电机)的简单结构源于它没有永磁体、转子导体和电刷,且在较宽的调速范围都具有高的系统效率。因此,相对于永磁直流无刷电机和感应电机,开关磁阻电机是有潜力的替代品。

➢ In a new design of a parallel hybrid vehicle where the size of components can be sized per design requirement, the ICE (Internal Combustion Engine) can be downsized because dynamic power is provided by the dynamic power source—the electric motor and battery bank—and the ICE (Internal Combustion Engine) can be sized so that its operating points lie mostly in the high-efficiency region.

新设计的并联式混合动力车辆的零件尺寸可以按要求设计。由于动力由动力源(电动马达和电池组)提供,内燃机的尺寸可以缩小。内燃机的大小也可以设计,使其操作点主要集中在高效区。

➢ The loads a structure is subjected to are divided into dead loads, which include the weights of all the parts of the structure, and live loads, which are due to the weights of people, movable equipment, etc.

一个结构物受到的荷载可分为静载与活载两类。静载包括该结构物各部分的重量。活载则是由于人及可移动设备等的重量而引起的荷载。

➢ The isolation of the rural world because of distance and lack of transport facilities is compounded by the paucity of the information media.

因为距离远,交通工具缺乏,农村社会与外界隔绝。这种隔绝,又由于信息媒介不足,而变得更加严重。

➢ Manufacturing process may be classified as unit production with small quantities being made and mass production with large numbers of identical parts being produced.

制造过程可分为单件生产和批量生产。单件生产就是生产少量的零件,批量生产是指生产大量相同的零件。

➢ The research work is being done by a small group of dedicated and imaginative scientists who specialize in extracting from various sea animals substances that may improve the health of the human race.

一小部分富有想象力和敬业精神的科学家正在进行这项研究。他们的研究专注于从各种海洋动物中提取能增进人类健康的物质。

4. 纲举目张——变序法

有时英语长句语法成分繁多，层次复杂，可以根据句子及其修饰语的主次、逻辑、时间先后，打乱原文顺序，有顺有逆综合处理，所以变序法又可称为综合法。

➢ Although it is the power used by a fuse which causes it to blow, fuses are rated by the current which they will conduct without burning out, since it is high current which damages equipment.

虽然正是通过熔丝的电使它烧断，但是只有过大的电流才会损坏设备，所以熔丝在额定值内不会被烧断，能够传导电流。

➢ Nonetheless, in 1995, after years of intense study, the Intergovernmental Panel on Climate Change (IPCC), sponsored by the United Nations, concluded tentatively that "the balance of evidence suggests that there is a discernible human influence on global climate".

尽管如此，经过数年的精心研究，由联合国赞助的政府间气候变化委员会（IPCC）在1995年初步得出结论："所有的证据都表明人类对气候变化有显著影响"。

➢ And so far as observation had gone, it seems unlikely that amid the whole of the heavens there are as many as a hundred stars whose light reaches us in less than twelve or fifteen years.

就现有的观测来看，在整个太空中，其光线能在12年到15年以内到达地球的星球不可能超过100个。

➢ The net rate at which the body loses heat by radiation is the difference between the rate at which it receives energy and the rate at which it loses energy.

物质由于辐射而失去热量的净速率就是物体获得能量的速率和失去能量的速率之差。

➢ Those functions that describe how the computer software reacts to mechanical design, called application functions, are more often important to the engineer in engineering applications such as analysis, calculation, and simulation in connection with mechanical design because he wishes to know how they will work in use to which he wants to apply them.

描述计算机软件如何适应机械设计的软件功能（被称为软件应用功能），对从事与机械设计有关的诸如分析、计算和模拟仿真工作的工程师来说是很重要的，因为他希望了解这些软件功能在他所从事的工作中是如何运作的。

➢ If we are to continue these trends we will have to develop a new "post-lithographic" manufacturing technology which will let us inexpensively build computer systems with mole quantities of logic elements that are molecular in both size and precision and are interconnected in complex and highly idiosyncratic patterns.

如果保持这种趋势，我们将会研发出一种新型的"后光刻"制造技术，它将会使我们可以用逻辑元素摩尔量(在规模和精度达到分子级别且相互间以复杂独特的方式相关联)来廉价地建立电脑系统。

➢ In conjunction with this result, a total available capacity expression that involves the temperature, charge-discharge rate, and running mileage as variables is reconstructed by the actual operation data to improve the model accuracy for application to electric vehicles.

结合这一结果,通过实际操作数据,重新构造以实时运行的电池温度、充放电速度和运行里程作为参数变量来描述的总可用电量表达式,从而提高用于电动汽车模型的准确性。

➢ Finally, based on the above modeling and analysis, the main aim of this paper is to investigate the dynamic behavior of the space manipulator, concerning the flexibility of the space manipulator and the harmonic hysteresis phenomenon.

最后,基于以上的模型和分析,考虑到空间机械臂的柔性和谐波滞后现象,本文着重探讨空间机械臂的动力行为。

➢ The self-adaption controller made by utilizing technology of self-adaption will adjust parameters of acceleration, velocity and shock degree of vehicle according to practical load degree and gear shifting principle with driving condition by calibration to realize self-adaption controlling and improve the characteristic of flexible driving in various load degrees and complex driving conditions.

利用自适应技术制造的自适应控制器,将会在车辆驱动条件下,根据实际负载程度和齿轮换挡原理,校准加速度、速度和振动参数实现自适应控制,并在不同的负载程度和负载的行驶条件下提高灵活驾驶特性。

➢ It's clear now that the pathogens can survive the gentle heating we give our rare hamburgers, the USDA (United States of Department of Agriculture) advises cooks at home to heat ground beef until it's no longer pink and reaches a temperature of 160°F.

美国农业部建议在家中烹饪加热碎牛肉时,应该加热到牛肉不再是粉红色并且温度达到华氏160°,这是因为现在我们都知道病原体能在只进行微热加工的含生肉的汉堡包中存活。

➢ Aluminum remained unknown until the nineteenth century, because nowhere in nature is it found free, owing to its always being combined with other elements, most commonly with oxygen, for which it has a strong affinity.

铝通常会跟其他元素结合,尤其是氧,因为铝和氧有很强的亲和力。由于这个原因,在自然界找不到游离状态的铝,所以人们在19世纪才发现铝。

➢ It's Monday afternoon inside Toyota Motor Corp.'s Valenciennes plant in northern France, where workers turn and bend swiftly over the assembly line to meet demanding hourly production targets.

这是星期一下午,在法国北部的丰田汽车制造公司的瓦朗西安工厂里,为了达到每小时的生产指标,工人们在生产线上忙碌着。

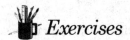 *Exercises*

1. Translate the long sentences in your professional literature with the skills introduced in this unit.

2. Translate following sentences by the learned skills flexibly.

1) Since the Industrial Revolution began by putting water and steam to work, machines using electricity, gasoline, and other energy sources have become so widespread that they now do a very large proportion of the work of the world.

2) For any machine whose input force and output force are known, its mechanical advantage can be calculated.

3) A cat, whose eyes can take in more rays of light than our eyes, can see clearly in the night.

4) We have to oil the moving parts of the machine, the friction of which may be greatly reduced.

5) The diode is coated with a thin layer of hard glass which eliminates the need for a hermetically sealed package.

6) To meet both pollution reduction requirements and plant performance goals, these markets are demanding a more cost-effective, in-process approach, which optimizes the combustion system to prevent emission generation.

7) So to address this question, we will assume that "alternative" refers to those fuels that are produced from a non-fossil source or to those fuels (fossil or otherwise) that would require substantial changes in automotive design or in the distribution and marketing infrastructure.

8) Battery electric vehicles have been dismissed as a colossal flop, so hybrid-electric vehicles, which use an internal-combustion engine for long journeys and an electric motor in town, will be a stop-gap to cut pollution and comply with laws limiting vehicle emissions.

9) But now that politicians and the green lobby are getting more worked up about emissions of global-warming gases, European car makers are terrified that regulations will be brought in to limit carbon dioxide emissions from cars, in the same way that toxic gases such as carbon monoxide or nitrogen oxides are subject to ever-falling statutory limits.

10) As the pandemic grows, it forces the world to see what it may not want to see: that diseases arising among specific populations—prostitutes (known to HIV/AIDS specialists as "sex workers") and their customers, drug users, and gay men—can flare into greater pandemics.

11) But now it is realized that supplies of some of them are limited, and it is even possible to give a reasonable estimate of their "expectation of life", the time it will take to exhaust all known sources and reserves of these materials.

12) It is necessary to use a component of power able to provide a strong power to starting and to assist the vehicle accelerate, the lifecycle of this energy storage device must be in adequacy

with stop & go technology.

13) An approximate model was generated from the optimal simulations or the normalized city cycles, and we tested the approximation model in forward simulations.

14) The contact stresses at the interface of braked racing tyre with the ground surface have been studied in part 1 of this article with a previously described and validated finite-element (FE) model.

15) The trip information recorded with a Global Navigation Satellite System (GNSS) receiver in an onboard unit (OBU) provides a convenient and flexible means to support automated road-use fee collection.

16) Various machine parts can be washed very clean and will be as clean as new ones when they are treated by ultrasonics, no matter how dirty and irregularly shaped they maybe.

17) Rocket research has confirmed a strange fact, which had already been suspected there is a "high temperature belt" in the atmosphere with its center roughly thirty miles above the ground.

18) The American economic system is, organized around a basically private-enterprise, market-oriented economy in which consumers largely determine what shall be produced by spending their money in the marketplace for those goods and services that they want most.

19) Thus, in the American economic system it is the demand of individual consumers, coupled with the desire of businessmen to maximize profits and the desire of individuals to maximize their income, that together determine what shall be produced and how resources are used to produce it.

20) It is often said television keeps one informed about current events, allow one to follow the latest developments in science and politics, and offers an endless series of programmes which are both instructive and entertaining.

21) It should be realized that when we assign a magnitude and direction to the velocity of a body, we are really expressing its velocity relative to something which is, for this particular purpose, imagined to be stationary.

22) Energy is the currency of the ecological system and life becomes possible only when food is converted into energy which in turn is used to seek more food to grow, to reproduce and to survive.

23) During precipitation water infiltrates into the ground, under the influence of gravity, this water travels downwards through the minute pore spaces between the soil particles until it reaches a layer of imperious bedrock, through which it cannot penetrate, the excess moisture draining downwards then fills up all the pore spaces between the soil particles, displacing the soil air.

24) Decision must be made very rapidly after physical endurance is tested as much as perception, because an enormous amount of time must be spent making certain that the key figures act on the basis of the same information and purpose.

25) Concrete is artificial stone made from Portland cement and inert filler materials called aggregates, which are mixed with water to a plastic consistency and placed in forms to harden and gain strength.

26) All commercial iron and steel contains iron as chief constituent, but the percentages of carbon and other elements and the methods by which iron and steel is produced, as well as the processes to which may be subjected, so change the characteristic properties that there are many distinct forms of iron and steel, some of which have properties so different as to appear like different metals.

27) The technical possibility could well exist, therefore, of nationwide integrated transmission network of high capacity, controlled by computers, inter-connected globally by satellite and submarine cable, providing speedy and reliable communications throughout the world.

28) Where an foreign enterprise is willing and able to develop the finished products that are not subject to the unified operation by the State, through joint efforts with the industrial enterprises in Tianjin, particularly in respect of machinery and electronic products and refined chemical products, by means of technology transfer, introduction of technical personnel, technical assistance and economic support, and to provide for foreign companies the finished products through the sales channel of the foreign parties, they may apply to the Municipal Commission of Foreign Economic Relations and Trade for the expansion of the business of joint development.

29) Modern scientific and technical books, especially textbooks, require revision at short intervals if their authors wish to keep pace with new ideas, observations and discoveries.

30) Up to the present time, throughout the eighteenth and nineteenth centuries, this new tendency placed the home in the immediate suburbs, but concentrated manufacturing activity, business relations, government, and pleasure in the centers of the cities.

参考译文
Reference Translation for Exercises

Unit 2

Exercises 2

1) 注意,当转向角为零时,a = b = 0.5,这意味着驱动力将会平均分配在机动车的左、右两侧。
2) 全球定位系统和惯性量测装置已经被证明是一个测量车况的有效手段。
3) 在设计建设跨海大桥时,桥跨下方的平均海水高度应该加以充分考虑。
4) 对机动车的稳定性控制已经展开了大量研究。
5) 在[10]中提出了电动车制动控制方法,研究对象是前后电机独立驱动的车,而不是轮毂电机驱动。
6) 我们知道市场崩盘不一定导致经济灾难。
7) 越来越复杂的车用电子设备增加了对配有更多嵌入式非易失性存储器的高性能 32-b 型微控制器(32-b MCUs)的需求。
8) 转换后变量的均值和方差精确到泰勒级数展开式的二阶。
9) 该隧道采用钻爆法施工。
10) 最基本的停车辅助系统是单个倒车雷达,后来,摄像系统也被用来作为停车辅助装置。
11) 通过显示屏,驾驶员能看见倒车图像、地图导航、夜间图像显示以及移动电视等。
12) 这封信背面的图表着重写明了你的存款情况。
13) 这种设计手段通常产生设计冲突,使设计人员不断重复地修改各种子系统的设计,需要开展各种试验才能完成振动系统的开发,从而导致产品研发周期长,大大影响了产品设计和检测的成本。
14) 这是研究胚胎发育的理想系统。
15) 该概念设计是基于最先进的桥梁技术的设计。
16) 在世界的贫困地区,有许多方式增加农业生产效率。
17) 如果不专注目标付出努力,你将失去影响力和效率并浪费你的资源,最终不能做成你真正想做的事。
18) 预修人工岛是为了安装首节沉管。
19) 老板正在编写招标文件。
20) 所有的桥梁梁段必须在工厂预制。

Unit 3

Exercises 3

1）我们要完全掌握集成电路技术，还必须经过三个阶段。

2）这本书对一般技术员来说也许内容太深。

3）把原料加工成成品的最简单方法是精密铸造。

4）在学会上经常进行广泛的思想交流。

5）这种仪器很昂贵，使其应用受到限制。

6）工业化发展似乎伴随着环境的退化。

7）在对污染物进行微生物转化的过程中，生物会清除毒素或在消耗其他物质时把这些毒素分解。

8）对处于静息状态的吸烟者所做的研究表明，吸烟者比非吸烟者消耗的热量要多。

Exercises 4

1）要了解力的作用，我们必须懂得力的三要素。

2）在高频条件下，积分时间很短，结果会接二连三地快速显示出来，用户可能来不及把答案记录下来。

3）钻床的功能是钻孔。

4）由于能量太小，必须采取措施防止信号完全丢失。

5）这种方法的发明者所表现的远见卓识和渊博知识，给人以良好的印象。

6）对于那些想戒烟但又不想发胖的吸烟者来说，实验结果似乎给他们泼了冷水。

7）一般说来，设计过程不是一帆风顺的，而需要反复试验。

8）钢和铸铁在含碳量上也有所不同。

9）素混凝土是不含钢筋的混凝土。

10）混凝土养护对新浇混凝土的温度和湿度要求很高。

Unit 4

Exercises

1）然而，从行驶车辆中检测行人并不容易。

2）投票过程中，需要对每对像素 p 和 q 进行三次测量。

3）特别是它们会产生氮氧化物和碳氢化合物等微小颗粒物——源自柴油不完全燃烧。

4）之后，大概从 2007 年开始，以燃料电池驱动的环境友好型汽车就开始面世了。

5）原因是：自然过程会使（海洋）从空气中吸收尽量多的二氧化碳来维持平衡。

6）结果，车载网络使汽车技术发生了悄然演变，从而消除曾用于控制电路笨重的布线。

7）该系统采用两个关键参数——冲击和失控，来决定是否启动安全气囊。

8）我们的河水被污染了，我们的海洋被污染了，我们的自然环境被破坏了。

9）功的大小取决于所施加的力与物体所移动的距离。

10）煤油不像汽油那样容易挥发。

11）下次地震将在什么时候发生？

12) 他们肯定能在短期内建成那座工厂。
13) 从全球变暖到臭氧层空洞,人类被认为应该对大量的环境问题负责。
14) 居住条件改善了许多。
15) 试件的长度应与所使用的装置相适应。
16) 热是能的一种形式,其他一切能的形式都能转化为热能。
17) 收音机在广播。
18) 如果开关接通,电流就流过线路。
19) 这两个物体相距很远,它们之间的吸引力可以忽略不计。
20) 他昨天把机器拆开了。
21) 由于分子运动而引起的力使分子分离。
22) 经过仔细研究之后,他们发现这个设计落后了。
23) 在发达国家,机动车辆是空气污染的主要来源,在落后的城市,这种污染也将增加。
24) 这个化学试验延误了十分钟。
25) 一个真正的市场式治理的演变可能将很快实现。
26) 本文利用安装在后轮轴上的强劲电动机,研究了插入式混合动力汽车的横摆力。
27) 在先进的悬架设计方面,数值仿真技术起着非常重要的作用,运用这种仿真技术我们可以把路面输入视为一个随机过程。
28) 随着每一次(气候)的改变,各式各样的物种都会顺应而生。
29) 考虑到这一点,用作参考模型的线性二自由度车辆模型可以用于计算车辆的期望横摆角速度,控制器尝试将车辆的非线性运动与之匹配。
30) 水银的重量约为水的十三倍。
31) 网络和电子商业将会造就一大批自由职业者,从而将对社会结构产生深远的影响。
32) 个人计算机使整个世界更新了工作、娱乐和通讯方式。
33) 他的目标是当一名计算机专家。
34) 在生命过程中,动物的活动方式与植物相反。
35) 电流的变化与电动势成正比,与电阻成反比。
36) 冰的密度比水小,因而能浮在水面上。
37) 生产成本的差异与能源密切相关。
38) 玻璃的可溶性比石英大。
39) 温度不变,则气体压力和体积成反比。
40) 这两种化合物都是酸,前者是强酸,后者是弱酸。
41) 大气层的厚度约为11000米。
42) 钢含碳量越高,强度和硬度就越大。
43) 虽然我们看不见空气,可我们周围到处都有空气。
44) 如果没有引力,人们就会一直掉到地球的中心。
45) 最普通的加速度是自由落体加速度。
46) 尽管能量的形式可以转换,但能量既不能被创造,也不能被消灭。

47) 无线电波与光波相似,只不过无线电波的波长要长一些。
48) 我们所需要的频率,甚至比我们称作高频率的还要高。
49) 越来越多的证据表明,许多塑料制品的化学成分会迁移到食物或流体上去,最终进入人体内。
50) 氧是物质世界的重要元素之一,其化学性质很活泼。
51) 操作系统的质量决定着计算机的应用效能。
52) 印度拥有软件设计方面的技术,而且拥有成千上万能说英语、精通技术的软件工程师。
53) 展望未来可以看到石油将在世界上起到令人鼓舞的作用。
54) 在自然界所存在的物质中,只有铀-235可以用作获得核能的材料。
55) 直到40年代初,化学家们才开始将这种技术用于分析工作。
56) 机制5a与机制5b有明显的差异,因为整个车体转动方向是相反的,并且车头与地面的碰撞在更低的速度(平均1.9m/s)发生。
57) 主动转向系统的另一个显著优点是以电子的方式增强了驾驶员的转向输入来稳定车辆的能力。
58) 让网络空间比大型商场、电视、公路和其他地方更加诱人的准确原因是方式不同。
59) 电子计算机的广泛应用,对科学技术的发展有极大的影响。
60) 自前工业化时代以来,随着人类活动对气候的改变产生影响,地球的气候系统在全球和地区范围内已经有了明显的改变。
61) 令人不可思议,柴油被认为是未来的环保燃料。
62) 电子计算机和微处理器对我们来说都十分重要的。
63) 中国设计的核动力系统十分精确。
64) 在一定场合下摩擦是绝对必要的。
65) (服用新药的)病人也将终生都要服药。但由于价格昂贵、疗程复杂,对于那些发展中国家的病人来说,十有八九都不能享用这些药物。
66) 医生们正在给病人做手术,可病人(的神经)一直十分紧张。
67) 使用雷达探测水下目标是没有用的。
68) 一些老板们非常积极地鼓励雇员们增强环保意识,更换小车。
69) 只要稍微修理一下,这台老式发动机就可使用。
70) 在科学研究、设计和经济计算方面广泛地应用电子计算机,可以使人们从繁重的计算劳动中解放出来。
71) 在过去的几年中,激光器件发展迅速,从而为(光)通讯系统的快速进步打开了通路。
72) 经常抽烟有害健康。
73) 每种型号只要稍加改动就能用于这三种系统。
74) 我们仔细地研究了这些化学元素的特性。
75) 水在4℃以下不断膨胀,而不是不断收缩。

Unit 5

Exercises

1) 多年来,同汽油机相比效率低且污染大的柴油机已经变得更加清洁。

2) 接下来的几个部分将展示现代规划的方法和相关的问题,详细地描述后现代方法以及它和现代方法的不同。

3) 尽管本世纪内温度增长比过去几百个世纪要迅速得多,但本世纪观察到的变暖现象可能是由于自然界的各种变化而引起的。

4) 行星地质学家们试着统计行星和月球表面的陨石坑数量以及大小分布,以获得它们的绝对年龄。

5) 在这个意义上说,许多汽车企业如丰田、本田、雪佛兰、马自达和福特,已经投入了大量的人力物力来研发混合动力汽车。

6) 尽管存在一些不确定性因素,用来模拟地球气候的计算机程序正得到迅速的改进。

7) 美国、日本、欧洲正在严格执行更加严厉的条例以减少各类汽车的污染排放。

8) 此外,由于电机和电池技术有很多实质性改善,电动车的驾驶性能指标能够与内燃机车相媲美。

9) 在欧洲以微弱优势取胜的丰田,在争夺第三世界各条公路更大市场份额的竞争中正成为令人生畏的市场力量。

10) 作为电动机最有效率的控制器——模糊逻辑控制器已经出现。

11) 在争夺第三世界各条公路更大市场份额的竞争中,丰田公司正成为令人生畏的市场力量。

12) 尽管存在一些不确定因素,用来模拟地球气候的计算机程序正在迅速得到改进。

13) 但是,目前还没有这方面的知识储备。

14) 因此,整个车辆的动态模型和主要组件将被忽略,只考虑动力运动分析。

15) 近几年混合动力汽车正变得流行起来。

16) 这种假设的影响已经由 Steeman 做出了论述。

17) 美国、日本以及欧洲正在制定更为严格的法令来减少汽车污染物的排放。

18) 但是现在,政治家们和绿色组织团体正致力于解决温室气体排放的问题。

19) 人类现在无法直接控制大气中的水的体积。

20) 随着电子行业和汽车行业的结合,汽车电子技术正在迅速发展。

21) 中国已经成为全球最大的石油产品进口国之一,主要是为了满足日益增长的汽车和卡车的需求。

22) 关于地球碳循环和海洋在二氧化碳吸收(碳"汇")中所扮演的角色,我们还有许多需要了解。

23) 在先前的研究中,我们已经证明智能压实技术带来的即期效益至少包括以下几点。

24) 人们期待以从传统碳氢化合物中提取的氢为燃料的车辆最终能取代汽油和柴油汽车。

25) 我们有几种方法解决能量管理控制问题。

26) 为了更好体现本文提出的控制器的有效性,在同样行驶路面的条件下,将未经控制器控制的车辆行驶性能与经控制器控制的车辆性能进行了对比。
27) 人们广泛认为交通应该发展成未来可持续发展的事业。
28) 我们周围的物质变化有两种,物理变化与化学变化。
29) 通常,仿造商们必须提供令人难以相信的保证和担保来区分其他同行的产品,从而获得竞争优势。
30) 首先,网络空间里人与人之间可以进行电子邮件交流,这种交流类似于电话交谈。
31) 问题在于其他减少氮氧化物排放的方法都依赖于能与燃料中的硫发生不良化学反应的催化剂,而该方法会将催化剂消耗殆尽。
32) 至少对于汽车制造商来说,汽车造型越小巧,看起来就越好看。
33) 为了满足工厂减排增效的目标,市场需要成本效益好的过程性方法来优化燃烧体系,防止污染的产生。
34) 或许我们可以抛开公路、新领域等比喻,把信息空间看作房地产。
35) 毫无疑问,欧洲的汽车生产商肯定会与丰田公司展开寸土必争的激烈市场竞争。
36) 北美植物的生长季节已经延长了大约一周。
37) 路波号称是世界第一台3升汽车,这个"3"不是指它的发动机大小,而是代表着它较低的耗油量。
38) 除此之外,人类对气候变化的影响将会在我们的知识累积到一定程度和科研模型有很大提高时才能确定。
39) 这就保证了柴油机能像汽油机那样安静平稳地工作,并且提供更好的燃油经济性。
40) 大部分的升温现象发生在晚上,大概是由于白天更多的云层遮挡着陆地,而到了晚上云层也阻挡了热量的散发。
41) 带有计算机病毒的软盘会使病毒传到计算机上。而病毒会传到其他任何使用于这台计算机的软盘上。因此专家建议用户最好给自己的信息软盘写保护。
42) 氢和氧化合,就形成水。
43) 由于柴油发动机燃烧需要更少的燃料,所以产生更少的二氧化碳排放。
44) 信息空间之所以具有如此大的诱惑力,正是因为它不同于商场、电视、公路或地球上其他的地方。
45) 假如没有重力,地球周围就没有空气。
46) 铝由于具有较好的导热性和导电性,在工业上得到了广泛的应用。
47) 除铜以外,还有许多别的金属也是良导体。
48) 安培、欧姆、伏特这三个单位是分别根据三位科学家的姓氏而命名的。
49) 声音的频率、波长与速度三者密切相关。
50) 个人计算机有台式和笔记本式两种。
51) 这篇文章总结了电子计算机、人造卫星和火箭等三个领域的新成就。
52) 电流的主要效应有磁效应、热效应和化学效应三种。

Unit 6

Exercises

1) 化学反应的速度和反应物的浓度成正比。
2) 三极管的基本功能是作电流放大器。
3) 它是在地质统计学中描述空间变化或均匀性的常用工具。
4) 通过软件来建立包括道路和车辆的虚拟场景。
5) 最近对各种数码相机的几何稳定性进行了测试。
6) 在表1中描述了车辆计算效率的结果。
7) 连接点的数量和复杂性对结构分析和设计的时间有决定性影响。
8) 剩余的能量用来使地球升温并且成为天气变化的动力。
9) 液体像固体一样,都有一定的体积。
10) 信号增大到10倍,增益降低到1/8。
11) 医院里如果使用计算机,就会使诊断更加快速、更加准确。
12) 牛顿晚年在神学研究上浪费了很多时间。
13) 他的左臂瘫痪了,没有知觉。
14) 人们对云层的作用知之甚少,但我们知道云层通过反射太阳能使地球冷却,通过吸收地面反射的热量让地球升温。
15) 同性电荷相斥,异性电荷相吸。
16) 在深海区,水温非常稳定,终年保持不变。
17) 领跑者将会远远甩开跟风者,以真正的优势提供更好的产品。
18) 水冷却到一定程度便成冰。
19) 气温升高会蒸发更多的水,融化更多海洋里和陆地上的冰。
20) 细菌也可以在海绵体中隐藏和繁殖,腐蚀木板、擦碟毛巾、洗涤槽、刀具以及台面板。
21) 碳酸盐能通过往这种水溶液中添加强碱而制得。
22) 与此同时,网络技术、光纤、蓝牙技术、局域网技术都将广泛地应用于汽车上,大大提升汽车的网络体系。
23) 气体受热时所发生的变化与液体完全一样。
24) 在当今时代,很难找到一块空间可以随心所欲,而不必担心影响你的邻居。
25) 力为正,偏心块位置就向下,正位移也向下。
26) 正如微软Word程序可以自动检测单词拼写错误那样,EHS专家现在也可以通过工具来自动监测空气排放的数据与信息。
27) 气压低,沸点就低。
28) 大概从2007年起,燃料电池驱动的环境友好型汽车就开始面世了。
29) 我们呼吸的空气是我们活得多彩的原因。
30) 实际上,一些农民很乐意听到这样的好消息。
31) 每次气候变化都有各种生物顺应而生。
32) 它们的药效只是把艾滋病毒感染者的死亡判决推迟一段时间。

33) 测试设备系统简图如图 1 所示。
34) 未来的纳米技术将让我们脱下拳击手套。
35) 本研究侧重于设计和开发的小型电动汽车轮毂电机。
36) 这场战争持续了 4 年,最后北方取胜。
37) 这意味着柴油机最符合汽车制造商对本产业的中期思考。
38) 几乎所有的车辆都在仪表板仪表安装了具有各种报警功能的报警器或扬声器。
39) 2000 年有 300 万人死于艾滋病。
40) 文章第三节包含了提出的检测方法和最先进的方法进行的对比。
41) 尽管气温增长比过去几百个世纪都迅速得多,但本世纪观察到的变暖现象可能是由于自然界的各种变化而引起的。
42) 通常分析的原始数据如图 6 所示。
43) 很难判断什么因素是主要的、次要的或者不重要的参数。
44) 行星越小,越容易受亚尔科夫斯基效应的影响。
45) 因此,专家认为,帮助人们妥善处理食物是非常重要的。
46) 那么,很有必要校准其灵敏性。
47) 普遍认为,接触应力是导致路面损坏的主要原因,尤其是路面的裂缝和车辙。
48) 据估计,现代装备精良的汽车采用了 50 多个微控制器。
49) 当太阳能穿过地表,转化成热能,而热能会迅速地向上辐射出去。
50) 我希望让员工确信去接受这种责任并参与进去,这将是值得努力的。
51) 对于汽车悬架控制问题而言,不可能测量到所有状态变量。
52) 然而,美中不足。
53) 一般来说,有两个相应的方法来开发汽车试验平台。
54) 市内短距离运输系统受到越来越多的关注,如轻轨、地铁和单轨。
55) 另一方面,证据表明有些现象可能在几十年内急剧地改变气候。
56) 两种通用的方法可以解决确定性的最优控制问题。
57) 通过其他微妙的例子展现了个人主义和集体主义思想在国家商业文化中的表现方式。
58) 尤其是 20 世纪 50 年代以来,人们对高质量汽车悬架做了广泛的研究。
59) 中国已经成为世界上石油产品进口最多的国家之一,主要是为越来越多的汽车提供燃料。
60) 一是配置一台真实的汽车进行实际的道路测试。
61) 启发式方法并不涉及明显的最小化或优化,相反,能量管理控制策略是基于工程直觉的规则来实现的。
62) 通常情况下,山寨厂商必须提供令人难以置信的承诺来使他们的产品与其他类似制造商区分开来。
63) 我认为这不是一种进步,而且这些刚刚复兴的公司不会长时间持续地服务客户。
64) 这项政府计划十分重要。
65) 技术就是在工业上应用科学方法和科学知识以满足我们物质上的需求。

Unit 7

Exercises

1) 温室效应的加剧<u>也有可能</u>给我们带来积极的影响。
2) Fi 和 Fb <u>只能单独出现</u>,Fi 不能出现在水平坐标上。
3) 那些<u>一直在亏损</u>的欧洲汽车制造商,如菲亚特、欧宝和福特,将会感到有压力。
4) 然而,仅仅简单地减少通风率<u>会</u>影响室内空气质量。
5) <u>很难</u>判断什么因素是主要的、次要的或不重要的参数。
6) 然而,<u>可以肯定的是</u>人类对地球上动植物产生破坏性的影响。
7) <u>所有人</u>都无法确定将来是否有这样的事情会发生。
8) 然而,开关磁阻电机的速度控制<u>还有提升的空间</u>。
9) 我们<u>应该关注</u>汽车制造业发生的巨大变化。
10) 那台机器有两个严重<u>缺陷</u>。
11) 规则<u>总有例外</u>。
12) 月球是一个<u>毫无生机</u>的世界,是多山的<u>不毛之地</u>。
13) 对青霉素过敏的患者<u>不得</u>使用本药。
14) 这种装置迄今为止已被订购 100 台以上,<u>限于篇幅</u>,<u>不能逐一列出</u>。
15) 镜面<u>一般不宜</u>擦拭。
16) 还有多种其他能源<u>尚未</u>开发。
17) 海拔高的地方冰雪常年<u>不化</u>。
18) 由于橡胶<u>不导电</u>,所以被用作绝缘材料。
19) 我们对你方条款<u>没有异议</u>。
20) 这份说明书<u>不够详尽</u>。
21) 精密仪器必须保持<u>无尘</u>。
22) 铁箱能使地球磁场<u>无法影响</u>指南针。
23) 我们<u>无权</u>签此合同。
24) 他们公司在产品包装和宣传上明显<u>比不上</u>竞争对手。

Unit 8

Exercises

1) <u>没有人</u>确定这些事情会不会发生。
2) 这<u>不是</u>谈论午餐的菜单,而是关于由食品引起的全国性暴发疾病的检讨。
3) 复杂的是:<u>还没有</u>明显的解决问题的方法。
4) 太阳能是清洁、安静、丰富和可再生的能源,对环境<u>不会</u>产生任何污染。
5) 假设虚拟体<u>没有</u>质量。
6) 但<u>无法</u>确定影响稳定性的真正原因。
7) 大家都很重视,但是<u>没人</u>有办法制止它。

8）尽管进行了几十年的科学研究,没人知道人类的活动带给环境多大的伤害。
9）很显然,延迟收获毫无经济意义。
10）没有转基因动物产品流入市场。
11）我们还不能在地球上创建一个完美的社会,在网络空间也不能。
12）红外线图像不依赖于场景的照明。
13）基因修改不是一件新奇的事情。
14）燃油并非总在最佳压力下喷射。
15）它并不总是进入我们的食物,但一旦进入,它会导致免疫系统脆弱的人患上脑炎或脑膜炎,如果是孕妇,就会发生流产或死胎。
16）最后,并不是所有的不确定性都是重要的。
17）大量的变量使调查不能完全彻底地进行。
18）环境不能完全被控制,因此总有遇到障碍物的未知概率。
19）然而,并不是所有第一代系统问题都可以解决。
20）机遇对每个人来说都是平等的,但当机遇真的到来时,并非每个人都有准备。
21）任何规则都有例外。
22）有一利必有一弊。
23）利用这个程序,对失效概率有较低影响的不确定性不容忽视。
24）一分耕耘,一分收获。
25）事实上,可以想象汽车在泵站能够添加氢气作为燃料。
26）一个物体对另一物体施加作用力必然会受到这另一物体的反作用力。
27）热转换成某种能,这一过程中不可能没有损耗。
28）不到安装时,不应打开轴承的包装箱或包装纸。
29）如果水分不够,生理过程就无法正常运行。
30）如果没有外力作用,静止的物体就不会移动。
31）在推崇个人主义价值的社会里,工人将质疑这种新方法,直到弄清楚该方法将如何直接影响他们作为个体的存在时,他们才会认可。
32）直到年末,我们才在始于1998—1999年的欧洲和北美第一次跟踪中确定这一证据。
33）一个感染 HIV 的人,会因为病毒严重损坏免疫系统而染上艾滋病,这时的免疫系统十分脆弱,有些人因此致死。
34）温室效应的增强也会带来积极的影响。
35）矿泉水是最解渴的饮料。
36）杀虫剂会造成很大危害,所以使用杀虫剂时应特别小心。
37）这些科学家完全相信居里夫妇。
38）受污染的庄稼竟高达 25%。
39）应特别强调适当进行润滑的重要性。
40）然而,药膏里有只苍蝇(美中不足)。
41）可持续管理被看作是一种实用和经济的保护物种免于灭绝的方式。
42）但是蛋白酶抑制剂通常与其他艾滋病药物如 AZT 结合,不是用来预防或治疗的。

43) 由于大多数合法企业意识到公众强烈的反垃圾邮件的情绪,所以他们就不使用它(垃圾邮件)了。
44) 对于云的作用人们知之甚少,但是大家都知道其通过反射太阳能来给地球降温,通过阻止地表热量辐射来给地球升温。
45) 广告商很少直接发送垃圾邮件。
46) 发展中国家的妇女几乎不可能与性伙伴谈论性安全,想尝试协商常常会招致虐待。
47) 我们发现他们往往由于不能正确推理而陷于本可避免的错误。
48) 绝缘体接上电源后,电不会像通过导体那样通过绝缘体。
49) 这些自由电子通常以不规则的方式运动。
50) 与通常想法不同,地球并不是在空无一物的空间中运转的。
51) 必须强调,任何病人如有明显喘鸣,切不可施行全身麻醉。
52) 一般说来,物理变化不形成新的物质。
53) 发动机不是因为燃料用完而停止的。
54) 各行星不是以匀速绕太阳运转。
55) 我们认为融化不是化学反应。
56) 医生们认为那位乳癌病人难以康复。

Unit 9

Exercises 2

1) 通过选择性地将一半的排放气体回送到发动机,参与燃烧的氧气量将会减少。
2) 这种工作方式效率(使发动机燃油利用率)低下,因为燃油并非总是在最佳压力下喷射。
3) 现有的预测方法大致可以分为基于经验的方法、基于模型(或基于物理模型)的方法和数据驱动的方法。
4) 但输油泵通过发动机驱动,所以喷油压力随着发动机的转速起伏。
5) 虚拟技术广泛应用于各种汽车试验平台。
6) 第三,单轨系统可以建立在交通拥挤的城市地区,因为它具有急转弯和爬坡功能。
7) 通风与缓解全球变暖的基本节能原理有关。
8) 在主动探测中,特殊的测试信号被输入进一个未被激活的相电路中。
9) 检测是通过寻找与人身体相似温度的分布来实现的。
10) 当车辆在路面运动时,路面不平整造成的随机振动通过轮胎和悬架系统传递到车身。
11) 为了探测月球表面,人们一次又一次地发射火箭。
12) 如果原子失去了一个或多个电子,我们就说该原子带正电荷。
13) 另外还有一项改进:人们使用尾气再循环系统来减少柴油机所排放的氮氧化物。
14) 本文详述了这种测量技术,工程测试中得到的试验数据表明了振动响应的性质。
15) 我们通过调用库函数 MLIB / MTRACE 读出控制信号。
16) 我们假设车体和两个转向架(前、后转向架)是具有侧向、旋转、侧偏自由度的刚体。
17) 在第一阶段,解决诸如运动重物的最简单动载荷作用下梁的运动特性问题时,我们可以使用两种基本方法。

18) 人们将重点转向环保或可持续建筑，寻求维持或进一步增加我们习惯的舒适度而且同时大大降低与人类生活方方面面相关的能源使用的理念。

19) 本文介绍了转向灵敏度、转向操作稳定性的概念和定量表达式。

20) 网络空间应该强制实施社区标准，但这些标准应该由网络空间社区自己来制定，而不是华盛顿的法院或政治家。

21) 人们发现只有第二种方法是成功的，即"发动机"通过 MLIB/MTRACE 读取 DS1103 平台接口数据的功能。

22) 然而，众所周知，传统的 PI 控制器通常不适合非线性系统。

23) 但发动机驱动输油泵，所以喷油压力随着发动机的转速起伏。

24) 第 2 节介绍了信号处理的方法。

25) 在这篇论文中，通过动载荷分析和对时间的一步积分过程解决了上述问题。

26) 然而，几乎没有用不同方法实现需求控制排气通风性能的文献资料。

27) 社区标准应该被强制实施，但应该由网络空间社区自己制定这些标准，而不是华盛顿的法院或政治家。

28) 摄入受污染的食物或饮料能引起食源性疾病。

29) 使用软件来建立一个包括道路和车辆的虚拟场景。

30) 针对四轮独立驱动电动汽车提出了一种车辆稳定控制方法。

31) 基于该车辆平台开发了先进的遗传—模糊主动转向控制器。

32) 车辆高速行驶时一个最值得关注的问题是，当某个驱动电机发生严重的故障时，必须考虑车辆的安全问题。

33) 从 Monty Python 短剧中衍生出了术语"垃圾邮件"（荷美尔肉类产品的商标）的用法。

34) 要求根据研究领域和网格得到的尺寸评估 CFD 模型的性能。

35) 可能需要注意的是，主动防倾杆系统是一种常见的、理想的重型车辆控制器。

36) 可用作一个起动机与发电机的集成，也可用来改善内燃机的燃油消耗。

37) 在高倍率放大下，可以看见竞争者的材料主要由直径 1~4 微米的纤维构成，许多纤维直径在 1~2 微米，几乎没有直径低于 1 微米的纤维。

38) 在这项研究中，假定 S15C 钢的热性质和 S45C 钢材是相同的。

39) 已经注意这种现象了。

40) 曾试图研究出一种培育水稻品种的新技术。

41) 无疑要考虑到现代通讯的惊人速度。

42) 它们可能一直是类地行星的一部分大气的来源。它们还被认为是构成外行星以及其卫星的一种类似微星的基础材料。

43) 多年来，工具和技术本身作为根本性创新的源泉，在很大程度上被科学史学家和科学思想家们忽视了。

44) 政府是以减少技术的经费投入来增加纯理论科学的经费投入，还是相反，这往往取决于把哪一方看作是驱动的力量。

45）石油的供应可能随时会被中断；不管怎样，以目前的这种消费速度，只需 30 年左右，所有的油井都会枯竭。

46）最后，结论被列于第 5 章。

47）从全球变暖到臭氧层空洞，人类被认为应该对大量的环境问题负责。

48）考虑地理参数和气候条件，他们的方法将被修改和调整，以适用于科威特。

49）在这些情况下，城市搜救移动机器人能够被派遣到垮塌的建筑帮助救援人员完成搜救任务。

50）电梯驱动系统被安装在建筑物的底部。

51）虚拟技术被广泛应用于各种汽车试验平台。

52）多种品牌和传感器的相机都已被评估。

53）整个过程被叫作温室效应。

54）其余的(热量)都被留在了低空层，其中包含了许多如水蒸气、二氧化碳、甲烷等可以吸收红外线的气体。

55）为了指定土壤中的底部边界条件，两种方法被提出来。

56）在本节中，建筑几何模型的实现将首先被讨论，紧随其后的是使用性能评估参数的概述。

57）在 ECMS 中，在使用燃油和电力之间的等效燃油消耗参数被定义为两个常数，根据电池状态进行切换。

58）在主动探测中，特殊的测试信号被输入进一个未被激活的相电路中。

59）不同车辆的研发过程中，这种方法也被充分应用在了不同种类的自动变速器平台上。

60）平衡悬架结构被广泛应用于实现轴载分配。

Unit 10

Exercises 2

1）C 是 B 的 1/2。

2）把激光管长度缩短到 1/10，就可以获得单模运作。

3）氢原子比氧原子大约轻 15/16。

4）如果把距离增大 2 倍，其万有引力就减少 8/9。

5）水星的向阳面上每平方英里吸收的热量是地球上同等面积所吸收热量的 7 倍。

6）美国的人均耗能量是世界上最贫穷国家人均耗能量的 100 倍以上。

7）无线电波的传播速度几乎比声音快 100 万倍。

8）正在兴建的实验室将比这个实验室大 1 倍。

9）我们厂今年的产量比去年增加了 1 倍。

10）两国计划于星期二签订一项长期协定，预计该协定将使两国的贸易额增加 1 倍。

11）当电压升高 10 倍时，电流强度降低到 1/10，因此功率保持不变。

12）冬季，水位比平均水位下降 2/3。

Unit 11

Exercises 2

1）大家都知道金属为什么在工业上会得到广泛的应用。
2）物质热胀冷缩是一个普通的物理现象。
3）电视摄像机的功能就是把图像分解成许许多多由小光点组成的线条。
4）一个物体究竟是处于运动状态还是静止状态，总是相对的。
5）太阳究竟有多热，简直难以用文字描述。
6）这就是第二运动定律的含义。
7）酸的另一个特性是它们能够与称为碱的化合物化合。
8）这是因为载流导体周围有一个磁场。
9）伽利略最光辉的业绩在于，在1609年，他成为第一个把新发明的望远镜对准天空的人，证实了行星是围绕太阳旋转，而不是围绕地球旋转。
10）事实上（真相就是），人类是从类人猿进化而来的。
11）我们可以说，物体的能量就是物体做功的能力。
12）你应当确定下列函数中哪一个是解析的。
13）电路的电导率就是电流通过该电路的难易程度的一种度量。
14）电子总是朝电位较高的地方运动。
15）我们必须知道被测物体处在多远的位置。
16）我们必须懂得函数斜率的含义（是什么）。
17）一般说来，有运动就有摩擦。
18）毫无疑问，基因工程是一项崭新而奇妙的新技术。
19）铜和铝广泛用来制作电缆，这是人所共知的事实。
20）医生们认为大多数人不能活过100岁。
21）但是将化学符号写成反应式，并不意味着所表示的反应确实会发生。

Unit 12

Exercises 2

1）使用生物锁的人再也不必担心忘记带钥匙了。
2）我们可以看见盛食物和饮料的玻璃瓶罐里面所装的东西。
3）使铁氧化物脱氧的化学过程很复杂。
4）机器人装备大量传感器（诸如视觉、触觉、受力和临近传感器）的时候很快就要到来了。
5）胃切除可以用许多方法。
6）计算机是一种装置，它接收一系列含有信息的电脉冲。
7）计算机在工程技术上已经获得广泛应用，它使人们摆脱复杂的测量和计算劳动。
8）这些电波以光的速度传播，它们通常被称为无线电波。
9）伽利略是著名的意大利科学家，他进一步证明了哥白尼学说是正确的。
10）为了求得压力，将力除以所作用的面积，从而得出单位面积上的压力。

11) 我们不能在月球上生存,因为那里没有空气,也没有水。

12) 变压器不能通直流电,因为直流电会烧坏变压器的线圈。

13) 由于氧化薄膜阻止氧气、水蒸气和其他气体的进入,反应常因形成氧化薄膜而减弱。

14) 这个方案富于创造性,独出心裁,并且很有魄力,所以他们都很喜欢。

15) 物质具有一定的特征或特性,因此我们很容易识别各种物质。

16) 这台发电机正在发电,发出的电是用来照明的。

17) 我们必须给机器的传动部分加油,以便使摩擦大大地减少。

18) 铁片如果被扔在雨里就会生锈。

19) 工厂虽小,但它每天都生产出大量的机器。

20) 抛光表面比无光泽表面反射的热量多,而无光泽表面比抛光面吸收的热量多。

21) 有轨电车多年前就在英国销声匿迹了,现在还有几个欧洲城市在使用。

22) 新联盟是在当地形成并且得到了当地政府的有力扶持,这一情况对于美国来说应该具有很大的诱惑力,更何况美国自身的利益也要求它对新联盟给予支持。

23) 正如许多人猜想的那样,蜘蛛不属于昆虫类,甚至与昆虫一点近亲关系也没有。

24) 众所周知,静止的物体没有外力作用,就不会移动。

25) 如实验所示,杠杆和滑轮改变了运动的方向。

26) 这本书写于1940年,是当时有关无机化学最好的参考书。

27) 没有一种材料在力的作用下一点也不变形的。

Unit 13

Exercises 2

1) Meroney 等人报告说,长宽比等于1时,污染物浓度几乎是独立于风速的。

2) 当涉及保护生物多样性的地区,如世界热带森林,可持续管理是否实用仍然存在许多问题。

3) 当海啸的波浪接近陆地的时候,它们的外形和行为取决于几个当地因素。

4) 当温水聚集在一个地方时,蒸发和云的积累可能会增加。

5) 当电子束扫描图像时,图像光强度的变化转化为电强度的变化。

6) 人们习惯于在丰年储存能量,靠它挨过荒年。但是如果坏年景总也不来,这些能量就很难处理了。

7) 收入所得税的提高可能会阻止人们去多挣钱,所以这种办法不切实际。

8) 由于人体的免疫系统遭到破坏,病人几乎没有什么能力来抵抗许许多多其他疾病的侵袭。

9) 撒哈拉沙漠在过去的四年中由于降水量充足而后退了40公里。

10) 由于月球的引力只有地球引力的六分之一,所以一个体重200磅的人在月球上仅有33磅重。

11) 如果峡谷外的风速低于临界值,就不会有上层和第二层的重合区域。

12) 如果统计数据是真实的,大多数美国人都要时不时忍受这方面的问题。

13) 如果行人与背景的温度差是显著的,边界区域的清晰度就更高。
14) 如果参数选择合适,Newmark-β法的优点是无条件稳定的积分。
15) 除非已知一个正方形或一个正方体的边长,否则就无法求出这个正方形的面积或这个正方体的体积。
16) 尽管行人的运动被假设为线性的,但装在汽车上的相机的运动不是线性的。
17) 虽然我们仅得到太阳辐射总能量的一小部分,但是,与我们的实际需要量相比,这已绰绰有余了。
18) 能量既不能创造,也不能消失,尽管其形式可以转变。
19) 虽然雷达应用无线电波,但与无线电和电视略有区别。
20) 尽管物质的形式各不相同,但它们都是运动中的物质。
21) 虽然身高是一种明显的遗传特征,但是个体的实际身高取决于基因和环境的相互作用。
22) 尽管这个问题很复杂,但是用电子计算机只要两小时就能解决。
23) 一切生物,不管是动物还是植物,都是由细胞组成的。
24) 火箭必须获得每秒大约5英里的速度才能把卫星送入轨道。
25) 铁制品常常涂以保护层,以免生锈。
26) 电缆通常铺设在地下,以延长使用寿命。
27) 升高温度使水变成蒸汽。
28) 一般来讲,哪里有工厂,哪里的空气就会被严重污染。
29) 哪里水源充足,就在哪里修建大批的水电站。
30) 如果没有阳光、水和空气,动植物都不能生存。
31) 因此,在很容易达到附着极限的湿滑路面上行驶时,使用转向干预而不是制动干预产生校正横摆力矩是很有好处的。

Unit 14

Exercises 2

1) 自从工业革命采用水能和蒸汽能之后,用电、汽油和其他能源的机器已非常普及,它们现在干着世界绝大部分的工作。
2) 对于任何机器来说,如果知其输入力和输出力,就能求出其机械效率。
3) 因为猫的眼睛比人的眼睛所吸收的光线要多,所以猫在黑夜里能看得很清楚。
4) 我们必须给机器的运动部件加润滑油,以使摩擦大大减少。
5) 因二极管的表面有一层薄薄的硬玻璃,故无须使用密封的管壳。
6) 为了达到减排增效的目标,市场要求本轻利厚、过程性的方法,以便能优化燃烧系统,防止污染排放的产生。
7) 所以为了解决这个问题,我们将采用"替代燃料"。"替代燃料"是指那些非化石燃料,或者是那些需要对汽车设计和分销以及营销基础设施进行大量改进的能源(化石燃料或其他能源)。
8) 电池电动汽车被认为是一个巨大的失败而遭淘汰,因此有了混合动力汽车。这种车能在长途旅程中使用内燃机提供动力,在城市则使用电动机,这将是减少污染和符合汽车减排法律限制的权宜之计。

9) 但因为政治家和环保团体正致力于温室气体的减排,欧洲汽车制造商担心,新出台的法规将限制二氧化碳的排放量,就像有毒气体如一氧化碳或氮氧化物正遭受着不断降低排量的法律限制。

10) 疫情的发展使世界看到那些不想看到的现象:娼妓(艾滋病专家称为"性工作者")和嫖客、吸毒者、同性恋等特定人群产生的疾病可以演变为大规模的流行病。

11) 可是现在人们意识到有些(矿物)供给是有限的,甚至还可以估计出"可使用/开采的时间",也就是说,经过若干年后,这些矿物的全部已知矿源和储量将消耗殆尽。

12) 有必要使用能量组合件在起动汽车和协助车辆加速时提供有力的动力,这种能量储备系统的生命周期必须符合启停技术。

13) 从最优仿真或者标准城市循环工况可以得到一个近似模型,我们用前向仿真测试了这个模型。

14) 在本文的第一部分,我们用之前描述且验证过的有限元模型的方法研究了赛车刹车时轮胎和路面接触的界面所受的接触压力。

15) 车载单元(OBU)中全球导航卫星系统(GNSS)接收器记录的旅行信息提供了方便、灵活的手段来支持道路使用自动收费。

16) 各种机器零件无论多么脏,不管形状多么不规则,当用超声波处理后,都可以清洗得非常干净,甚至像新零件一样。

17) 火箭研究证实了早就引起怀疑的一个奇异的事实:大气层中有一个"高温带",其中心在距地面约 30 英里高的地方。

18) 美国的经济体系是一个基本上以私有企业为主的市场经济。在这样的经济体中,消费者通过花钱购买他们最需要的服务和商品,很大程度上决定了生产。

19) 因此,在美国这个经济体中,个体消费者的需求以及商人试图将其利润最大化和个人试图将其收入最大化的欲望一起决定了应该如何利用资源来生产他们所共同需要的东西。

20) 人们常说,通过电视可以了解时事,掌握科学和政治的最新动态。从电视里还可以看到层出不穷,既有教育意义又有娱乐性的新节目。

21) 应当认识到,当我们确定某一物体速度的大小和方向时,实际上我们表示的是相对于某一参考物的速度,对于这一特定场合来说,可以设想该参考物是静止不动的。

22) 能量是生态系统的货币,只有当食物变为能量,能量再被用来获取更多的食物以供生长、繁殖和生存,生命才成为可能。

23) (在降雨其间,)水渗入地下,在重力的影响下,这种水通过土壤微小孔隙空间向下流动直至到达不透水岩层为止。向下移动的动量水分,充满了土壤颗粒之间的空隙,挤出了土壤的空气。

24) 必须把大量时间花在确保关键人物均根据同一情报和目的行事,而这一切对身体的耐力和思维能力都是一大考验。(因此,一旦考虑成熟,)决策者就应迅速做出决策。

25) 混凝土是由硅酸盐水泥和填补料一起制成的人造石,加水搅拌达到可塑的稠度后,浇入模壳,待其逐渐硬化而增加强度。

26) 所有商用钢铁都以铁为主要成分,但由于碳和其他元素的含量不同,钢铁冶炼方法以及加工过程不同,改变了其特性,从而产生多种不同的钢铁,其中有些钢铁的特性极不相同,看上去就像不同的金属一样。

27) 建立全国统一的大容量的通信网络,由计算机进行控制,通过卫星和海底电缆在全球提供快速可靠的通信服务,这种可能性从技术上来讲是完全存在的。

28) 凡外商投资企业有能力也愿意与天津市工业企业通过技术转让、引进人才、技术帮助、经济支持等途径,共同开发国家统一经营以外的制成品,特别是开发机电产品和精细化工产品,并通过外方的销售渠道直接为外国公司提供制成品,可以向市外经贸委申请扩大联合开发的业务。

29) 对于现代科技书籍,特别是教科书来说,要是作者希望自己书中的内容能与新概念、新观察和新发现同步发展的话,那么就应该常常将书中的内容重新修改。

30) 到目前为止,经历了18和19两个世纪,这种新的倾向是把住宅安排在城市的近郊,而把生产活动、商业往来、政府部门以及娱乐场所都集中在城市的中心地区。

中 篇
学术英语写作篇

Unit 1 论 文 简 介
Introduction

Questions for thought:

Do you often read academic research papers? What kinds of subjects do you usually read?

Have you ever written academic research papers?

Where do you usually find the materials you need for your paper?

What do you want to learn from this course?

1. Some essential definitions

Subject: an area of interest that can be narrowed down to a suitable topic; subjects are either too broad or too loosely defined to serve as topics for research papers.

Topic: a reasonably narrow, clearly defined area of interest that could be thoroughly investigated within the limits set for a given research assignment.

Are they subjects or topics? Why?

adolescent behavior; America's political troubles; Shakespeare's tragedies; prehistoric animals; acid rain; cancer cures; computer-assisted education; illegal immigration

Compare the subjects with the topics and say what's the difference between them.

➢ Adolescent behavior

The effect of parental attitudes on teenage alcoholism

➢ America's political troubles

The effects of terrorism on the social policies of the American government over the last ten years

➢ Shakespeare's tragedies

The relationship between young women and their fathers in several Shakespearian tragedies

➢ Acid rain

Acid rain's effect on the recent deterioration of forests and lakes in the Northeast

➢ Computer-assisted education

The effectiveness of computer programs in the remediation of writing problems

➢ Illegal immigration

The effect of illegal immigration on unemployment in the Southwest

➢ Cancer cures

The role of emotions in the cure of certain cancers

➢ Prehistoric animals

The role of humans in the extinction of large prehistoric mammals

Thesis: a general statement that announces the major conclusions you reached through a thoughtful analysis of all your sources.

Hypothesis: your prediction, made sometime before reading the sources, as to what your research will reveal about the topic; that is, what answers you expect to find for the major questions raised by the topic.

2. Differences between *Research Papers* and *Reports*

1) *Reports*

- recording the facts you discovered and handing in the result
- only compiling information without evaluating or interpreting it
- simply recording a series of facts that you found, often from a single source
- no evaluation or interpretation, none of your own ideas

2) *Research Paper*

- to evaluate or interpret or in some other way add to and participate in what you write
- to consider the why and how of the topic you choose
- to develop a point of view toward your material, take a stand, express some original thought
- to analyze, interpret, evaluate the information you gather, and then to draw conclusions from it

A *report* can be on one subject alone: whales, direct mail advertising, etc..

In a *research paper*, however, you narrow down the general area by taking a specific approach to the material, an approach which is often reflected in the thesis or underlying idea of the research paper.

3. Qualities of *Research Paper*

Qualities a *research paper* has:

- It synthesizes your discoveries about a topic and your judgment, interpretation, and evaluation of those discoveries.
- It is a work that shows your originality.
- It acknowledges all sources you have used.

4. Misunderstanding of *Research Paper*

- A summary of an article or a book (or other source material) is not a research paper.
- The ideas of others, repeated uncritically, do not make a research paper.

- A series of quotations, no matter how skillfully put together, do not make a research paper.
- Unsubstantiated personal opinion does not constitute a research paper.
- Copying or accepting another person's work without acknowledging it, whether the work is published or unpublished, professional or amateur, is not research—it is plagiarism.

5. Importance of *Research Paper*

- The skills in writing research paper—making decisions about a subject, developing an inquiring attitude, gathering information, examining it critically, thinking creatively, organizing effectively, and writing convincingly—are crucial to academic success. They are also basic to business, professional, and private life.
- It offers you the chance to investigate something you may have wanted to know about, or to find out about a subject you think you may be interested in, or to look at something related to a course you would like to take but have no time to schedule at the moment.
- Writing a research paper requires you to exercise that form of judgment called critical thinking.

6. Parts of *Research Paper*

A *research paper* usually includes the following parts:
Title page, Outline, Abstract, Text of the paper, Works Cited, Appendix

7. Steps in writing *Research Paper*

Five steps to a *research paper*:
Choosing the topic →Collecting information →Evaluating materials →Organizing ideas →Writing the paper

Assignments

1. Explain the difference between a subject and a topic with more than three examples.
2. Which of the following items seem likely to work out well as topics for research papers? Explain your reasons.
- ➢ Working women in America today
- ➢ The way FM radio signals are sent and received
- ➢ The CIA's role in Nicaragua
- ➢ The invention of gunpowder
- ➢ The cause of measles
- ➢ The cause of cancer

- The British colonization of Africa in the nineteenth century
- Programs for prevention of child abuse
- The real author of Shakespeare's plays
- The cause of teenage alcoholism
- The generation gap
- The role of computers in business today
- Automation in heavy industry
- The effectiveness of capital punishment in reducing the crime rate
- The arms race as a threat to peace
- The effect of illegal immigration on the economy of the Southwest
- The effect of high salaries on the quality of baseball being played today
- The ability of some people to see the future in their dreams

Unit 2 论文选题
Negotiating a Topic

Questions for thought:

- What is the main purpose of a research paper itself?
- Why should we form a hypothesis before searching for sources?
- What is an effective hypothesis?

1. Choosing a subject

Step 1: Deciding what question the research will answer and what problem will be worthwhile exploring.
- "I want to write about the trouble in the Middle East."
- "I want to know more about dinosaurs."
- "I am interested in some problems faced by the Catholic Church today."
- "I've always been fascinated by the Salem witchcraft trials."

Step 2: How do I know the subject is any good?
- You must like the subject well enough to spend a good many days and nights working on it.
- The subject must lead to a good topic—one that raises some questions which have not been answered to the satisfaction of all the authorities in the field.
- Such uncertainty among the experts gives you the opportunity to examine the different points of view and arrive at those conclusions that will become your paper's thesis.
- The best subjects are those that suggest a good many interesting topics to choose from.

2. Kinds of topics

Assigned topics, Field-of-Study topics, Free-Choice topics.

Assigned topics:

Assigned topics are those selected by an instructor and presented to you, often as a list of actual writing subjects to choose from.

Often what are called "Assigned Topics" are actually subjects; they already have been narrowed and are ready for investigation.

Sometimes a rather general Assigned Topic is presented and you need to choose a specific subject for research.

Assigned topic:
- Write on some subject related to our study of language

   You might choose:
- to investigate censorship of language on television
- whether whales actually communicate with a language

Field-of-Study topics:

Field-of-Study topics are those that you choose, so long as they are related to the course for which the paper is assigned.

Some General Reference Sources:

Your textbook, Course materials, Encyclopedias, Card catalog, Periodical indexes, Your own interests

Free-Choice topics:

Free-Choice topics are those that give you free rein to investigate any area you choose.

The best way to develop a Free-Choice Topic:

Expand on a familiar area——Look to an area new to you——Try a textbook——Work from your strengths——Become a browser in the library——"Get inside" the library catalog system

3. Finding a topic

A good topic raises questions that have no simple answers.
- Why is the sky blue?
- How does vitamin C help the body fight disease?
- Why did the popes leave Rome for southern France in the 1300s?
- Why did Guiteau shoot President Garfield?

Specific topics make better papers than very broad or general ones.

Compare:
➢ Importance of Economics

   International Cooperation Exemplified by the World Bank
➢ Surgery

   Growing Scandal of Unnecessary Surgery
➢ Philosophers and Their Philosophies

   Aristotle's Theory of Tragedy in the Movie High Noon

Look for significant points on which the experts disagree such as highly controversial issues and less well-known questions.
➢ Value of a new, expensive weapon
➢ Causes of alcoholism
➢ Long-range benefits of a particular vitamin, such as C or E

- Emily Dickinson's reasons for not publishing her poems
- Possibility of extending the human life span

4. Qualities of a good topic

- The topic will enable you to fulfill the assignment.
- The topic interests you enough to work on it.
- The topic will teach you something.
- The topic is of manageable scope.
- You can bring something to the topic.
- Enough information on the topic is available to you.
- The topic is suitable for your audience.
- The topic lets you demonstrate all your abilities that a research paper is meant to show.

Can you find enough information to meet the specified length?

Is the topic really related to the course for which it will be written?

If your instructor has already dealt with this topic in class, how will your writing augment what was included in the course?

Examples:
- American Foreign Policy
- Religion

No matter how interesting or exciting a topic seems, work with it only if you can give to it the kind of time it will require of you.

5. Topics to avoid

You should probably avoid topics in which the controversy derives solely from opinion.
- Is football too violent?
- Was Ali the greatest boxer ever?
- Should public schools be allowed to mandate that pupils pray?
- Should selling marijuana be legalized?
- Should abortion be banned?

You must beware of topics involving the paranormal because almost all the "sources" consist of personal accounts of occult phenomena or weird sightings.

Examples: UFOs ESP
- Air Force's response to reports of UFO sightings
- Scientific techniques for investigating ESP

What is being done in this area?

Assembling information from various sources

Dealing with very current events

➢ Use of genetic engineering to detect and cure disease

➢ Use of computers in banking or education

Avoid the following problems when choosing your topic:

- Do not reuse a paper you have written for another instructor.
- Do not choose a topic on which you do not plan to do all the work yourself.
- Do not choose a topic that is too broad for a research paper.
- Do not choose a topic for which a single source will provide all the information you need.
- Do not choose a topic about which your conclusions will be irrelevant.
- Do not start work on any topic unless you think it will hold your interest long enough to complete the paper.
- Do not choose a topic unsuited for your audience.
- Do not pursue a topic that seems to go nowhere for you.
- Be wary of choosing a topic so neutral that you cannot express an attitude toward it.
- Consider avoiding topics that have been particularly popular among students.
- Consider avoiding a highly controversial topic unless you think you can bring something new and special to the subject.

Examples:

➢ How Ford should have designed the Edsel

➢ Commercial by-products of the Fishing Industry

➢ Rock music of the '80s

➢ Relative merits of ways to investigate gory murders

➢ Inside of a marine engine

Assignments

1. What must be your first concern when looking for a topic?

2. Start your own research paper, following the steps. You may use the list of subject areas below, choose one subject area, and then do sufficient background reading to find two or three potential topics for a seven-to-ten-page research paper.

➢ Choose a subject—one of the following or any other that meets the requirements of this course

➢ Go to three or more background sources and find two to five potentially workable topics

➢ Select the topic that seems most interesting and/or most workable.

Subject areas:

——Asian or Italian or Irish immigration to the United States

——The banking industry and the Great Depression

——Endangered species

- Environmental controls on large industries
- Safety and the automobile industry
- Group therapy for emotional problems
- The US judicial system's problems
- The welfare system
- Causes of urban decay
- Organized crime in America
- Genetic experimentation
- Government's role in medical care
- Theodore Roosevelt, conservationist, imperialist
- Martin Luther King, Jr., civil rights leader of the 1960s
- James Hoffa, union leader accused of being involved with organized crime
- Mother Jones, union organizer of early twentieth century
- Elizabeth I, queen of England in a crucial era
- Eleanor Roosevelt, humanitarian
- Mohandas Gandhi, leader of Indian independence movement
- Winston Churchill, leader of England during World War II
- Japanese businesspeople: their customs, their ethics, their relations with labor and government
- South Africa's system of racial segregation, apartheid
- Brazil's economy, growing pains of a Third World nation of enormous potential
- OPEC, the troubles that come with instant wealth
- Harry Truman, controversial president in critical postwar period, 1945—1952

Unit 3 题目确定
Narrowing the Topic

1. Background reading or preliminary research

Background reading consists of looking up your subject or topic in general reference works.

General encyclopedias, Specialized or subject-specific encyclopedias, Subject-specific dictionaries, Almanacs, Handbooks, Periodical articles from full text databases, Biographical sources, Other sources via the catalog

Example:

Subject: Astronomy

Topic: The Beginning of the Universe

➢ look up "the Universe" in an encyclopedia;
➢ read the section on astronomy in an atlas such as Earth and Man;
➢ read ahead, or reread, the section on astronomy in other sources.

The purpose behind background reading is twofold:

● You want to feel certain that you have chosen the best available topic;
● Even if your original idea for a topic was a fine one, you will benefit from refreshing your knowledge of the subject.

Do not read entire books during preliminary research:

➢ Martin Luther King, Jr.
➢ Martin Luther King's relationship with militant black leaders

In taking notes, avoid recording detailed factual information.

2. Brainstorming

Brainstorming consists of wide-open, no-holds-barred thinking about some subject, in which your mind is free to produce any and all ideas that come along.

Note:

● Do not reject any idea during the brainstorming session;
● Record every thought;
● Stop after about fifteen minutes and review your notes;

- Check off the ideas that seem best;
- Put all the notes aside and review them again in a fresh light the next day.

Topic: Dinosaurs

➢ What exactly was a dinosaur?

➢ How do we know what it was, aside from the bones?

➢ When did people first find dinosaur bones?

➢ Where did they live? What did they eat?

➢ Did any other creatures prey on them?

➢ What caused dinosaurs to die out?

➢ How long were they around?

➢ Did they evolve from earlier life forms? From sharks? From little lizards?

➢ Are crocodiles really modern dinosaurs?

➢ Are there any other dinosaurs around now, possibly in some unexplored jungle or on a deserted island?

➢ Someone said birds evolved from dinosaurs—are they right?

➢ What caused the extinction of dinosaurs?

➢ Did they just become too big? But what about the smaller ones?

➢ Did they run out of food? If so, how could that happen?

➢ Did they become unfit for survival? How?

➢ Were other creatures smarter than they were? How could we know how smart they were?

➢ Their brains were probably larger than ours. How do we know about these long-gone beasts? Or don't we know? Is it all guesswork?

➢ Do we find each skeleton all in one spot, or do we assemble possible skeletons from a mixed heap of bones?

➢ How come no animals are that big today (except whales)?

➢ Why are today's lizards and other reptiles no larger than alligators?

Possible Themes:

➢ Why did dinosaurs become extinct?

Topic: cause of extinction

➢ What exactly was (or is) a dinosaur?

Topic: their place in evolution

➢ How do we know what we say we know?

Topic: the basis of our knowledge of prehistoric creatures

3. Forming a Hypothesis

Begin to form a hypothesis while you are choosing your topic.

The key to successful research lies in forming a reasonable hypothesis as early as possible, for you cannot rely entirely on the topic to guide you through this complex process.

There are two good reasons for starting out with a hypothesis.

First, a hypothesis points you in the right direction by indicating the specific questions you need answers for.

Second, the hypothesis can test the thoroughness of your research.

Example:
- Intelligence is inherited.
- Advocates: Arthur Jensen, F. O. Wilson, etc.
- Critics: Steven Rose, Stephen Jay Gould

Conclusion:

A carefully limited topic will ensure that you will be working with a manageable number of sources; but you will need a hypothesis to help you decide what ideas and facts in each source will be most useful in your effort to cover the topic thoroughly, intelligently and efficiently.

4. Forming a Hypothesis by Brainstorming

Example 1:
Subject: Dinosaurs
Topic: Causes for their extinction
Hypotheses:
- Did the evolution of smaller, smarter animals somehow lead to the extinction of the slow-witted dinosaurs? Were these new creatures (mammals)?
- Did major climatic changes bring about the extinction by eliminating the tropical swamplands in which the dinosaurs thrived? How fast might such changes take place?
- Could a meteor striking the Earth cause such a change?
- Did deadly radiation from an exploding nearby star do them in? In that case, wouldn't some have survived?
- Did dinosaurs become so large they could not find enough food in their environment?

The newest Hypothesis:
- Radiation from an exploded star caused the Great Extinction.

Another Hypothesis:
- A meteor hit the Earth 65 million years ago drastically cooling the atmosphere and killing off the dinosaurs.

Example 2:
Subject: Alcoholism
Topic: Treatment of alcohol addiction
Hypotheses:
- How well do support therapies, such as Alcoholics Anonymous, work in their efforts to treat al-

coholism? Does the addict have to be religiously inclined for such therapies to work?
➤ How successful are aversion therapies that use chemicals to make liquor repellent? Doesn't the effect wear off?
➤ How effective are cognitive therapies that try to get alcoholics to stop drinking by showing them films of their own drunken behavior? Is psychotherapy able to treat alcoholism by helping the patients understand the unconscious reasons for their drinking? How would knowing why you drink help you stop?

Hypothesis:

Of the four most common alcoholism therapies, none seems to have convinced its critics that it offers a strong likelihood of success.

Thesis:

The success of a particular alcoholism therapy depends almost entirely upon the personality of the individual addict.

Narrow the topic to a specific subject before starting to gather information.

Example 3: Presidency
➤ The changing role of the president in relation to Congress over the past fifty years
➤ How John Kennedy handled the Cuban missile crisis?
➤ The effect of Ronald Reagan's appointment of the first woman justice to the Supreme Court

5. Three Limitations

The required **length** of the paper you will write, The source **material** available to you, The **audience** who will read (or hear about) your paper.

1) Length

The subject you decide on, after narrowing a topic, should have sufficient range and depth to show your work as that of a serious student. Don't choose a subject so broad that you must be superficial in order to fit work into a required length.

Example 1:

Modern American Writers——Arthur Miller——Arthur Miller as a Playwright——Biographical Elements in Arthur Miller's *A Memory of Two Mondays*

Example 2:

Television Programs——Violence on Television——The Influence of TV Violence on Children——The Effects of TV Cartoon Violence on Children

2) Materials available

● If you choose a topic too narrow, you may find that you can't locate enough information for a paper of the length demanded.

- Before deciding definitely on a subject for your research, go to the principal library you plan to use, look through the card catalog, and check the holdings of the library against one or two of the most relevant periodical indexes to make sure there is enough information available to you.
- Investigate the availability of nonprint materials before you make a final decision about your subject.

3) Audience

Who are they? What know they? How will they respond to what you write?

6. Focusing on a Subject for Research

Methods to Find a Focus:
Subdividing, Free Association, Asking Questions, Using the Online Catalog

1) Subdividing

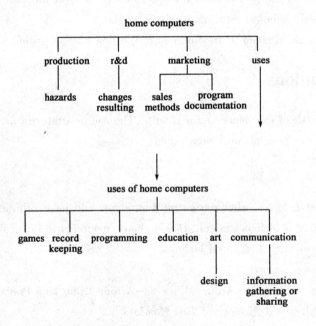

2) Free Association

Crime

police	laws
riots	deterrents
prevention	big cities
white-collar	growing rates
punishment	penal system
repeat offenders	death penalty
citizen activities	

White-collar Crime

```
offices            department stores
perpetrators       internal security systems
deterrents
"Internal Security Systems to Prevent White-Collar
 Crime"
"Lie Detector Tests as a Prerequisite for Employment"
```

Combined Method. The subject of a research paper can be arrived at by a combination of two of the methods we have been reading about.

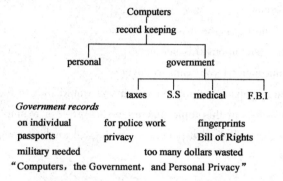

Government records

```
on individual      for police work        fingerprints
passports          privacy                Bill of Rights
military needed    too many dollars wasted
```
"Computers, the Government, and Personal Privacy"

3) Asking questions

①The five "W"s

Who——people

What——problems, things, ideas

Where——places

When——past, present, future

Why——causes, reasons, results, conditions

Example 1:

Television (the broad topic)				
Who?	**What?**	**Where?**	**When?**	**Why?**
Show hosts	Violence	Satellite transmission	Commercial beginnings	Election
Actors and actresses	News	Remote places	New channels to come	Interference with studies
Directors	Religion	Hollywood	Broadcast times	Persuasive power
Johnny Carson	Commercials	New York	Technical development	Selling to children
Lucille Ball	Videodiscs VTR	Local stations		Education

Example 2:

Television News (partially narrowed subject)				
Who?	**What?**	**Where?**	**When?**	**Why?**
Anchorpersons	Getting a job as manipulator of audience	Local coverage	Immediacy of election coverage	Limits
Weather reporters	Compared to print media	Networks	Topics and times of broadcast	
On-site crews Tom Brokaw	Sports coverage	Remotes		

②Asking other questions

Topic: Government funding of the arts

What do you already know about this subject?

Is there a specific time period you want to cover?

Is there a geographic region or country on which you would like to focus?

Is there a particular aspect of this topic that interests you? For example, public policy implications, historical influence, sociological aspects, psychological angles, specific groups or individuals involved in the topic, etc.

Topic Narrowing:

government funding of the arts	
General topic	Government funding of the arts
Time span	1930s
Place	USA
Event or aspects	New Deal, painting
Narrowed topic sentence	Federal funding of painters through New Deal programs and the Works Progress Administration

4) Using the Online Catalog

Subheadings that define geographical locations, material types, or specific aspects of a topic *Search also under* or *See also* notes and links that identify other related or narrower subjects.

7. Broaden Your Topic

1) Topic broadening

If a topic is too new and sources to your research questions may not yet exist, think of parallel and broader associations for your subject to find a broader topic that will be easier to research.

Example:

Topic: The effect of deforestation on Colombia's long-term ability to feed its citizens

Consider the following questions
- Could you examine other countries or regions in addition to Colombia?
- Could you think more broadly about this topic? Give thought to wider topics like agriculture and sustainable development.
- Who are the key players in this topic? The government? Citizens? International organizations?
- What other issues are involved in this topic? Such as, how can natural resources be allocated most economically to sustain the populace of Colombia?

Specific topic	What is the effect of deforestation on Columbia's long-term ability to feed its citizens?
Alternative focus	Agriculture, sustainable development
Alternative place	South America
Alternative person or group	United Nations and its subgroups
Alternative event or aspect	Birth Control
Broadened topic sentence	How can the United Nations encourage South American countries to employ sustainable development practices?

2) Using the Online Catalog

Click on "about" after a subject heading. This link will take you to a scope note that defines what kinds of materials are cataloged under that heading. Often links to broader terms can be found within these scope notes.

8. Finding an Approach

Finding an approach before you start collecting material helps you determine the method you will use to deal with the material; you then know what to look for and have some notion of how to present it.

Method: Glancing at probable sources

Two important and practical purposes:
- A way of finding an approach to your subject;
- A prelude to your own exercise of critical thinking, of being selective about what information you need to include and what kind of support each approach demands.

Five approaches toward the subject

Examining or analyzing, Evaluating or criticizing, Comparing and contrasting, Relating, Arguing or persuading.

1) Examining or analyzing

Examples:
Examine the stylistic devices in a work of literature;

- Tom Jones as a Picaresque Novel
- Gulliver's Travels as Political Satire

Examine the intellectual, scientific or sociological background of a person or an historical period:
- Labor Union Movement in Golda Meir's Youth
- Pre-Sputnik Space Exploration

Examine variations of a work of art or examine how the artist revised it:
- How Picasso Developed Guernica
- Versions of "Sailing to Byzantium"

Analyze the evolution of a business practice:
- The Phenomenon of Record Sales Promotions on Television
- Solar Heaters as a Growth Industry

Warning:
Don't fall into the trap of just enumerating a series of pieces of information.
- The Anthropological Films of Robert Flaherty

2) Evaluating or criticizing

Examples:
Evaluations of individuals, works or ideas:
- The Effectiveness of the Seat Belt Law
- Rachel Carson's Writings and Ecological Awareness
- Computer Games as Learning Tools

Choose a critical approach to many ideas:
- The Role of the Brother in *The Glass Menagerie*
- Dorothy Parker as Spokesperson for Women of Her Time
- Practical Applications of Space Shuttle Experiments
- "Win Big Money" Offers in Ads
- Government Limitation of Boating Down the Colorado River
- Foreign Policy toward Panama in the Past Decade
- The Ethics of a Death Penalty

3) Comparing and contrasting

To compare is to find similarities, and to contrast is to find differences.
Examples:
Making a comparison of critical receptions of a work or of views about an individual or of ideas:
- 1984 at Publication and in 1984
- Views of Ronald Reagan's Presidency

- Various Buddhist Sects

Compare and contrast events as viewed by different countries or as viewed by people in different situations:
- Israeli and Arab Views of the Six-Day War
- Oil Company and Consumer Views of the Need for Underwater Oil Exploration
- Unappreciative Daughters in Two Shakespeare Plays
- High Noon and Shane as Archetypal Western Films
- Nutritional Values of Three Popular Diets
- Translations of Faust by Kaufmann, Raphael, and Wayne

4) Relating

Establishing and supporting relationships is a distinctive kind of approach.

Examples:

Show the relationship between a theory and its practical application:
- The Psychology of the Underdog in "Peanuts"

Show the relationship between a person's work or thought and life:
- Martin Luther King, Jr., as an Effective Leader of Civil Rights Activists

Relate an individual to a specific event or attitude:
- Cesar Chavez and Effective Boycotts
- Impact of ZPG on Marketing
- Influence of Numerology on Medieval Church Architecture
- Mendelian Theory in the Selective Breeding of Cattle
- Search for Adequate Written Characters for Spoken Eskimo Languages
- Production Lines for Productive Working Environments
- Chimps Learn Language like Children

5) Arguing or persuading

At the heart of argumentative or persuasive writing is a thesis or overriding principal idea that is logically supported by evidence.

Examples:

Defend a position:
- The Word "Amateur" should be Dropped from Sports
- Nobel Literature Prizes are Often Conferred for Political Rather than Literary Reasons

Justify an action:
- Frequent Auto Design Changes are Necessary

Prove a belief:
- Horror Movies are Needed in Our Society
- Common Stocks of Companies X and Y are Good Investments

9. Wording Approaches and Final Titles

Formulate your approach statement as a two-part phrase: the subject and the approach.
- Obesity
- *Peter Rabbit* as shown in story and film
- Mica mining techniques to meet commercial demands

Note that none of these sample subjects or approaches is in the form of a question.

If you find yourself thinking in terms of a question, simply rephrase it into a statement.

Example:
- How has Richard Ⅲ been depicted in different eras?
- Richard Ⅲ as depicted by Shakespeare and by twentieth-century historians.

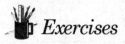 *Review Questions*

1. What is the value of brainstorming? At what point(s) in the research process is this activity likely to help you?
2. What is the purpose of background reading? If you know your topic from the start, should you skip this step?
3. Why is it a good idea to look for a controversy of some sort when trying to come up with a topic?
4. Why do you need to form a hypothesis if you have an excellent topic? How does a hypothesis help at various stages of research?

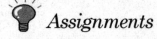 *Exercises*

Find a proper thesis or theme by following the five steps: (1) choose one subject area, (2) do sufficient background reading, (3) find two or three potential topics for a seven-to-ten-page research paper, (4) do some brainstorming to find a proper topic, (5) form a reasonable hypothesis by brainstorming to find a proper thesis or theme.

Assignments

1. Try one or two of the three methods explained in class to narrow one of the following topics to a workable subject for research.
   ——Energy conservation
   ——Rat control in town
   ——Paintings of a particular artist
   ——E-learning
2. Decide one or two approaches you may take toward the following subjects and explain the

reason for your choice:

——On relationships between translated and original texts
——A quality evaluation of SLA/FLT experimental studies by Chinese researchers
——A comparative study of the structural syllabus and the notional-functional syllabus
——Internal structure of EFL motivation at the tertiary level in China
——An exploration of Sweet's influence on the study of Chinese grammar
——The function of language transfer and the analysis and countermeasure of written English
——A cognitive-pragmatic analysis of language report in English and Chinese
——A study of the style of editorial English
——A cognitive-psychological analysis of the second language acquisition process
——On the process of metaphor understanding and its characteristics

Unit 4 文 献 笔 记
Taking Notes

1. Evaluating Source Materials

- Don't try to take detailed or extensive notes at first; just try to get familiar with the subject so you can be selective enough to take effective notes.
- Previewing or general reading before you take notes gives you a feel for your subject before you begin working intensively on it and helps you define the subject as much as possible.
- If you need to use every source you can find, you will want to know how to evaluate them to get better information. Also, the more closely you evaluate material, the more refined you make your judgment and the more you have your independent thinking abilities.

1) Before you read

- Are the resources enough to:
  Support your argument
  Include a variety of viewpoints and materials
- Are there different resources?
  Primary Sources
  – Contemporary accounts of an event and original documents
  – Examples: letters, diaries, audio-recordings of speeches, newspaper articles
    Secondary Resources
  – Retrospective sources based on primary resources; include scientific or scholarly analysis
  – Examples: books, articles, editorials, reviews, scientific studies
- Which authors seem outstanding in the field?
  An author's publication quantity
  An author's credentials may be a useful guide to his or her standing in a field.
- What is the date of publication?
  Current Events Research: Use resources that are recent and reflect current attitudes.
  Historical Research: Use a variety of resources from different time periods including both primary and secondary resources.
- How credible does a source seem?
  The reputation of a publisher is worth considering.
  The bases of the author's conclusions should be reliable.

If your resource is a book, you can find out how it was received by the critics from reviews.

The extent of documentation an author provides to support statements is another measure of a source's credibility.

If your resource is a person, make sure it is someone qualified to give you the information you are looking for.

2) When you read

- What does the language of a source tell you?

Language reveals something of the beliefs and attitudes of the writer.

- Which sources seem to give you the most information?

Some reference materials will tell you more than others about the subject you are researching.

- What facts keep reappearing in your reading?

If information is repeated in several sources, it is probably particularly important.

2. Qualities of Good Notes

- Legibility:

Take notes on 10cm × 15cm cards.

Take notes in ink.

Write on only one side of a card.

Put only one idea on a card.

Use whatever abbreviations you find convenient for notes.

- Accuracy:

Read your research material carefully.

Record precisely.

Distinguish among fact, inference, and opinion.

A *fact* is a statement that can be verified by evidence from the senses.

An *inference* is an educated guess based on one fact or more.

Opinion expresses a belief held by an individual, but is not observable or verifiable.

- Completeness:

Identify the source of what appears on each card.

Note the page numbers from which you obtained information.

Identify the subject of each card.

> **Language learning**   Babbie 153-154
>
> "Our language is simply too complicated for anyone to learn totally from scratch, Chom-/sky and his followers argue."
>
>   Quotation

3. Conventions of Writing Notes

- Quotations:

All wording taken completely from a written or spoken source must be acknowledged in two ways: both by quotation marks and by crediting the source.

> Danger   Rowan, 18
>
> "The federal government has an average of eighteen separate records on each citizen. The danger is that any person can be analyzed by looking at a compilation of computer entries about him."
>
>   Quotation

- Quotations at page breaks:

> **Language learning**   Babbie 153-154
>
> "Our language is simply too complicated for anyone to learn totally from scratch, **Chom-/sky** and his followers argue."
>
>   Quotation

- Quotations within quotations:

> "'**It** said I owed 50 cents to my high school for not returning my locker key,' he told a reporter. 'That shows the kind of stuff your high school **keeps**.'" (Sherick 53)

- Punctuation for quotations:

> Senator Sam Ervin pointed out that during the hearings he conducted in 1969, many cases "**to** coerce citizens into supplying personal information for statistical data banks in the Census Bureau and other federal agencies were **documented**." (5)

> "**Sometimes** the issue of threats to individual rights is presented only alter a data system has **developed**," wrote Senator Sam Ervin, "**and** only alter practical problems are raised which were not envisioned on **paper**." (6)

- Poetry quotations:

> "**Busy** old fool, unruly sun, / Why dost thou thus, / Through windows, and through curtains, call on **us**?"

- Words omitted from a quotation:

> The Data Bank hearing committee defined privacy as "the capacity … to determine what information about the individual will be collected and disseminated to ethers." (Bouchard 73)

> So pervasive has computer record-keeping become that even our most ordinary activities "are likely to leave distinctive electronic tracks in the memory of a computer…" ("Surveillance Society" 25)

- Titles within sources:

If you have occasion in your notes to write the names of books, plays, pamphlets, long poems, periodicals, films, computer software, record albums, radio or television programs, paintings or sculptures, even spacecraft—underline them. If such titles are within a passage you are quoting, retain the underlining.

Put in quotation marks the titles of short stories, poems, essays, chapters in books, newspaper or magazine articles, songs, lectures or speeches, and individual episodes of radio and television series.

- Italicized or foreign words:

If a word within a quotation is in italics, underline it in your notes and in the text of your research paper.

If you write or quote a foreign word or phrase, underline it, also, even though it does not appear that way in your source.

- Interpolations:

Relate a pronoun to its antecedent noun when the noun doesn't appear in the quoted passage.

> "**It** [**new technology**] has removed the quality of mercy from our institutions by making it impossible to forget, to forgive, to understand, to tolerate." (Ervin 7)

Show that something is copied accurately, even though it's wrong.

> "'when,' as Senator Ervin had pointed out, 'people fear surveillance, whether it exists or not, when they grow afraid to speak their minds and hearts freely to their government or to anyone else, '**then** [sic] we shall cease to be a free society.'" (Barth ix)

Express a personal comment:

> Ervin wrote that the army has 25,000,000 records [**that was in 1971—think of the increase by now!**] of people " who have undergone security investigations as present or former members of armed forces, civilian employees of the Department of Defense, or employees of defense contractors." (4)

4. Reading to Take Notes

- Skimming:

Looking through the work quickly in order to get an overall impression of it

- Scanning:

Looking for specific information quickly, without reading word by word or, in better reading technique, phrase by phrase

5. Kinds of Taking Notes

The four basic kinds of notes:

Summary, Paraphrase, Direct quotation, Personal comment

- Summary:

To record in your own words the essence of a passage and omit examples or explanations.

The summary reports *only* the central idea of *what an author has said* and must not include your own interpretation or a comment on the meaning.

Summary must follow the organization or order of the original source.

> Language learning   Babbie 153-154
>
> Language is the most important set of symbols a person learns. Behaviorists believe it takes place through reward for correct imitation of sounds. Chomsky believes all languages have a basic grammar and that everyone is born with the ability to use it.
>
> **Summary**

- Paraphrase:

A paraphrase states the ideas of a source in your own words, but follows the original writing phrase by phrase; therefore, a paraphrase not only has the same organization as the original, but it is also approximately the same length.

> Language learning   Babbie 153-154
>
> Language is a learned series of symbols transmitted through a culture. However, there is no agreement about how such learning takes place. Behavioral psychologists believe language is learned by "selective reinforcement". That is, children are rewarded by adults for behaving in approved ways and punished if they don't. B. F. Skinner believes children are rewarded for imitating the language sounds of people from whom they gain approval.
>
> **Paraphrase**

Paraphrased notes are often preferable to summaries because they are more detailed and specific. They are often preferable to quotations because the text is in your own words rather than in someone else's.

Be sure that when you incorporate a paraphrased note into your paper you give proper documentation.

Paraphrasing is a *complete rewriting*, not just a game of rearranging words.

- Direct quotation:

Direct quotation notes are useful when the original wording of a research source is important, especially in the three instances:

— The words of your source are written in a *style* so perfect, so suitable, or so vivid that they seem beyond changing.

— The material is so *significant* or *controversial*, or its source so *authoritative*, that it must be stated with utmost accuracy.

— The wording of a source needs to be *transmitted accurately* and you want to be sure to do so. Sometimes wording is so succinct that to tamper with it is to violate a piece of fine writing, so you might decide to use a quotation note.

Remember these two customs:

If anything you are quoting has a quotation from another source within it, you show that by using single quote marks within the double ones.

You must show page breaks within a quotation by using a slash mark with a space on either side of it and then both page numbers.

Sample note card for a quotation showing a page break by the slash mark (/). Both page numbers show at top right with name of source.

> Language learning   Babbie 153-154
>
> "Our language is simply too complicated for anyone to learn totally from scratch, **Chom-/sky** and his followers argue."
>
> **Quotation**

- Personal comment:

You will undoubtedly have comments to make on information while you gather it as well as on ideas that you read and think through.

Record all these thoughts on separate note cards rather than run the risk of losing what might be the most helpful part of your work.

Use essentially the same form for your own comments as you do for other note cards, except that you will not need a title source in the upper right-hand corner.

Sample note card for a personal comment:

> Language learning
>
> The approving response Skinner believes leads people to speak their language must take many different forms. How can a child figure out what all of them signify?
>
> **Personal Response**

6. Combination

A summary and personal comment or a paraphrase and quotation are sometimes appropriate combinations, especially if a quotation is brief and you want to put it into context for the sake of sense.

If a combination note includes a quotation, be sure you record the source in the upper right-hand corner so you can give accurate attribution when you use this note card in writing your paper.

> Language learning   Babbie 154
>
> Chomsky says all people are born with the ability to understand the basic structures of language. "This position is in striking contrast to conventional social science, yet Chomsky makes a compelling case, one that has had an enormous impact within the discipline of linguistics."
>
> **Summary + Quote**

7. Plagiarism

Plagiarism is using someone else's words or ideas without giving proper credit to the person who devised them.

The most obvious kind of plagiarism is submitting another person's paper as your own.

A more subtle kind of plagiarism is to let your reader think that certain words, phrases, or ideas are your own when they are, in fact, the property of other people you fail to acknowledge.

People tend to commit plagiarism at either of two stages in the research paper process.
- The first stage is in taking notes
- The other stage is in writing the paper

You will NOT commit plagiarism if you will do the four following things:
- Use quotation marks around all words and phrases that you get from any of your research sources and cite the source both in note cards and in your paper.
- Credit the source of any ideas, including summaries and paraphrases, you get from any of your research sources by documentation when you write your paper.
- Be sure every source in your documentation is also in the Works Cited.
- Give an adequate introduction or otherwise clearly delineate borrowed words and ideas.

ORIGINAL PASSAGE:

Experiments with frogs' and cats' eyes suggest that adaptation to darkness is in part due to regeneration of visual pigment (bleached during exposure to white light) in the retina. The pigment appears to be bleached only minimally with exposure to red light; hence the use of red light bulbs in photo-developing labs and in other situations where workers alternate between darkness and light. Once the eyes are dark-adapted, they will continue to be so following exposure to red light. (Guy R. Lefrancois, Psychology, 2nd ed. Belmont: Wads-worth, 1983:128.)

UNACCEPTABLE SUMMARY:

Experiments with animals' eyes suggest that their adaptation to darkness occurs because visual pigment in the retina regenerated. Red light bleaches the pigment only minimally so people who work in photo-developing labs and other places where they alternate between light and darkness use red lights to help their eyes become dark-adapted and continue to be so.

ACCEPTABLE SUMMARY:

Visual pigment that bleaches out of the retina in white light acts differently in red light. Thus, a red light is easier on the eyes of people who work in enclosures where there is continual change between dark and light.

Red light illumination helps people adapt to changes between dark and light within a work area.

UNACCEPTABLE PARAPHRASE:

Experiments with the eyes of frogs and cats suggest they can adapt to darkness partly because of the regeneration of their visual pigment in the retina, which was bleached when it was subjected to white light. The pigment seems to bleach only a little with exposure to red light; therefore, red light bulbs are used in photo-developing labs and in other places where workers' eyes have to alternate between dark and light. Once their eyes are adapted to dark, they will continue that way after being exposed to red light.

ACCEPTABLE PARAPHRASE:

Experiments with animals' eyes led to the conclusion that part of the reason humans' eyes can adapt to darkness is that visual pigment in the retina is regenerated, even alter it is bleached when exposed to white light. Since exposing the eyes to red light seems to bleach it much less, people who work in photo-developing labs and other places where they must go between light and darkness now work under red light bulbs so their eyes will continually adapt to the darkness under their working conditions.

Common knowledge:

Common knowledge is information so basic to a study or so well known that it doesn't have to be documented.

You may not always be sure whether a specific statement can properly be considered common knowledge or whether it requires documentation. In such cases the safest rule is, "When in doubt, give credit."

A Note about Photocopying:

Photocopying book pages or even complete magazine articles is no substitute for taking careful notes—not even if passages in the photocopy are underlined or otherwise marked for attention.

If you use a computer...

If you use a database program for taking notes on a microcomputer, you should set up the same basic information you would on a note card: author, perhaps title, page number(s), library call number (for books), type of note, and key word.

Review Questions

1. What problems should be considered while evaluating source materials?
2. What are the qualities of good notes?
3. What is the difference between a summary and a paraphrase? How are they similar?
4. What are the advantages of paraphrasing and summarizing rather than copying passages from sources?
5. When paraphrasing, do you have to change every word that appeared in the original? Explain your answer.
6. For what reasons might you quote rather than paraphrase a statement found in a source?
7. How to avoid plagiarism in note taking?

Assignments

1. Take a full set of notes on the following excerpt from a lecture. Be sure to follow the direction indicated by the hypothesis when deciding what information belongs in your notes. Remember not to put too much information on individual cards. If you quote something, mark it clearly, and, in parentheses, give a reason for quoting—accuracy, memorable words, conciseness, authority.

Topic: the causes of violence in America today

Hypothesis: "Although some observers blame violence on television and the economy, the cause may lie in our past, going back to the lawless West and to Prohibition."

2. Take a full set of notes on this magazine article. Be sure to follow the direction indicated by the hypothesis when deciding what information belongs in your notes. Remember not to crowd information on your cards. If you quote something, mark it clearly, and, in parentheses, give your reason for quoting—accuracy, memorable words, conciseness, authority. Also, make up bibliography cards for any potential sources you discover in this article.

Topic: preservation of world's forests

Hypothesis: "The continued loss of the world's forests will have disastrous effects on both nature and civilization."

Unit 5　写作准备
Preparing to Write the Paper

Take a long, hard look at what you've gathered, evaluate the notes, and organize those you select.

When you organize your ideas, you also need to think again about the audience for this research paper you are writing.

Consider again the approach you determined to take toward your subject.

1. Organizing your note cards

Lay all your note cards out on a table, arranging them into groups according to subtopics.

Look through your notes carefully and consider each card on its own merits.

Sift through your notes and consider how each one will fit into a general scheme.

Add cards expressing your own opinions.

Go through the note cards and decide what you want to emphasize about your subject, what you want to build your work around.

2. Composing a thesis statement

A *thesis statement* is a specific declaration that summarizes the point of view you will take in your paper.

A *thesis statement* expresses the main ideas of your paper and answers the question or questions posed by your paper.

A *thesis statement* generally consists of two parts: your topic, and then the analysis, explanation(s), or assertion(s) that you're making about the topic.

The characteristics of a successful thesis statement:
- It is limited so it can give direction to the paper.

  Compare:
  ➢ Some kinds of mining interfere with an area.
  ➢ Strip mining permanently injured the ecology of eastern Pennsylvania by destroying vegetation.
- It is narrow, rather than broad.

  Compare:
  ➢ The American steel industry has many problems.

> The primary problem of the American steel industry is the lack of funds to renovate outdated plants and equipment.
- It is specific.

Compare:
> Outdoor furniture is made of various materials.

Wood, aluminum, and wrought iron outdoor furniture have properties that make them suitable for differing climates.
> Hemingway's war stories are very good.

Hemingway's stories helped create a new prose style by employing extensive dialogue, shorter sentences, and strong Anglo-Saxon words.
- A thesis statement has one main point rather than several main points. More than one point may be too difficult for the reader to understand and the writer to support.

Compare:
> Stephen Hawking's physical disability has not prevented him from becoming a world-renowned physicist, and his book is the subject of a movie.
> Stephen Hawking's physical disability has not prevented him from becoming a world renowned physicist.
- It is a way to unify the ideas in the paper.
- It is an aid to coherence for your paper.

3. Warnings for writing a thesis statement

- A promise or statement of purpose cannot serve as a thesis statement.

Compare:
> In this paper I am going to show how the ancient Egyptians were able to build so many huge temples and tombs.
> The ancient Egyptians, were able to build so many huge temples and tombs because the dependence on agriculture left seasons when farmers had time to do other kinds of work, the religion encouraged people to do work that glorified their gods and pharaohs, and busy masses were necessary for political and economic stability.
- A topic or subject by itself cannot serve as a thesis statement.

Examples:
> New Land for Public Parks
> Social Security and Old Age
> Continuing changes in the Social Security System make it almost impossible to plan intelligently for one's retirement.
- A few words added to a title, but not forming a complete sentence, cannot be a thesis statement.

Compare:

- ➤ What new land ought to be taken for public parks and why
- ➤ Citizens should work through governmental agencies to set aside land for public use before business interests destroy natural beauty and natural resources.
- A question cannot serve as a thesis statement.

  Compare:
- ➤ What are Leni Riefenstahl's contributions to film?
- ➤ Leni Riefenstahl's use of unconventional camera angles and dramatic editing introduced an artistic perspective to the filming of sporting events.
- A thesis statement is an assertion, not a statement of fact or an observation.

  Compare:
- ➤ People use many lawn chemicals.
- ➤ People are poisoning the environment with chemicals merely to keep their lawns clean.
- A thesis takes a stand rather than announcing a subject.

  Compare:
- ➤ The thesis of this paper is the difficulty of solving our environmental problems.

  Solving our environmental problems is more difficult than many environmentalists believe.
- ➤ Leni Riefenstahl's methods gave new perspective to filming sports.

  Leni Riefenstahl's use of unconventional camera angles and dramatic editing introduced an artistic perspective to the filming of sporting events.

4. Generating a thesis statement with assigned topic

Distill the assignment into a specific question.

Example:

Assignment: Write a report to the local school board explaining the potential benefits of using computers in a fourth-grade class

Question: What are the potential benefits of using computers in a fourth-grade class?

Answer: The potential benefits of using computers in a fourth-grade class are…

Answer: Using computers in a fourth-grade class promises to improve…

5. Generating a thesis statement with unassigned topic

A good thesis statement will usually include the following four attributes:
- Take on a subject upon which reasonable people could disagree
- Deal with a subject that can be adequately treated given the nature of the assignment
- Express one main idea
- Assert your conclusions about a subject

Example: Steps to Generate a Thesis Statement

Topic: Problems posed by drug addiction

Your interest: The problems of crack babies

General subject: Crack babies

Narrow the topic: Programs for crack kids

Take a position on the topic: More attention should be paid to the environment crack kids grow up in.

Use specific language: Experts estimate that half of crack babies will grow up in home environments lacking rich cognitive and emotional stimulation.

Make an assertion based on clearly stated support: Because half of all crack babies are likely to grow up in homes lacking good cognitive and emotional stimulation, the federal government should finance programs to supplement parental care for crack kids.

The thesis answers the question: Why should anything be done for crack kids and who should do it?

6. Ways of organizing content

Some subjects dictate the best order to use such as chronology or problem to solution.

Often the thesis statement points the way toward organizing the content of your paper.

1) Analytical Thesis Statements

In an analytical paper, you are breaking down an issue or an idea into its component parts, evaluating the issue or idea, and presenting this breakdown and evaluation to your audience.

Example:

An analysis of barn owl flight behavior reveals two kinds of flight patterns: patterns related to hunting prey and patterns related to courtship.

2) Expository (Explanatory) Thesis Statements

In an expository paper, you are explaining something to your audience.

Example:

The lifestyles of barn owls include hunting for insects and animals, building nests, and raising their young.

3) Argumentative Thesis Statements

In an argumentative paper, you are making a claim about a topic and justifying this claim with reasons and evidence.

Example:

Barn owls' nests should not be eliminated from barns because barn owls help farmers by eliminating insect and rodent pests.

Effect-to-cause organization

Thesis statement: The ancient Egyptians were able to build so many huge temples and tombs because the dependence on agriculture left seasons when farmers had time to do other kinds of work, the religion encouraged people to do work that glorified their gods and pharaohs, and busy masses were necessary for political and economic stability.

Problem to solution organization

Thesis statement: Good citizens should work through governmental agencies to set aside land for public use before business interests destroy natural beauty and natural resources.

Specific to general

Thesis statement: Leni Riefenstanl's use of unconventional camera angles and her dramatic editing introduced an artistic perspective to the filming of sporting events.

Thesis statement: Individuals need to guard their right to privacy as computers make federal government information gathering, storage, and dissemination increasingly easy and more extensive.

Problem: (1) The federal government has gathered a great deal of information about its citizens and stored it in computers. (2) Computer storage and dissemination has inherent problems that affect personal privacy.

Solution: Individuals must be on guard to be sure their personal privacy is not violated as a result of information about them in government computers.

Six possible ways of organizing information:
- Time.

    Examples
    - Examine varying critical receptions of a novel over a period of time
    - Detail the changing demography of a city
    - Persuade a plant supervisor to install a new manufacturing process
- Known to unknown or simple to complex

    Examples:
    - On the effects of prolonged space trips
    - On the theater of the absurd
- Comparison and contrast.

Comparison dwells on the similarity while contrast concentrates on dissimilarity.

A comparison / contrast essay usually follows one of these two patterns: the point-by-point pattern or the subject-by-subject pattern.

The subject-by-subject pattern works better in short essays where few aspects are considered, or where the writer's interest is in the whole.

The point-by-point pattern is preferable in long essays where many aspects are mentioned, for a long discussion of the various aspects of one item puts too much burden on the reader's memory.

In the point-by-point pattern, the writer discusses both items under each of the various aspects compared / contrasted.

Thesis statement: Film X is better than film Y.
Ⅰ. Direction
   A. X
   B. Y
Ⅱ. Script
   A. X
   B. Y
Ⅲ. Acting
   A. X
   B. Y
Ⅳ. Photography
   A. X
   B. Y
Ⅴ. Set decoration
   A. X
   B. Y

In the subject-by-subject pattern, the writer discusses the various aspects of one item before going on to the other.

Thesis statement: Film X is better than film Y.

Ⅰ. X	Ⅱ. Y
Direction	Direction
Script	Script
Acting	Acting
Photography	Photography
Set decoration	Set decoration

Examples:
➢ The platforms of candidates for elective office
➢ The relative merits of three sites being considered for a new sports stadium
➢ An analysis of two different publications addressed to members of the same profession

● General to particular or particular to general.

Material that follows the organizational pattern of general to particular begins with some fairly broad ideas or statements and then arranges the remainder of the information as a series of specific points in support.

Examples:
➢ Developing economic independence of a newly formed nation
➢ The short stories of James Agee (or any other writer)

● Problem to solution or question to answer.

If your research has been about how to solve a particular problem, you might use the problem-to-solution organization for your paper.

Example:
➢ Food distribution problems in a community

Many business and technical papers are written to seek solutions to problems.

Sometimes a question is posed and a paper is developed around an answer to it.

Example:
➢ How it is possible to establish the authenticity of Shakespeare's work.
● Cause to effect or effect to cause.

Examples:
➢ How plastics have influenced industrial design
➢ Applications of the Taft-Hartley Act since it went into effect
➢ The Russian boycott of the 1984 summer Olympics
➢ How reorganizing the administration in a county office would bring about more effective service to people and more efficient use of employees' time

7. Outlines

An outline is an orderly plan, in writing, showing the division and arrangement of ideas.

Its principal function is to indicate the relationship of ideas to each other, to show which are important and which are subordinate.

The outline for your paper is put together after you have decided on the thesis statement.

Reasons of writing an outline:

You are likely to forget some things you thought you had firmly in mind when you started.

In an outline you can rearrange ideas without difficulty.

You can judge the effectiveness of the organization of your whole paper when you see all the content in a plan before you.

Don't be surprised if your outline isn't "perfect" the first time you put it down on paper.

An outline is to a completed research paper what a blueprint is to a completed house.

By the time you have done research and are ready to write your paper, you pretty much know what you want to present.

If you don't find these main ideas readily, prompt yourself with a bit of role playing.

The final outline:
– will show where to put the key ideas of your paper and how to provide details on one or more levels where they are required;
– will indicate the emphases that will make your finished research paper;
– shouldn't be so minutely detailed that it becomes a paper in itself;
– shouldn't be so brief or vague that you need to guess about what is meant in order to get a general picture of a paper from reading its outline.

8. Forms of Outlines

Topic outlines, Sentence outlines, Paragraph outlines, Decimal outlines

- **Topic outline:**

The *topic outline* is one of the most widely used of all outline forms because the wording is succinct.

Try to use a parallel (and consistent) grammatical structure throughout a topic outline.

Example:

I. Principles of polygraph

II. Uses by private business

    A. Discourage thievery

    B. Screen out undesirable characteristics

- **Sentence outline:**

The *sentence outline* presents statements as grammatically complete sentences.

Example:

I. The polygraph measures physiological changes in response to questions.

II. Private business uses polygraph testing for at least two reasons.

    A. Employees are tested to thwart thievery.

    B. Potential employees are tested to discover the existence of characteristics that would make them undesirable employees.

- **Paragraph outlines:**

A *paragraph outline* has the same symbols as topic and sentence outlines, but each symbol is followed by several sentences——that is, by a paragraph.

- **Decimal outline:**

1.
    1.1
        1.1.1
        1.1.2
        1.1.3
    1.2
        1.2.1
        1.2.2

2.

…

Phrases, rather than sentences, follow each numerical designation.

9. Outline Conventions

- Numbers and letters are used alternately in an outline (except in the case of a decimal outline) so ideas of equal importance in the overall concept of the paper will have the same kind of symbol.
- Symbols in an outline must always appear at least in pairs.

　　I.
　　　　A.
　　　　B.
　　　　C.
　　　　　　1.
　　　　　　2.
　　　　　　3.
　　　　　　　　a.
　　　　　　　　b.
　　II.
　　　　A.
　　　　　　1.
　　　　　　2.
　　　　　　　　a.
　　　　　　　　　　1).
　　　　　　　　　　2).
　　　　　　　　b.
　　　　B.

- Every symbol in an outline is followed by a period (except those in a decimal outline).
- Capitalize the first letter of the first word after every symbol.
- Grammatically complete sentences require normal sentence punctuation.
- All symbols of the same kind should be in a vertical line.
- Begin succeeding lines of writing under the first word after a symbol.

　Example:

　A. This is an especially long statement and requires four lines, so the subsequent lines begin under the first word after the symbol

- Type an outline in double spacing.

　Example:

　Computers, Government Files and Personal Privacy

　Thesis: Individuals need to guard their right to privacy as computers make federal government information gathering, storage, and dissemination increasingly easy and more extensive.

Ⅰ. Bases of personal privacy
　　A. Constitution
　　B. Definition
Ⅱ. Fears of government intrusiveness
　　A. Government takeovers
　　B. Private autonomy
Ⅲ. Government record keeping
　　A. Extent of individual record storage
　　B. Sources of information

10. Outline Content

Some guides for making the content of your outline meaningful:
- Every word in your outline should say something about the content of your paper.

Thesis: Professionally made videotapes are better for classroom teaching than those made in classrooms.

Compare:
Ⅰ. In-class taping
　　A. who does it
　　B. why used
Ⅱ. Professional
　　A. who does it
　　B. why used

Ⅰ. In-class taping
　　A. Camera operators
　　　　1. Students
　　　　2. School media specialists
　　B. Advantages
　　　　1. Immediacy
　　　　2. Student involvement
Ⅱ. Professional preparation
　　A. Sources
　　　　1. Specialists within school
　　　　2. Businesses
　　　　3. Educational TV stations
　　B. Advantages
　　　　1. Variety of subject matter
　　　　2. Slick production techniques
　　　　3. Time saving

- The information for each subheading must be directly related to, and subordinate to, the heading under which it appears.

Thesis: Arthur Miller used elements of a sophisticated mistress in one story and a childlike wife in another to develop the character of Roslyn Taber in his cinema-novel The Misfits.

Compare:

> Ⅰ. "The Misfits" was published in 1957.
>   A. The story concerned three cowboys on a mustang hunt. Roslyn meets them.
>   B. Roslyn is an eastern sophisticate.

> Ⅰ. Roslyn appears in "The misfits" published in 1957.
>   A. She meets three cowboys going on a mustang bunt.
>   B. She is an eastern sophisticate.

> Ⅰ. Roslyn is an eastern sophisticate in "The Misfits" (1957).
>   A. She enjoys new sights and experiences.
>   B. She feels sorry for hurt animals.
> Ⅱ. Roslyn is a charming…

- Make relationships clear by using the same symbol (that is, Roman numerals, capital letters, Arabic numerals, and so on) for ideas of equal importance.

Thesis: Hemingway's writing evolved from his own life.

Compare:

> Ⅰ. Early journalistic career
> Ⅱ. Participation in WWI
> Ⅲ. <u>The Sun Also Rises</u>
>   A. Other successful early novels
>   B. <u>A Farewell to Arms</u>
> Ⅳ. Sympathetic to Loyalists
>   A. <u>For whom the Bell Tolls</u>
>   B. Participation in Spanish Civil War

> Ⅰ. Early journalistic career
> Ⅱ. Participation in WWI
> Ⅲ. Expatriate novelist years
>   A. <u>The Sun Also Rises</u>
>   B. <u>A Farewell to Arms</u>
> Ⅳ. Participation in Spanish Civil War

- Only principal points appear in an outline.

Include in it the main points you want to make in your paper and not the illustration, amplification, and development of those points.

11. Structures of Qualitative dissertation outline and quantitive dissertation outline

QUALITATIVE DISSERTATION OUTLINE	QUANTITATIVE DISSERTATION OUTLINE
Chapter 1: Introduction ● Background of the Problem ● Statement of the Problem ● Purpose of the Study ● Research Questions ● Importance of the Study ● Scope of the Study ● Definition of Terms ● Delimitations and Limitations	*Chapter 1: Introduction* ● Background of the Problem ● Statement of the Problem ● Purpose of the Study ● Theoretical Framework ● Research Hypotheses ● Importance of the Study ● Scope of the Study ● Definition of Terms ● Summary
Chapter 2: Review of the Literature (often reviewed after rather than before data collection in qualitative studies)	*Chapter 2: Review of the Literature*
Chapter 3: Research Methods ● Qualitative Paradigm ● Qualitative Methods ● Researcher's Role ● Data Sources ● Data Collection ● Data Analysis ● Verification ● Ethical Considerations ● Plan for Narrative ● Pilot Study Results	*Chapter 3: Research Methods* ● Research Design ● Participants ● Instrumentation ● Research Procedures ● Pilot Testing ● Data Analysis ● Assumptions of the Study ● Limitations of the Study ● Summary
Chapter 4: Research Findings	*Chapter 4: Research Findings*
Chapter 5: Conclusions, Discussion, and Suggestions for Future Research ● Summary ● Conclusions ● Discussion ● Suggestions for Future Research	*Chapter 5: Conclusions, Discussion, and Suggestions for Future Research* ● Summary ● Conclusions ● Discussion ● Suggestions for Future Research

12. Review——Prewriting

Prewriting exercises help you...

Focus intellectually;

Narrow and define topics for your paper;

Develop logical or architectural structure to topics you have identified;

Provide a context for "project management".

Four exercises in prewriting:

- **Focused free writing.**
  - Use a blank paper or computer screen and set a time limit of 5 -15 minutes.
  - Summarize the topic in a phrase or sentence; generate a free flow of thought.
  - Write anything that comes to mind, whether on topic or off, for the period of time you chose.
  - Don't pause, don't stop, don't rush; work quickly.
  - Don't review what you have written until you have finished.
  - At the end of your time, refer back to the beginning: rephrase the initial topic. Repeat a word, phrase, or important thought or emotion that makes sense.
  - Review: are there words or ideas you can grab onto for the topic? Is there a main idea within this sequence of ideas?

- **Brainstorming.**
  - Use a blank paper or computer screen and set a time limit of 5 - 15 minutes.
  - Summarize the topic in a phrase or sentence; generate a free flow of thought.
  - Write down everything that comes to mind to generate a free flow of thought.
  - Think of ideas related to this topic, the crazier the better: be wild and amuse yourself; eliminate nothing.
  - Make up questions and answers about the topic, no matter how strange: Why am I doing this? What could be interesting about this to me? Why don't I like this? What color is it? What would my friend say about it?
  - Review: are there words or ideas you can grab onto for the topic? Is there a main idea within this sequence of ideas?

- **Mind mapping.**
  - Think in terms of key words or symbols that represent ideas and words.
  - Take a pencil (you'll be erasing!) and a blank (non-lined) big piece of paper or use a blackboard and (colored) chalk.
  - Write down the most important word or short phrase or symbol in the center. Think about it; circle it.
  - Write other important words outside the circle. Draw over-lapping circles to connect items, or use arrows to connect them (think of linking pages in a web site). Leave white space to grow

your map for further development, explanations, action items.
- Work quickly without analyzing your work.
- Edit this first phase; think about the relation of outside items to the center; erase and replace and shorten words for these key ideas; relocate important items closer to each other for better organization; use color to organize information; link concepts with words to clarify the relationship.
- Continue working outward.

Freely and quickly add other key words and ideas (you can always erase!). Think weird: tape pages together to expand your map; break boundaries. Develop in directions the topic takes you—don't bet limited by the size of the paper. As you expand your map, tend to become more specific or detailed.

- **Listing and outlines.**

This is a more structured and sequential overview of your research to date. You may also outline to organize topics built from free writing, brainstorming, or mind mapping:
- Arrange items or topics, usually without punctuation or complete sentences.
- List topics and phrase them in a grammatically similar or parallel structure (subjects, verbs, etc.).
- Sequence topics in importance, defining what "level" of importance they are. Items of equal importance are at the same level.

Example: Study Guides & Strategies

I. Preparing to learn
   A. Learning to learn
   B. Managing time
   C. Setting goals/making a schedule

II. Studying
   A. Thinking critically
   B. Memorizing
   C. Organizing projects

III. Writing Essays
   A. Basic of essays
     1. Prewriting
       a. Definitions
       b. Basics of prewriting
       c. Exercises
       d. …
     2. Rough drafts
       a. Definition
       b. Basics of drafts

                    c. Exercises
                    d. ...
            3. ...
        B. Types of essays
            1. Five paragraph essays
            2. Essays for a literature class
            3. Expository essays
            4. Persuasive essays
            5. ...

Review Questions

1. What is the function of an outline?
2. What are some problems that you might encounter in constructing an outline?

 Assignments

1. Compare the following thesis statements and then decide which ones are weak thesis statements and which ones are strong thesis statements. Explain the reason.

① *Thesis statement* 1: There are some negative and positive aspects to the Banana Herb Tea Supplement.

Thesis statement 2: Because Banana Herb Tea Supplement promotes rapid weight loss that results in the loss of muscle and lean body mass, it poses a potential danger to customers.

② *Thesis statement* 1: My family is an extended family.

Thesis statement 2: While most American families would view consanguineal marriage as a threat to the nuclear family structure, many Iranian families, like my own, believe that these marriages help reinforce kinship ties in an extended family.

③ *Thesis statement* 1: Companies need to exploit the marketing potential of the Internet, and web pages can provide both advertising and customer support.

Thesis statement 2: Because the Internet is filled with tremendous marketing potential, companies should exploit this potential by using web pages that offer both advertising and customer support.

④ *Thesis statement* 1: World hunger has many causes and effects.

Thesis statement 2: Hunger persists in Appalachia because jobs are scarce and farming in the infertile soil is rarely profitable.

⑤ *Title*: Compare and contrast the reasons why the North and South fought the Civil War.

Thesis statement 1: The North and South fought the Civil War for many reasons, some of which were the same and some different.

Thesis statement 2: While both sides fought the Civil War over the issue of slavery, the North ought for moral reasons while the South fought to preserve its own institutions.

Thesis statement 3: While both Northerners and Southerners believed they fought against tyranny and oppression, Northerners focused on the oppression of slaves while Southerners defended their own rights to property and self-government.

⑥ Write an analysis of some aspect of Mark Twain's novel Huckleberry Finn.

Thesis statement 1: Mark Twain's Huckleberry Finn is a great American novel.

Thesis statement 2: In Huckleberry Finn, Mark Twain develops a contrast between life on the river and life on the shore.

Thesis statement 3: Through its contrasting river and shore scenes, Twain's Huckleberry Finn suggests that to find the true expression of American democratic ideals, one must leave "civilized" society and go back to nature.

2. Write an outline for your term research paper.

Unit 6 摘要撰写
Writing an Abstract

If you need to write an abstract for an academic or scientific paper, don't panic; your abstract is simply a summary of the work or paper that others can use as an overview. It will help your reader to understand the paper and it will help people searching for a particular work to find it and decide whether it suits their purposes. Seeing as an abstract is only a summary of the work you've already done, it's easy to accomplish!

1. Getting Your Abstract Started

1) Write your paper first.

Even though an abstract goes at the beginning of the work, it acts as a summary of your entire paper. Rather than introducing your topic, it will be an overview of everything you write about in your paper.

- A thesis and an abstract are entirely different things. The thesis in a paper introduces the main idea or question, while an abstract works to review the entirety of the paper, including the methods and results.
- Even if you think you know what your paper is going to be about, always save the abstract for last. You will be able to give a much more accurate summary if you do just that—summarize what you've already written.

2) Review and understand any requirements for writing your abstract.

The paper you're writing is likely not of your own accord, and relates back to a specific assignment for work or school. As a result, you may also be presented with specific requirements for your overall essay and abstract. Before you start writing, refer to a rubric or guidelines you were presented with to identify important issues to keep in mind.

- Is there a maximum or minimum length?
- Are there style requirements?
- Are you writing for an instructor or a publication?
- Consider your audience. Will other academics in your field read this abstract, or should it be accessible to a lay reader or somebody from another field?

3) Determine the type of abstract you must write.

Although all abstracts accomplish essentially the same goal, there are two primary styles of abstract: descriptive and informative. You may have been assigned a specific style, but if you haven't, you will have to determine which is right for you. Typically, informative abstracts are used for much longer and technical research while descriptive abstracts are best for shorter papers.

- Descriptive abstracts explain the purpose, goal, and methods of your research but leave out the results section. These are typically only 100-200 words.
- Informative abstracts are like a condensed version of your paper, giving an overview of everything in your research including the results. These are much longer than descriptive abstracts, and can be anywhere from a single paragraph to a whole page long.
- The basic information included in both styles of abstract are the same, with the main difference being that the results are only included in an informative abstract and an informative abstract is much longer than a descriptive one.

2. Writing Your Abstract

1) Identify your purpose

You're writing about a correlation between lack of lunches in schools and poor grades. So what? Why does this matter? The reader wants to know why your research is important, and what the purpose of it is. Start off your descriptive abstract by answering one or all of the following:

Why did you decide to do this study?

Why is this research important?

Why should someone read your entire essay?

2) Explain the problem at hand

So the reader knows why you wrote your paper or why you think your topic is important, but now they need to know what the primary issue your paper deals with is. You can sometimes combine the problem with your motivation, but it is best to be clear and separate the two.

What problem is your research trying to better understand or solve?

What is the scope of your study—a general problem, or something specific?

What is your main claim or argument?

3) Explain your methods

Motivation-check. Problem-check. Methods? Now is the part where you give an overview of how you accomplished your study. If you did your own work, include a description of it here. If you reviewed the work of others, it can be briefly explained.

Discuss your own research including the variables and your approach.

Describe the evidence you have to support your claim.

Give an overview of your most important sources.

4) Describe your results (informative abstract only)

This is where you begin to differentiate your abstract between a descriptive and an informative abstract. In an informative abstract, you will be asked to provide the results of your study.

What is it that you found?

What answer did you reach from your research or study?

Was your hypothesis or argument supported?

What are the general findings?

5) Give your conclusion

This should finish up your summary and give closure to your abstract. In it, address the meaning of your findings as well as the importance of your overall paper. This format of having a conclusion can be used in both descriptive and informative abstracts, but you will only address the following questions in an informative abstract.

What are the implications of your work?

Are your results general or very specific?

3. Formatting Your Abstract

1) Keep it in order

There are specific questions your abstract must provide answers for, but the answers but be kept in order as well. Ideally it should mimic the overall format of your essay, with a general "introduction" "body" and "conclusion".

2) Provide helpful information

Unlike a topic paragraph which may be intentionally vague, an abstract should provide a helpful explanation of your paper and your research. Word your abstract so that the reader knows exactly what you're talking about, and isn't left hanging with ambiguous references or phrases.

Avoid using direct acronyms or abbreviations in the abstract, as these will need to be explained in order to make sense to the reader. That uses up precious writing room, and should generally be avoided.

If your topic is about something well-known enough, you can reference the names of people or places that your paper focuses on.

3) Write it from scratch

Your abstract is a summary, yes, but it should be written completely separate from your paper. Don't copy and paste direct quotes from yourself, and avoid simply paraphrasing your own sentences from elsewhere in your writing. Write your abstract using completely new vocabulary and phrases to keep it interesting and redundancy-free.

4) Use key phrases and words

If your abstract is to be published in a journal, you want people to be able to find it easily. In order to do so, readers will search for certain queries on online databases in hopes that papers, like yours, will show up. Try to use 5-10 important words or phrases key to your research in your abstract.

For example, if you're writing a paper on the cultural differences in Schizophrenia, be sure to use words like "schizophrenia" "cross-cultural" "culture-bound" "mental illness" and "societal acceptance". These might be search terms people use when looking for a paper on your subject.

5) Use real information

You want to draw people in with your abstract; it is the hook that will encourage them to continue reading your paper. However, do not reference ideas or studies that you don't include in your paper in order to do this. Citing material that you don't use in your work will mislead readers and ultimately lower your viewership.

6) Avoid being too specific

An abstract is a summary, and as such should not refer to specific points of your research other than possibly names or locations. You should not need to explain or define any terms in your abstract a reference is all that is needed. Avoid being too explicit in your summary and stick to a very broad overview of your work.

7) Be sure to do basic revisions

The abstract is a piece of writing that, like any other, should be revised before being completed. Check it over for grammatical and spelling errors and make sure it is formatted properly.

4. Tips

- Abstracts are typically a paragraph or two and should be no more than 10% of the length of the full essay. Look at other abstracts in similar publications for an idea of how yours should go.
- Consider carefully how technical the paper or the abstract should be. It is often reasonable to assume that your readers have some understanding of your field and the specific language it en-

tails, but anything you can do to make the abstract more easily readable is a good thing.
- An abstract may have a formal tone, but avoid using the passive voice ("the experiment was performed") unless the publication requires it.

Assignments

1. **Analyze abstracts in your professional papers.**
2. **Write an abstract for your own paper.**

Unit 7 论文写作
Writing the Paper

You must plan to write at least three versions of your paper:
Writing the rough draft, Revising the rough draft, Writing the polished, final draft

1. Writing the rough draft

Writing Style ⟶ Starting the Paper ⟶ Writing the Body of the Paper ⟶ Integrating Resource Information ⟶ Ending the Paper ⟶ Selecting a Title

1) Writing Style

- Research papers are usually written in the third person.
  Writing in the first person focuses attention on the author;
  Writing in the second person draws the attention of the audience to itself;
  Using the third person directs the reader's entire attention to what you have to say in your research paper.
- Your research paper should be written in a straightforward style that is neither artificially formal nor as loose and relaxed as you would use for a personal letter.
- No matter how much of a person's work you have read, never refer to that individual except by full name (given and surnames) or by last name alone.
- The wording of the research paper should be as accurate as possible and thus not carry unsubstantiated generalizations.
- Be cautious that your writing doesn't show bias toward a person's age, sex, race, political attitudes, religious beliefs, sexual orientation, or national origin.

2) Starting the Paper

(1) Good Openings
a. Clarify the topic you are going to write about.
The language used in cigarette advertisements in magazines and newspapers has long been governed by the guidelines of various organizations. Despite such restrictions, differences in word emphasis and other elements of slanting make it possible to trace changes in cigarette ads over the last twenty-five years.

b. State your position on the topic you have chosen.

Seldom do we have the chance to watch a dramatic character develop throughout various works by the same author. It is, therefore, a fascinating glimpse into the mind of playwright Arthur Miller to follow the growth of Roslyn. She is first apparent in the thoughts of the cowboys, Gay, Perce, and Guide in "The Misfits", but does not actually appear in the story. Roslyn is unmistakable, however, in another short story, "Please Don't Kill Anything," although she is not named but is referred to as "the girl". Miller finally combined the two characters for the Roslyn of The Misfits, which he called a cinema-novel because it used the perspective of film and its images; it was also the basis of the screenplay he wrote for the film of the same name.

c. Relate your topic to something current or well known.

In a scene from Woody Allen's movie Annie Hall, Alvy Singer (Allen) asks Annie Hall (Diane Keaton) why she would not go out with him that night. Her reply is, "The Grammy Awards are on TV tonight, Alvy. I wouldn't miss those for anything!" Annie is just one of the many people who are hopelessly hooked on award shows, and there are enough of such programs on television to make the addiction almost incurable.

d. Challenge some generally held assumptions about your topic.

People living in the public eye, particularly political leaders, always have a great deal written about them. If they are eminent leaders, their early lives and their most private moments become favorite topics for journalists. If they have been eminent leaders for a long time, so much has probably been written about them over a period of years that little, if anything, can remain secret or hidden. Joseph Stalin would seem to offer the perfect example of how the public record reveals a man's private life. He ruled the Soviet Union for so many years and was so constantly in the news that it seems impossible for any facet of his life to remain secret. Yet the truth is that few people really know anything about Stalin's life. He himself undoubtedly destroyed most of the records which might have shed some light on his true personality and character. During his rule in the Soviet Union, the history of his life underwent repeated revisions. Since his death and subsequent "disgrace", so many other changes occurred that the "real" Stalin may never be truly known.

e. Show something paradoxical about your topic or about the material you will present.

Television is certainly one of the most influential forces on society in this last half of the twentieth century. Yet though it is called "educational", it teaches little. Though it is called "real", it is fakery of the worst sort. Though it is said to be a disseminator of American values, it has worked to destroy them. It encourages violence, passivity, complacency, and illiteracy simultaneously.

f. Use a brief quotation if you can find an applicable one that is provocative or that makes a general statement about your topic.

In Horizons West, Jim Kitses writes: in an increasingly utilitarian age, one of film technology and "participational media", the word "art" can seem to have a narrow and effete ring to it. Yet to study the art of the western in any depth, we must embrace both mass culture and the individual film-maker, the industry and the star, film history, American history, and film language. The western movie is indeed more than simple escapism, more than wish fulfillment. It is a cinema genre with its own archetypal patterns and a form so all-embracing that to study it requires one to range over unsuspected areas.

g. State some striking facts or statistics you have discovered about your topic.

In 1974 a Senate Subcommittee reported that it had surveyed 54 federal agencies and discovered that together they maintained 858 data banks on individuals. Although there were no figures for 93 of those data banks, 765 of them contained 1,245,699,494 records! Furthermore, 84% of the data banks were operating without explicit legal authority (Neier 14). If there were so many data banks and so many individual records stored by the government in 1974, think of how those numbers must surely have increased by now. Retail credit reporting companies are the next largest users of data banks, and businesses with many employees follow behind. Chances are that everybody in the United States is listed on one of these data banks, sometimes in less than flattering ways and sometimes with untruths.

h. Place your topic in time by giving some historical or chronological information.

For as long as there have been liars, there have been attempts to find the truth. Those on trial in ancient China were made to chew rice powder while testifying. If the powder was dry when the suspect spat it out, he was judged guilty because it was assumed that nervousness over telling lies had dried the saliva in the suspect's mouth. Other ordeals were set up for suspected liars in other times including being subjected to boiling water or red-hot stones ("lie Detectors in Business" 69). Finally, with the invention of the modern polygraph (commonly called a lie detector) in 1921, it seemed that there was at last a foolproof way of finding out if people answering questions were lying or being truthful.

i. Give a brief description or background resume of some person or event of significance to your topic.

Lady Murasaki Shikibu was born about 978 AD. and died about 1030. She had the enviable position of being a member of the Fujiwara clan and a member of a family which produced mikados, statesmen, and at least one celebrated Japanese poet. Because she was of the nobility, she had the time and the education to write. Her book Genii Monogatari, known in English as The Tale of Genji, is now the West's chief source of information about court life in 11th century Japan.

(2) Bad Openings

Getting a good start should obey the following rules:

Don't repeat the title.

Don't tell explicitly what you propose to do in the paper.

Don't feel compelled to repeat the thesis statement completely in the opening of the paper.

Don't ask a question.

Don't give a dictionary definition.

Don't write a cute or folksy opening.

3) Writing the Body of the Paper

(1) Each paragraph should have:

A specified topic or thesis stated in a topic sentence

Information, evidence, explanations etc. expanding on the topic sentence

Connection or links with previous and following paragraphs

(2) To link ideas one should:

- Clarify the relationship between ideas and use words that express that relationship, eg. an example of this is ..., by way of contrast..., a further development was..., similarly ..., another approach to the problem ..., this is realized in practice by ..., secondly ....

- Use known information at the beginning of sentences; introduce new information later in the sentence.

- Refer explicitly to previously given information, eg. a variation on this theme ... .

- Use words from the question to give a cohesive framework to your answer.

(3) Before completing the first draft one need to:

- Develop each paragraph by integrating evidence to support the points you are making.

- Read the assignment task again to check that you have actually followed the directions to meet the task requirements, eg. *Have you "critically examined" your beliefs and developed arguments?*

- Write an Introduction and a Conclusion for your paper.

- Proof-read, edit and redraft your paper until you are happy with the final product.

(4) Some qualities of good writing:

a. Unity and coherence.

- A unified paper is one that deals with a single subject and a single idea.

- A coherent piece of writing is one that hangs together well, that not only holds the attention of readers but also helps them move from one point to another.

Ways of Making Writing Coherent:

- Use transitional words and phrases, eg. *"therefore" "moreover" "however" "in the second place" "at the same time" "as a result" "first" "second" "furthermore"*.

- Use pronouns for important nouns, eg. *"he" "she" "it" "they" "them" and "those"*.

- Establish some logical order, eg. *cause to effect, general to particular*.

- Use repeated key words and phrases, eg:

  ➢ ...Of the 15 states licensing *polygraph operators*, none provides for internship or schooling in the profession and not all require operators to be bonded.

  ➢ Certainly adequate training and screening of *polygraph operators*...

(The first sentence is the end of one paragraph; the second sentence is the beginning of the next paragraph)

- Use a consistent point of view.
- Integrate information.

  Some advice on integrating information:
  - Use your sources as support for your insights, not as the backbone of your paper. A patchwork of sources stuck in a paper like random letters in a ransom note does not make a research paper.
  - Summarize (condense a text by stating the main ideas in your own words) and paraphrase (say the same thing in a different way) much more often than you use direct quotes (same words as the original, in quotation marks).
  - Don't use direct quotes as fillers except that the author says something so aptly or dramatically that a paraphrase would lose that power. Or, if you're analyzing the language of a passage.
  - If do you use a direct quote, the explanation should be twice as long as the quote. Even summaries and paraphrases don't become your own thoughts just because they're in your own words. You have to explain them too. Readers have to know why you include source material where you do.
  - If multiple sources say the same thing, summarize what they say and put a few key names in brackets at the end of the sentence. This can both add credibility and reduce space!
  - When you do use direct quotes, the most fluid way to integrate them is to incorporate key words right into your text.
  - Don't summarize plots of primary sources. Assume your audience has read the work. Only explain as much as you need to to establish context for an example.

  b. Adequate Support.

  Ways of making adequate support:

  Offer statistics, Give examples, Offer documentation, Give specific details, Use authoritative sources

  c. Emphasis.

  Ways of emphasizing:
  - by proportion (the amount of space devoted to an idea)
  - by repetition (of words and ideas you believe are important)
  - by position

  d. Concreteness and Specificity.
- Concrete words name those things you can ascertain through the senses: what you see, hear, smell, touch, and taste.

  "A blue two-story house with red shutters"
- Abstract words, on the other hand, name feelings, beliefs, ideas.

  "Beauty" "happiness" "honor" "democracy" "the American way"

  Compare:
- ➢ Cortes was impressed by the beauty of Monteztima's clothing.

➤ When Cortes reached Tenochtitian, he was met by Montezuma wearing his ceremonial clothing. Cortes could not help but be impressed by Montezuma's wide, sweeping cape with its intricate design of great delicacy worked in the multicolored feathers of unknown birds.
- General words encompass many ideas.
"animals" "boats"
- Specific words limit the multiple concepts.
"female humpback whale" "yellow catamaran"

Compare:
➤ The polygraph records physical responses.
➤ The polygraph senses and records physiological responses such as blood pressure, respiration, and heart rate.

4) Integrating Resource Information

When you are writing about other people's ideas your readers need to know *whose voice* they are hearing. Readers need to know whether they are reading the original author's *actual* words or your *interpretation* of the original source. To manage this combination of different "voices", you need to:
- Use quotes, paraphrases or summaries of the original material and make sure you *acknowledge* the source by referencing it.
- Be familiar with *words* and *phrases* which are used to introduce the ideas of others in a quote, paraphrase or summary form.
- Show clearly *where* and *why* you differ from the points other writers have made by constructing sentences and paragraphs which qualify or criticize what others have written. [Eg. *by using ... but, although, however, while, on the other hand ... and then giving your reasons*]
- Show that you have thoughts of your own by expressing your own opinion, making suggestions or putting forward some conclusions [Eg. *by using ... thus, therefore, consequently, in this case ... and then stating your thesis*].

The key to a successful paper is to integrate your documented material into the text that the audience follows the flow of words and ideas without being distracted by your resource information and its documentation.

5) Ending the Paper

(1) Good endings

a. If you have written an argumentive or persuasive paper, remind the audience of what you want them to do or think in order to respond to your presentation.

Example:
The computer has created problems of quantity, sensitivity, and variety of data about us that never existed before because never before has information been so easy and cheap to store, retrieve,

and move about. If we are to retain our right of privacy, and therefore of control over our personal lives, we ought to pay attention once more to Thomas Jefferson's observation that "eternal vigilance is the price of liberty."

b. Use a brief quotation that summarizes the ideas or attitudes you have expressed throughout the paper.

Example:

Thucydides made mistakes, to be sure, but the historical significance of his work cannot be disputed. Like any great leader, he needed courage to break away from tradition and to introduce new ideas. His contributions are summed up this way by Finley:

For he, as clearly as any tragedian, indeed as any Greek author, possessed the greatest of Greek abilities, the ability to observe the actualities of life with unflinching candor, yet at the same time, without falsifying these actualities, to reduce them to their generic and hence their lasting patterns. To have performed this feat both of record and of simplification on a plane of strict reality, and at a time when the basic political ideas of western man were at issue is Thucydides' monumental triumph.

c. Make some statement about your thesis, instead of merely repeating it.

Example:

We have seen the Roslyn of the original story, whom the men wanted too much to please, become the charming but somewhat cloying girl of a later Miller story. When she was transformed into a major character in The Misfits, Roslyn grew in complexity and lost the simple definition of innocence or sophistication that each of her "ancestors" had. In these three works, Miller has provided us with an excellent view of the development of a dramatic character from first sketches to boldly colored completeness.

d. Return to some initial generalization and show how you have proved, disproved, or enlarged upon it.

Example:

Don Quixote, then, was not simply a mad old man. Rather, he was a person of deep humanity whose misadventures stemmed mainly from attempts to help the oppressed. Furthermore, what seemed to be his foolish dreams are really the hopes of the sanest and least foolish people everywhere; what seemed to be his useless persistence is really idealism; what seemed to be his inability to cope with his time is really the doubt and tension every human lives with. The character Cervantes created cannot be called "mad" unless each of us is willing to accept that label also, for he is a composite of us all—and each of us has within the self a bit of Don Quixote.

e. Link what you have written either to something known or to what seems a future possibility.

Example:

When the Marquis de Sade published a novel in the early 19th century in France dealing with the raising and seduction of a child, the public was outraged. This story and others by him, were so immoral, so heinous, that the Marquis gave birth to a word which denotes all that is evil in human behavior. Today and in 19th century of France, the acts described in other portions of this paper are considered immoral. Yet in 11th century of Japan, they were evidently accepted as part of a way of life. And it is evident that today, in this country, as already noted, morality, like sanity, is a relative factor which depends greatly on the prevailing environmental influences.

f. State a conclusion you have reached about your subject.

Example:

The polygraph has been called "inherently intrusive... [and the testing] invades privacy and degrades human dignity" (Pear). Added to that, results are often inaccurate and operators are unreliable. The evidence against using the polygraph to screen employees in private businesses seems overwhelming. Relatively few people are dishonest. To seek them out with a lie detector does not justify the intimidation and heartbreak of polygraph testing for the many honest people.

(2) **Bad Endings**

If you want to get an impressive ending, you should follow the following practice:

Don't bring up a new idea.

Don't stop abruptly or simply trail off.

Don't ask a question.

Don't make any statement or suggestion that needs extensive clarification.

Don't fumble.

Don't tell explicitly what you have done in the paper.

Don't make a change in your style.

6) Selecting a Title

Don't choose a title that is general or vague.

Avoid choosing a title that is coy.

Avoid choosing a long, detailed research paper title.

Don't use a question in place of a title.

Never use a thesis statement as a title.

Compare:

➢ Ship Salvaging

   Rightful Ownership of Treasure Salvaged in Florida Waters

➢ A Look at William Dean Howells

   The Concept of Work in the Novels of William Dean Howells

➢ Auto Insurance Rates

   Legislative Influences on Auto Insurance Rates

➢ Who's Pushing the Puffs?

   Changing Language in Printed Cigarette Ads

➢ An Examination of the Setting as Metaphor in the Films of John Ford with Particular Reference to *Fort Apache*

Setting As Metaphor in John Ford's Films

2. Revising the Paper

Become your own toughest critic.

Become the author again.

Examine the revised essay very closely.

Approach your revision in an orderly way, by thinking of the task on four levels of organization: The whole paper, Paragraphs, Sentences, Individual words and phrases

1) Reconsidering the organization

- Switch the order of the subtopics, stating the opposing case first and rebutting it with your case
- Cut the two passages out of the paper and tape or paste them back in the new order
- Rewrite them and revise the transitions to make the new order effective
- Rewrite drastically and thereby produce a new "first" draft to work with

2) Revising paragraphs

- Think of a paragraph as a group of sentences that work together to support a controlling idea
- See if the rewriting (or addition) of a topic sentence will clarify your thoughts
- Focus on two additional features of paragraph structure
  - the order in which you have presented the details in support of your topic sentence
  - the smoothness with which you have moved from one sentence to the next or from one idea to another
- Rearrange the details until you have found the most effective order for them

3) Revising sentences

- Check the length of your sentences

Compare:

a) Throughout the war, many Southerners came to think of Lincoln as a power-hungry autocrat, who, in spite of the public speeches in which he advocated peace and reconciliation, was in reality determined to destroy anyone, in the North or South, who stood in the way of his gaining absolute control of the nation he had been elected to govern.

b) Throughout the war, many Southerners came to think of Lincoln as a power-hungry autocrat, in spite of the public speeches in which he advocated peace and reconciliation. They believed that he was in reality determined to destroy anyone, in the North or South, who stood in the way of his gaining absolute control of the nation he had been elected to govern.

c) Throughout the war, many people detested Lincoln. They considered him to be power-hungry. His speeches called for peace and reconciliation. But these people did not believe him. They included Northerners as well as Southerners. They believed that he intended to destroy anyone who opposed him. They thought he desired to gain absolute control of the country. They saw his election as part of his plan to rule as a dictator.

d) Throughout the war, many people detested Lincoln, whom they considered power-hungry. Although his speeches called for peace and reconciliation, these people did not believe him. Both Northerners and Southerners thought that he intended to destroy anyone who opposed him and sought dictatorial control of the country he had been elected to govern.

- Check the patterns of your sentences to see if you have repeated one pattern monotonously

Compare:

Hartman says that ... Anna Freud states that ... Mahler claims that ... And now Kohut states that...

Hartman says that ... Further support comes from Anna Freud ... Nahler agrees, for the most part, claiming that ... Recently, Kohut added further support to this idea when he stated ...

4) Revising word choice

- Finding Variety.

Compare:

A young, idealistic anthropologist, on first venturing into a primitive society, is likely to suffer severe disillusionment. For one thing, most such societies live under physical conditions that no one coming from American society can possibly anticipate. But far more dispiriting is the fact that these societies often practice customs radically opposite to the ideal life in nature that naive students like to imagine: a society of simple folk, yes, but a society that knows the true value of love, kindness, sharing, and mutual respect. The Yanomamo society provides an example that could try the soul of any young idealist searching for simple, natural virtues. Their social practices include...

A young, idealistic anthropologist, on first venturing into a primitive society, is likely to suffer severe disillusionment. For one thing, most such people live under physical conditions that no one coming from America can possibly anticipate. But far more dispiriting is the fact that these communities often practice customs radically opposite to the ideal life in nature that naive students like to imagine: a society of simple folk, yes, but one that knows the true value of love, kindness, sharing, and mutual respect. The Yanomamo tribe provides an example that could try the soul of any young idealist searching for simple, natural virtues. Their social practices include...

- Avoiding Vagueness.

Compare:

> The evidence against the polygraph seems overwhelming.

Evidence against using the polygraph to screen employees in private businesses seems overwhelming.

➢ With all the different stories and the conflicting details, there was one person who could have cleared up all the questions: Megan Marshack.

One person could have cleared up all the different stories and conflicting details: Megan Marshack.

➢ Napoleon was a great man.

Napoleon was a brilliant military strategist.

➢ Sarah Bernhardt was an outstanding actress.

Sarah Bernhardt played a wide variety of roles to perfection.

➢ Einstein was a fantastic thinker.

Einstein's theories reshaped the world of modern physics.

➢ Oedipus Rex is a first-rate play.

The play Oedipus Rex provides meaningful insights into human behavior.

● Avoiding Slang and Colloquialisms

Compare:

➢ The women in Rubens's paintings are very sexy.

The women in Rubens's paintings are very sensuous.

➢ The CIA has been blasted recently for failing to perform its duties with sufficient restraint.

The CIA has been sharply criticized recently for failing to perform its duties with sufficient restraint.

➢ The prosecutor called upon a well-known shrink to testify that the defendant was not really crazy.

The prosecutor called upon a well-known psychiatrist to testify that the defendant was not legally insane.

● Taking care to make jargon into what is readily understandable.

Compare:

➢ Soon Dorothy Liebes's trademark became her skip dent warps of textured and metallic yarns with unusual weft materials.

➢ Soon Dorothy Liebes's trademark became the fabrics she designed of unevenly spaced textured and metallic yarns crossed by unusual threads or even by thin strips of wood or metal.

● Paying attention to transitional words and phrases

● Make sure that modifiers are near the words they modify

3. Writing the Polished, Final Draft

There are two more jobs you must do before you begin to prepare the manuscript of your paper. You must write a complete set of notes acknowledging the source of each quotation or paraphrase in the paper, and you must prepare a final version of your bibliography.

Review Questions

1. At least how many versions of a research paper must you write? Why?
2. What are the characteristics of a good opening?
3. What are the qualities of good writing?
4. What are the ways of making writing coherent?
5. List some of the ways of writing good endings.
6. Briefly outline the steps in revising a rough draft.

Assignments

1. Accord to the outline you made last week to write the first part *Introduction* of your term research paper.
2. Accord to the outline you made the week before last to finish the second part *Review of the Literature* of your term research paper.

Unit 8 文 献 注 释
Documentation

1. Why is Documentation Necessary?

Legal, Practical, Ethical

What is plagiarism? (review)

Plagiarism is the unacknowledged use of someone else's words or ideas.

Example of plagiarism:

Passage from the journal *Lancet*

After forty years of research and an international bibliography of over 3000 studies, reviews, commentaries, and meta-analyses, it is clear that television violence can lead to harmful aggressive behaviour.

Passage from *The Christian Science Monitor*

The simplicity of the experiment at the Minneapolis day-care center and the starkness of the results stunned the parents. When a class of two- to five-year-olds watched public television's big-hearted purple dinosaur, "Barney", they sang along, marched along, held one another's hands, and laughed together. The next day, the same class watched the aggressive teenage avengers, "Power Rangers". Within minutes, they were karate-chopping and high-kicking the air, and one another.

Passage from a student essay

Over forty years of research and an international bibliography of over 3000 studies, reviews, commentaries, and meta-analyses make it clear that television violence can lead to harmful aggressive behavior. For example, an experiment at a Minneapolis day-care center stunned parents. When the children watched PBS' big-hearted dinosaur, "Barney", they sang and marched along while holding hand and laughing. The next day, the same class watched the aggressive teenage avengers, "Power Rangers". And within minutes, they were karate chopping and high-kicking the air, and one another.

2. What should one acknowledge in a research paper?

①Direct quotations
②Borrowed ideas (including paraphrases and summaries)
③Visual material such as maps, charts, diagrams, and pictures that you did not devise.
(Visual materials are acknowledged by a statement of the source below the chart, map, or graph.)

Common knowledge (review):

To decide if a point is common knowledge, ask yourself these questions:

Is the information unusual, technical, strange, or specific to some profession or discipline?

Is the information difficult to verify in a common reference source, like a dictionary or encyclopedia?

Is the information potentially controversial?

Some documentation systems used in different discipline:

- Parenthetical documentation (the Modern Language Association's *MLA Handbook for Writers of Research Papers*);
- The Chicago (footnotes or endnotes) style;
- The numbered style (the *CBE Manual: A Guide for Authors, Editors, and Publishers in the Biological Sciences*;)
- The APA style (*Publication Manual of the American Psychological Association*).

3. Parenthetical Documentation

(1) Introduction of Parenthetical documentation

- The most recent standard recommended by the Modern Language Association's *MLA Handbook for Writers of Research Papers*, second edition (MLA System).
- The MLA system consists of two interrelated elements:

  Parenthetical notes in the text

  A bibliography (works cited page) attached to the text
- Parenthetical documentation gives brief and specific information—usually only the author's surname or a title plus the exact page number—about a source at each point in your research paper that requires such recognition.
- Parenthetical documentation is paired with an entry in the Works Cited at the end of your paper.
- The aim of parenthetical documentation is to give required information without interrupting the flow of reading (and writing).

(2) Qualities of Parenthetical Documentation

—makes typing easy

—makes reading easy

—widely used in the social sciences natural sciences and humanities

(3) General Guidelines

- Type your paper or write it on a computer and print it out on standard-sized paper.
- Double-space your paper.
- Set the margins of your document to 1 inch on all sides.
- Create a header that numbers all pages consecutively in the upper right-hand corner, one-half

inch from the top and flush with the right margin.
- Use either underlining or italics throughout your essay for highlighting the titles of longer works and providing emphasis.
- If you have any notes, include them on a page before your works cited page and format them the same way as your works cited list.

(4) Formatting the first page of your paper
- Do not make a title page for your paper unless specifically requested.
- Provide a double-spaced entry in the top left corner of the first page that lists your name, your instructor's name, the course, and the date.
- Create a header numbering all pages consecutively in the upper right-hand corner, one-half inch from the top and flush with the right margin.
- Center your title on the line below the header with your name.
- Begin your paper immediately below the title.

Sample first page of an essay in MLA style:

```
                                                              Purdue 1
Pete Purdue
Dr. B. Boilermaker
English 101
12 November 2000
              Building a Dream: Reasons to Expand
                      Ross-Aide Stadium
   During the 2000 football season, the Purdue Boilermakers won the Big
Ten Conference Title, earned their first trip to the Rose Bowl in thirty-four
years, and played consistently to sold-out crowds. Looking ahead...
```

(5) Formatting your works cited list
- Begin your works cited list on a separate page from the text of the essay.
- Label the works cited list Works Cited (do not underline the words Works Cited nor put them in quotation marks) and center the words Works Cited at the top of the page.
- Double space all entries and do not skip spaces between entries.

Compare

Parenthetical Notes	Works Cited
Einstein notes, "There is hardly a simpler law in physics than that according to which light is propagated in empty space" (17)	Einstein, Alber. *Relativity: The Special and the General Theory*. Trans. Robert W. Lawson. New York: Crown, 1961.
Almost all Canadian households include at least one television set ("Box" 16)	"Viewing the Box." *Canada and the World Backgrounder*. Oct. 2001: 16 + .

Continue

Parenthetical Notes	Works Cited
"It was the worst of times, it was the best of times" (Dickens, Two Cities 1)	Dickens, Charles. *A Tale of Two Cities*. 1859. New York: Bantam, 1983
Dickens satirizes the Lancastrian model of education in the character of Mr. M'Choakumchild (Hard Times 4-6)	*Hard Times*. 1854. Ware, Hertfordshire: Wordworth Editions Ltd., 1995.

(6) How to incorporate parenthetical documentation in a text

- Identify author or title and page in parentheses.

Examples:

Those in the first category comprise only 1/5 to 1/3 of the reports and questionnaires about citizens generated by the government (Miller 59).

Such information may be used "to intimidate and to inhibit the individual in his freedom of movement, associations, or expression of ideas within the law" (Uncle Sam 7).

- If the work you are making reference to has no author, use an abbreviated version of the work's title. For non-print sources, such as films, TV series, pictures, or other media, or electronic sources, include the name that begins the entry in the Works Cited page.

Example:

An anonymous Wordsworth critic once argued that his poems were too emotional ("Wordsworth Is A Loser" 100).

- Identify the author or title in the text; put page number(s) in parentheses.

Examples:

Sherick points out (53-54) that there is a government file on you if you have ever worked for a federal agency or a government contractor, participated in a federally financed project...

"Computers" reports that three categories of personal data systems are now kept in computers (31).

More Examples:

Wordsworth stated that Romantic poetry was marked by a "spontaneous overflow of powerful feelings" (263).

Romantic poetry is characterized by the "spontaneous overflow of powerful feelings" (Wordsworth 263).

Wordsworth extensively explored the role of emotion in the creative process (263).

- Committee or corporate authorship.

Compare:

The report said that the polygraph "should be proscribed on intrusiveness grounds" (United States Privacy Protection Study Commission 239)

The United States Privacy Protection Study Commission felt that the polygraph "should be proscribed on intrusiveness grounds" (239).

- Use the last name of an author or the title of an article in the text if you make a reference to the complete work.

Examples:

Cowan shows how the government is using bugging, informers, subpoenas, and other methods to invade individual rights and civil liberties.

Ciardi's translation of The Divine Comedy clearly shows the rhyme scheme of the work.

(7) Special Kinds of Parenthetical Documentation

- More than one work by an author in the Works Cited.

If you use more than one work from a single author, when you refer to either of the sources, give the author's last name, an abbreviated title of the work, and the relevant page number(s). A comma separates the author's last name and the title; however, there is no punctuation between the title and the page number(s).

Example:

When calculating the number of homeless animals in the United States, the author comically stated that "Maybe man would not overrun the planet, but his pet poodles and Siamese cats might" (Westin, Pethood 6). She then further stated that there are 50 million homeless animals in the country (Westin, "Planning" 10).

Note: If you mention the author's last name in the sentence, you do not need to include the author's last name in parentheses.

- Multiple Authorship.

Examples:

Also among computer records were 5.4 million dossiers on people who got FHA loans (LeMond and Pry 139).

Maimon et al. give examples of writing in humanities, social sciences, and natural sciences.

- Work in multiple volumes.

Examples:

Antonin Dvorak is called "Old Borax", although the source of the nickname is never explained (Huneker 2: 65-69).

Huneker calls Antonin Dvorak "Old Borax" (2: 65-69), although he never explains the source of the nickname.

- Use the abbreviation if the reference is to an entire volume in a multivolume work.

Example:

The articles about New York show that he was an inveterate name-dropper (Huneker, vol. 2).

- One work quoted within another work.

Example:

Miller said, "This will be true despite the 'softness' or 'imprecision' of much of the data" (qtd. in Hoffman 23).

- Works of Literature or drama.

Examples:

> - **Tamburlaine** crowns himself, to the acclaim of the crowd **(2.7)**
> - "Not all the curses which the Furie breathe I shall make me leave so rich a prize as this" **(Tamburlaine 2.7)** or **(Tamburlaine II. Vii)**.

(act → 2, scene → 7)

- Classical poems or verse plays: the first number is the book, canto, or part and the second the precise line numbers.

Examples:

> - We know a great deal about the battle dress of the early Greeks by reading a description of Agamenon **(Iliad 11. 15-44)**.

(Book, canto or part → 11; Line number → 15-44)

- Classical prose works in several editions: show first the page number on which you found the information, then the part, chapter, section, or book, with appropriate abbreviations such as "ch." or "bk." to specify the larger unit.

Example:

Candide finally found a place where even the children wore gold brocade and where their toys were gold, emeralds and rubies (31; ch. 17).

- Different locations of information within the same work cited at the same time.

Example:

Westin points out the six trends and how the speed of a computer is pushing them toward reality (158-162, 166).

- Citing multiple works in one parenthetical reference

Example:

Several writers have expressed concern about the confidentiality of information on federal tax returns ("Big Brother"; Linowes 54; "Restoring Privacy").

- Documenting nonprint materials.

Examples:

One would hardly call a song of farewell to an overcoat realistic (La Boheme 4), yet it fits easily into the opera.

The famed farewell to an overcoat (Great Moments in Opera, side 3) is one of many arias from "realistic" operas.

The reporter finally locates Kane's former wife (reel 3).

(8) Documenting Quotations

- Prose (whether fiction or nonfiction) or dramatic dialogue of four or fewer typed lines.

Examples:

"Privacy also involves a subjective sense of self-determination and control over personal information" (Sobel 9).

According to some, dreams express "profound aspects of personality" (Foulkes 184), though others disagree.

According to Foulkes's study, dreams may express "profound aspects of personality" (184).

Is it possible that dreams may express "profound aspects of personality" (Foulkes 184)?

Cullen concludes, "Of all the things that happened there/ That's all I remember" (11-12).

- Quotations of more than four lines.

Examples:

As LeMond and Fry write:

> The right to privacy is generally the first right to be legislated out of existence in a modern police state. But in the United States the growing rise in dossier-accumulation might soon accomplish the same end without the necessity of any tedious and time-consuming passage of the appropriate legislation. (137)

Nelly Dean treats Heathcliff poorly and dehumanizes him throughout her narration:

> They entirely refused to have it in bed with them, or even in their room, and I had no more sense, so, I put it on the landing of the stairs, hoping it would be gone on the morrow. By chance, or else attracted by hearing his voice, it crept to Mr. Earnshaw's door, and there he found it on quitting his chamber. Inquiries were made as to how it got there; I was obliged to confess, and in recompense for my cowardice and inhumanity was sent out of the house. (Brontë 78)

- Poetry quotations.

Quotations of three or fewer lines poetry

Example:

The nonsense wording "Twas brillig, and the slithy toves / Did gyre and gimble in the wabe" (Carroll 79) illustrates the structure of English.

Quotations of more than three lines of poetry:

> Shakespeare wrote about old age in **sonnet 73**:
>
> > That time of year thou may'st in me behold
> > When yellow leaves, or none, or few, do hang
> > Upon those boughs which shake against the cold—
> > Bare ruin'd choirs where late the sweet birds sang.

> Shakespeare wrote metaphorically about old age in these lines:
>   That time of year though may'st in me behold
>   When yellow leaves, or none, or few, do hang
>   Upon those boughs which shake against the cold—
>   Bare ruin'd choirs where late the sweet birds sang.
> (**Sonnet 73**)

> In her poem "Sources", **Adrienne Rich** explores the roles of women in shaping their world:
>   The faithful drudging child
>   the child at the oak desk whose penmanship,
>   hard work, style will win her prizes
>   becomes the woman with a mission, not to win prizes
>   but to change the laws of history. (23)

4. Documenting Visual Material

- A table.

    Example:

    Table 1
    Personal Experiences with Privacy Invasions

Violation of Privacy by	Is Violated	Not Violated	Not Sure
Computers which collect a lot of information about you	19%	71%	10%
The government when it takes a census	14	84	2
Employment interviews	11	83	6

    Source: Westin, Alan F., and Michael A. Baker. <u>Databanks in a Free Society: Computers, Record-Keeping and Privacy.</u> (New York: Quadrangle, 1972): 477. (Source: Westin and Baker 477.)

- Other illustrative material such as charts, maps, photographs, or diagrams.

    Example:

    Figure 1.1

    U.S.---Japan Merchandise Trade: 1975-78

    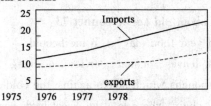

    Source: U.S. Bureau of the Census, <u>Statistical Abstract of the United States: 1979</u> (Washington: GPO, 1979) 920.

5. Using Notes with Parenthetical Documentation

- To avoid impeding the flow of the reading the problem, put a superscript number at the place in the text where the comment, explanation, or other information are needed, then use a matching superscript number with them at the end of the paper on a page headed "Note" (or "Notes").
- Use a separate note to list a series of bibliographic citations that would be too long to appear as parenthetical documentation. Semicolons between the entries show that these are separate citations.

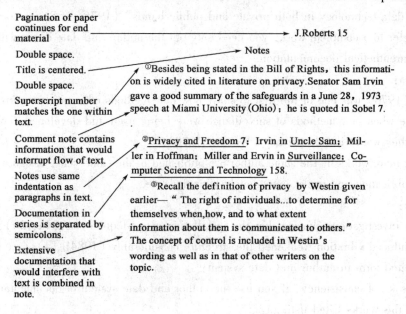

6. Author and date system

- Show the author's last name (or a shortened form of the title if the work is anonymous), the date (year) of the publication, a comma, and then the page on which you found the information.

Examples:

Those in the first category comprise only 1/5 to 1/3 of the reports and questionnaires about citizens that are generated by the government (Miller 1971, 59).

"Data derived from a computer carries an impact disproportionate to its actual value" (Bouchard and Franklin 1980, 42).

That such information may be used "to intimidate and to inhibit the individual in his freedom of movement, associations, or expression of ideas within the law" (Uncle Sam 1971, 7) was a special concern of Senator Ervin.

- Documentation using the author and date system is as flexible as the parenthetical documentation forms explained earlier.

Examples:

Miller wrote that the first category comprises only 1/5 to 1/3 of the reports and questionnaires about citizens that are generated by the government (1971, 59).

In 1971 the first category comprised only 1/5 to 1/3 of the reports and questionnaires about citizens that were generated by the government (Miller 59).

Neier (1975, 190) notes that the FBI is a good data collector for the private sector.

Even former president Nixon said that careers and people "have been destroyed by the misuse and abuse of data technology in both private and public hands" (1976, 165), according to Sobel.

- If you refer to a complete work, you need only put the author and date either within the text or in the parenthetical documentation.

Examples:

Westin (1970) was one of the first to study how new methods of surveillance invaded privacy.

At a time when new methods of surveillance were being used and developed, concern was expressed that they would invade privacy (Westin, 1970).

- If two or more works by the same author are published in the same year, assign a lowercase letter to each publication and use it immediately after the date.

Example:

David's investigations showed that the installation was adequate (1984a, 28), but that both natural and induced vibration weakened the structure considerably (1984b, 4).

- Works cited form in author and date system:

For the sake of consistency, if you use the author and date system of documentation, you must also use it in the Works Cited listing.

The form is essentially the same as in the Works Cited used with other documentation systems except that the date of publication is typed two spaces after the period following the author's name (or the title of an article) and omitted from its usual place after the name of the publisher or the date of a periodical.

Examples:

Carroll, John M. 1975. Confidential Information Sources: Public and Private. Los Angeles: World

David, Michael. 1984a. "Adequate Installations Take Time." Buildings Feb.-Mar.: 27-30.

- - - . 1984b. "Sure Ways to Undermine Your Work." Buildings Oct.-Nov.: 4+.

- Full in-text documentation:

Full in-text documentation might be convenient if you have only a few sources to document.

If you use such full in-text documentation, it may not be necessary to prepare a separate bibliography or list of Works Cited because the information in either will only be redundant.

Examples:

Ford Rowan reported that the government had an average of eighteen different records on each citizen [Technospies (New York: Putnam, 1978) 18].

In "The Assault on Privacy," Richard Boeth [(Newsweek 27 July 1970) 19] reports about Ralph Nader's concern with the issue of privacy.

Of all federal data banks surveyed, 84% were operating "without explicit authority of law" (John M. Carroll. Confidential Information Sources: Public and Private. [(Los Angeles: Security, 1975) 169)].

7. APA System

- If the author's last name and the date of a publication cannot be included easily within the text, use parenthetical documentation.

Examples:

Westin (1970) was one of the first to study how new methods of surveillance invaded privacy.

At a time when new methods of surveillance were being used and developed, concern was expressed that they would invade privacy (Westin, 1970).

- If no author is shown for a work you quote or borrow ideas from, cite it by title and date.

Examples:

"Big Brother Is a Big Worry" (1979) reports the follow-up Louis Harris poll.

Louis Harris also published a follow-up to his original poll ("Big Brother," 1979).

The transcription excerpts in Uncle Sam Is Watching You (1971) give a unique insight into the workings of a Senate subcommittee.

The transcription excerpts (Uncle Sam, 1971) give a unique insight into the workings of a Senate subcommittee.

- To cite specific parts of a source parenthetically within the text, such as a page number or a chapter, shows the author's last name, the date of the publication, and the page or chapter where the specific material is located. Each of the three units is separated by a comma and a space, and the whole is enclosed within parentheses.

Examples:

He states, "Occupation is another critical determinant of social standing in many societies" (Babbie, 1983, p. 241).

Various kinds of social inequality are considered at length (Babbie, 1983, chap. 8).

- If the passage to be cited occurs at the end of a sentence, put the documentation before the period, as in the examples above.
- If the quotation (or other borrowed idea) is in the middle of a sentence, put the parenthetical documentation immediately after what needs to be cited, then continue the sentence.

Example:

"Occupation is another critical determinant of social standing in many societies" (Babbie,

1983, p. 241), yet such standings may be affected by many additional factors.
- Documentation using the author and date system is as flexible as the parenthetical documentation forms explained earlier. Examples:

Babble (1983) wrote, "Occupation is another critical determinant of social standing in many societies" (p. 241).

In 1983 Babbie wrote, "Occupation is another critical determinant of social standing in many societies" (p. 241)

- When a work has two or more authors, cite the names of all authors the first time you mention the work. After that, cite both authors, if there are only two.
- If there are three to five authors, cite all names the first time but subsequently use only the surname of the first person named and et al. to signify the others.

Examples:

The most extensively documented explanation of the two acts (Bouchard and Franklin 1980) also includes information about locating personal information.

The writing exercises of Schorer, Durham, Jones, and Johnston (1984) make a variety of demands on their readers.

The writing exercises of Schorer et al. (1984) make a variety of demands on their readers.

- If you use one work by six or more authors, both first and subsequent citations are by surname of the first author followed by *et al.*
- Should you have citations by *two* or *more authors with* the *same last name*, obviously you have to signal the reader which author you are referring to. Therefore, use initials with the last name (rather than the last name alone) in each reference.
- You may cite two or more works within the same parentheses. If they are works by the same author, give the dates in chronological order and separate them with commas.
- If the works were published in the same year, assign them lowercase letters, alphabetically by title, to distinguish the works; use the same letters when you cite these works in the reference list.

Examples:

He showed that individual privacy was not to be taken for granted (Westin, 1970, 1979).

The extensive research reported by David (1984a, 1984b, 1984c, in press—1985) shows the lengths to which people will go to avoid dealing with computerized information.

- If the works are by different authors, arrange them alphabetically by surname (of the first author) and separate the references by semicolons.

Example:

The excellent record-keeping qualities of government computers have often been cited (Kirchner, 1984; Westin & Baker, 1972).

- Cite letters, interviews, telephone conversations, and similar personal communications only in the text. Because many of these sources are ephemeral and cannot be found by another person, they are not included in the reference list. Therefore, give the initials and the surname of people from whom you got information, as well as the date of the communication.

Examples:

D. D. Glenn (personal communication, April 11, 1985) found that the supposedly simple procedure of obtaining his records led him to hire an attorney in Washington.

Despite the supposedly simple procedure of obtaining personal records, many people hire attorneys in Washington to make the search for them (D. D. Glenn, personal communication, April 11, 1985).

8. Numbered System

- This system is used widely in the natural sciences such as medicine, chemistry, physics, engineering, computer science, and mathematics.
- In these sciences, writers rarely quote their sources directly; however, if you quote, the page number must be included in the note.
- Documentation in the text is an Arabic numeral, sometimes underlined, followed by a comma, a space, and then by an exact page reference; all the information is then enclosed within parentheses.
- The numerals must be coordinated with the entries in the list of Works Cited.

Examples:

"The right to privacy is generally the first right to be legislated out of existence in a modern police state," (1, 137) is pointed out by LeMond and Fry.

Of all federal data banks surveyed, 84% were operating "without explicit authority of law" (2, 169).

The Works Cited for these two sources would be written this way:

Examples

1. Lemond, Alan, and Ron Fry. No Place to Hide. New York: St. Martin's, 1975.

2. Carroll, John M. Confidential Information Sources: Public and Private. Los Angeles: Security, 1975.

- Even if you do not mention the author within your text, place only the number assigned to it in the note. If you refer to more than one source at the same time, include the number assigned to each source.

Examples:

Recent experimentation (6, 7, 8) seems to indicate...

9. Footnotes and Endnotes

(1) Footnotes

- Footnotes may either give the documentation for borrowed words and ideas or they may contain

your own comments about the text that are put separately to avoid interrupting the flow of reading the research paper.
- Allow two double spaces between the end of the text and the beginning of the footnotes on the page.
- A superscript number at the point in the text where acknowledgment is needed is coordinated with the same number preceding a footnote on the same page.

(2) **Endnotes**
- Give documentation (and, sometimes, comments) at the end of the research paper.
- Begin on a page headed "Notes" following the last page of the paper itself and before the Works Cited.
- Work in pairs between the text and the page of documentation.
- Put a number immediately after a quotation or a borrowed idea in the text and then use the same number to give the complete documentation information on the page of endnotes at the conclusion of the research paper.
- Endnotes give four pieces of information about the source you used:
    - the author
    - the title of the work
    - publication information
    - the actual page or pages the information was on
- The forms or conventions vary according to whether there is one author or several, whether the work appeared in a periodical paged by the issue or by the year, whether the author is unknown, whether the pamphlet is unpaged, which computer system a program runs on, and other variables.

(3) **Differences in punctuation between a documentation note and the same source listed in the Works Cited**
- The units are separated by commas or parentheses in documentation. They are separated by periods in the Works Cited.
- The author's name is written in the usual order in documentation: that is, given name and then surname. The order is reversed in the Works Cited.
- The numbers of pages in printed material that you used for specific information are noted in documentation notes. Page numbers do not appear in entries for books in Works Cited.

Compare:

[2] Chu-Kia Wang, and Charles G. Salmon, <u>Introductory Structural Analysis</u> (Englewood Cliffs: Prentice, 1983)158.

Wang, Chu-Kia, and Charles G. Salmon. <u>Introductory Structural Analysis.</u> Englewood Cliffs: Prentice, 1983.

	J.Roberts 15
Your name and the successive page numbeber.	
Double space.	Notes
Title is centered.	①Besides being stated in the *Bill of Rights*, this information is widely cited in literature on privacy. Senator Sam Irvin gave a good summary of the safeguards In a June 28, 1973 speech at Miami University (Ohio); he is quoted in Sobel7.
Double space.	
Superscript number matches the one within text.	
Comment note contains information that would interrupt flow of text.	②<u>Privacy and Freedom</u> 7; Irvin <u>in Uncle Sam</u>; Miller in Hoffman; Miller and Ervin in <u>Surveillance Computer Science and Technology</u> 158.
Notes use same indentation as paragraphs in text.	
Documentation in series is separated by semicolons.	③Recall the definition of privacy by Westin given earlier— "The right of individuals...to determine for themselves when, how, and to what extent information about them is communicated to others." The concept of control is included in Westin's wording as well as in that of other writers on the topic.
Extensive documentation that would interfere with text is combined in note.	

(4) Note Numbering System

- The identifying numbers in both text and endnotes are written as superscript.
- Within the text, put the note numbers at the end of a phrase, clause, or sentence that needs documentation and after any punctuation mark (except a dash).
- The coordinated note number begins a documentation entry in the endnotes; it is followed by a space, then the author or title that begins the entry.
- In neither text nor endnote is there any period or other mark before or after the superscript numeral.

A. First References: Books

The basic form for the first reference of a book:
- the author's name one space after the note number
- a comma after the name, one space
- the title of the book, underlined, another space
- in parenthesis, the place of publication, a colon and a space
- the name of the publisher, a comma, a space
- the date of publication, one space after the closing parenthesis
- the exact page (or pages), a period

[1] Candice Bergen, <u>Knock Wood</u> (New York: Linden, 1984) 45.
[1] Candice Bergen, <u>Knock Wood</u> (N.p.: Linden, 1984) 45. ← Place of publication unknown
[1] Candice Bergen, <u>Knock Wood</u> (New York: n.p., 1984) 45. ← Name of publisher unknown
[1] Candice Bergen, <u>Knock Wood</u> (New York: Linden, n.d.) 45. ← Date of publication unavailable

Examples of first references for books in endnotes
Book by Two or Three Authors

[2] Chu-Kia Wang, and Charles G. Salmon, Introductory Structural Analysis (Englewood Cliffs: Prentice 1983)158.

Book by More Than Three Authors

[3] Elaine P. Maimon, et al., Writing in the Arts and Sciences(Boston: Little, 1981) 278.

Organization or Institution as Author

[4] American Camping Association, Camp Standards with Interpretations for the Accreditation of Organized Camps, rev. ed. (Martinsville: American Camping Assoc., 1980)34.

Book in Collaboration

[5] A J. Foyt with William Neely, A J (New York: Times, 1983) 78.

Book with Single Editor or Compiler of

[6] Harrison E. Silisbury, ed., Vietnam Reconsidered: Lessons from a War(New York: Harper, 1984) 65-67.

Anthology with No Editor Given

[7] The Oxford Book of Verse in English Translation(Oxford: Oxford UP, 1983) 543.

Work in an Anthology

[8] Gwendolyn Brooks, "The Rites for Cousin Vit," The Harper Anthology of Poetry, ed. John Frederick Nims (New York: Harper, 1981) 185.

[9] Anna Maria Ortese, "A Pair of Glasses," trans. Frances Frehaye, Stories of Modern Italy, ed. Ben Johnson (New York: Modern Library Random, 1960) 406.

Introduction by Other Than Author

[10] Aian Schneider, introduction, Five Plays, by Michael Weller (New York: NAL, 1982) ii-iv.

Work in Several Volumes

[11] Richard Crashaw, The Complete Works of Richard Crashaw, 2 vols. (New York: AMS, 1983) 1: 234-37.

Translated Book

[12] Yasunari Kawabata, Beauty and Sadness, trans. Howard Hibbett (New York: Perigee, 1981)57.

Edition of a Book

[13] Audrey J. Roth, The Research Paper: Process, Form, and Content, 5th ed. (Belmont: Wadsworth, 1986) 156-58.

Republished Book

[14] Harold S. Kushner, When Bad Things Happen to Good People (1981; New York: Avon, 1983)89.

B. First References: Periodicals

— the note number in superscript, a space

— the author's name in first-last-name order, a comma, a space

— the title of the article in quotation marks, a comma inside the ending quote mark, another space

- the name of the magazine, underlined, the date, month, and year, a colon, another space
- the specific page numbers, a period

[15] Ed Magnuson, "Stirring Up New Storms," Time 9 July 1984: 9.

The following examples show the way to record various kinds of first references for periodicals in the endnotes (or footnotes).

Magazine Article by Known Author, Pagination by Issue

[15] Ed Magnuson, "Stirring Up New Storms," Time 9 July 1984: 9.

Magazine Article by Known Author, Pagination by Volume

[16] Daniel R. Schwarz, "The Originality of E. M. Forster," Modern Fiction Studies 29(1983): 634-35.

Magazine Editorial

[17] Ian Ledgerwood, "Dear Reader," editorial, Modern Maturity Dec. 1984-Jan. 1985:4.

Book or Film Review in Magazine

[18] Michael Holroyd, "A Life Upon the Wicked Stage," rev. of Mrs. Pat: The Life of Mrs. Patrick Campbell, by Margot Peters, New York 26 Mar. 1984:87.

Newspaper Article by Known Author

[19] Heather Dewar, "School Summer Programs Get the Ax," Miami News 7 June 1984, final home ed.: A5.

Newspaper Editorial, No Author Shown

[20] "Opportunity at the Summit," editorial, Wall Street Journal 7 June 1984:28.

Book or Film Review in Newspaper

[21] Vincent Canby, "Film: Malle's 'Crackers,' with Donald Sutherland," New York Times 17 Feb. 1984: C19.

Published Interview

[22] Goldie Hawn, "Playboy Interview," with Lawrence Grobel, Playboy Jan. 1985: 71.

C. First References: Other Print Sources

Follow the same general set of rules for books, periodicals, and other print sources.

Separate each unit of information by commas (rather than by periods as you do in the Works Cited) and single spaces.

Examples:

Document from an Information Service

[23] Hugh Burns, "A Writer's Tool: Computing As a Mode of Inventing," ERIC 1980, ED 193 693.

Unpublished Thesis or Dissertation

[24] Audrey Joan Dynner, "Resources for Writers," diss. Union Graduate School, 1976, 125.

Pamphlet by Known Author

[25] Jim Parker, Drugs and Alcohol: A Handbook for Young People (Phoenix: Do It Now Foundation, 1981) 6.

Letter, Personal or Unpublished

[26] Sharon Lee, letter to the author, 22 Nov. 1985.

Government Publications

[27] United States, House, Committee on Government Operations A Citizen's Guide on How to Use the Freedom of Information Act and the Privacy Act in Requesting Government Documents: 13the Report (Washington: GPO, 1977)8-11.

D. First References: Nonprint Sources

Indent five spaces, the superscript number that coordinates with the number in the text, a space.

Author, title, publication data, separate by commas, end with a period.

Examples:

Cartoon or Illustration

[28] Garrv Trudeau, "Doonesbury," cartoon, Miami Herald 22 Dec. 1984: 6C.

Works of Art

[29] Pierre-Auguste Renoir, San Marco, Minneapolis Institute of Arts, Minneapolis.

[30] Hanukah Lamp from Poland, Jewish Museum, New York.

[31] Constantin Brancusi, Sleeping Muse, Metropolitan Museum of Art, New York.

Personal or Telephone Interview

[32] Judith A Matz, personal interview, 4 Aug. 1984.

[33] Nancy Tuck Davis, telephone interview, 12 Nov. 1985.

Radio, Television, or Recorded Interview

[34] Leonard Ciro, interview, Know Your Community, WFCM, Miami, 28 Nov. 1984.

Lecture

[35] Janice C. Redish, "The Language of Bureaucracy," Literacy in the 1980s Conference, Ann Arbor, 25 June 1981.

Recorded Speech or Lecture

[36] John Kenneth Galbraith, "Economics and the Press: A Working Guide to the Gullible," address to the National Press Club, audiocassette, Washington, Natl. Pub. Radio Ed. Services, NP-820419, 1982(38 min.).

Computer Software

[37] Word Juggler lie, computer software, Quark, 1983.

Material from a Computer Service

[38] J. Kirchner, "Poll Reveals Americans See Computer As Friend, Foe," Infoworld 9-16 Jan. 1984: 100 (DLALOG file 275, item 129230).

Radio or Television Program

[39] You and the Law, writ, and prod. Alan Roy, WDC Special Report, WSVN Miami, 10 Oct. 1983.

[40] "School's Out!" writ. Norman Raymonds, Lookin' Local, created and dir. By Martin

Matte, KWP, Belmont [CA] 2 Sept. 1982.

Feature-Length Film

[41] Dir. Orson Welles, Citizen Kane, RKO, 1941.

[42] Ball of Fire, dir. Howard Hawks, prod. Samuel Goldwyn, MGM, 1941.

Short Film, Filmstrip, Videotape, or Slide Program

[43] Arla Sorkin and Terry Kahn, Filmmakers, Scarcity and Planning, Walt Disney, 1977 (16 mm. color sd., 17 min.)

[44] National Defense, 2 filmstrips, 2 audiocassettes, writ. Kate Griggs, photo ed. Wendy Davis, Prentice Hall Media, 1982 (84 fr., color, 17/8 ips, mono, 27 min.).

Phonograph Record or Audiotape

[45] Franz Joseph Haydn, Symphony no. 101 "The Clock," cond. Leonard Bernstein, New York Philnarmonic Orch., Columbia, M33531, 1975.

[46] Martin Luther King, Jr., "I Have a Dream," Free at Last, Motown, 3150, 1988.

Live Theatrical or Musical Performance

[47] La Cage Aux Folles, dir. Arthur Laurents, with Gene Barry and George Hearn, Palace Theater, New York, 21 Mar. 1984.

[48] Giacomo Puccini, Manon Lescaut, prod. By Gian Carlo Menotti, cond. Nello Santi, with Teresa Zylis-Gara and Vasile Moldoveanu, Metropolitan Opera, Metropolitan Opera House, New York, 31 Mar. 1984.

[49] Mike Nichols, dir., The Real Thing, by Tom Stoppard, with Jeremy Irons and Laila Robins, Plymouth Theater, New York, 3 Jan. 1985.

E. Subsequent References

Once you have recorded the full information about a source, you can shorten the citation the next time you refer to the work.

After the superscript number and a space, record the author's name and the specific page or pages you are citing.

Examples:

[50] Lance J. Hoffman, ed. Security and Privacy in Computer Systems (Los Angeles: Melville, 1973) 29.

[51] Hoffman 42-43.

[52] "Big Brother Is a Big Worry," Newsweek 14 May 1979, 42.

[53] "Big Brother" 42.

If you are citing more than one work by the same author, include the title of the work or a shortened form of it with the author's name as a subsequent reference.

Examples:

[54] Alan F. Westin, Computer Science and Technology: Computers, Personnel Administration, and Citizens Rights (Washington: GPO, 1979) 45.

[55] Alan F. Westin, Privacy and Freedom (New York: Atheneum, 1970) 98-99.

⁵⁶ Westin, Privacy 87-90.
⁵⁷ Westin, Computer Science 135.

Review Questions

1. What should one acknowledge in a research paper?
2. What disciplines are MLA system mainly used in?
3. What information must be given if we use MLA system?
4. What information must be given in documenting visual material?
5. What disciplines are Author and date or Author-year system mainly used in?
6. What information must be given if we use Author and date or Author-year system?
7. What disciplines are Number-system or CBE system mainly used in?
8. What information must be given if we use Number-system or CBE system?
9. What information must be given if we use footnotes or endnotes?
10. What disciplines are APA System mainly used in?
11. What information must be given if we use APA System?

Assignments

1. Accord to the outline you made the week before last to finish the third part *Research Methods* of your term research paper. Remember to acknowledge all the sources and document completely all materials in your text that is not original.

2. Accord to the outline you made the week before last to finish the fourth part *Research Findings* of your term research paper. Remember to acknowledge all the sources and document completely all materials in your text that is not original.

Unit 9　文献格式
Works Cited Format

To be useful to your reader, a bibliography or a list of works cited must answer several basic questions about each source.

What is its full title?

Who wrote or created it?

Where and when was it published? And by what publisher?

For articles in periodicals and for essays in books, on what pages can it be found?

The three categories of listing sources:

Books——name, title, location, publisher, date...

Periodicals——name, title, date, page number, volume and issue numbers...

Nonprinting and computer materials——narrator of a television program, director of a film, speed of an audiotape, distributor of a computer program ...

1) Conventions

①Start the list of Works Cited on a new page, but continue numbering pages from the text of your research paper.

Works Cited

"Big Brother Is a Big Worry." Newsweek 14 May 1979: 42. Boeth, Richard. "The Assault on Privacy." Newsweek 27 July 1970: 15+.

Bouchard, Robert F., and Justin D. Franklin. Guidebook to the Freedom of Information and Privacy Acts. New York: Boardman, 1980.

---

②Center the heading Works Cited (or Annotated List of Works Cited or whichever title describes your list) one inch down from the top of the page.

Works Cited

"Big Brother Is a Big Worry." Newsweek 14 May 1979: 42. Boeth, Richard. "The Assault on Privacy." Newsweek 27 July 1970: 15+.

Bouchard, Robert F., and Justin D. Franklin. Guidebook to the Freedom of Information and Privacy Acts. New York: Boardman, 1980.

③Double-space between the heading and the first entry, as well as between lines of each entry and between items on your list.

④Use hanging indentation. That is, begin each entry at the left margin you establish. However, if you need more than one line to give all the necessary information, indent subsequent lines five spaces from the left margin.

⑤Entries are listed alphabetically according to the last name of the author (or the first author, if there is more than one person). If no author's name is shown, begin with the title of the work and use the first word to determine the alphabetical placement.

⑥If there are several entries by the same author, use the name only for the first entry. Substitute three hyphens in place of the name for subsequent works by that person.

Works Cited

Westin, Alan F. Computer Science and Technology: Computers, Personnel Administration, and Citizen Rights. Washington: GPO, 1979.

—. Privacy and Freedom. New York: Atheneum, 1970.

—, and Michael A Bsker. Databanks in a Free Society: Computers, Record-Keeping and Privacy. New York: Quadrangle, 1972.

---

⑦No distinction is made between a hardbound and a softbound book.

⑧Continuous underlining, including spaces, is easy to type for titles. However, underline only the words, not the spaces, if you choose.

⑨Only special information about the edition of a book (rev., alt., 5th ed., and so on) is noted. Otherwise, it is assumed to be a first edition and you do not record that fact.

Works Cited

"Big Brother Is a Big Worry." Newsweek 14 May 1979: 42. Boeth, Richard. "The Assault on Privacy." Newsweek 27 July 1970: 15+.

Columbia Human Rights Law Review Staff, eds. Surveillance, Dataveillance, and Personal Freedom. Fair Lawn: Burdick, 1973.

---

⑩A dictionary or encyclopedia is treated as a book, but the author's name or chief editor is omitted.

⑪Alphabetically arranged entries in encyclopedias, dictionaries, and other reference works do not need either volume or page numbers noted.

> **Works Cited**
>
> "Big Brother Is a Big Worry." <u>Newsweek</u> 14 May 1979: 42. Boeth, Richard. "The Assault on Privacy." <u>Newsweek</u> 27 July 1970: 15+.
>
> Columbia Human Rights Law Review Staff, eds. <u>Surveillance, Dataveillance, and Personal Freedom</u>. Fair Lawn: Burdick, 1973.
>
> "Newton, Isaac." <u>The New Columbia Encyclopedia</u>. 1975.

⑫ Specific page numbers used within a book are not noted unless your source was a work in an anthology or a collection. Begin page numbers within an anthology two spaces after the period that signifies conclusion of publication information; end with another period.

> **Works Cited**
>
> Howard, William. "Emily Dickinson's Poetic Vocabulary." <u>PMLA</u> 72 (1957). 225-48.
>
> Thomas, Owen. "Father and Daughter: Edward and Emily Dickinson." <u>American Literature</u> 40 (1960). 510-23.

⑬ The page number of a periodical item begins one space after the colon that ends other publication information; it, too, concludes with a period. Omit any abbreviation for the word "page(s)". Show inclusive and successive pages with a hyphen but only the last two digits of a three-digit number, if the first number remains the same. Thus, use 634-42 but 897-927. If the pages of an article are not successive (that is, pages of advertising or other text intervene), follow the initial page number by a +.

> **Works Cited**
>
> "Big Brother Is a Big Worry." <u>Newsweek</u> 14 May 1979: 42. Boeth, Richard. "The Assault on Privacy." <u>Newsweek</u> 27 July 1970: 15+.
>
> Wellborn, Stanley N. "Big Brother's Tools Are Ready, but..." <u>U. S. News & World Report</u> 26 Dec. 1983: 88-89.

⑭ Long poems appearing in book form, such as Paradise Lost or The Rime of the Ancient Mariner, are treated as books.

⑮The Bible and the names of books within it are not underlined (or italicized). The King James Version is assumed unless you state otherwise.

⑯Only the city of publication for books is noted; omit the name of the state where it is located.

⑰The names of publishers are recorded in abbreviated form, usually by only the first word shown. However, if the company bears a person's name such as "Charles Scribner's Sons" only the last name, Scribner's, is used. A university press is designated UP, and other customary abbreviations (such as "Rev." for "Review" and "Assn." for "Association") are used. Omit corporate designations (such as "Company" or "Incorporated"). Therefore, Wadsworth Publishing Co. is listed simply as Wadsworth.

⑱Months in periodicals are abbreviated, except for May, June and July.

⑲Never number the entries in a list of Works Cited.

⑳Punctuation and spacing are important within each entry.

㉑End each work cited with a period.

2) APA Reference Forms

- Type the word Reference at the center of the first line of a new page to begin the list.
- Start the first line of an entry at the left margin, but indent the second and succeeding lines of each entry three spaces from that margin.
- Type the list double spaced, in alphabetical order by author (or title, if no author is shown).
- If you have two or more works by the same author in the reference list, put them in the order of publication (and repeat the full author entry unit).
- Works by people with the same surname are alphabetized by first initial.
- Alphabetize corporate or agency authorship by the first significant word in the name.
- Each entry in the reference list contains four units, in this order: the author, the year of publication, the title, and the publication information. The units end with periods and are separated from each other by a single typewriter space.

Reference

Berndt, T. J. (1996). Exploring the effects of friendship quality on social development. In W. M. Bukowski, A. F. Newcomb, & W. W. Hartup, (Eds.), *The company they keep: Friendship in childhood and adolescence*. (pp. 346-365). Cambridge, UK: Cambridge University Press.

Berndt, T. J. (2002). Friendship quality and social development. *Current Directions in Psychological Science*, 11, 7-10.

Wegener, D. T., & Petty, R. E. (1995). Flexible correction processes in social judgment: The role of naive theories in corrections for perceived bias. *Journal of Personality & Social Psychology*, 68, 36-51.

Customs to be adhered to in the APA reference style:

①Allow just one space between each unit of the citation: author, date, title, and publisher's location and name. End each unit with a period, unless an author's name with a period ends the unit.

> Berndt, T. J. (1996). Exploring the effects of friendship quality on social development. In W. M. Bukowski, A. F. Newcomb, & W. W. Hartup, (Eds.), *The company they keep: Friendship in childhood and adolescence.* (pp. 346-365). Cambridge, UK: Cambridge University Press.

②Give the surnames and initials of all authors, no matter how many there are. Separate the names with commas and use an ampersand (&) between the last two names.

> Wegener, D. T., Kerr, N. L., Fleming, M. A., & Petty, R. E. (2000). Flexible corrections of juror judgments: Implications for jury instructions. *Psychology, Public Policy, & Law*, 6, 629-654.

③If there is more than one author, give each in surname/given-name order. Use an ampersand (&) between names instead of the full word.

> Wegener, D. T., & Petty, R. E. (1994). Mood management across affective states: The hedonic contingency hypothesis. *Journal of Personality & Social Psychology*, 66, 1034-1048.

④If a book is the work of one or more editors, enclose the abbreviation "Ed." or "Eds." (without the quotation marks, of course) in parentheses after the name of the last editor.

> Columbia Human Rights Law Review staff (Eds.). (1973). *Surveillance, dataveillance and personal freedom.* Fair Lawn, NJ: Burdick.

⑤Enclose the date of publication in parentheses. For magazines and newspapers, put a comma after the year, then the month-written out in full-and the date.

> Wellborn, S. N. (1983, December 26). Big brother's tools are ready, but... *U. S. News & World Report*, pp. 88-89.
> Fisher, M. (1985, April 8). Many can't join the club, or visit. *The Miami Herald*, pp. 1A, 12A.

⑥Capitalize only the first word of a book or article title, and the first word of a subtitle (if there is one); type the remaining words entirely in lowercase letters. However, capitalize each word in the title of a periodical.

> Ortony, A, Turner, T. J., & Larson-Shapiro, N. (1985). Cultural and instructional influences on figurative language comprehension by inner city children. *Research in the Teaching of English*, L9, 25-36.

⑦Italicize the titles of books and periodicals. Do not use quotation marks around the titles of articles within these longer works.

⑧If a book appears in any special edition—that is, as a revised, alternate, or subsequent edition—enclose that information in parentheses after the title. If edition information appears, put the period to end the title after the parentheses.

> Roth, A J. (1986). *The research paper: Process, form, and content* (5the ed.). Belmont, CA: Wadsworth.

⑨Show the state in which a publisher is located, unless the city is well known. Use the standard two-letter postal abbreviation for states. Put a colon after the location.

> Jaffe, A (1964). Symbolism in the visual arts. In C. G. Jung (Ed.), *Man and MB symbols* (pp. 230-271). Garden City, NY: Doubleday.

⑩Be as brief as possible in the name of the publisher (omit such words as "Company" or "Incorporated"), but do spell out the names of associations and university presses.

> Berndt, T. J. (1996). Exploring the effects of friendship quality on social development. In W. M. Bukowski, A. F. Newcomb, & W. W. Hartup, (Eds.), *The company they keep: Friendship in childhood and adolescence.* (pp. 346-365). Cambridge, UK: Cambridge University Press.

⑪Publication information for a journal article consists of the name of the publication, a comma, the volume number followed by a comma, and the inclusive pages on which the article is printed. Do not use abbreviations for either "volume" or "pages."

> Green, M. (1985). Talk and doubletalk: The development of metacommunication knowledge about oral language. *Research in the Teaching of English* 19, 9-24.

⑫The actual page numbers on which a newspaper article appears are shown following the name of the paper and a comma. Use the abbreviation "p." or "pp." before the first page number; separate page numbers by commas and end the unit with a period.

> Fisher, M. (1985, April 8). Many can't join the club, or visit. *The Miami Herald*, pp. 1A, 12A.

⑬An article or chapter within a book is treated simply as an article or chapter through the first three units: author, date, and title. Then, add the word "In" and give the author or editor's name, the book title, then parentheses enclosing the abbreviation "pp." and the exact page numbers. Then give the publisher's location and name, followed by a period.

> Jaffe, A (1964). Symbolism in the visual arts. In C. G. Jung (Ed.), *Man and MB symbols* (pp. 230-271). Garden City, NY: Doubleday.

3) APA Typing Customs

①Double-space throughout the paper; indent paragraphs five spaces from the left margin; allow two spaces after periods and colons, but one space after commas, semi-colons, and initials.

②Use quotation marks around all quoted material, but use single quotation marks to show a quote within a quote. A quotation of up to forty words should be included in the text. Any quotation longer than that should be typed double spaced as a block indented five spaces from the normal left margin.

③Try to include both author and date before the block. Then, after the concluding period of a quotation, allow one space and enclose the page number of the source in parentheses; no punctuation mark follows.

④A research paper that follows the APA style has two special differences from the final presentation style: it has a title page, and each page has a running head rather than the name of the author.

⑤Type the title in uppercase and lowercase letters in the center of the page. Under it, put your name as author. About two-thirds of the way down from the top of the page and lined up at the right margin, on succeeding lines write the course abbreviation, your instructor's name, and the date on which the paper is due.

⑥On succeeding pages in the text of your paper, show only the running head and the page number for identification.

⑦If there is an abstract, put it immediately after the title page and before the text begins; write the heading "Abstract" in the center of the page with a double space between it and the page number, as well as between it and the first line of text. Continue the running head and page number for each page of references.

4) Standard Forms for Works Cited

BOOKS:

Three kinds of information
- Author, title, and publication details
- A period and two spaces show the end of the first two units and a period concludes the entry.

Location:
Show only the name of the city
Example:

Belmont	Belmont, California
Dubuque	Dubuque, Iowa
Englewood Cliffs	Englewood Cliffs, New Jersey

The publisher's name: either a single word or a shortened form of the whole name.
Example:

Farrar	Farrar, Straus, & Giroux, Inc.
Harper	Harper & Row, Publishers, Inc.
St. Martin's	St. Martin's Press, Inc.
Pocket	Pocket Books
Free	The Free Press

If the publisher's name is that of one person record just the last name:
Example:

Bowker	R. Bowker Co.
Knopf	Alfred A. Knopf, Inc.
Putnam	G. P. Putnam's Sons

Omit business abbreviations (such as Co., Inc., or Corp.), articles, and descriptive words (such as Press or Publishers) that are part of the publisher's full name:
Example:

Wadsworth	Wadsworth Publishing Co.
Boardman	Clark Boardman Co., Ltd.
Allen	George Allen and Unwin Publishers, Inc.

A book published by a university press is recorded by the name of the university together with the initials "U" (for University) and "P" (for Press or Publishers).
Example:

Oxford UP	Oxford University Press
Princeton UP	Princeton University Press
U of Chicago P	University of Chicago Press
Johns Hopkins UP	The Johns Hopkins University Press

Use standard abbreviations for words that are part of the publisher's name:

Harvard Law Rev. Assn.	Harvard Law Review Association
Acad. for Educ. Dev.	Academy for Educational Development, Inc.

Use familiar capital letter combinations if that is how the name of a publisher is customa-

rily shown.

GPO U. S. Government Printing Office
NCTE National Council of Teachers of English

If you believe readers may not know the acronym or letter combination, use abbreviations in preference:

Mod. Lang. Assn. rather than MLA.

If you cannot find the place of publication, write N. p. where the city would ordinarily appear.

If no publisher is given, write n. p. after the colon and where the name of the publisher would be.

If no date of publication is available, use the letters n. d. after the comma where you would provide the date; you do not then need another period at the end of the entry.

5) Assembling a List of Works Cited in Your Paper

Books:

① Basic Forms for books

> Author, A. A. (Year of publication). *Title of work: Capital letter also for subtitle.* Location: Publisher. (APA)
>
> Author, Aaa Aaa. *Title of work: Capital letter also for subtitle.* Location: Publisher, Year of publication. (MLA)

② Basic forms for a book chapter or an article in a collection

> Author, A. A., & Author, B. B. (Year of publication). Title of chapter. In A. Editor & B. Editor (Eds.), *Title of book* (pages of chapter). Location: Publisher. (APA)
>
> Author, Aaa Aaa, and Author, Bbb Bbb. "Title of chapter". In A. Editor & B. Editor (Eds.), *Title of book* (pages of chapter). Location: Publisher. (Year of Publication). (MLA)

③ Basic forms for electronic books

> Author, A. A., & Author, B. B. (Year of publication). *Title of book.* Location: Publisher. Date you accessed the site. Address of the site. (APA)
>
> Author, Aaa Aaa, and Author, Bbb Bbb. *Title of book.* Location: Publisher. (Year of publication). Date you accessed the site. Address of the site (MLA)

④Basic forms for An article on a web site

> Author(s). (Date of posting/revision). Article Title. *Name of web site*. Name of institution / organization affiliated with site. Date of access <electronic address>. (APA)
>
> Author(s). "Article Title." Name of web site. Date of posting/revision. Name of institution/organization affiliated with site. Date of access <electronic address>. (MLA)

Examples:

Book by Single Author

APA	Fleming, T. (1997). *Liberty!: The American Revolution*. New York: Viking.
MLA	Fleming, Thomas. *Liberty!: The American Revolution*. New York: Viking, 1997.
APA	Bergen, C. (1984). *Knock Wood*. New York: Linden.
MLA	Bergen, Candice. *Knock Wood*. New York: Linden, 1984.

Two books by the same author

APA	Palmer, W. J. (1993). *The Films of the Eighties: A Social History*. Carbondale: Southern Illinois UP. Palmer, W. J. (1997). *Dickens and New Historicism*. New York: St. Martin's.
MLA	Palmer, Wiiliam J. *Dickens and New Historicism*. New York: St. Martin's 1997. —. *The Films of the Eighties: A Social History*. Carbondale: Southern Illinois UP, 1993.

Book by Two or Three Authors

APA	Sennett, R., & Cobb, J. (1972). *The hidden injuries of class*. New York: Vintage Books.
MLA	Sennett, Richard, and Jonathan Cobb. *The Hidden Injuries of Class*. New York: Vintage Books, 1972.

APA	Wang, C. F., & Salmon, C. C. (1983). *Introductory Structural Analysis*. Englewood Cliffs, NJ: Prentice.
MLA	Wang, Cha-Fia, and Charles C. Salmon. *Introductory Structural Analysis*. Englewood Cliffs: Prentice, 1983.

Book by More Than Three Authors

APA	Schwartz, D., Ryan, S., & Wostbrock, F. (1995). *The encyclopedia of TV game shows*. New York: Facts on File.
MLA	Schwartz, David, Steve Ryan, and Fred Wostbrock. *The Encyclopedia of TV Game Shows*. New York: Facts on File, 1995.
MLA	Malmon, Elaine P., et al. *Writing in the Arts and Sciences*. Boston: Little, 1981.

Organization or Institution as Author

APA	American Camping Association. (1980). *Camp Standards with Interpretations for the Accreditation of Organized Camps* (rev. ed.). Martinsviile, Indiana: American Camping Assoc.
MLA	American Camping Associateion. *Camp Standards with Interpretations for the Accreditation of Organized Camps*, rev. ed. Martinsviile: American Camping Assoc., 1980.

Book in Collaboration

APA	Foyt, A. J., & Neely, W. (1983). *A. J.* New York: Times.
MLA	Foyt, A. J., with Wifijam Neely. *A. J.* New York: Times, 1983.

Anonymous Book

APA	*Fire of Life: The Smithsonian Book of the Sun*. (1981). New York: Norton
MLA	*Fire of Life: The Smithsonian Book of the Sun*. New York: Norton, 1981.

Author's Name Absent from Book but Known from Another Source

APA	[Dynner, E.] (1984). *Camera TechniQues*. Miami: Travelogue.
MLA	[Dynner, Eugene.] *Camera TechniQues*. Miami: Travelogue, 1984.

Book by Pseudonymous Author but Real Name Supplied

APA	Carr, P. [Hibbert, E.] (1983). *Knave of Hearts*. New York: Putnam.
MLA	Carr, Philippa [Eleanor Hibbert]. *Knave of Hearts*. New York: Putnam, 1983.

Book in Which Illustrator is Important

APA	Biamonte, D. (illus.), Kavanaugh, J. J. (text). (1980). *A Fable*. New York: Dutton.
MLA	Biamonte, Daniel, illus. *A Fable*. Text by James J. Kavanaugh. New York: Dutton, 1980.
APA	Kavanaugh, J. J. (1980). *A Fable*. D. Biamonte (Illus.). New York: Dutton.
MLA	Kavanaugh, James J. *A Fable*. Illus. Daniel Biamonte. New York: Dutton, 1980.

Book Condensation of Longer Work

APA	Thompson, T. (1975). *Lost*. (Cond.). Pleasantvilie, NY: Digest.
MLA	Thompson, Thomas. *Lost*. Cond. From *Lost*. Pleasantvilie: Digest, 1975.

Book with Single Editor or Compiler of a Collection

APA	Salisbury, H. E., (ed.). (1984). *Vietnam Reconsidered: Lessons from a War*. New York: Harper.
MLA	Salisbury, Harrison E., ed. *Vietnam Reconsidered: Lessons from a War*. New York: Harper, 1984.

Book with Two or More Editors or Compilers

APA	Huey, R. B., Pianka, E. R., & Schoener, T. W., (eds.). (1983). *Lizard Ecology: Studies of a Model Organism*. Cambridge: Harvard UP.
MLA	Huey, Raymond B., Eric R. Pianka, and Thomas W. Schoener, eds. *Lizard Ecology: Studies of a Model Organism*. Cambridge: Harvard UP, 1983.

Anthology with No Editor Given

APA	*The Oxford Book of Verse in English Translation*. (1983). Oxford: Oxford Up.
MLA	*The Oxford Book of Verse in English Translation*. Oxford: Oxford Up. 1983.

Poem in Anthology

APA	Brooks, G. (1981). The Rites for Cousin Vit. *The Harper Anthology of Poetry* (p. 684). J. F. Nims (ed.). New York: Harper.
MLA	Brooks, Gwendolyn. "The Rites for Cousin Vit." *The Harper Anthology of Poetry*. Ed. John Frederick Nims. New York: Harper, 1981. 684.

Article, Chapter, Story, or Essay in a Collection

APA	Vincent, D. (1982). The Decline of the Oral Tradition in Popular Culture. *Popular Culture and Custom in Nineteenth-Century England* (pp. 20-47). R. D. Storch (ed.). New York: St. Martin's.
MLA	Vincent, David. "The Decline of the Oral Tradition in Popular Culture." *Popular Culture and Custom in Nineteenth-Century England*. Ed. Robert D. Storch. New York: St. Martin's, 1982. 20-47.
APA	Ortese, A. M. (1960). A Pair of Glasses. F. Frehaye (trans.). *Stories of Modern Italy* (406-27). B. Johnson (ed.). New York: Modern Library-Random.
MLA	Ortese, Anna Maria. "A Pair of Glasses." Trans. Frances Frehaye. *Stories of Modern Italy*. Ed. Ben Johnson. New York: Modern Library-Random, 1960. 406-27.

Book Edited by Other Than Author of Contents

APA	Truman, H. S. *Letters Home*. M. M. Poen (ed.). New York: Putnam, 1984.
MLA	Truman, Harry S. *Letters Home*. Ed: Monte M. Poen. New York: Putnam, 1984.

Work of Author Contained in Collected Works

APA	Miller, A. (1981). *After the Fall. Arthur Miller's Collected Plays* (Vol. II, pp. 125-242). New York: Viking.
MLA	Miller, Arthur. *After the Fall. Arthur Miller's Collected Plays* (Vol. Volume II). New York: Viking, 1981. 125-242.

Several-Volume Work under General Title, with Each Volume Having Separate Title

APA	Martin, D. M. (1982). *Social Sciences*. Handbook of Latin American Studies (No. 43). Austin: U of Texas P.
MLA	Martin, Dolores Mayano. *Social Sciences*. Handbooks of Latin American Studies, No. 43. Austin: U of Texas P, 1982.

Book in Series Edited by Other Than Author

APA	Standley, A. R. (1981). *Auguste Comte*. S. E. Bowman (ed.). Twayne's World Author Series (No. 825). Boston: Twayne.
MLA	Standley, Arline R. *Auguste Comte*. Ed. Sylvia E. Bowman. Twayne's World Author Series No. 825. Boston: Twayne, 1981.

Introduction by Other Than Author

APA	Schneider, A. (1982). Introduction. *Five Plays* (11-vi). By M. Weller. New York: NAL.
MLA	Schneider, Alan. Introduction. *Five Plays*. By Michael Weller. New York: NAL, 1982. 11-vi.

Encyclopedias

APA	Lumiansky, R. M. (1998). Chaucer. In *The new encyclopaedia Britannica* (Vol. 15, pp. 745-748). Chicago: Encycloaedia Britannica.
MLA	Lumiansky, R. M. "Chaucer." *The New Encyclopaedia Britannica: Macropaedia.* 15th ed. 1998.

Work in Several Volumes

APA	Crashaw, R. (1983). *The Complete Works of Richard Crashaw* (2 vols). New York: AMs.
MLA	Crashaw, Richard. *The Complete Works of Richard Crashaw* 2 vols. New York: AMS, 1983.

Translated Book by Known Author

APA	Kawabata, Y. (1981). *Beauty and Sadness.* H. Hibbett (trans.). New York: Perigee.
MLA	Kawabata, Yatrunari. *Beauty and Sadness.* Trans. Howard Hibbett. New York: Perigee, 1981.
APA	Ibsen, H. (1978). *Pillars of Society. Henrik Ibsen. The Complete Major Prose Plays* (pp. 10-45). R. Fjelde (trans.). New York: Farrar.
MLA	Ibsen, Henrik. *Pillars of Society. Henrik Ibsen. The Complete Major Prose Plays.* Trans. Rolf Fjelde. New York: Farrar, 1978. 10-45.
APA	Hibbett, H. (trans.). (1981). *Beauty and Sadness.* By Yasunari Kawabata. New York: Perigee.
MLA	Hibbett, Howard, trans. *Beauty and Sadness.* By Yasunari Kawabata. New York: Perigee, 1981.

Translated Book (Author's Name Included in Title)

APA	*The Poems of Catullus: A Bilingual Edition.* (1983). P. Whigham (trans.). Berkeley, California: U of California P.
MLA	*The Poems of Catullus: A Bilingual Edition.* Trans. Peter Whigham. Berkeley: U of California P, 1983.

Edition of a Book

APA	Roth, A. J. (1986). *The Research Pagper: Process, Form, and Content* (5th ed.). Belmont: Wadsworth.
MLA	Roth, Audrey J. *The Research Paper: Process, Form, and Content.* 5th ed. Belmont: Wadsworth. 1986.
APA	Belles, R. N. (1983). *What Color Is Your Parachute? A Practical Manual for Job-Hunters and Career Changes* (rev. and enl. 扩充 ed.). Berkeley: Ten Speed.
MLA	Belles, Richard Nelson. *What Color Is Your Parachute? A Practical Manual for Job-Hunters and Career Changers.* Rev. and enl. ed. Berkeley: Ten Speed, 1983.

Privately Printed Book

APA	*Poetry in Crystal.* (1963). New York: Steuben.
MLA	*Poetry in Crystal.* New York: Steuben, 1963.

Signed Article in Reference Book

APA	Turner, R. H. (1981 ed.). Collective Behaviour. *New Encyclopedia Britannica: Macropaedia.*
MLA	Turner, Ralph H. "Collective Behaviour." *New Encyclopedia Britannica: Macropaedia.* 1981 ed.
APA	Cleary, E. W. (1984 ed.) Privacy, Right of. *The World Book Encyclopedia.*
MLA	Cleary, Edward W. "Privacy, Right of." *The World Book Encyclopedia.* 1984 ed.

Unsigned Article in Reference Work

APA	Space Travel. (1980 ed.). *Compton's Encyclopedia.*
MLA	"Space Travel." *Compton's Encyclopedia.* 1980 ed.
APA	Reagan, Ronald. (42nd ed. 1982-1983). *Who's Who in America.*
MLA	"Reagan, Ronald." *Who's Who in America.* 42nd ed. 1982-1983.

Republished Book or Modern Reprint of Older Edition

APA	Kushner, H. S. (1983). *When Bad Things Happen to Good People* (1981). New York: Avon.
MLA	Kushner, Harold S. *When Bad Things Happen to Good People.* 1981. New York: Avon, 1983.
APA	James, G. W. (1974). *Indian Blankets and Their Makers* (1914). New York: Dover.
MLA	James, George Wharton. *Indian Blankets and Their Makers.* 1914. New York: Dover, 1974.

6) Standard Forms for Works Cited

Periodicals:

- Three kinds of information: author, title, and publication data (name of the periodical the article is in, date of publication, and pages on which it appears)
- A period and two spaces follow the name of the author and the title; a period concludes the information.
- Parts of the publication information are separated by a single space; a colon precedes page numbers.
- Write the inclusive page numbers on which an article appears, but if it is not on successive pages (that is, there is intervening print, text, photograph, or advertising) put a + immediately after the first page number, then a period to end the entry.
- Some scholarly journals or other publications continue page numbers throughout a volume (that is, through a year of publication rather than beginning with page number 1 in each issue). When you cite such a periodical, right after the title put the number of the volume, the year of publication in parentheses, then the inclusive page numbers of the article you used.
- The headlines of newspaper articles are considered their "titles". Authorship is shown in a by-

line, except if you are citing a letter to the editor, which is signed at the end.

①Basic Forms for An article in a periodical:

Author, A. A. , Author, B. B. , & Author, C. C. (Year). *Title of article. Title of periodical*, *volume number*, pages. (APA)
Author, A. A. , Author, B. B. , and Author, C. C. "Title of article". *Title of periodical*, volume number (Year): pages. (MLA)

②Basic Forms for an Article in an Internet Periodical

Author, A. A. , & Author, B. B. (Date of publication). Title of article. Title of journal, volume number (issue number if available). Retrieved month day, year, from address. (APA)
Author, A. A. , and Author, B. B. "Title of article". Title of journal, volume number (issue number if available). (Date of publication). Retrieved month day, year, from http://Web address. (MLA)

Examples:

Magazine Article by Known Author, Pagination by Issue

APA	Magnuson (ed.). (9 July 1984). Stirring Up New Storms. *Time*, 8-11.
MLA	Magnuson, Ed. "Stirring Up New Storms." *Time* 9 July 1984: 8-11.
APA	Gawande, A. (2001, July 9). The man who couldn't stop eating. *The New Yorker*, 77, 66-75.
MLA	Gawande, Atul. "The Man Who Couldn't Stop Eating." *New Yorker* 9 Jul. 2001: 66-75.
APA	Malveaux, Julianne. "Black Women and Stress." *Essence* Apr. 1984:74+.

Magazine Article by Known Author, Pagination by Volume

APA	Brown, E. (1996). The lake of seduction: Silence, hysteria, and the space of feminist theatre. *JTD: Journal of Theatre and Drama*, 2, 175-200.

MLA	Brown, Erella. "The Lake of Seduction: Silence, Hysteria, and the Space of Feminist Theatre." *JTD: Journal of Theatre and Drama* 2 (1996): 175-200.
APA	Schwarz, D. R. (1983). The Originality of E. M. Forster. *Modern Fiction Studies* 29, 623-41.
MLA	Schwarz, Daniel R. "The Originality of E. M. Forster." *Modern Fiction Studies* 29 (1983): 623-41.
APA	Harlow, H. F. (1983). Fundamentals for preparing psychology journal articles. *Journal of Comparative and Physiological Psychology*, 55, 893-896.

Articles from a Multiple Authors

APA	Jones, G., Hanton S., & Connaughton, D. (2002). What is this thing called mental toughness? An investigation of elite sport performers. *Journal of Applied Sport Psychology*, 14, 205-218.
MLA	Jones, Graham, Sheldon Hanton, and Declan Connaughton. What is This Thing Called Mental Toughness? An Investigation of Elite Sport Performers. *Journal of Applied Sport Psychology* 14 (2002): 205-218.
APA	Kernis, M. H., Cornell, D. P., Sun, C. R., Berry, A., & Harlow, T. (1993). There's more to self-esteem than whether it is high or low: The importance of stability of self-esteem. *Journal of Personality and Social Psychology*, 65, 1190-1204.

Full Text Magazine Article from a Database

APA	Gore, R. (2001, April). Pharaohs of the sun. *National Geographic*, 199. Retrieved August 21, 2001, from Expanded Academic ASAP database.
MLA	Gore, Rick, "Pharaohs of the Sun." *National Geographic* Apr. 2001. *Expanded Academic ASAP*. Gale Group. Duke U Lib., Durham. 21 Aug. 2001.

APA	Holton, W. (1994). The Ohio Indians and the coming of the American Revolution in Virgina. *The Journal of Southern History*, 60, 453-478. Retrieved July 31, 2001, from JSTOR database.
MLA	Holton, Woody. "The Ohio Indians and the Coming of the American Revolution in Virginia." *The Journal of Southern History* 60. 3 (1994): 453-478. *JSTOR*. Duke U Lib., Durham. 31 July 1998 <http://www.jstor.org>.

Magazine Article by Unknown Author

APA	How Disney Is Circling the Wagons. (4 June 1984). *Business Week*, 35.
MLA	"How Disney Is Circling the Wagons." *Business Week* 4 June 1984:35.

Magazine Editorial

APA	Ledgerwood, I. (Dec. 1984). "Dear Reader." Editorial. *Modern Maturity* Jan. 1985, 4.
MLA	Ledgerwood, Ian. "Dear Reader." Editorial. *Modern Maturity* Dec. 1984 Jan. 1985: 4.

Book or Film Review in Magazine

APA	Salinger, S. V. (2001). [Review of the book *Not all wives: Women of colonial Philadelphia*]. *The Journal of American History*, 88, 184-185.
MLA	Salinger, Sharon V. Rev. of *Not All Wives: Women of Colonial Philadelphia*, by Karin Wulf. *The Journal of American History* 88 (2001): 184-185.
APA	Holroyd, M. A Life Upon the Wicked Stage (26 Mar. 1984). Rev. of *Mrs. Pat: The Life of Mrs. Patrick Campbell*, 86-87, by Margot Peters. New York.
MLA	Holroyd, Michael, "A Life Upon the Wicked Stage." Rev. of *Mrs. Pat: The Life of Mrs. Patrick Campbell*, by Margot Peters. New York 26 Mar: 1984:86-87.

Newspaper Article by Known Author

APA	Holden, S. (1998, May 16). Frank Sinatra dies at 82: Matchless stylist of pop. *The New York Times*, pp. A1, A22-A23.
MLA	Holden, Stephen. "Frank Sinatra Dies at 82: Matchless Stylist of Pop." *New York Times* 16 May 1998, natl. ed.: A1+.
APA	Dewar, H. (7 June 1984). School Summer Programs Get the *Ax*. *Miami News*, final home ed, A5.
MLA	Dewar, Heather. "School Summer Programs Get the Ax." *Miami News* 7 June 1984, final home ed.: A5.

Newspaper Article by Unknown Author

APA	2 Prison Escapees Sighted Near Camp. (5 June 1984). *Chicago Tribune*, Midwest ed., sec. 1,1.
MLA	"2 Prison Escapees Sighted Near Camp." *Chicago Tribune* 5 June 1984, Midwest ed., sec. 1:1.

Newspaper Editorial

APA	Opportunity at the Summit (Editorial). (7 June 1984). *Wall Street Journal*, 28.
MLA	"Opportunity at the Summit." Editorial. *Wall Street Journal* 7 June 1984: 28.

Book or Film Review in Newspaper

APA	Canby, V. (17 Feb. 1984). Film: Malle's 'Crackers,' with Donald Sutherland. *New York Times*, C19.
MLA	Canby, Vincent. "Film: Malle's 'Crackers,' with Donald Sutherland." *New York Times* 17 Feb. 1984: C19.

Newspaper Supplement in Magazine Format

APA	Monet, D. (10 July 1983). Cold Soup. *Tropic in Miami Herald*, 10-13.
MLA	Monet, Dorothy. "Cold Soup." *Tropic in Miami Herald* 10 July 1983: 10-13.

Article from an Online Newspaper

APA	Wright, S. (2001, January 25). Curriculum 2000 draws criticism. *The Chronicle*. Retrieved November 7, 2001, from http://www. chronicle. duke. edu.
MLA	Wright, Steven. "Curriculum 2000 Draws Criticism." *The Chronicle* 25 Jan. 2001. 7 Nov. 2001 <http://www. chronicle. duke. edu/story. php? article_id = 21459 >.

Article from an Online Database

APA	Cowell, A. (2001, September 3). Britain faces flurry of illegal migrants using channel tunnel. *New York Times*. Retrieved October 19, 2001, from Expanded Academic ASAP database.
MLA	Cowell, Alan. "Britian Faces Flurry of Illegal Migrants Using Channel Tunnel." *New York Times* 3 Sept. 2001, late ed. *Expanded Academic ASAP*. Duke U Lib., Durham. 19 Oct. 2001 <http://infotrac. galegroup. com/menu >.

An article in an online journal or magazine

APA	Evnine, S. J. (2001). The universality of logic: On the connection between rationality and logical ability [Electronic version]. *Mind*, 110, 335-367.
MLA	Evnine, Simon J. "The Universality of Logic: On the Connection between Rationality and Logical Ability." *Mind* 110. 438 (2001). 31 July 2001 <http://www3. oup. co. uk/mind/ >.
APA	Saletan, W. (2001, August 16). The ethicist's new clothes. *Slate*. Retrieved August 17, 2001, from http://slate. msn. com/framegame/entries/o1-08-16_113959. asp
MLA	Saletan, William. "The Ethicist's New Clothes." *Slate* 16 August 2001. 17 August 2001 <http://slate. msn. com/framegame/entries/01-08-16_113959. asp >.

Other Sources

①Basic forms of other print sources:

Author, A. A. (Year of publication). Title of work: Capital letter also for subtitle. Location: Publisher. (APA)

Author, A. A. Title of work: Capital letter also for subtitle. Year of publication. Location: Publisher. (MLA)

②Basic Forms for Nonperiodical Internet Document (e.g., a Web page or report):

Author, A. A., & Author, B. B. (Date of publication). Title of article. Retrieved month date, year, from http://Web address. (APA)

Author, A. A., and Author, B. B. "Title of article". (Date of publication). Retrieved month date, year, from http://Web address. (MLA)

③Basic Forms for Part of Nonperiodical Internet Document:

Author, A. A., & Author, B. B. (Date of publication). Title of article. In Title of book or larger document (chapter or section number). Retrieved month date, year, from http://Web address. (APA)

Author, A. A., and Author, B. B. "Title of article". In Title of book or larger document (chapter or section number). (Date of publication). Retrieved month date, year, from http://Web address. (MLA)

Document from an Information Service

APA	Burns, H. (1980, ed.) A Writer's Tool: Computing As a Mode of Inventing. ERIC, 193 693.
MLA	Burns, Hugh. "A Writer's Tool: Computing As a Mode of Inventing." ERIC, 1980. ED 193 693.

Unpublished Thesis or Dissertation

APA	Dynner, A. J. (1976). Resources for Writers. (Diss.). Union Graduate School.
MLA	Dynner, Audrey Joan. "Resources for Writers." Diss. Union Graduate School, 1976.

Mimeographed Report

APA	Michaels, D. (n.d.). Instructions for Students in English 101. (Mimeo.). Miami, n.p.
MLA	Michaels, David. "Instructions for Students in English 101." Mimeo. Miami: n.d., n.p.

Pamphlet by Known Author

APA	Parker, J. (1981). *Drugs and Alcohol: A Handbook for Young People*. Phoenix: Do It Now Foundation.
MLA	Parker, Jim. *Drugs and Alcohol: A Handbook for Young People*. Phoenix: Do It Now Foundation, 1981.

Pamphlet by Unknown Author

APA	*World Military Expenditures and Arms Transfers*, 1972-1982. (1984). Washington: U. S. Arms Control and Disarmament Agency.
MLA	*World Military Expenditures and Arms Transfers*, 1972-1982. Washington: U. S. Arms Control and Disarmament Agency, 1984.
APA	Research and Training Center on Independent Living. (1993). *Guidelines for reporting and writing about people with disabilities* (4th ed.) [Brochure]. Lawrence, KS: Author.

Letter, Personal or Unpublished

APA	Lee, S. (22 Nov. 1985). Letter to the author.
MLA	Lee, Sharon. Letter to the author. 22 Nov. 1985.
APA	Nightingale, F. (3 Feb. 1898). Letter to Sir Arthur Landrow. Sheffield Historical Society, Sheffield, England.
MLA	Nightingale, Florence. Letter to Sir Arthur Landrow. 3 Feb. 1898. Sheffield Historical Society, Sheffield, England.

Letter, Published

APA	Arbogast, E. R. (8 Dec. 1984). AMA: Profit Motives. (Letter). *Miami Herald*, final ed. A26.
MLA	Arbogast, Eugene R. "AMA: Profit Motives." Letter. *Miami Herald* 8 Dec. 1984, final ed. A26.
APA	Bendig, B. (Letter). (Nov. 1984). *Weight Watchers Magazine*, 6.

MLA	Bendig, Betfy. Letter. *Weight Watchers Magazine* Nov. 1984: 6.
APA	Kaye, S. H. (1985). A Comment on 'Response to Writing'. (Letter). *College English* 47, 181-82.
MLA	Kaye, Susan H. "A Comment on 'Response to Writing'. Letter. *College English* 47 (1985): 181-82.
APA	Schwartz, M. (1985). Mimi Schwartz Responds. (Letter). *College English* 47, 183-84.
MLA	Schwartz, Mimi. "Mimi Schwartz Responds." Letter. *College English* 47 (1985): 183-84.

Government Publication

APA	*Hate Crimes Prevention Act of 1998: Hearing before the Committee on the Judiciary, United States Senate*, 105th Cong., 2nd sess. 1 (1998).
MLA	United States. Senate. Committee on the Judiciary. *Hearing on the Hate Crimes Prevention Act of 1998.* 105th Cong., 2nd sess. S. J. Res. 1529. Washington: GPO, 1999.
APA	National Institute of Mental Health. (1990). *Clinical training in serious mental illness* (DHHS Publication No. ADM 90-1679). Washington, DC: U. S. Government Printing Office.
MLA	*Cong. Rec.* 16 July 1981: H4421.
APA	United States. Cong. Office of Technology Assessment. (1980). *Energy from Biological Processes.* Washington. GPO.
MLA	United States. House. Committee on Government Operations. *A Citizen's Guide on How to Use the Freedom of Information Act and the Privacy Act in Requesting Government Documents*: 13th Report. Washington: GPO, 1977.

MLA	United States. Cong. Office of Technology Assessment. *Energy from Biological Processes*. Washington: GPO, 1980.
APA	United States. Senate. Committee on Finance. (1983). *Hearings on the Administration's Assessment of the 1982 Meeting of the Ministers to the GATT*. 89th Cong., 1st sess. Washington: GPO.
MLA	United States. Senate. Committee on Finance. *Hearings on the Administration's Assessment of the 1982 Meeting of the Ministers to the GATT*. 89th Cong., 1st sess. Washington: GPO, 1983.
APA	State of Florida. Department of Transportation. (1982). *Road Design Standards*. Tallahassee.
MLA	State of Florida. Department of Transportation. *Road Design Standards*. Tallahasseee, 1982.

Published Interview

APA	Hawn, G. (Jan. 1985). Playboy Interview. With Lawrence Grobel. *Playboy*, 71+.
MLA	Hawn, Goldie. "Playboy Interview." With Lawrence Grobel. *Playboy* Jan. 1985: 71+.

Cartoon or Illustration

APA	Trudeau, G. (22 Dec. 1984). Doonesbury. (Cartoon). *Miami Herald*, C6.
MLA	Trudeau, Garry. "Doonesbury." Cartoon. *Miami Herald* 22 Dec. 1984: C6.
MLA	Burrola, Ann. Photograph. *Life* Jan. 1985: 62.

Personal or Telephone Interview

MLA	Elloie, P. H. (Speaker). (1994). Interview with K. Ellis. (cassette recording). *Behind the veil: Documenting African-American life in the Jim Crow South*. Rare Book, Manuscript, and Special Collections Library, Duke University.

APA	Elloie, Pealie Hardin. Interview with Kate Ellis. Rec. 15 July 1994. Audiotape. *Behind the Veil: Documenting African-American in the Jim Crow South*. Rare Book, Manuscript, and Special Collections Lib., Duke U.
MLA	Matz, J. A. (4 Aug. 1984). Personal interview.
APA	Davis, Nancy Thok. Telephone interview. 12 Nov. 1985.

Questionnaire You Develop

APA	Malcolm, M. (21 Dec. 1984). Questionnaire.
MLA	Questionnaire. 15 Dec. 1983.

Radio, Television, or Recorded Interview

APA	Ciro, L. (28 Nov. 1984). Interview. *Know Your Community*. WFCM, Miami.
MLA	Ciro, Leonard. Interview. *Know Your Community*. WFCM, Miami. 28 Nov. 1984.

Lecture

APA	Redish, J. C. (25 June 1981). The Language of Bureaucracy. Literacy in the 1980s Conference. Ann Arbor.
MLA	Redish, Janice C. "The Language of Bureaucracy." Literacy in the 1980s Conference. Ann Arbor, 25 June 1981.

Works of Art

APA	Renoir, Pierre-A. *San Marco*. Minneapolis Institue of Arts, Minneapolis.
MLA	Renoir, Pierre-Auguste. *San Marco*. Minneapolis Institute of Arts, Minneapolis.
APA	Hanukah Lamp from Poland. Jewish Museum, New York.
MLA	Brancusi, Constantin. *Sleeping Muse*. Metropolitan Museum of Art, New York.
APA	Rodin, A. (1981). *Meditation*. Musee Rodin, Paris. (Illus. 5.6). in *Rodin Rediscovered*. A. E. Elsen. (Ed). Washington: National Gallery of Art.

MLA	Rodin, Auguste. *Meditation*. Musee Rodin, Paris. Illus. 5.6 in *Rodin Rediscovered*. Ed. Albert E. Elsen. Washington: National Gallery of Art, 1981.

Recorded Speech or Lecture

APA	Gaibraith, J. K. (1982). Economics and the Press: A Working Guide to the Gullible. Address to the National Press Club. (Audo-cassette). Washington: Natl. Pub. Radio Ed. Services, NP-820419.
MLA	Gaibraith, John Kenneth. "Economics and the Press: A Working Guide to the Gullible." Address to the National Press Club. Audio-cassette. Washington: Natl. Pub. Radio Ed. Services, NP-820419, 1982.

Computer Software

APA	*Word Juggler lie*. (1983). Computer software. Quark.
MLA	*Word Juggler lie*. Computer software. Quark, 1983.

Material from a Computer Service

APA	Kirchner, J. (1984). Poll Reveals Americans See Computer As Friend, Foe. *Infoworld* 9 Jan. -16 Jan, 100. DIALOG file 275, item 129230.
MLA	Kirchner, J. "Poll Reveals Americans See Computer As Friend, Foe." Infoworld 9 Jan. -16 Jan. 1984: 100. DIALOG file 275, item 129230.

Radio or Television Program

APA	*You and the Law*. (10 Oct. 1983). Alan Roy. (Writ. and prod.). WDC Special Report WSVN, Miami.
MLA	*You and the Law*. Writ. and prod. Alan Roy. WDC Special Report WSVN, Miami. 10 Oct. 1983.
APA	Bellisario, D. L. (Producer). (1992). *Exciting Action Show*. [Television series]. Hollywood: American Broadcasting Company.

MLA	"School's Out!" Writ. Norman Raymonds. *Lookin' Local*. Created and dir. by Martin Matte. KWP, Belmont, CA. 2 Sept. 1982.

Feature-Length Film

APA	Welles, O. (dir.). (1941). *Citizen Kane*. With Welles, Joseph Cotton, and others. EKO.
MLA	Welles, Orson, dir. *Citizen Kane*. With Welles, Joseph Cotton, and others. EKO, 1941.
MLA	Agnes Moorehead, actress. *Citizen Kane*. Dir. Orson Welles. With Welles, Joseph Cotton, and others. RKO, 1941.
MLA	Mankiewicz, Herman J., and Orson Welles, screenwriters. *Citizen Kane*. Dir. Orson Welles. With Welles, Joseph Cotton, and others. RKO, 1941.
MLA	*Ball of Fire*. Dir. Howard Hawks. Prod. Samuel Goldwyn. Screenplay by Charles Brackett and Billy Wilder. Photography by Gregg Toland. Music by Alfred Newman. With Gary Cooper, Barbara Stanwyck, Dana Andrews. MGM, 1941.

Basic forms for a motion picture or video tape:

Producer, P. P. (Producer), & Director, D. D. (Director). (Date of publication). Title of motion picture [Motion picture]. Country of origin: Studio or distributor. (APA)

Producer, P. P. (Producer), and Director, D. D. (Director). Title of motion picture [Motion picture]. Date of publication. Country of origin: Studio or distributor. (MLA)

Short Film, Filmstrip, Videotape, or Slide Program

APA	Kopelson, A. (Producer), & Stone, O. (Writer/Director). (1986). *Platoon* [Motion Picture]. United States: Hemdale Film Corporation.
MLA	*Platoon*. Prod. Around Kopelson. Dir. Oliver Stone. Perf. Tom Berenger, Willem Dafoe, and Charlie Sheen. Videocassette. Hemdale Film Corporation. 1986.

APA	Smith, J. D. (Producer), & Smithee, A. F. (Director). (2001). *Really Big Disaster Movie* [Motion picture]. United States: Paramount Pictures.
MLA	Sorkin, Arla, and Terry Kahn, filmmakers. *Scarcity and Planning*. Dir. Terry Kahn. Walt Disney Educational Media, 1977. 16mm. color sd., 17 min.
APA	*National Defense*. 2 filmstrips, 2 audiocassettes. Written by Kate Griggs. Photo ed. Wendy Davis. Prentice-Hall Media, 1982. Each 84 fr. color., $1^7/_8$ ips, mono, 27 min.
MLA	Harris, M. (Producer), & Turley, M. J. (Director). (2002). *Writing Labs: A History* [Motion picture]. (Available from Purdue University Pictures, 500 Oval Drive, West Lafayette, IN 47907).
APA	*Taxes: Why We Have Them*. Videocassette. BFA Educational Media, 1979. 3/4", 14 min.
MLA	Blackwood, Michael, prod. And dir. *Pablo Picasso: The Legacy of a Genius*. Videocasstte. Blackwood Productions, 1982. 90 min.

Live Theatrical or Musical Performance

APA	*La Cage Aux Folles*. (21 Mar. 1984). Dir. Arthur Laurents. By Harvey Fierstein. Music by Jerry Herman. With Gene Barry and George Hearn. Palace Theater, New York.
MLA	*La Cage Aux Folles*. Dir. Arthur Laurents. By Harvey Fierstein. Music by Jerry Herman. With Gene Barry and George Hearn. Palace Theater, New York. 21 Mar. 1984.
MLA	Bailey, Pearl, and Louie Bellson Jazz Quartet. Kinaroth Hall, Ein Gev, Israel. 8 May 1981.
MLA	Nichols, Mike, dir. *The Real Thing*. By Tom Stoppard. With Jeremy Irons and Laila Robins. Plymouth Theater, New York. 3 Jan. 1985.

Basic forms for a television broadcast or television series:

Producer, P. P. (Producer). (Date of broadcast or copyright). Title of broadcast [Television broadcast or Television series]. City of origin: Studio or distributor. (APA)

Producer, P. P. (Producer). Title of broadcast [Television broadcast or Television series]. Date of broadcast or copyright. City of origin: Studio or distributor. (MLA)

Basic Forms for a single episode of a television series:

Writer, W. W. (Writer), & Director, D. D. (Director). (Date of publication). Title of episode [Television series episode]. In P. Producer (Producer), Series Title. City of origin: Studio or distributor. (APA)

Writer, W. W. (Writer), and Director, D. D. (Director). Title of episode [Television series episode]. In P. Producer (Producer), Series Title. (Date of publication). City of origin: Studio or distributor. (MLA)

Broadcast or Telecast of Performance

APA	*Cost Fan Thtte*. By Wolfgang Amadeus Mozart. With Carol Vaness, Julie Murray, David Randall. Cond. Jeffrey Tate. Metropolitan.
MLA	*Cost Fan Thtte*. By Wolfgang Amadeus Mozart. With Carol Vaness, Julie Murray, David Randall. Cond. Jeffrey Tate. Metropolitan.
APA	Important, I. M. (Producer). (1990, November 1). *The Nightly News Hour*. [Television broadcast]. New York: Central Broadcasting Service.
MLA	Opera. Texaco-Metropolitan Opera Radio Network. WTMI, Miami. 22 Dec. 1984.

Basic forms for a music recording

Songwriter, W. W. (Date of copyright). Title of song [Recorded by artist if different from song writer]. On Title of album [Medium of recording]. Location: Label. (Recording date if different from copyright date) (APA)

Songwriter, W. W. "Title of song" [Recorded by artist if different from song writer]. On Title of album [Medium of recording]. (Date of copyright). Location: Label. (Recording date if different from copyright date) (MLA)

Phonograph Record or Audiotap

APA	Puccini, G. (1964). *Tosca*. With Zinka Milanov, Jussi Bjoerling, and Leonard Warren. Cond. Erich Leinedort. Rome Opera House Orch. And Chorus. RCA Victrola, VICS 6000.

MLA	Puccini, Giacomo. *Tosca*. With Zinka Milanov, Jussi Bjoerling, and Leonard Warren. Cond. Erich Leinedort. Rome Opera House Orch. and Chorus. RCA Victrola, VICS 6000, 1964.
APA	Taupin, B. (1975). Someone saved my life tonight [Recorded by Elton John]. On *Captain fantastic and the brown dirt cowboy* [CD]. London: Big Pig Music Limited.
MLA	Haydn, Franz Joseph. Symphony no. 101 "Clock" and Symphony no. 103. Cond. Leonard Bernstein. New York Philharmonic Orch. Columbia, M33531, 1975.
APA	*Marilyn Home Live at La Scala*. Martin Katz, piano/kiavier. CBS Masterworks, M37819, 1983.
MLA	King, Martian Luther, Jr. "I Have a Dream." *Free at Last*. Motown, 3150, 1968.
APA	Lowell, Robert. *Robert Lowell Reads His Works*. Carillon, YP 301, 1961.
MLA	Poe, Edgar Allan. *The Pit and the Pendulum*. Cassette. Read by Raymond Harris. Jametown, TC-5527, 1982. 29 min., mono.
MLA	Britton, James N. *Writing to Learn and Learning to Write*. Cassette. Rec. 18 Apr. 1972 Troy State College. Urbana, NCTE. 4914.

A web site.
- Important Elements:

Author / Title of article / Title of magazine / Volume number (if needed) / Date of Access / Address of Site

- It is necessary to list your date of access because web postings are often updated, and information available at one date may no longer be available later. Be sure to include the complete address for the site.

Electronic Book

APA	Norman, R. (1998). *The moral philosophers*. New York: Oxford University Press. Retrieved August 14, 2001, from Duke University, Duke University Libraries, netLibrary Web site: http://www.netlibrary.com.

MLA	Norman, Richard. The Moral Philosophers. New York: Oxford UP, 1998. Duke University Libraries, Durham, NC. 14 Aug. 2001 <http://www.netlibrary.com>.

An article on a web site

APA	Using Modern Language Association (MLA) Format. (2003). *Purdue Online Writing Lab*. Purdue University. 6 Feb. 2003 <http://owl.english.purdue.eduhandouts/research/r_mla.html>.
MLA	"Using Modern Language Association (MLA) Format." *Purdue Online Writing Lab*. 2003. Purdue University. 6 Feb. 2003 <http://owl.english.purdue.eduhandouts/research/r_mla.html>.
MLA	Poland, Dave. "The Hot Button." *Roughcut*. 26 Oct. 1998. Turner Network Television. 28 Oct. 1998 <http://www.roughcut.com>.

An article/publication from an electronic database

MLA	Smith, Martin. "World Domination for Dummies." *Journal of Despotry* Feb. 2000: 66-72. *Expanded Academic ASAP*. Gale Group Databases. Purdue University Libraries, West Lafayette, IN. 19 February 2003 <http://www.infotrac.galegroup.com>.
APA	Smyth, A. M., Parker, A. L., & Pease, D. L. (2002). A study of enjoyment of peas. *Journal of Abnormal Eating*, 8(3). Retrieved February 20, 2003, from PsycARTICLES database.

Article in a reference database on CD-ROM

MLA	"World War II." *Encarta*. CD-ROM. Seattle: Microsoft, 1999.

Article from a periodically published database on CD-ROM

MLA	Reed, William. "Whites and the Entertainment Industry." *Tennessee Tribune* 25 Dec. 1996: 28. *Ethnic NewsWatch*. CD-ROM. Data Technologies. Feb. 1997.

An Online Image or Series of Images

MLA	Smith, Greg. "Rhesus Monkeys in the Zoo." No date. Online image. Monkey Picture Gallery. 3 May 2003. < http://monkeys. online. org. /rhesus. jpg >

E-mail (or other personal communications)

APA	Note: In APA style, email message should not be included in the Works Cited list, because they are personal communications and cannot be retrieved by a third party. They should, however, be cited in text (see APA: In-text Parenthetical Citations.)
MLA	Baker, Virginia. "Tips for finding sources." E-mail to Jane Robinson. 28 Oct. 2002.

E-mail to you

MLA	Kunka, Andrew. "Re: Modernist Literature." E-mail to the author: 15 Nov. 2000.

Email communication between two parties

MLA	Neyhart, David. "Re: Online Tutoring." E-mail to Joe Barbato. 1 Dec. 2000.

Online Posting

APA	Casper, K. (2001, October 1). Re: watered down curricula. Message posted to http://mathforum. org/ epigone/ math-teach.
MLA	Casper, Karl. "Re: Watered Down Curricula." Online posting. 1 Oct. 2001. Math Forum. 26 Oct. 2001 http://mathforum. org/epigone/math-teach/wheebrelwhing/7zq2783 aznop@ forum. mathforum. com.
APA	Frook, B. D. (1999, July 23). New inventions in the cyberworld of toylandia [Msg 25]. Message posted to http://groups. earthlink. com/forum/messages/00025. html.

MLA	Karper, Erin. "Welcome!" Online posting. 23 Oct. 2000. Professional Writing Bulletin Board. 12 Nov. 2000 http://linnell.english.purdue.edu/ubb/Forum2/HTML/000001.html.

 Review Questions

What should be included in works cited?

 Assignments

1. Arrange the following publication information in its proper order.

①Author: Alexander W. Astin Title: Achieving Educational Excellence. Publication information: Washington: Jossey-Bass, 1985.

②Author: Charles Darling Title: "The Decadence: The 1890s." Publication information: Humanities Division Lecture Series. Capital Community College, Hartford. 12 Sept. 1996.

③Author: Gloria Anzaldua Title: Borderlands/La Frontera: The New Mestiza. Publication information: San Francisco: Spinsters/ Aunt Lute, 1987.

④Author: J. Anderson Title: "Keats in Harlem." Publication information: New Republic 204.14 (8 Apr. 1991): n. pag. Online. EBSCO. 29 Dec. 1996.

⑤Author: Joe Feinberg Title: "Freedom and Behavior Control." Publication information: Encyclopedia of Bio-ethics, I, 93-101. (MLA) New York: Free Press, 1992.

⑥Author: John S. Christie Title: "Fathers and Virgins: Garcia Marquez's Faulknerian Chronicle of a Death Foretold." Publication information: Latin American Literary Review 13.3 (Fall 1993): 21-29.

⑦Author: Larry Williams Title: "Powerful Urban Drama Builds in Bell's Tense 'Ten Indians'." Publication information: Rev. of Ten Indians, by Madison Smartt Bell. Hartford Courant 1 Dec. 1996: G3.

⑧Author: Lauren P. Burka Title: "A Hypertext History of Multi-User Dimensions." Publication information: MUD History. URL: http://www.ccs.neu.edu/home/lpb/mud-history.html (5 Dec. 1994).

⑨Author: Lewis Mumford Title: Highways Around the World. Publication information: New York: Prentice, 1967.

⑩Author: Lewis Mumford Title: The Highway and the City. Publication information: New York: Harcourt Brace and World, 1963.

⑪Author: M. Pikarsky and Christensen, D. Title: Urban Transportation Policy and Management. Publication information: Boston: D. C. Heath, 1976.

⑫Author: Margot C. Hennessy Title: "Listening to the Secret Mother: Reading J. E. Wideman's Brothers and Keepers." Publication information: American Women's Autobiography: Fea (s)ts of Memory. Ed. Margo Culley. Madison, WI: U. Wisconsin P, 1992. 302-314.

⑬Author: N. M. Metheny, and W. D. Snively. Title: Nurses' Handbook of Fluid Balance. Publication information: Philadelphia: Lippincott, 1967.

⑭Author: Natalie Angier Title: "Chemists Learn Why Vegetables are Good for You." Publication information: New York Times 13 Apr. 1993, late ed. : C1. New York Times Ondisc. CD-ROM. UMI-Proquest. Oct. 1993.

⑮Author: Pamela Schneider Title: Seniors: What Keeps Us Going. Publication information: Interview. With Linda Storrow. Natl. Public Radio. WNYC. New York. 11 July 1988.

⑯Author: Richard H. C. Seabrook Title: "Community and Progress." Publication information: cybermind@jefferson.village.virginia.edu (22 Jan. 1994).

⑰Author: Robert Redford Publication information: Personal Interview. 24 Sept. 1996.

⑱Author: Ronald E. Pepin Title: Literature of Satire in the Twelfth Century. Publication information: Lewiston: Edwin Mellen P, 1988.

⑲Author: U.S. Dept. of Commerce. Title: U.S. Industrial Outlook. Publication information: Washington, D.C., Government Printing Office, 1990.

⑳Author: V.S. Jones, M.E. Eakle, and C.W. Foerster. Title: A History of Newspapers. Publication information: Cambridge, Eng. : Cambridge UP, 1987.

㉑Author: Webb Shaw Title: "Professionals are Required to Report Abuse." Publication information: Akron (Ohio) Beacon Journal, Nov. 11, 1984 (Located in NewsBank [Microform]. Welfare and Social Problems, 1984, 51: D12-14, fiche).

㉒Title: "Money." Publication information: Compton's Precyclopedia. 1977 ed., X, 80-91.

㉓Title: "The Political Problems of Arms-Treaty Verification." Publication information: Technology Review May/June 1986: 34-47.

㉔Title: "U.S. troops capture chief aide to warlord." Publication information: Hartford Courant 22 Sept. 1993: A5.

㉕Title: "What's a Hoatzin?" Publication information: Newsweek 27 Sept. 1993: 72.

㉖Title: Creation vs. Evolution: "Battle of the Classroom." Publication information: Videocassette. Dir. Ryall Wilson, PBS Video, 1982. (MLA) 58 min.

㉗Title: Creation vs. Evolution: "Battle of the Classroom." Publication information: Videocassette. Dir. Ryall Wilson, PBS Video, 1982. (MLA) 58 min.

2. Construct a Works Cited page for the following sources, putting all of the information in the correct order according to the learned format.

①Your research led you to a book titled Emily Dickinson: A Collection of Critical Essays, in which you found an essay called Emily Dickinson and the Limits of Judgment. The book was edited by Richard B. Sewall, and the essay was the work of Yvor Winters. The essay began on page 38 and ended on page 56. The book was published in 1963 by Prentice-Hall, located in Englewood Cliffs, New Jersey.

②Your research uncovered an essay, Father and Daughter: Edward and Emily Dickinson, which was published in a journal, American Literature, in January 1960. This was volume 40, and the essay covered pages 510 to 523. The writer was Owen Thomas.

③When quoting Emily Dickinson's poetry, you used a collection called The Complete Poems of Emily Dickinson, which was published in 1960 by Little, Brown and Company, located in Boston, Massachusetts. The person who edited the poems was Thomas H. Johnson.

④When quoting the poet's letters, you used a three-volume collection called The Letters of Emily Dickinson, which was published in Cambridge, Massachusetts, by the Harvard University Press in 1958. The editors were Thomas H. Johnson and Theodora Ward.

⑤You read a book written by the critic Paul J. Ferlazzo in 1976. The book was titled Emily Dickinson and was published by Twayne Publishers, which is located in Boston, Massachusetts.

⑥You read a tribute to the poet, called The First Lady of Mt. Holyoke, which appeared in the South Hadley (Massachusetts) Gazette on December 10, 1980. This unsigned essay appeared on the second and third pages of the second section of the newspaper.

⑦You also wrote a letter to a professor at Mt. Holyoke College, Joanna Caldwell, who is an authority on the poet and her works. You quoted a remark from her reply to you, which was written on November 4, 1980.

⑧You read an article in the magazine Psychology Today, written by John Forsyte, Joanna Caldwell, and Edgar Polishook. The article, titled Emily Dickinson: Inhibited Genius, appeared in the July 1979 issue on pages 68 to 80.

⑨You read a review of Ferlazzo's book (see item 5), written by Joanna Caldwell, which was published in PMLA, volume 65, pages 343 to 345. This issue was published in May 1980.

Unit 10 论文终稿 Final Presentation

1) First Page

- The following information appears on the title page: the title, your name, your instructor's name, the course and section number, and the date on which the paper is submitted.
- If you are to follow MLA style, do not use a title page. Instead, type your name, your instructor's name, the name of the course, and the date, each on its own line in the upper left-hand corner, double-spaced.
- Double-space again and center the title on your paper, begin each word except articles, conjunctions, and short prepositions with a capital letter.

```
            The title

               By
              XXX

       Academic Writing
           Section
       Professor ×××
          The Date
```

MLA:

- Underline or put in quotation marks titles of books, films, or short stories.

- If your title requires more than one line of type, double-space between them.
- Use a quadruple space (two double-spaces) between the end of your title and the beginning of the text of the paper.
- Begin with the usual five-space indentation from the left margin for the first paragraph.

2) Outline Page

- Put the outline before the text, using the same heading (name, instructor, course, date) and centering the title as on the first page of your paper.
- Double-space after the title (and throughout the thesis statement and outline) and write the thesis of your paper, adhering to established left and right margins for typing.
- Center the designation "Outline" (without the quotation marks), then double-space and begin writing your outline.
- If you need more than one page for the outline, put your name at the top right in the usual place and use consecutive small Roman numerals.
- Should you have several pages of front matter before the text, such as an outline, preface, or synopsis, number those pages with consecutive small Roman numerals (i, ii, iii) just after your name.

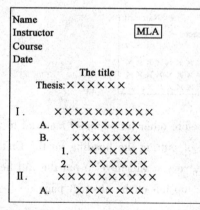
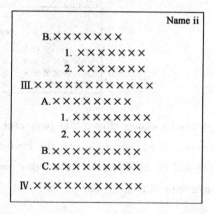
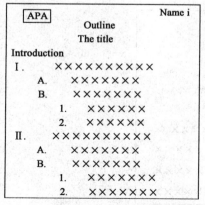
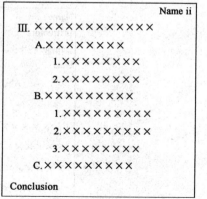

3) Abstract

- Business, technical, and scientific research works sometimes have an abstract of the study.
- Center the heading "Abstract," without the quotation marks, in capital and lowercase letters, one inch down from the top of the paper.
- Write no more than one page summarizing the contents of your research paper.
- Observe the usual margins of one inch on each side, and remember to number the page with small Roman numerals if it is part of other front matter; if it isn't, omit any number.

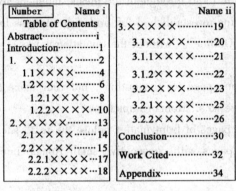

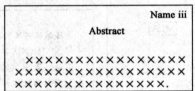

- This page usually comes after a title page and before other introductory material to the paper itself. However, if you are following the custom of putting the heading on the first page of the text, there will be no title page before this one, so you will have to put the full heading (your name, instructor's name, course, date) at the top left of the abstract page.

MLA:

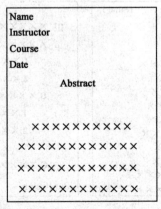

4) The Text

- Follow the conventions of style and documentation you've learned when you type the text of your research paper.
- Be sure you have acknowledged all material that isn't original within the text.
- Type the entire text double spaced on only one side of each page and leave one-inch margins all around.
- Indent the beginning of each new paragraph five spaces from the left margin.
- If you begin with a long quotation, however, follow the indentation you would anywhere else in the paper: start each line ten spaces from the left margin and end each a few spaces before the right margin you set for yourself.

5) Page Numbering

- Number all pages of the text, appendixes, works cited, and so on, consecutively in the upper right-hand corner, one-half inch down from the top.
- Put each number one space after your first initial and last name; check spacing so the line will end one inch in from the right-hand side of the paper.
- If you are to follow APA style, type the first word (or first two words) of your title, rather than your name, next to the page number.
- Begin with the number 2 because the first page of the text is assumed to be 1, even though it isn't numbered.

MLA:

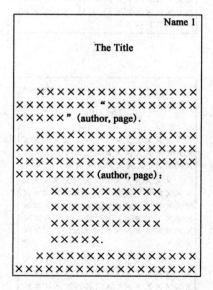

APA:

```
                                    Title 1
                                  The Title

            ××××××××××××××
        ××××××××"××××××××
        ××" (author, year, page). ×××××
        ×××××××××.

            ××××××××××××××
        ××××××××××××××××
        ×××××"××××××××××
        ×××××××"(author, year, page).
        ××××××××××××××.

            ××××××××××××××
        ××××× (author, year, page):
              ××××××××××
              ××××××××××
```

Number:

```
                                    Name 1
                                  The Title

            ××××××××××××××
        ××××××××"××××××
        ××××××" (1, page). ×××××.

            ××××××××××××××
        ××××××××××××××××
        ××××××××(2). ××××××
        ×××××××××
        ××××××.

            ××××××××××××××
        ××××××××××××××××
        ××××××× (3, 4, 5). ×××××
        ×××××××
```

Notes:

```
                                    Name 1
                                  The Title

            ××××××××××××××
        ××××××××××××××××
        ××××[1]. ×××××××××××.

            ××××××××××××××
        ××××××××××××××××
        ××××××××[2]. ×××××××
        ××××××××××××××××
        ×××.

            ××××××××××××××
        ××××××××××××××××
        ×××××××[3]. ×××××××××
        ××××××××××××××××
```

6) End notes

- If you are not using in-text parenthetical documentation, you will have numbered all material that needs documentation or other comment by successive superscript numbers within the text of your paper.
- You then need to supply the explanation for each by matching the superscript number and listing all such material in end notes.
- Center the title "Notes" (without the quotation marks) on the first page one inch from the top.
- Double-space, indent five spaces from the left margin, and begin typing the information for each note with the appropriate superscript Arabic number.
- Omit punctuation after the number, but allow one space before you begin the reference.
- Double-space all lines.
- Begin second and subsequent lines for each reference at the left margin.
- Continue the page numbering successively from the text of your paper.
- Make a final check to be sure the note numbering on these pages corresponds to the notes in the text of your paper.

Notes:

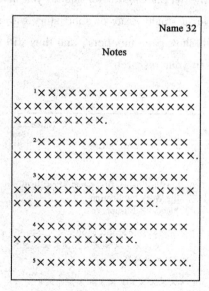

7) Works Cited

- Begin this list on a new page at the end of your text by putting your name and the page (numbered consecutively after other material) half an inch below the top at the right-hand corner of

the paper and then centering the title one inch from the top of the paper.
- Double-space and begin the first entry at the left margin.
- Continue typing double spaced throughout the Works Cited.
- The first line of each entry begins at the left margin but subsequent lines are indented five spaces.
- Works Cited are always presented in alphabetical order by the last name of the author or editor (except the numbered system).
- In the case of multiple authorship or editorship, alphabetize by the name of the first person shown on the title page.
- If neither such name is available, alphabetize the work by the first word of its title, beginning the entry at the left margin just as you would a person's name.
- If the first word of a title you are alphabetizing is a, an, or the, use the second word for alphabetizing, but write the title as it actually appears.
- If an author is represented by more than one item, put the person's works in alphabetical order by title.
- Instead of repeating the name when you type the list of Works Cited, substitute three hyphens followed by a period and two spaces before starting the next title.
- Never number the items in the Works Cited. Nor should you note the page numbers you consulted within a book (except for a single essay or short story within a collection).
- Only periodical citations will show page numbers, and they will be for the whole article, even if just half a page was useful in your research.

MLA:

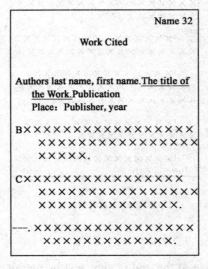

APA:

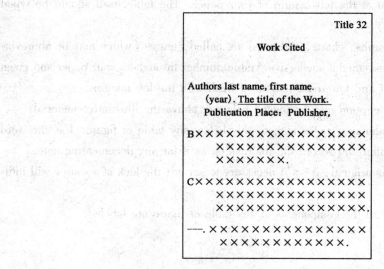

Number:

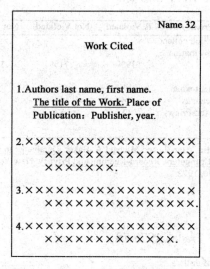

Illustrative Materials: Charts, Tables, Graphs, Pictures.
- Put illustrative materials as close as you can to the portion of the text they illustrate in order to make your research paper most easily read and understood.
- Since visual representations of complex ideas are sometimes helpful to readers, plan on using whatever will fit your subject.
- A table is labeled in capital and lowercase letters above the visual and is followed by an Arabic number showing successive tables in your research paper.

- On a second line, a caption in capital and lowercase letters tells what the table shows. Both the label and the caption begin at the left margin of your paper. The table itself should be typed double spaced.
- Photographs, drawings, graphs, charts, and maps are called Figures (which may be abbreviated as "Fig."). Each is assigned a successive Arabic number throughout your paper and given a title or caption in capital and lowercase letters set flush with the left margin.
- Both the label and title or caption may be placed below or above the illustrative material.
- Give the source of any explanatory notes immediately below any table or figure. Use the word "Source" followed by a colon and record the information as if for any documenting note.
- If the illustrative material is original, it isn't necessary to say so; the lack of a source will indicate that it is.
- As a final check, be sure all the components of any table or figure are labeled.

8) A table

Example:

Table 1

Personal Experiences with Privacy Invasions

Violation of Privacy by	Is Violated	Not Violated	Not Sure
Computers which collect a lot of information about you	19%	71%	10%
...			
The government when it takes a census	14	84	2
Employment interviews	11	83	6
...			

Source: Westin, Alan F., and Michael A. Baker. <u>Databanks in a Free Society: Computers, Record-Keeping and Privacy.</u> New York: Quadrangle, 1972.

Figure 1

U. S.—Japan Merchandise Trade: 1975-78

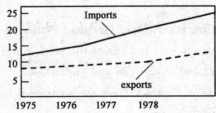

Source: U.S. Bureau of the Census, <u>Statistical Abstract of the United States: 1979.</u> Washington: GPO, 1979.

9) Annotation

- An annotation is a short statement, often not even a sentence, that tells what is important or characteristic about a source.
- If you are asked to make annotations, head the page on which they begin "Annotated List of Works Cited" and begin each annotation after the period that ends the citation entry. Continue the hanging indentation form.
- Annotations begin with capital letters and end with periods. They follow the same hanging indentation form of the entry.
- Keep annotations brief; one or two remarks will suffice.

Example:

Miller, Arthur R. The Assault on Privacy. Ann Arbor: U of Michigan P, 1971. How new technology and information-gathering methods point to need for new legal framework and reexamination of attitudes.

- Annotations are particularly helpful to anyone who wants to decide whether or not to consult the sources you have used in preparing your research paper.
- If you know you will have to supply annotations to the works you cite in your paper, you should write comments on your Works Cited cards as you search various sources.
- Annotations do one or more of the following, as each example shows:
  - ➤ State the general content of a source:
    Supports the author's contention that <u>Painted Veils</u> was written in only six weeks.
  - ➤ Make a judgment about the source:
    Particularly lucid explanation of physiology of polygraph testing.
  - ➤ Point out valuable properties or qualities of the source:
    Contains photographs by the author.
  - ➤ Note the viewpoint or bias of the author:
    Notably lacking are suggestions of or allowances for alternate viewpoints.
  - ➤ Tell something about the author of the source:
    Author is political science professor who has published widely on privacy.

A sample Annotated List of Works Cited:

Examples:

"Big Brother Is a Big Worry." Newsweek 14 May 1979: 42. Contains Louis Harris poll.

Bouchard, Robert F., and Justin D. Franklin. Guidebook to the Freedom of Information and Privacy Acts. New York: Boardman, 1980. Extensively documented explanation of two acts noted in title.

Carroll, John M. Confidential Information Sources: Public and Private. Los Angeles: Security, 1975. Complete course in how to make personal investigations using existing medical, credit, law, etc. records.

Columbia Human Rights Law Review Staff, eds. Surveillance. Dataveillance. and Personal Freedom. Fair Lawn: Burdick, 1973. Articles by various authors on use and abuse of information technology, especially how computers and data banks interfere with personal privacy.

"Computers: The Limits of Use in a Democratic Society." U. N. Chronicle Apr. 1983: 30-32. Describes present uses of computerized personal data systems and need for privacy safeguards.

Hoffman, Lance J. ed. Security and Privacy in Computer Systems. Los Angeles: Melville, 1973. Technical aspects of security problems and significant comments in the field.

10) Appendix

- An *appendix* lets you include additional illustrations or other materials that amplify the text without interrupting your reader's concentration in going through the research paper.
- Put an appendix (appendixes or appendices) after the Works Cited.
- Appendixes containing material relevant to your research and illustrating or supporting it are sometimes put at the end of the paper.
- You might need to include illustrative materials such as pictures, graphs, or charts with the text or as appendixes to it.
- Write the word in capital letters and centered, one inch down from the top of the first page.
- If you have more than one appendix, give each one an identifying capital letter, beginning with A.
- Continue with successive page numbers as you do through the text of the research paper; however, do not write a number on the first page of the first appendix, even though you count that as a page.

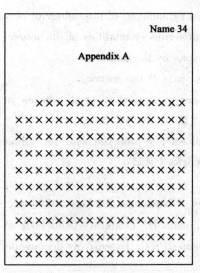

11) Proofreading

- It's imperative to correct any errors.

- Take time to proofread your entire research paper before turning it in.
- If you find any errors you have overlooked, you can correct them in ink.
- Any page that requires extensive corrections should be retyped.

12) Organization

ABSTRACT

Tell what is to be, why it is important and what you hope to do. Keep it short. No more than one page.

TABLE OF CONTENTS

Self-explanatory.

Part One: Chapter I

Introduction

Problem Statement

Background

Purpose

Theoretical Foundation/Conceptual Foundation

Assumptions

Limitations

Scope

Definition of Terms

Hypotheses or Research Questions

Significance

Summary

Chapter II——Literature Review

Your literature review needs to look at several important aspects.

①It should give research, which utilizes the same design or methodology you will be using.

②Demonstrate that you have examined a great deal of relevant research concerning your project.

③The literature review is a fine place to develop your theoretical underpinnings, again giving fairly current sources to substantiate your use of this theoretical and conceptual background.

④Use primary sources as much as possible. When using secondary sources, make certain you identify them.

⑤Finally, but actually the very first activity in the Literature Review, is to describe the organization.

Chapter III——Methodology

- Introduction. Tell us again what the problem is, the purpose and a little background.
- Design of the Study. It must include:
  ➤ Description of the target population.

- If you are going to use a sample, show how you will obtain this sample, where it comes from and how many you anticipate will participate.
- Tell how many will be in the sample.
- Tell what you intend to do with this sample.

Chapter IV——Results, Presentation of the Data
- Start with a brief Introduction. Restate the Problem. Give us again a description of the population and the sample. Briefly tell us again how you obtained the data when and where.
- Do this in answering your research questions or in supporting or rejecting your hypotheses.
- Summarize.

Chapter V——Summary, Conclusions and Recommendations
- What can you draw from your findings? Give your question a brief discussion of the finding and the conclusion drawn from it.
- Show how your results reflect or reject the theoretical foundation or conceptual organization. Show how this study impacted social change.
- Finally, give recommendations for a future study—what you might have done differently.

Assignments

Write an academic research paper in your research field according to the guide to the process you've learned in class. You may refer to the samples.

    Word limit: 5000 words

    Time limit: date-month-year

    Hand in your typed writing

参考答案
Answers to Exercises

Unit 1

Assignments 1

Subject: an area of interest that can be narrowed down to a suitable topic; subjects are either too broad or too loosely defined to serve as topics for research papers.

Examples: ...

Topic: a reasonably narrow, clearly defined area of interest that could be thoroughly investigated within the limits set for a given research assignment.

Examples: ...

Assignments 2

(omitted)

Unit 2

Assignments 1

- The subject must lead to a good topic.
- The topic should raise questions that have no simple answers.
- The topic should be specific rather than broad or general.
- The topic should be highly controversial or less well-known.

Assignments 2

- Choose a subject—one of the following or any other that meets the requirements of this course
- Go to three or more background sources and find two to five potentially workable topics
- Select the topic that seems most interesting and/or most workable.

Unit 3

Review Questions 1

Brainstorming is a useful approach to finding the best topic. If you are already fairly familiar with your subject area, a little brainstorming may turn up a number of good possibilities for research. Brainstorming consists of wide-open, no-holds-barred thinking about some subject, in which your mind is free to produce any and all ideas that come along.

Review Questions 2

The purpose behind background reading is twofold. First, you want to feel certain that you have chosen the best available topic. Other possibilities may appear during your background reading, and one of them might be even better than your first one. Second, even if your original idea for a topic was a fine one, you will benefit from refreshing your knowledge of the subject, thereby giving yourself a better handle on the many new facts and ideas your research will uncover.

Review Questions 3

A good topic raises questions that have no simple answers. When there is no single, accepted answer, the experts will disagree to some extent, which is just what you want. If topics can be fully covered by reading just one, or two sources, or if it has had an accepted answer, there is no need for you to research. Although you may use different examples and different words to express the idea, there is no challenge in such a topic.

Review Questions 4

There are two good reasons for starting out with a hypothesis, even if it may prove to be somewhat inaccurate. First, a hypothesis points you in the right direction by indicating the specific questions you need answers for. As you look for information that either agrees or disagrees with your hypothesis, you move closer to the "truth", and that will be your thesis. Second, the hypothesis can test the thoroughness of your research. If your conclusions are to be considered valid, you must consult a variety of sources representing different viewpoints. You should not try to defend your hypothesis by using only those sources that support it. Your mission is to present readers with the full picture so they will have enough information to evaluate your conclusions.

Unit 4

Review Questions 1

Before you read, you should consider:

——Which authors seem outstanding in the field?

——What is the date of publication?

——How credible does a source seem?

When you read, you should consider:

——What does the language of a source tell you?

——Which sources seem to give you the most information?

——What facts keep reappearing in your reading?

Review Questions 2

– Legibility

– Accuracy

– Completeness

Review Questions 3

(1) Summary

To record in your own words the essence of a passage and omit examples or explanations.

The summary reports only the central idea of what an author has said and must not include your own interpretation or a comment on the meaning.

Summary must follow the organization or order of the original source.

(2) Paraphrase

A paraphrase states the ideas of a source in your own words, but follows the original writing phrase by phrase; therefore, a paraphrase not only has the same organization as the original, but it is also approximately the same length.

Review Questions 4

Paraphrased notes are often preferable to summaries because they are more detailed and specific. They are often preferable to quotations because the text is in your own words rather than in someone else's.

Review Questions 5

No, there is no need to do so. A paraphrase states the ideas of a source in your own words, but follows the original writing phrase by phrase; therefore, a paraphrase not only has the same organization as the original, but it is also approximately the same length.

Review Questions 6

The words of your source are written in a style so perfect, so suitable, or so vivid that they seem beyond changing.

The material is so significant or controversial, or its source so authoritative, that it must be stated with utmost accuracy.

The wording of a source needs to be transmitted accurately and you want to be sure to do so. Sometimes wording is so succinct that to tamper with it is to violate a piece of fine writing, so you might decide to use a quotation note.

Review Questions 7

Use quotation marks around all words and phrases that you get from any of your research sources and cite the source both in note cards and in your paper.

Credit the source of any ideas, including summaries and paraphrases, you get from any of your research sources by documentation when you write your paper.

Be sure every source in your documentation is also in the Works Cited.

Give an adequate introduction or otherwise clearly delineate borrowed words and ideas.

Unit 5

Review Questions 1

- To indicate the relationship of ideas to each other
- To show which are important and which are subordinate
- To remind you of the order of presentation
- To make you rearrange ideas without difficulty
- To judge the effectiveness of the organization of your whole paper

Review Questions 2

- What kind of outlining is best for our paper?
- What are the outline conventions?
- How to make the content of the outline meaningful and helpful to our final writing?

Unit 7

Review Questions 1

We must write at least three versions of the paper: a rough draft, a revised draft, and a polished final manuscript suitable for submission. Writing is a complex activity that involves constant thinking of ideas and searching for the best wording and phrasing. New thoughts will occur to us as we write.

Review Questions 2

(1) Clarify the topic you are going to write about.

(2) State your position on the topic you have chosen.

(3) Relate your topic to something current or well known.

(4) Challenge some generally held assumption about your topic.

(5) Show something paradoxical about your topic or about the material you will present.

(6) Use a brief quotation if you can find an applicable one that is provocative or that makes a general statement about your topic.

(7) State some striking facts or statistics you have discovered about your topic.

(8) Place your topic in time by giving some historical or chronological information.

(9) Give a brief description or background resume' of some person or event of significance to your topic.

Review Questions 3

(1) Unity and coherence

(2) Adequate support

(3) Emphasis

(4) Concreteness and specificity

Review Questions 4

(1) Use transitional words

(2) Use pronouns for important nouns

(3) Establish some logical order

(4) Use repeat key words and phrases

(5) Use a consistent Point of view

(6) Integrate information

Review Questions 5

(1) If you have written an argumentive or persuasive paper, remind the audience of what you want them to do or think in order to respond to your presentation.

(2) Use a brief quotation that summarizes the ideas or attitudes you have expressed throughout the paper.

(3) Make some statement about your thesis, instead of merely repeating it.

(4) Return to some initial generalization and show how you have proved, disproved, or enlarged upon it.

(5) Link what you have written either to something known or to what seems a future possibility.

(6) State a conclusion you have reached about your subject.

Review Questions 6

(1) Reconsidering the organization

(2) Revising paragraphs

(3) Revising sentences

(4) Revising word choice

Unit 8

Review Questions 1

Direct quotations

Borrowed ideas (including paraphrases and summaries)

Visual material such as maps, charts, diagrams, and pictures that you did not devise

Review Questions 2

Social, natural sciences and humanities

Review Questions 3

Author's last name or title and the page

Review Questions 4

Complete information about the source as appears in the Works Cited: author, title, publication place, publication name, publication year, pages

Author's last name and pages

Review Questions 5

English and humanities

Review Questions 6

Author's last name or title, the date of publication and the page

Review Questions 7

Natural sciences such as medicine, chemistry, physics, engineering, computer and mathematics

Review Questions 8

Arabic numeral and the page if it is a quotation

Review Questions 9

The author, the title of the work, publication information (place of publication, the name of the publisher and the date of publication), and the page

Review Questions 10

In social science

Review Questions 11

The author's last name or the title, the date

Unit 9

Review Questions

Author's full name. Title of work: Capital letter also for subtitle. Location: Publisher, Year of publication.

Assignments 1

Anderson, J. "Keats in Harlem." *New Republic* 204. 14 (8 Apr. 1991): n. pag. Online. EBSCO. 29 Dec. 1996.
Angier, Natalie. "Chemists Learn Why Vegetables are Good for You." *New York Times* 13 Apr. 1993, late ed.: C1. *New York Times Ondisc*. CD-ROM. UMI-Proquest. Oct. 1993.
Anzaldua, Gloria. *Borderlands/La Frontera: The New Mestiza*. San Francisco: Spinsters/Aunt Lute, 1987.
Astin, Alexander W. *Achieving Educational Excellence*. Washington: Jossey-Bass, 1985.
Burka, Lauren P. "A Hypertext History of Multi-User Dimensions." *MUD History*. URL: http://www.ccs.neu.edu/home/lpb/mud-history.html (5 Dec. 1994).
Christie, John S. "Fathers and Virgins: Garcia Marquez's Faulknerian *Chronicle of a Death Foretold*." *Latin American Literary Review* 13. 3 (Fall 1993): 21-29.
Creation vs. Evolution: "Battle of the Classroom." Videocassette. Dir. Ryall Wilson, PBS Video, 1982. (MLA) 58 min.
Darling, Charles. "The Decadence: The 1890s." Humanities Division Lecture Series. Capital Community College, Hartford. 12 Sept. 1996.

Feinberg, Joe. "Freedom and Behavior Control." *Encyclopedia of Bioethics*, I, 93-101. (MLA) New York: Free Press, 1992.

Hennessy, Margot C. "Listening to the Secret Mother: Reading J. E. Wideman's *Brothers and Keepers*." *American Women's Autobiography: Fea(s)ts of Memory*. Ed. Margo Culley. Madison, WI: U. Wisconsin P, 1992. 302-314.

Jones, V. S., M. E. Eakle, and C. w. Foerster. *A History of Newspapers*. Cambridge, Eng.: Cambridge UP, 1987.

Metheny, N. M., and W. D. Snively. *Nurses' Handbook of Fluid Balance*. Philadelphia: Lippincott, 1967.

"Money." *Compton's Precyclopedia*. 1977 ed., X, 80-91.

Mumford, Lewis. *The Highway and the City*. New York: Harcourt Brace and World, 1963.

—. *Highways Around the World*. New York: Prentice, 1967.

Pepin, Ronald E. *Literature of Satire in the Twelfth Century*. Lewiston: Edwin Mellen P, 1988.

Pikarsky, M. and Christensen, D. *Urban Transportation Policy and Management*. Boston: D. C. Heath, 1976.

"The Political Problems of Arms-Treaty Verification." *Technology Review* May/June 1986: 34-47.

Redford, Robert. Personal Interview. 24 Sept. 1996.

Schneider, Pamela. Interview. *Seniors: What keeps Us Going*. With Linda Storrow. Natl. Public Radio. WNYC. New York. 11 July 1988.

Seabrook, Richard H. C. "Community and Progress." cybermind@jefferson. Village. Virginia. edu (22 Jan. 1994).

Shaw, Webb. "Professionals are Required to Report Abuse." *Akron (Ohio) Beacon Journal*, Nov. 11, 1984 (Located in NewsBank [Microform]. Welfare and Social Problems, 1984, 51: D12-14, fiche).

Sixty Minutes. CBS. WFSB, Hartford. 3 May 1991.

U. S. Dept. of Commerce. *U. S. Industrial Outlook*. Washington, D. C., Government Printing Office, 1990.

"U. S. troops capture chief aide to warlord." *Hartford Courant* 22 Sept. 1993: A5.

"What's a Hoatzin?" *Newsweek* 27 Sept. 1993: 72.

Williams, Larry. "Powerful Urban Drama Builds in Bell's Tense 'Ten Indians'." Rev. of *Ten Indians*, by Madisoon Smartt Bell. *Hartford Courant* 1 Dec. 1996: G3.

Assignments 2

Caldwell, Joanna. Letter to the author. 4 November, 1980.

Caldwell, Joanna. Rev. of <u>Emily Dickonson</u>, by Paul J. Ferlazzo. <u>PMLA</u> vol. 65. May 1980: 343-345.

Dickinson, Emily. <u>The Complete Poems of Emily Dickenson</u>. Ed. Thomas H. Johnson. Boston: Little, 1960.

—. <u>The Letters of Emily Dickenson</u>. Ed. Thomas H. Johnson and Theodora Ward. 3 vols. Cambridge, MA: Harvard UP, 1958.

Ferlazzo, Paul J. <u>Emily Dickonson</u>. Boston: Twyne, 1976.

"The First Lady of Mt. Holyoke." <u>South Hadley (Massachusetts) Gazette</u>. December 10, 1980: sec. 2: 2-3.

Forsyte, John, Joanna Caldwell, and Edgar Polishook. "Emily Dickinson: Inhibited Genius?". <u>Psychology Today</u> July 1979: 68-80.

Thomas, Owen. "Father and Daughter: Edward and Emily Dickenson." <u>American Literature</u> 40 (1960): 510-23.

Winters, Yvor. "Emily Dickens and the Limits of Judgement." <u>Emily Dickenson: A Collection of Critical Essays</u>. Ed. Richard B. Sewall. Englewood Cliffs: Prentice, 1963.

下 篇
实用英语写作篇

Unit 1　求学简历
CVs

　　个人简历是个人经历的概述,主要用在求职和求学。在英文中,简历既可以说是 CV(curriculum vitae),也可以说是 Resume。那么,这两个词有什么区别呢? 二者在长度、内容和应用范围上都有所不同。现在常常有人把 CV 和 Resume 混起来称为"简历",其实 CV 应该是"履历",Resume 才是"简历"。Resume 概述了与求职有关的教育准备和经历,是经验技能的摘要,其主要目的在于说服用人单位雇佣自己;而 CV 则集中说明学术工作,重视与文化程度和学习成绩有直接关系的方面。

　　CV 的长度由其内容确定,有时可长达十页,年轻人的履历一般长度在二至四页,而老资历的通常也有六至八页。内容应包括:姓名、地址、电话号码及电子邮件地址;文化程度;受何奖励和大学奖学金;教学相关经历;有何论著发表;语言或其他技能,课外活动及个人爱好。

　　Resume 大多只需一页,而长度为两页的是具有广泛工作经验的人才。内容应包括:姓名、地址、电子信箱(可选)和电话号码(当地和固定的);工作岗位(可选);教育;获何荣誉奖励;有关功课(可选);经历——应列出组织、地址、日期、工作名称、成绩和职责的简述。

　　综上可见,求学简历叫 CV 似乎更为准确一些。

　　申请国外院校入学或是奖学金资助,提交个人简历时应说明申请人具备了相应的教育背景、技能和工作经历。如果申请人是申请研究生及以上的学历,那么简历中还需要包括相关教学和研究经历、出版的论文或专著、获得的研究资助、加入的专业团体、获奖情况等信息。这些内容能够大大增加被录取的可能性,因为这些可以充分证明申请人的学术能力。

　　留学简历一般包括以下内容:
①申请人基本信息(包括姓名、性别、国籍、婚姻、联系方式等);
②教育背景(即学校、主辅修专业课程、成绩等);
③专业经历(和本专业直接或间接相关的学术活动、工作、实习等);
④社会活动(如社团活动、志愿者经历等);
⑤个人爱好(写出自己强项和闪光点);
⑥其他技能(语言、计算机等)。

　　简历的写作需要注意:
①语言简练,一般省略主语;
②排版清晰,重点突出,可适当运用斜体、大写、加粗、下划线等方式突出重要信息,以便审阅者审阅;
③学术著作、出版物的表达方式以及相关信息(如作者、发表时间、标题、出版刊物等)的顺序要按照国际惯例或专业惯例排列,体现出较好的专业素养;
④简历重点是体现学术能力部分,如出版物等,内容尽量丰富,这无疑将为自己增分不少。

当然,一定要实事求是,切忌无中生有,否则会弄巧成拙。

1. 本科生简历

PERSONAL INFORMATION

 Name:*Li Ming*
 Gender:male
 Date of Birth:28/06/1992
 Telephone: +86-18986852000, +86-28-62652700
 E-mail:liming@ yahoo. cn
 Address: × × × × ×
 Citizenship:People's Republic of China

EDUCATIONAL BACKGROUND

 Bachelor of Science in Financial Engineering
 Economics and Management School, Sichuan University, expected 2016.
 ***General GPA*:3.75 *Major GPA*:3.79 *Ranking*: 3/70**
 Core Courses: Financial Engineering, Financial Economics, Corporate Finance, Securities Investment Analysis, Derivative Security, Fixed Income of Securities, Dynamic Optimization, Time Series Analysis.

RECORDS OF STANDARD TESTS

 TOEFL 102 (Reading 28, Listening 29, Speaking 21, Writing 24) Sep. 2014.
 GRE 1290 (V 520, 65%, Q 770, 88%) AW 4.5, 54% Jun. 2014.
 IELTS 7 (Listening 7.5, Reading 7.5, Writing 6, Speaking 7) May. 2014.

WORKING EXPERIENCES

 China Construction Bank, Sichuan Branch, Chengdu, China July. 2014-Aug. 2014.
 Summer Intern*, *Personal Financial Department
 ◆Assisted with service of personal credit card.
 ◆Participated in the bank's strategic transformation and training program of customer service quality.
 Bank of China, Sichuan Branch, Chengdu, China July. 2013-Aug. 2013.
 Summer Intern*, *Personal Consumption and Loan Department
 ◆Assisted in Housing Mortgage Loans and Auto Loans transactions.
 ◆Helped arrange official files.

◆Participated in the market investigation of Auto Loans which covered more than 90% staff in the bank and obtained more than 100 pieces of useful information.

IMPORTANT PROJECTS

Program of Chinese National Natural Science Foundation
Prof. Assistant and Asset Pricing 2013-2014
◆Collecting relevant materials and papers.
◆Data Analysis and Processing.
◆Assisting with constructing and consummating the pricing model.

PUBLICATIONS

◆Relationship between interest rate and stock price index in China. **X monthly**, Oct. 2015
◆Empirical Research on Return Volatility of Aluminum Futures Market in China. ***Communication in Finance and Accounting***, to be published

ACADEMIC HONORS

◆*Second-class scholarship and "Excellent Student"*, Sichuan University, Sep. 2015
◆*Second Prize of the "National Case Study Competition"*, Dec. 2014
◆*First Prize of the "Competition of economic cases of Industries"*, Dec. 2014
◆*Second-class scholarship and "Excellent Student"*, Sichuan University, Sep. 2014
◆*Second-class scholarship and "Excellent Student"*, Sichuan University Sep. 2013

SKILLS

◆Computer skills: Proficient in Microsoft Word, PowerPoint, Access, Excel and Eviews
◆Other skills: Passed the Highest Level (Level 10) of National Piano Amateur Grade Testing
◆Detail-oriented, team-spirited, responsible and motivated

个人信息

姓名:李明
性别:男
生日:1992年6月28日
电话:+86-18986852000, +86-27-62652700
邮件:liming@yahoo.cn
地址:×××××
国籍:中华人民共和国

教育背景

金融工程学学士

四川大学经管学院,2016 年毕业。
全科 GPA：3.75　专业课程 GPA：3.79　排名：3/70
主要课程:金融工程学、金融经济学、公司理财、证券投资分析、衍生证券、固定收益债券、动态优化、时间序数分析。

标准测试成绩

托福：102(阅读28,听力29,口语21,写作24);测试时间:2014 年 9 月
GRE：1290(V520,65%, Q770,88%) 写作4.5,54%;测试时间:2014 年 6 月
雅思：7(听力7.5,阅读7.5,写作6,口语7);测试时间:2014 年 5 月

工作经历

2014.7—2013.8　　　中国建设银行四川分行 中国成都
暑期实习　私人金融部
- 协助私人信用卡业务
- 参与该行的战略转型以及客服质量的培训项目

2014.7—2013.8　　　中国银行四川分行　中国成都
暑期实习　私人消费信贷部
- 协助房贷、车贷业务
- 协助安排办公档案
- 参与车贷市场调查,该调查覆盖该行90%以上的员工,获得100多份有用信息。

重要项目

中国国家自然科学基金
2013—2014　　　教授助理,资产定价
- 收集相关资料和论文
- 数据分析和加工
- 协助建立健全定价模型

出版论文

中国利率和股价指数之间的关系[J]. X 月刊,2015.10
中国铝期货回报波幅实证研究[J]. 金融会计通讯,将要付梓

学术荣誉

2015.09　　　四川大学二等奖学金和"优秀学生"称号
2014.12　　　"国家案例研究竞赛"第二名
2014.12　　　"行业经济案例竞赛"第一名
2014.09　　　四川大学二等奖学金和"优秀学生"称号
2013.09　　　四川大学二等奖学金和"优秀学生"称号

技能

计算机:熟练掌握 MS Word,PowerPoint,Access,Excel 和 Eviews
其他技能:通过国家业余钢琴十级(最高级)
个人描述:注重细节,团队合作,有责任心,富有激情

2.硕士简历

Li Wei

liwei@gmail.com
Address:×××××

Education

University of California, Berkeley-School of Information
◆Master of Information Management, May 2016
◆Concentration in Human-Computer Interaction, User Interface Design, Information Visualization and Database Management
◆3.79 GPA

Keene State College
◆Bachelor of Science, Mathematics, Minor:Art, May 2008
◆Member of Kappa Mu Epsilon, Mathematics Honor Society
◆3.53 GPA cum laude

Experience

Interaction Designer-Educational Technology Services-UC Berkeley
October 2015—present
◆Designed user interaction for an online equipment reservation system
◆Performed heuristic evaluation and provided design recommendations for open source course management system

Helpdesk Administrator-Sapient-TEK Systems
November 2010—February 2011
◆Provided first level technical support to advanced users
◆Participated in support team, 70% field support and 30% call tracking in Remedy Help Desk

Helpdesk Technician-Keene State College-Campus Technology Services
October 2008—September 2010
◆Managed daily activities of a technical support center in all academic setting including seven technicians

- ◆ Provided first line technical support for over 550 faculty and staff members
- ◆ Created and maintained documentation related to technical policies and procedures

Projects

iBuyRight
www.proiectibuyright.com
- ◆ Served as Project Manager for Masters final project team to set project goals and milestones as well as to communicate progress with stakeholders
- ◆ Played a key role in the visual and interaction design of mobile prototypes
- ◆ Performed needs and usability analysis using interview, surveys and comparative analysis

Empty Orchestra
http://dream.sims.berkeley.edu/~kbryant/emptyorchestra.php
- ◆ Designed and implemented a database of karaoke studios and song that alleviates search and browse problems with current karaoke systems
- ◆ Implemented design using MySQL and PHP and documented system design in a written report

UFOViS
http://www.sims.berkeley.edu:8000/academics/courses/is247/f05/projects/ufovis
- ◆ Created a visualization of UFO sighting data to facilitate potential spatial and temporal pattern recognition for information visualization course
- ◆ Implemented design using Yahoo! Maps API

Skills

- ◆ Very familiar with principals of graphic design and visual communication
- ◆ Strong logical and analytical approach to problem solving
- ◆ Experience with the following software:
  Photoshop, Illustrator, Indesign, GoLive, Flash including ActionScript, Flash Lite, Dreamweaver, Fireworks, Omnigraffle, Microso Office products, MS Project, Visio
- ◆ Knowledge of HTML, CSS, Javascript, PHP, mySQL, Java, XML

李伟

邮箱：liwei@mail.com
地址：×××××

教育背景

伯克利大学信息学院
- 信息管理硕士学位，2016.5
- 主修人机互动、用户界面设计、信息可视化和数据库管理

- GPA：3.79

基恩州立学院
- 理学学士学位，数学（专业）(2008.5)，辅修：艺术
- 数学荣誉协会 Kappa Mu Epsilon 成员
- GPA：3.53（优等）

工作经历

2015.10—今　伯克利大学教育科技服务　互动设计师
- 为一家在线设备预订系统设计用户界面
- 进行启发性评估，并为开放课程管理系统提供设计建议

2010.11—2011.02　TEK 系统 Sapient 服务服务台管理员
- 为高级用户提供一流技术支持
- 在客服部门参与支持团队，70% 外场支援，30% 客户电话跟踪

2008.10—2010.09　基恩州立学院校园技术服务部服务台技术员
- 在一个学术团队的技术支持中心处理日常事务，该团队包括 7 名技术员
- 为 550 多名教师和员工提供一流技术支持
- 制订并维护与技术政策和程序相关的文件

参与项目

iBuyRight 项目
相关网址：www.proiectibuyright.com
- 在硕士结业项目组中担任项目经理，制订项目目标、项目重点，与相关方交流项目进展
- 在动态原型的视觉和互动设计中扮演重要角色
- 通过走访、调查和比较分析来进行需求和可用性分析

Empty Orchestra 项目
相关网址：http://dream.sims.berkeley.edu/~kbryant/emptyorchestra.php
- 设计并使用了一种卡拉 OK 录音棚和歌曲数据库，缓解了当前卡拉 OK 系统在搜索和浏览方面的问题
- 用 MySQL 和 PHP 将设计付诸实践，在一份文件报告中记录系统设计

UFOVis 项目相关网址：http://www.slims.berkeley.edu:8000/academics/courses/is247/f05/projects/ufovis/
- 作为信息可视化课程的一个项目，将 UFO 目击数据可视化，为潜在时空模型认知提供了便利
- 用 Yahoo! Maps API 实现了设计

技能

- 熟知图形设计和视觉交流原则

- 在解决问题过程中具有较强的逻辑和分析能力
- 熟悉以下软件：Photoshop, Illustrator, Indesign, GoLive, Flash including ActionScript, Flash Lite, Dreamweaver, Fireworks, Omnigraffle, Microsoft Office products, MS Project, Visio
- 对 HTML、CSS、Javascript、PHP、mySQL、Java、XML 等也有一定的掌握。

3. 博士简历

Li Peng

  Department of Computer and Information Science
  University of Pennsylvania
  Cell phone：(732)668-7728
  Office：(215)573-7736
  lipeng@ cis. upeen. edu

Education

  University of Pennsylvania, Philadelphia, PA, USA Ph. D. candidate 2011—Present.
  Department of Computer and Information Science
  Dissertation: Towards High-performance Word Sense Disambiguation by Combining Rich Linguistic Knowledge and Machine Learning Approaches (to be defended in July, 2016)
  Advisor: Martha S. Palmer
  Committee Members: Joshi K. Aravind, Claire Cardie (external examiner), Mitch P. Marcus (chair), Lyle H. Ungar
  University of Pennsylvania, Philadelphia, PA, USA M. S. 2010—2011
  Department of Computer and Information Science
  Tsinghua University, Beijing, China M. E. 2008—2010, B. S. 2004—2008
  Department of Computer Science and Technology

Research Experience

  Department of Computer and Information Science, University of Pennsylvania
  Ph. D. Candidate 2011—2016
  ……
  Department of Computer Science & Technology, Tsinghua University, Beijing, China
  Master Student, Senior College Student 2007—2010
  ……

Honors and Awards

  ◆ Graduate student research fellowship from the Department of Computer and Information Sci-

ence, University of Pennsylvania. Sept. 2010—present.
- ◆ Tsinghua-Motorola Outstanding Student Scholarship, top 3 among over 50 graduate students in the Department of Computer Science and Technology, Tsinghua University. Oct. 2009
- ◆ Honor of Excellent Student of Tsinghua University, top 10 among over 150 undergraduate students in the Department of Computer Science and Technology, Tsinghua University. Nov. 2007
- ◆ Honor of Excellent Student of Tsinghua University, top 10 among over 150 undergraduate students in the Department of Computer Science and Technology, Tsinghua University. Nov. 2005
- ◆ First Prize in the Tenth National High School Student Contest in Physics in Tianjin, sponsored by Chinese Physical Society and Tianjin Physical Society. Top 10 among over 1,000 competition participants in Tianjin area. Nov. 2003.

Publications

- ◆ Li Peng and Martha Palmer. Clustering-based Feature Selection for Verb Sense Disambiguation. In Proceedings of the 2015 IEEE International Conference on Natural Language Processing and Knowledge Engineering (IEEE NLP-KE 2015), PP. 36-41. Oct. 30-Nov. 1, Wuhan, China, 2015.

Oral Presentations

- ◆ "Towards Robust High Performance Word Sense Disambiguation by Combining Rich Linguistic Knowledge and Machine Learning Methods", in the 7th Penn Engineering Graduate Research Symposium, Feb. 15, 2016.

Other Professional Activities

- ◆ Organizer of the weekly seminar, the Computational Linguists' Lunch (CLUNCH), attended by about 30 faculty members and students mainly from the Department of Computer Science and Information and the Department of Linguistics, University of Pennsylvania. Spring, 2013
- ◆ Teaching assistant for the graduate-level course CIT594 II—Programming Languages and Techniques, which is oriented to master students in the Department of Computer and Information Science, University of Pennsylvania. Spring, 2012

Reference

Joshi K. Aravind, PhD (joshi@linc.cis.upenn.edu, 215-898-8540)
Martha S. Palmer, PhD (Martha.Palmer@colorado.edu, 303-492-1300)
Lyle H. Ungar, PhD (ungar@cis.upenn.edu, 215-898-7449)

李鹏

宾夕法尼亚大学计算机与信息科学系
手机:(732)668-7728
办公室电话:(215)573-7736
邮箱:lipeng@ cis. upenn. edu

教育背景

2011 至今　宾夕法尼亚大学　美国宾夕法尼亚州费城　博士在读
计算机与信息科学系
论文:《通过结合丰富的语言知识和机器学习方法达到高性能词义消歧》(答辩时间 2016 年 7 月)
　　指导老师:玛莎·S·帕莫
　　委员会成员:霍什·K·阿瑞文,克莱尔·卡尔迪(校外监考员),米奇·P·马尔卡斯(主席),莱尔·H·恩格
2010—2011　宾夕法尼亚大学　美国宾夕法尼亚州费城　理科硕士
计算机与信息科学系
2004—2008　清华大学　中国北京　理学学士;2008—2010　清华大学　中国北京　教育学硕士
　　计算机系

研究经历

宾夕法尼亚大学计算机与信息科学系 博士生在读　2011—2016
　…(从略)
中国北京　清华大学计算机系　研究生、大四本科生　2007—2010
　…(从略)

荣誉和奖励

2010.9 至今宾夕法尼亚大学计算机与信息科学系研究生研究员
2009.10 清华大学计算机系"清华-摩托罗拉优秀学生奖学金",50 名研究生中前 3 名
2007.11 清华大学计算机系"清华优秀学生"荣誉称号,在 150 名本科生中前 10 名
2003.11 第十届全国高中生物理竞赛天津赛区一等奖,成绩位列天津赛区 1000 多名参赛者的前 10 名。该竞赛由中国物理协会和天津物理协会主办。

出版论文

　李鹏,玛莎·帕莫. 在动词语义消歧上以聚类为基础的特征选择. 2015 年电气与电子工程师协会自然语言处理和知识工程学国际会议论文集(IEEE NLP-KE 2015),PP. 36-41. 10. 30-11.1,中国武汉,2015.

......（从略）

口头报告

"通过结合丰富的语言知识和机器学习方法达到强大而高性能的语义消歧",第七届宾夕法尼亚工程学研究生研究专题报告会,2016年2月15日.

......（从略）

其他专业活动

- 2013年春每周研讨会"计算机语言午餐"(CLUNCH)的组织者。该研讨会由约30位宾夕法尼亚大学计算机系和语言学系的教师和学生参加。
- 2012年春研究生课程CIT594 Ⅱ——编程语言和技术的助教。该课程针对宾大计算机系的研究生开设。

......（从略）

推荐人

霍什·K·阿瑞文,博士(joshi@linc.cis.upenn.edu, 215-898-8540)

玛莎·S·帕莫,博士(Martha.Palmer@colorado.edu, 303-492-1300)

莱尔·H·恩格,博士(ungar@cis.upenn.edu, 215-898-7449)

Unit 2　申请过程中与大学的各种联络信件
Application Correspondence

　　申请留学是个比较复杂的过程,申请信在其中则显得格外重要,可以说是申请成功的关键。申请留学大致分为三个阶段:申请阶段、接到录取通知阶段以及动身出国阶段。由于来回往复的各种信件较多,这里就几个关键步骤做简要的介绍。

　　①索取入学申请表。你可以采用信函或填写索取表格的方式向所申请学校的招生办索取入学申请表以及简章等。有些申请表格可以直接到相关学校的网站上下载。填写申请表时,要写清个人信息、学习的专业、中学或大学学习的课程、其他学术背景、工作经历、英语水平等。有些大学还要求填写附表,证明经济能力。

　　②告知校方已经寄出相关材料。填写好表格后,往往可以把自己的简历、个人陈述、推荐信等材料一并寄出去,同时,还需要缴纳申请费。之后申请人和校方之间往往还会展开一系列关于申请材料的信件往来,这部分经常是通过电邮完成的,既高效又经济。

　　③通知录取阶段。如果收到学校录取通知书,则需要先对校方表示感谢,然后继续询问后面的事宜,如住宿等。如果校方拒绝录取,建议还是礼貌性地回复一封。当然,如果对校方的拒绝理由不满意,那么还可以进行申诉(Appeal),说不定还有"柳暗花明"的可能。

1. 索取入学申请表

Dear Sir/Madam,

I am a senior student in Chongqing University, China and I am very much interested in the Software Design MA Program of your university and plan to apply for admission for the Fall of 2016. I would appreciate it very much if you would send me the application forms and further information about the program. My mailing address is shown on the top of this letter.

Thank you for your kind help.

Sincerely yours,

Li Ming

敬启者:

　　本人是中国重庆大学的一名大四学生,对贵校软件设计的研究生项目颇感兴趣,希望申请2016年秋季入学。倘贵处能回寄入学申请表以及关于该项目的详细信息,本人将不胜感激。本人通信地址见此信上方。

　　感谢您的帮助。

李明　谨上

2. 校方对索取信息的回复

Dear Mr. Li,

Thank you for your inquiry concerning our graduate program. I enclose an application form for financial aids and a brochure describing research activities in the Department of Computer Science. I am also enclosing a document about the general information of this department.

Please feel free to write if you have any questions.

Very truly yours,
John Chambers

亲爱的李同学：

感谢您询问我校的研究生项目。随信附上一份资助申请表和一份介绍计算机系研究活动的手册。同时寄上一份介绍计算机系概况的文件。

有问题请来信。

诚挚的约翰·钱伯斯

3. 告知校方已填好入学申请表

Dear Sir,

Thank you very much for the information you sent me about your financial aids and the application form, which I am returning herewith, duly filled in. Also enclosed is a money order from the Bank of China of 60 dollars for the application fee.

I look forward to hearing good news from you.

Sincerely yours,
Li Ming

尊敬的先生：

十分感谢您为我寄来贵校的相关资助信息和申请表。现将正式填好的申请表，连同一张支付申请费的中国银行开具的60美元汇票一同寄上。

期待着您的好消息。

李明 谨上

4. 告知校方各项材料正分别寄出

To whom it may concern,

Enclosed you will find my application materials for admission to MIT for the fall of 2016. I have included completed application forms, financial statement, academic statement and application fee.

As for other materials, I have requested ETS to send you the official reports of my TOEFL and GRE scores and my university to send the official records of my performances in the undergraduate studies. Three letters of recommendation will be mailed to you by suitable references of mine.

I would appreciate it if you could process these materials as expediently as possible. Please contact me at (+86)189 0000 0000 if there are any problems or questions. I look forward to hearing from you, and to attending MIT.

Thank you for your time and attention.

Regards,

Li Ming

敬启者：

随函附上我申请2016年秋季入麻省理工学院学习的材料。其中包括填好的申请表、财力证明、读书计划和申请费。

至于其他材料，我已经请求ETS寄去我的TOEFL和GRE成绩正式通知单，也已请求原大学寄去本科成绩单。三封推荐信也将由适当的推荐人寄去。

倘您能尽快处理这些材料，我将不胜感激。若出现任何困难或疑问，请通过电话(+86) 189 0000 0000联系我。期待您的来信，也期待进入麻省理工学院学习。

感谢拨冗阅信。

李明　敬启

5. 询问申请材料是否收到

To whom it may concern,

I am a Chinese applicant to your university's Software Design MA Program. I am writing to confirm whether you have received my application package via mail to the graduate admissions office about three weeks ago. Please let me know if anything is missing.

Thank you for your assistance with this matter and I look forward to hearing from you.

Sincerely yours,

Li Ming

敬启者：

本人是贵校软件设计研究生项目的一名中国申请者。来函确认贵处可否收到三周前本人通过邮局寄去的申请材料。若有任何遗漏，烦请告知。

感谢帮助。静候佳音。

李明　谨上

6. 告知校方 TOEFL 和 GRE 成绩已寄出

Dear Sir,

Thank you for your letter regarding my TOEFL and GRE scores.

I took the TOEFL and GRE examinations at the beginning of this year. I have written to the ETS and received a reply. They have agreed to send my scores to you as soon as possible.

To my knowledge, all my credentials have been sent to you or requested to send to you till now. Your kind attention to my application is much appreciated.

Faithfully yours,
Li Ming

敬启者：

感谢您来信询问我的 TOEFL 和 GRE 成绩。

我今年年初参加了这两项考试。我已给 ETS 去函，并已收到回函。他们已同意尽快将我的材料寄往你处。

据我所知，到目前为止，我的所有证明材料都已被寄往或是要求被寄住你处。谢谢您对我申请的关注。

李明　谨上

7. 告知已按要求补寄经济资助证明和成绩单等

Dear Sir,

Thank you for your message dated March 5th. 2016, with reference to my application materials.

As requested, I have enclosed a completed financial certificate and score reports from my current university, and hope that they can reach you in good condition.

If you need any further information concerning my application, please let me know.

Thank you for your time and attention.

Sincerely yours,
Li Ming

敬启者：

感谢贵处 2016 年 3 月 5 日关于本人申请材料的来信。

本人现已按要求附上一份本人当前就读大学开具的完整经济证明和成绩单，望贵处悉数收毕。

若在申请问题上还需任何材料，烦请告知。

劳烦览信，本人不胜感激。

李明　敬启

8. 询问申请进展情况

Dear Sir/Madam,

I am writing to inquire into the status of my application. I applied for admission into Computer Science School at your university, and my application number is 00000. Can I check my application status on line now? When can I find out about the admission results?

I look forward to hearing from you regarding my application status.

Thank you!

Sincerely,

Li Ming

敬启者：

本人望询问申请贵校的进展情况。本人申请进入贵校的计算机学院，申请号为00000。请问现在我可以在网上查看申请状态吗？我何时才能查出申请结果？

敬候佳音。

谢谢！

李明　谨上

9. 录取通知书

Dear Mr. Li,

It is my pleasure to inform you, on behalf of the Computer Science School, of your admission to the Ph. D. program at Standford University beginning at September, 2016. The size and strength of our applicant pool is such that only the strongest candidates can be admitted, and our offer of admission to you reflects our great confidence in your potential as a software engineer. The quality of the faculty and graduate students, combined with an outstanding academic atmosphere, makes the Computer Science School a unique place to pursue graduate study. We hope that you will join the school in September.

The Computer Science School is committed to continuing financial support of all graduate students in the school. Students in good standing will receive full tuition plus stipend in the form of Teaching and Research Assistantships for the duration of their graduate studies towards the Ph. D. degree. The University has not yet set the stipends for the 2016—2017 academic year. However, last year the stipend from Teaching and Research assistantships was $15,000, and we expect a modest increase for the 2016—2017 academic year.

Successful applicants ordinarily have a number of offers from which they must choose. In reaching a decision, you may find it helpful to communicate directly with our faculty members or graduate students whose interests parallel your own. Please feel free to call our student services officers, Lucy Lee at

(000)0000000, if you need assistance in obtaining names or phone numbers of people to talk to.

The high quality of our students is a distinguishing feature of our program. To facilitate planning and arrangement, we would like to hear your response to this offer as soon as you have made a decision, but in any case, no later than the formal deadline of April 30, 2016.

Sincerely yours,

John Chambers

Professor of Computer Science

Chair, Graduate Admissions Committee

亲爱的李先生：

我谨代表计算机学院，很高兴地通知您，您已经获得了斯坦福大学2016年9月博士生入学资格。此次申请者人数众多，实力强劲，因此只有最强的申请者才有资格被录取。而这份录取通知书正反映出了我们坚信您有成为一名软件工程师的潜质。计算机学院师资雄厚，生源一流，加之学术氛围浓厚，这些都使其成为不可多得的研习之地。我们期待您在9月份的加入。

斯坦福大学的计算机学院一直致力于给所有研究生提供经济资助。优秀学生将获得学费全免外加薪金的资助，薪金即学生在研究生到博士生的学习过程中担任助教或是科研助理所获得的报酬。我校暂时还没有定下2016—2017学年的薪金数额。但去年的助教助理薪金水平是15000美元，预计今年会有适度的增加。

成功的申请者一般都会有众多学校供其选择。为了帮助自己决策，您可以直接与我校的教师或是兴趣一致的研究生进行交流。如果您需要获得咨询人的姓名或手机号，请随时拨打我们学生处老师露西·李的电话(000)0000000。

一流的生源是我院研究生部的特点。为方便筹划和安排，我们希望您做出决定后尽快回复此函，但无论如何，请最迟于2016年4月30日前给予答复。

约翰·钱伯斯　谨上

计算机科学教授

研究生招录委员会主席

10. 拒绝通知书

Dear Sir,

Your application for admission to Harvard has been reviewed. It is my unpleasant duty to inform you that we are unable to approve your admission.

The volume of application for admission received by Harvard far exceeds the number of students we are able to accommodate and, as a result, admission is a selective process and highly competitive, for this reason we are able to accept only a limited number of undergraduate international students who present outstanding records of previous academic achievement. Your application was considered in competition with those of other undergraduate international applicants. Unfortunately, we were not able to select you for admission.

We appreciate your interest in Harvard and your understanding of the circumstances which place a limit on the number of students that we are able to accept. Our decision on your application does not in any way reflect on your ability to continue your education and we hope that you will not be discouraged from investigating the many opportunities that may be available to you at other institutions of higher education.

Sincerely yours,
John Chambers

尊敬的先生:

我们审核了您给哈佛大学的申请书。但是,遗憾地告知您,我们不能接受您的申请。

本校所收到的申请人数大大超过了我们可以招收的学生人数,竞争非常激烈,我们只能从中有选择地录取。因此,我们只招收了海外有限数目的成绩优异的大学本科毕业生。我们将您的成绩与别人的作了比较,但没能选择您。

非常感谢您对哈佛大学的兴趣和您对我们限制人数的理解。我们的决定丝毫不能说明您不能继续深造。希望您不要灰心,继续去其他高校寻找机会。

约翰·钱伯斯　谨上

11. 申请者表示同意入学

Dear Sir,

Thank you very much for your letter, stating that my application for admission to the undergraduate program at the University of California has been accepted and approved. It is an honor to notify you that I intend to enroll as an undergraduate, with my coursework beginning as of the fall semester of this year.

Please let me know what the next steps are, and l will be pleased to proceed with planning. I look forward to being a student at your fine university. Thank you again.

Sincerely,
Li Ming

敬启者:

非常感谢您来信,告知加利福尼亚大学研究生院已经接受并通过了我的入学申请。很荣幸地通知您,我愿意成为贵校的研究生,于今年秋季入学。

请告知接下来我需要做的事,我希望有计划地完成整个过程。期待成为贵校的学生。再次致谢。

李明　谨上

12. 申请者谢绝入学

Dear Sir,

Thank you very much for admitting me to your prestigious university. But I regret to inform you that before your letter arrived, I had accepted an offer of admission from another university.

Your assistance to my application, however, is appreciated and I will never forget it. Thank you again for admitting me to your university.

Sincerely yours,

Li Ming

敬启者：

非常感谢贵校录取。但是我很遗憾地告诉您，在您的信到来之前，我已然接受了另外一所学校的录取。

然而，我仍然非常感谢您在我申请过程中的帮助，对此我将永远铭记。再次感谢贵校的录取。

李明　谨上

13. 询问住宿问题

To whom it may concern,

I am already recruited by your esteemed university, and I have several questions about your housing situation.

Is on-campus housing available? If so, what does it cost and how do I apply? If on-campus housing is not available, is there off-campus housing in close proximity to the campus? What are my best resources for finding such housing?

Please contact me with any housing information you may have available, or please direct me to someone who can provide such information, such as a local real estate agent. I look forward to your reply.

Thank you very much for your time.

Regards,

Li Ming

敬启者：

本人已被贵校录取，现有几个关于住宿的问题。

请问可以住校吗？如果可以，费用如何，怎样申请？如果不可，请问校外有邻近学校的住宿吗？要获得这样的住宿，最好查看什么信息？

若您有任何关于住宿的信息，烦请联系我，或者将拥有这类信息的联系人的联系方式告知，比如当地的房地产中介。敬候佳音。

感谢拨冗阅信。

李明　敬启

14. 申请住校

To whom it may concern,

I accept your kind offer of a full-time scholarship with deep appreciation. This is to inform you that I wish to enroll in September. I am preparing for the enrollment now. I wish to live on campus.

If possible, would you please book me a two-bedroom apartment shared with an American boy student?

Thank you very much for your assistance.

Sincerely yours,

Li Ming

敬启者：

非常感谢贵校给我的全额奖学金。我写此信是告知您我决定9月份到贵校报到。现在正为报到做准备，并希望能够住校。

如果可能，您能否帮我订一间和美国男学生合住的双人房间？

多谢您的帮助。

李明　谨上

15. 申请延期入学

To whom it may concern,

I am writing to apply for a three-month deferment of my enrollment at your university as my father is sick and I just can't leave him here and go to the US, so I have to take care of him for several months.

Would you please let me know your acceptance of the deferment as soon as possible?

Should it require a fee or deposit to hold my place, please do not hesitate to contact me. Thank you in advance for your assistance. I look forward to attending your university then.

Thanks for your time and consideration.

Very truly yours,

Li Ming

敬启者：

由于父亲生病，需要本人照料数月，此时断不可前去美国而置其不顾，因此希望申请延期3个月入学。

请问可否尽快告知这份申请的通过情况?

倘若保留本人的入学资格需要额外的费用或是定金,请随时联系我。提前感谢您的帮助。期待进入贵校学习。

对您付出的宝贵时间和慎重考量,本人不胜感激。

李明　谨上

16. 通知校方已获得护照和签证

Dear Sir,

This is to inform you that I am going well with the preparation for the forthcoming trip to the United States. I have obtained my passport and visa. The travel agency is arranging my journey. As soon as my travel plan comes out, I will notify you of the time of my arrival.

Looking forward to meeting you in Standford.

Yours sincerely,

Li Ming

尊敬的先生:

写此信是通知您我的赴美准备工作一切顺利。我已经拿到了护照和签证,旅行社正在安排我的行程。一旦行程敲定,我会马上告知您我到达的时间。

期待早日在斯坦福见到您。

李明　谨上

Unit 3　申请奖学金 Scholarship

奖学金是大家都非常关心的问题。奖学金有以下几种：

①Fellowship：这是大家最喜欢的一种奖学金，不干活白拿钱，而且不用缴税；即使缴的话，税率还比 TA 或者 RA 低。

②Tuition Scholarship：帮你出全部或者部分学费。

③Teaching Assistantship(TA)：助教，一般是 1/2 的助教，教课、改作业、批卷子、组织本科学生讨论，一周一般干 20 小时的活，任务比较固定。1/2 的意思是一周只需要工作 20 小时（全职工作是每周 40 个小时，20 个小时正好是 1/2）。去当 TA，但是没有考过 TSE(Test of Spoken English 英语口语测试)的，一般学校会提前给你 TA 培训，这一般会要求你要比其他的人提前入学，不过这个培训也是学校出钱，所以不必担心。

④Research Assistantship(RA)：助研，一般就是帮忙在实验室打工，这个工作的辛苦程度就要看你老板要你去干什么了，可能没什么活干，那将非常轻松；也可能有很多活，比较累。

这所有奖学金都可以统称为 Scholarship。

申请奖学金的态度要诚恳，说清为什么申请，并且展示自己申请的资质（尤其在学术方面的）。

1. 提出奖学金申请

Dear Sir,

　　Your prominent school has the reputation of cultivating great engineers. A while ago, I heard the news that your school is giving out hundreds of scholarship to those who are commendable and wanted to become a civil engineer.

　　I want to grab this chance and apply for scholarship. I am a civil engineering graduate and wanted to learn more on how to become a full pledge engineer. I would be truly delighted if you can check out and view my scholarship application.

　　I want to be a part of your great college and learn more about engineering. Please do find my profile, essay and other qualifications that are attacked here with my application letter. Hope that you will call me back soon.

　　Sincerely Yours,
　　Li Ming

尊敬的先生：

贵校培养优秀工程师，声名远播。不久前，本人听说贵校发放了数百个奖学金名额，奖励那些优秀而有志成为土木工程师的学生。

本人希望争取这次申请奖学金的机会。本人是一名土木工程研究生，希望进一步学习如何成为一名真正的工程师。倘若贵校能检查并审核我的奖学金申请，本人将非常高兴。

本人希望成为贵校的一员，学习更多工程知识。请接收本人的简历、论文和其他随函附上的资质证明。期待早日回复。

李明 谨上

2. 索取奖学金申请表

Dear Sir,

I should like to apply for one of the scholarship that your school may be offering to students from other countries. Would you please send me the necessary application forms and any further details about the scholarships?

I am a postgraduate student of University of Science and Technology of China. I major in microelectronics engineering, and do some research work during my study years. I hope to have a further study and continue to do my research work if I succeed in obtaining the engineering scholarship.

Enclosed please find two letters of recommendation and my score report card. Thank you for your consideration. I look forward to your reply.

Respectfully yours,
Li Ming

敬启者：

本人有意申请贵校的外国留学生奖学金。请问可否寄来必要的申请表和任何有关奖学金的更多细节？

我是一名中国科技大学的学生。我的专业是微电子工程，在学习期间还做一些研究工作。如果我成功获得工程奖学金，我希望进行更深入的学习，并继续我的研究工作。

随函附上我的两封推荐信以及成绩单。感谢您的工作。静候佳音。

李明 敬启

3. 寄回填好的奖学金申请表

Dear Sir,

I am returning herewith, duly completed, the application form for scholarship which you have kindly sent me. Thank you again for your time and assistance.

Sincerely yours,
Li Ming

敬启者：
承蒙您的好意，寄给我奖学金申请表格。现已按要求填好，随函寄回给您。再次感谢您百忙之中的帮助。

李明　谨上

4. 感谢给予奖学金

Dear Mr. Chambers,

I wanted to show my great appreciation for awarding me the Civil Engineering Scholarship for two years. I want to thank you for providing the opportunity to continue my studies in your college. I am very grateful that with the entire applicants that applied for the scholarship, I was chosen to be one of those recipients.

I also want to pledge, that I will do my very best in my studies in order to get high grades every semester and graduate with flying colors from your university.

Once again, thank you so much for granting file the scholarship and for giving me the opportunity to let my dreams come true.

Yours Truly,
Li Ming

尊敬的钱伯斯先生：
我要对您给予我为期两年的土木工程奖学金表示深深的感谢。要感谢您给我机会在贵校继续深造。能在众多申请者中被选中，我深表感激。

同时，我保证将会尽全力学习深造，争取每个学期都拿到好成绩，以优异的成绩毕业。

再次感谢颁发奖学金，也感谢您给我实现梦想的机会。

李明　谨上

Unit 4　经济资助(助学金)及资助证明
Financial Aid & Certificates

　　校方提供的经济资助(Financial Aid),从某种程度上来说,也可以看成是奖学金,有时候就把它归类为奖学金,这类资助有"勤工俭学"的意思。有时经济资助不仅仅是校方提供的,还有家长、国家、公司单位等,这类就是真正意义上的"资助"了。

　　经济资助证明对于申请人的成功申请有着至关重要的作用,若在这一关卡住,那么前面的一切努力都化为乌有。资助证明由资助人开具,说明申请人有足够的经济能力支付学习、访问以及在外生活的一切费用。请注意以下几点:

　　①对于格式,每个学校没有统一标准。有些学校有一封写好的证明书,只需资助人或担保人填写。

　　②财力表现方式不限,可以是定期存款、活期存款、支票存款或是有价证券、国库公债、股票等形式。只要能显示其票额足够即可。

　　③开户人不一定是本人,可以是申请人的家人、亲戚、朋友,但要写清与申请人的关系。

　　④证明具有法律效力,一定要慎重填写。

1. 递交申请材料

To whom it may concern,

Enclosed you will find my completed financial aid application and all necessary information. Please examine the enclosed material to ensure that it has been filled out correctly and that no crucial information is missing.

If there is anything else you require to make your decision, please do not hesitate to contact me. I look forward to hearing from you soon.

Thank you.

Regards,

Li Ming

敬启者:

　　随函附上本人填好的经济资助申请表和所有必要的信息。请检查附件中的材料,确保其填写正确,并且没有重要信息遗漏。

　　如果您在做出决定前还需要其他材料,请随时联系我。静候佳音。

　　谢谢。

李明　谨上

2. 询问申请进展

To whom it may concern,

On March 8th I mailed you my completed application and additional information to be considered as a candidate for the X financial aid program. To date, I have not received any word from you regarding the results of that submission.

Please contact me at your earliest convenience and let me know whether or not I have been selected to receive financial aid, or whether you are still making your decisions. The information will help me make some of my plans for the coming year. You may reach me at 000 0000.

Thank you very much

Regards,

Li Ming

敬启者：

3月8日，本人向您寄去了填讫的 X 经济资助项目申请表以及其他信息。到目前为止，本人尚未收到贵处关于那份申请的任何回复。

烦请尽快告知本人是否已获得经济资助，或者贵处是否依然处于决定阶段。申请结果将影响到我来年的计划。您可以致电 000 0000 联系本人。

非常感谢。

李明　谨上

3. 学校通知获得经济资助

Dear Mr. Li,

It is our pleasure to inform you that our college, Fulton Institute, has selected you to be this year's sponsorship recipient. As you know, Fulton Institute has been existed for 35 years, being renowned for its high achievers annually.

We are happy to inform you that your application for a tuition fee waiver has been approved for the first year of your college studies, with possible sponsorship in the following year depending on your first year results. The Institute's board of trustees is proud to finance $1,500 towards your education to cultivate the potential we believe, is in you for excellence.

Please respond to this scholarship offer before the end of this month to facilitate the sponsorship progress.

We hope to hear from you soon.

Ms. Joan Chambers

Fulton Institute

Scholarship Department

亲爱的李先生：

非常高兴地通知您，富尔顿学院已经将您选为经济资助受益人。如您所知，富尔顿学院建院 35 年，以每年送出成功的毕业生闻名遐迩。

很高兴地告诉您，您关于减免学费的申请已经获得通过，您入学第一年的学费将被减免，若第一年成绩优异，次年也可能获得减免待遇。院董事会很荣幸资助您 1500 美元教育费用，我们相信您有出类拔萃的潜质，而这笔资金将助您将这种潜力开发出来。

请在月底前回复此函，推进申请进程。

静候佳音。

琼·钱伯斯
富尔顿学院奖学金部

4. 感谢提供经济资助

To whom it may concern,

I just wanted to write a brief note to express my sincere thanks and great pleasure at having been selected to receive financial aid from the X program. This will go a long way toward helping reach my educational and career goals.

Thank you again for selecting me.

Regards,

Li Ming

敬启者：

短短此函谨向贵校给予本人 X 项目经济资助表示诚挚的感谢，本人非常高兴。这对本人实现学术和职业目标将大有裨益。

再表谢意。

李明　谨上

5. 国家留学基金管理委员会出具的公派资助证明

China Scholarship Council

March 5, 2016

To whom it may concern,

This is to certify that Mr. Li Ming has been awarded a scholarship under the State Scholarship Fund to pursue his research in the United States as a visiting scholar. The awardee was selected through a rigid academia evaluating process organized by China Scholarship Council (CSC) in 2016. The scholarship totals $17,000 (covering the international airfare, stipend and other necessary allowances) for a period of 12 months. The Education Section of the Chinese Embassy for the Chinese Consulate General in your country is entrusted by CSC to look after the welfare of the awardee and make the payment to the individual.

CSC is a non-profit institution affiliated with the Ministry of Education of the P. R. China. It is entrusted by the Chinese Government with the responsibilities of managing the State Scholarship Fund and other related affairs. It sponsors Chinese citizens to study abroad and international students to study in China.

In accordance with the laws and regulations and related policies, the awardee has signed CSC an "Agreement for Study Abroad for CSC Sponsored Chinese Citizens". In this notarized Agreement, the awardee promises to return to China upon completion of his research within the set time.

中国国家留学基金管理委员会

敬启者：

兹证明李明先生获得中国国家奖学金基金下的奖学金，以此帮助其完成访学研究的工作。该获奖人在2016年由中国国家留学基金管理委员会（CSC）组织的一个严格的学术评价体系中脱颖而出。该奖学金共计17000美元（包括国际航班、薪金和其他必要的津贴），期限是12个月。中国驻贵国总领事馆的中国使馆教育部门受CSC委托，负责关照获奖人福利并为其颁发奖金。

CSC是中华人民共和国教育部下属的一个非营利性的机构。它受中国政府委托，负责管理国家留学基金以及其他相关事务。CSC支持中国公民赴境外留学，也支持外国来华留学生。

根据法律法规和相关政策，获奖人与CSC签署了《中国国家留学基金管理委员会资助中国公民留学协议》。协议中，获奖人保证在规定时间内完成研究后返回中国。该协议已经公证。

2016年3月5日

6. 单位出具的公派资助证明

To whom it may concern,

This is to certify that Li Ming has received the financial support from ×××Company to pursue a one-year study abroad. Li Ming has received a financial support totaling $12,000 covering international airfares, stipend and other allowances. Li Ming is now a promising employee in our company, and is permitted to study at Cambridge University form September 1, 2012 to August 20, 2013.

Yours Faithfully,
Zhang Ming

敬启者：

兹证明李明获得×××公司的经济资助，进行一年的出国学习。李明获得了共计12000美元的经济资助，其中包括国际航班、薪金和其他津贴。李明现为我公司一位很有潜力的员工，并被剑桥大学录取，深造时间是2016年9月1日至2017年8月20日。

张明　谨上

7. 家长资助证明

To whom it may concern,

I, Mr. Li Dawei, will support my son, Mr. Li Ming, during his 24 months study at Cambridge University.

I have attached bank statement of RMB 400,000, which amounts to USD 63,000 in total and assure that I can support his study with the money shown here and other funds not indicated here.

If you need any further information, please do not hesitate to contact me.

Sincerely yours,

Li Dawei

敬启者:

本人李大卫将为儿子李明在剑桥大学为期24个月的学习进行经济资助。

随函附上一份共计40万元人民币,约合6.3万美元的银行对账单,并保证本人可以用此单上显示以及未有显示的资金对其学习进行资助。

若您还需要任何其他信息,请随时联系本人。

李大卫　谨上

8. 家长担保函

Letter of Supporting

(time)

To: British Embassy

Dear Sir or Madam,

I am the applicant Li Ming's father and guarantor for his study in Britain, Li Dawei. I have been working as the sales manager in ××× Co. Ltd. since 1998 with annual income RMB 130,000 (excluding year-end bonus) after tax. For better development in the future, my son, Li Ming decided to go to Britain for further study. I am willing to provide my savings RMB 650,000 to support my son. I guarantee that my son Li Ming will have no economic difficulties in Britain and obey the laws and regulations. I am willing to bear all the responsibility if any problems happen.

Please give kind consideration to my son Li Ming's visa application. Thanks a lot!

I hereby to guarantee.

Li Dawei

Signature:____

担 保 信

致英国大使馆：

尊敬的签证官先生/女士：

我是申请人李明的父亲兼其在英国留学的担保人——李大卫,1998 年至今工作于×××有限公司,任销售部经理一职,年薪为人民币 13 万元(税后,不含年终奖金)。我的儿子李明为了将来能有更广阔的就业前景,计划赴英国学习,我愿意提供我的积蓄 65 万人民币的银行存款作为他赴英国留学的费用。我保证我儿子李明在英国期间不会在经济方面遇到任何困难,并保证他不会触犯任何法律,若有任何问题,我愿意承担一切责任！

希望签证官对我儿子李明的签证申请给予善意的考虑,谢谢！

特此担保！

李大卫
签名：____
（时间）

9. 资助人的单位收入证明

Certificate of Employment

To whom it may concern,

This is to certify that Mr. Li Ming, an interpreter of ××× Company, has worked in this company since the year 2005. He has an annual income (before tax) of RMB 110,000, including salary, rewards and year-end bonus (His personal income tax is deducted by relevant department automatically).

Sincerely yours,
Zhang Ming

单位收入证明

敬启者：

兹证明李明先生是×××公司的口译员,自 2005 年起在我公司工作。李先生税前年薪为人民币 110,000 元,其中包括薪水、奖励和年终奖金(其个人收入所得税已由有关部门自动扣除)。

张明　谨上

Unit 5　学历、学位、奖励、工作经历证明
Relevant Certificates

  无论是申请学校还是签证,学历证明、成绩单等都是非常必要的证明材料。这些文件都是校方和签证官做出决定的重要依据,用以判断申请人是否有能力完成学习和是否有资格得到签证。这些材料都需要有申请人就读学校的盖章。一般来说,申请人都会有一份中文的证明和成绩单。但在申请出国留学时,往往要先翻译成英文。一般来说,翻译稿的格式要尽量靠近原稿,然后再在适当的地方标注此为"the translation of the original piece"字样,翻译件同样要盖上学校公章。

  成绩单也是如此,翻译件格式要尽量接近原件格式,也需要盖上学校的公章。由于成绩单往往是一个巨大的表格,而且比较复杂,因此本单元暂不举例。

  同时,在申请过程中由于提到了自己的一些奖励情况、工作经历,因此有时有必要向校方提供这方面的证明。这就需要找奖状颁发单位以及工作单位的相关部门索取证明。如果证明是中文,需将其翻译为英文,同时注上此为翻译件。原件和翻译件都需盖上相关部门的公章。证明的信件一般言简意赅,用语正式严肃。工作证明可以适当写长一些,加上一些对申请人的评价等。

1. 本科学历证明

Education Certification

  This is to certify that student ×××(name), ×××(gender), born in ×××(Month), ×××(Year), studied a ×××-year undergraduate course at ××× University from ×××(Month), ×××(Year) to ×××(Month), ×××(Year), majoring in ×××. Having passed all courses stipulated in the teaching program, the above student received a graduation certificate in ×××(Month), ×××(Year).

(certificate serial number: ×××)
Academic Affairs Office
××× University
Date: Year-Month-Day

学历证明书

  ×××同学,×××(性别),×××年×××月生。×××年×××月至×××年××

×月在我校×××专业完成了×××年制本科教学计划规定的全部课程,成绩合格,于×××年×××月取得毕业证书。

（证书编号：×××）

×××大学教务处（盖章）
×××年×××月×××日

2. 硕士学历证明

Education Certification

This is to certify that student ×××(name), ×××(gender), born in ×××(Month), ×××(Year), studied a ×××-year postgraduate course at ××× University from ×××(Month), ×××(Year) to ×××(Month), ×××(Year), majoring in ×××. Having passed all courses stipulated in the teaching program, the above student received a graduation certificate in ×××(Month), ×××(Year).

(certificate serial number: ×××)
Graduate School
××× University
Date: Year-Month-Day

学历证明书

×××同学,×××(性别),×××年×××月生。×××年×××月至×××年××月在我校×××专业完成了×××年制研究生教学计划规定的全部课程,成绩合格,于×××年×××月取得毕业证书。

（证书编号：×××）

×××大学研究生院（盖章）
×××年×××月×××日

3. 本科学位证明

Academic Degree Certification

This is to certify that student ×××(name), ×××(gender), born in ×××(Month), ×××(Year), studied a ×××-year undergraduate course at Soochow University from ×××(Month), ×××(Year) to ×××(Month), ×××(Year), majoring in ×××. The student has duly completed the program and graduated. A Bachelor Degree of ××× is hereby conferred on the student in ×××(Month), ×××(Year) through verification in accordance with the requirement of PRC Regulations of Academic Degrees.

(certificate serial number: ×××)
Academic Affairs Office
Chongqing University
Date:

学 位 证 明

学生×××(姓名),×××(性别),×××年×××月生。自×××年×××月至×××年×××月在我校×××专业完成了×××年制本科学习计划,现已毕业。经审核符合《中华人民共和国学位条例》的规定,×××年×××月授予学士学位证书。

(证书编号:×××)

重庆大学教务处(盖章)
×××年×××月×××日

4. 硕士学位证明

Academic Degree Certification

This is to certify that student ××× (name), ××× (gender), born in ××× (Month), ××× (Year), studied a ×××-year postgraduate course at Soochow University from ××× (Month), ××× (Year) to ××× (Month), ××× (Year), majoring in ×××. The student has duly completed the program and graduated. A master Degree of ××× is hereby conferred on the student in ××× (Month), ××× (Year) through verification in accordance with the requirement of PRC Regulations of Academic Degrees.

(certificate serial number: ×××)
Graduate School
Chongqing University
Date:

学 位 证 明

学生×××(姓名),×××(性别),×××年×××月生。自×××年×××月至×××年×××月在我校×××专业完成了×××年制研究生学习计划,现已毕业。经审核符合《中华人民共和国学位条例》的规定,×××年×××月授予硕士学位证书。

(证书编号:×××)

重庆大学研究生院(盖章)
×××年×××月×××日

5. 奖励证明

Nov. 12, 2015

To whom it may concern,

This is to certify that Mr. Li Ming, a senior student in the Computer Science School of Chongqing University, received three ××× Awards, which only students among the top 5 percent are entitled.

Chongqing University

敬启者：

兹证明李明，重庆大学计算机学院大四学生，曾三度荣获×××奖学金，此项殊荣仅排名前5%的优等生才有资格获得。

重庆大学
2015 年 11 月 12 日

6. 工作经历证明

Working Certificate

21/12/2015

To British Embassy
Whom It May Concern,

××× Development Co. Ltd. was founded in 1995 with the registered capital of RMB 20,000,000. We mainly deal with X.

Mr. Li Ming has been working in our company since 2005. Due to his outstanding working behavior, Mr. Li was promoted to the sales manager. Mr. Li worked hard and had opening up wide market for our company, which made our company has a stable position in the keener competition. His yearly salary is RMB 48,000 and his personal income tax has been deducted and paid by our company.

For better development in the future, Mr. Li decided to go to Britain for further study. Our company needs high-qualified manager, so we totally agree with his study plan and sincerely hope that Mr. Li can come back to our company for further work after finishing his study.

Please do not hesitate to contact us if you require any further information!

Hereby certified!

Zhang Ming
General Manager
××× Co. Ltd.

工 作 证 明

致英国大使馆

尊敬的先生/女士：

×××有限公司成立于1995年，注册资金为人民币2000万元。公司的经营范围主要包括×。

李明先生于2005年加入我公司，后因工作业绩突出，被提升为销售部经理。李先生工作认真负责，为我公司开发了广阔的市场，使公司在竞争激烈的市场中占据了一席之地。公司给予李明的年薪为人民币4.8万元，其个人所得税由我公司代扣代缴。

李先生为了将来在国内有更好的发展，决定赴英国留学深造，我公司也十分需要高素质的管理人才，所以我们十分赞同其留学计划并真诚欢迎李明先生学成回国后能继续在我公司从事工作。如有进一步需要，欢迎与我公司取得联系！

特此证明！

总经理：张明

×××有限公司

2015年12月21日

参 考 文 献
References

[1] Al-Enezi, F. Q. & J. K. Sykulski. Modeling of a Photovoltaic Module Considering the Solar Energy Available from Horizontal Surfaces over Kuwait Area[J]. *Journal of Electronic Science and Technology*, 2012, 10(2): 173-180.

[2] Ahmada K., M. Khare & K. K. Chaudhry. Wind Tunnel Simulation Studies on Dispersion at Urban Street Canyons and Intersections[J]. *Wind Engineering and Industrial Aerodynamics*, 2005 (93): 697-717.

[3] Francesco, Braghin., et al. Tyre Wear Model: Validation and Sensitivity Analysis[J]. *Meccanica*, 2006 (41):143-156.

[4] Chris, K. & L. Sridhar. LANA: A Lane Extraction Algorithm that Uses Frequency Domain Features[J]. *IEEE Transaction on robotics and automation*, 1999(15): 143-150.

[5] Chung, S. Niahn., Liang L. Chun & Jou L. Nan., et al. Optimal Design for Passion of a Light Rail Vehicle using Constrained Multiobjective Evolutionary Search[C]. *IEEE Proc. International Conference on Networking, Sensing & Control*, 2004, 134-139.

[6] Deng, Dean. FEM Prediction of Welding Residual Stress and Distortion in Carbon Steel Considering Phase Transformation Effects[J]. *Journal of Materials and Design*, 2009 (30): 359-366.

[7] Dong Shaojiang & Luo Tianhong. Bearing Degradation Process Prediction Based on the PCA and Optimized LS-SVM Model[J]. *Measurement*, 2013(46): 3143-3152.

[8] Fathollahzadeh, M. H., G. Heidarinejad & H. Pasdarshahri. Prediction of Thermal Comfort and Energy Consumption in a Dense Occupancy Environment with the Under Floor air Distribution System[J]. *Building and Environment*, 2015(90): 96-104.

[9] Friedli, T., M. Hartmann, & J. W. Kolar. The Essence of Three-Phase PFC Rectifier Systems - Part II.[J] *IEEE Transactions on Power Electronics*, 2014, 29 (2):543-560.

[10] Gao Feng, Liu Guoliang, & Wang Guofu, et al. Development of an Intelligence Vehicle Experiment System[J]. *Journal of Mechanical Engineering*, 2010, 23(6):684-689.

[11] Hall, D. J., S. Walker & A. M. Spanton. Dispersion from Courtyards and Other Enclosed Spaces[J]. *Atmospheric Environment Report*, 1999(33): 1187-1203.

[12] Hatch, E. Basic Machining Operations and Cutting Technology[M]. London: Cambridge University Press, 2012.

[13] He Y, Liu XT, Zhang CB, & Chen ZH. A New Model for State-of-Charge (SOC) Estimation for High-power Li-ion Batteries[J]. *Applied Energy*, 2013(101):808-814.

[14] Huang, H. H. Active Roll Control for Rollover Prevention of Heavy Articulated Vehicles with Multiple-rollover-index Minimization[C]. *Proceedings of the ASME* 2010 *Dynamic Systems and Control Conference*. 2010, September 12-15, Cambridge, Massachusetts, USA.

[15] Jain, M. & S. S. Williamson. Suitability Analysis Of In-Wheel Motor Direct Drives For Electric And Hybrid Electric Vehicles[C]. Electrical Power & Energy Conference (EPEC), 2009 IEEE 2009:1-5.

[16] Jie, L. Z., S. Z. Yan & J. N. Wu. Analysis of Parameter Sensitivity of Space Manipulater with Harmonic Drive Based on the Revised Response Surface Method [J]. *Journal of Acta Astronautica*, 2014(98): 86-96.

[17] Kaltsoukalas, K., S. Makris, & G. Chryssolouris. On Generating the Motion of Industrial Robot Manipulators[J]. *Journal of Robotics and Computer-Integrated Manufacturing*, 2014 (32): 65-71.

[18] Laverge J., N. Van Den Bossche, N. Heijmans & A. Janssens. Energy Saving Potential and Repercussions on Indoor Air Quality of Demand Controlled Residential Ventilation Strategies [J]. *Building and Environment*, 2003(46): 1497-1503.

[19] Liu Wenwen, Qu Xian & Liu Xi. The Innovative Design for Automobile EPS System Based on Active Front-wheel Steering Technology [J]. *Journal of Jiangsu University*, 2004, 25(1): 21-25.

[20] Lorenzo, S., O. Simona & R. Giorgio. A Comparative Analysis of Energy Management Strategies for Hybrid Electric Vehicles[J]. *ASME Journal of Dynamic Systems, Measurement, and Control*, 2011(133): 1-8.

[21] Mirzaei, Parham A. & F. Haghighat. A Procedure to Quantify the Impact of Mitigation Techniques on the Urban Ventilation[J]. *Building and Environment*, 2012, 47 (1):410-420.

[22] Newmark, Peter. Approaches to Translation[M]. Shanghai: Shanghai Foreign Language Education Press, 2001.

[23] Oshieba A., H. Bazzi, H. A. Maksoud. &M. Khater. Sensorless Control of Switched Reluctance Motor Drive Systems [J]. *Journal of Energy and Power Engineering*, 2013 (7): 118-125.

[24] Remmlinge, J., M. Buchholz, T. Soczka-Guth & K. Dietmayer. On-board State-of-health Monitoring of Lithium-ion Batteries Using Linear Parameter-varying Models[J]. *Journal of Power Sources*, 2013(239): 689-695.

[25] Rieke-Zappa, D., W. Tecklenburg, J. Peipe, H. Hastedt & Claudia Haig. Evaluation of the Geometric Stability and the Accuracy Potential of Digital Cameras-Comparing Mechanical Stabilisation Versus Parameterization[J]. *Journal of Photogrammetry and Remote Sensing*, 2009, 6(4): 248-258.

[26] Torres, J. L., R. Gonzalez, A. Gimenez & J. Lopez. Enery Management Strategy for Plug-in Hybrid Electric Vehicles [J]. *Applied Energy*, 2014(113):816-824.

[27] Wang Rongrong & Wang Junmin. Stability Control of Electric Vehicles with Four Independent-

ly Actuated Wheels[C]. *Proceedings of the 50th IEEE Conference on Control and European Control Conference*, 2011, December 12-15, 2511-2516.

[28] Winai, C. & H. Prasert. Design of Efficient In-wheel Motor for Electric Vehicles[J]. *Energy Procedia*, 2014(56): 525-531.

[29] Wong, S. V. & A. M. S. Hamouda. Machinability Data Representation with Artificial Neural Network[J]. *Journal of Materials Processing Technology*, 2003(138): 538-544.

[30] Xu Q, Chang GK & Gallivan VL. Development of a Systematic Method for Intelligent Compaction Data Analysis and Management[J]. *Construction and Building Materials*. 2012 (37): 470-480.

[31] Zarei, J., M. A. Tajeddini & H. R. Karimi. Vibration Analysis for Bearing Fault Detection and Classification Using an Intelligent Filter[J]. *Mechatronics*, 2014(24): 151-157.

[32] Zhang Yingchao, Zhao Zhengming, Guo Wei & Sun Xiaoying. High Performance Position Control System Based on SR-PM Motor[J]. *Tsinghua Science and Technology*, 2007, 12 (5): 614-619.

[33] Zhao Wanzhong, et al. Integration Optimization of Novel Electric Power Steering System Based on Quality Engineering Theory[J]. *Journal of South University*, 2013 (20): 1519-1526.

[34] Zhong L., X. Han, S. Q. Zhou, Q. Ren, T. Yun. Research on Component Phases and Microstructure Shape of a Rapid Ion Nitriding Layer[J]. *Journal of Materials Engineering and Performance*, 2003, 12(6): 687-692.

[35] 常晨光,陈瑜敏. 功能语境研究[M]. 北京:外语教学与研究出版社,2011.

[36] 陈枫. 应用文写作案例大全[M]. 北京:中国水利水电出版社,2012.

[37] 但汉源. 英汉翻译理论与技巧[M]. 长沙:中南工业大学出版社,1999.

[38] 丁树德. 翻译技法详论[M]. 天津:天津大学出版社,2005.

[39] 张敏,杨秀芬. 科技英语阅读教程[M]. 北京:外语教学与研究出版社,2007.